W9-BUD-709

**Absolutism
and
Enlightenment**

1660 – 1789

1660–1789

Absolutism and Enlightenment

R. W. HARRIS

Master of Studies and
Head of the Department of History
in the
King's School, Canterbury

HUMANITIES PRESS
New York

© Blandford Press Ltd

First published
in the United States 1966
by Humanities Press Inc.
303 Park Avenue South
New York, N.Y. 10010

Library of Congress Catalog Card No. 66–23176

Printed in Great Britain by
Richard Clay (The Chaucer Press), Ltd
Bungay, Suffolk

Contents

LIST OF MAPS

List of Illustrations

(appearing between pages 214–215)

ACKNOWLEDGMENTS

The illustrations have been produced by permission of the following:

1 Victoria & Albert Museum
2, 3, 17, 18, 21 Radio Times Hulton Picture Library
4, 5, 6 Alinaris, Rome
7, 8 Instituto Italiano di Cultura
9 Musée du Louvre, Paris
10 National Gallery of Scotland
11 Deutscher Zentrale für Fremdenverkehr, Frankfurt AM
12 Das Kunsthistorisches Museum
13 Bundesbildstelle, Bonn
14 Musée de Versailles
15 Musée de Dijon
16 Nationalmuseum, Stockholm
19 Deutscher Kunstverlag
20 Mr. J. G. Morrison

The eighteenth century—

'*the great century*'
Michelet

'*the century of true renaissance*'
Georges Lefebvre

Introduction

Embarking upon a period of history, it is important to know what to look for, what questions to ask, what themes to expect. From one point of view it is sufficient to regard the period spanned by this book as one of remarkable personalities, Louis XIV, Peter the Great, Charles XII of Sweden, Frederick II of Prussia, Catherine II of Russia, the Empress Maria Theresa and her son Joseph II among the rulers; or Descartes, Newton, Locke, Bernini, Claude, Poussin, Montesquieu, Voltaire, Kant and Goethe in the world of the intellect and the spirit. For many people the fascination of history lies in the pursuit of the ultimate mystery of personality, and this is a perfectly reasonable approach. But for a full understanding of the position of any personality in history, one needs to view it in the context of the age, and we may indicate at the outset what that context was.

First, the period 1660–1789 was a great period of State-making. In 1660 most of the 'States' of Europe were still primarily 'Estates', that is to say, they lacked more than the beginnings of centralised government; they were still in some ways provincial and federal, with local laws and customs acting as a constant check upon the ruler. The work of Louis XIV, the Great Elector, and his successors, Peter the Great, Maria Theresa, Charles XI of Sweden and others, all had the same tendency towards administrative absolutism.

As this could be done only by curbing the feudal liberties of the nobility, it might be supposed that a consequent theme would be an extended battle between the ruler and his nobility. It was not quite like that. Most rulers obtained the acquiescence of their nobilities to administrative centralisation, either, as in France, by neutralising their power while confirming them in their social privileges, or, as in Prussia, by taking them to some extent into partnership, and relying upon them to fill administrative as well as military posts. As events turned out from the point of view of the Monarchy, the Prussian way seemed preferable, for in France during the eighteenth century there was a resurgence of the power of the nobility which went far to paralyse the effectiveness of the Monarchy. This led directly to administrative breakdown and the French Revolution. On the other hand Prussia and Austria (which in administrative matters substantially adopted the Prussian system) withstood the days of the French Revolution without themselves experiencing revolution (except, to some extent, in provinces near to France).

The tendency towards administrative absolutism was accompanied by a drive towards larger political units. This was, in one aspect, simply a matter of economics, for economic progress was stultified by tiny States, constant customs barriers, bad roads, different coinages and hampering local restrictions. Mercantilism was the first attempt to provide something approaching a single economic policy for a State, however imperfect this was in practice. European rulers learnt to encourage trade and industry as an essential part of the business of building up the strength of their States; and trade, industry and colonies played a larger part in the consciousness of most peoples as time went on.

The other aspect of this drive towards larger units was the tendency to aggression on the part of the stronger States. The same forces which led Louis XIV to subdue his nobility or his *parlements*, led him also to seek to absorb the Netherlands, Alsace and Franche Comté. The new centralised Prussian monarchy found irresistible the temptation to seize Silesia and West Prussia, just as the new-found strength of Russia under Catherine II sought to dismember the Ottoman Empire, as well as Poland. To retain European stability in face of such aggression, European statesmen paid lipservice to the principle of the balance of power, and often met aggression by alliances to redress the balance. But the system worked imperfectly, and there was in fact important changes in the balance of power between 1660 and 1789. One pattern of change reflected the decline of the Mediterranean and latin peoples, Spain, the Italian States, the Papacy, and to some extent France; and the rise of Britain, Prussia and Russia. Even more spectacular was the change in the balance of power in eastern Europe, with the catastrophic decline of Sweden, Poland and the Ottoman Empire, and the rise of Russia and Prussia. Less obvious, but equally important, is the remarkable way in which the character of the Habsburg power adapted itself to the changing conditions of Europe.

More important, perhaps, than all this, for the future of the world, was the intellectual revolution which is spanned by the dates 1660–1789. It was primarily a revolution in man's attitude to the Universe, consequent upon the birth of modern science in the age of Galileo and Newton. The Universe had come to be intelligible as a material and mechanical process, governed by mechanical laws. These laws were ascertainable by man's reason; they were keys which would unlock doors to unimaginable wealth and power. Thus there was born a new materialism, a new belief in the here-and-now, a new thirst for knowledge. The age of gadgets had begun.

The intellectual achievements of the age exalted men's reason. It could hardly be maintained in future that what seemed contrary to man's reason could be true. Nor, in political and social matters, could it be argued that institutions which did not accord with reason could any longer be justified. Government existed for the happiness of the citizens, for what other explanation seemed reasonable? Men were no longer merely the wicked offspring of Adam's Fall; they were also participators in godlike Reason. In this connection there took place an interesting instance of what psychologists call 'transference'. In the intellectual and philosophical world the man who stood at the apex of human achievement was he who discerned the laws of nature, Euclid, Pythagoras, Galileo, Descartes, Newton, Huygens, because upon such men rested the hopes for human progress. In the political sphere at the apex of things stood the ruler; upon him rested the hopes of man in society. Both were lawgivers, and, provided their laws were good laws, they deserved to be venerated and obeyed. Hence arose the idea of the Enlightened Despot.

The argument was well put in *L'ordre naturel et essentiel des sociétés politiques* (1767) by the French Physiocrat, Mercier de la Rivière. The Enlightened Despot is one whose laws are the true expression of the needs of society; he is the one from whom abundance arises, the one whose very glance 'makes the most barren land fruitful'. Just as Euclid is 'a true despot, and the geometric laws which he has handed down to us are truly despotic laws', and must be obeyed, so the laws of the Enlightened Despot should be obeyed because he is 'less a man than a beneficent deity', because his commands are the emanation of 'supreme reason'. Of course there are bad kings, tyrants, just as there are bad philosophers and scientists, but the Enlightened Despot is the true beneficiary of his people.

It is clear then that the new philosophy was a powerful ally of the new secular absolutism. The eighteenth century was the century of Enlightened Despotism. The *philosophes* were ready in their praises for any ruler who followed their teaching. Frederick the Great paraded his Enlightenment in his correspondence with Voltaire, as Catherine II did in her correspondence with Diderot. Joseph II declared that 'he made Philosophy the legislator of his Empire'. But Enlightenment reached also the smaller Courts of Europe. Maximilian III of Bavaria (d. 1777) was deeply influenced by the Enlightenment, founded an Academy of Sciences, made education compulsory, and was a patron of German literature. Frederick II of Hesse-Cassel (d. 1785) was a humanitarian ruler and a patron of the arts. Louise Dorothea in Gotha, Anna Amalia in Weimar, Charlotte Amalia in Meiningen, Duke Ferdinand of Brunswick, Count Collo-redo, Archbishop of Salzburg, were all accounted enlightened rulers in Germany. In Italy, Charles of Bourbon made an enlightened king of Naples before he left in 1759 to be king of Spain. His successor, Ferdinand IV, was too ignorant a ruler to account for much, but his wife Maria Carolina, daughter of Maria Theresa, brought with her much of the Habsburg authority, and their famous Minister Tanucci stood always for hostility to feudal privilege and the immunities of the Catholic Church. Peter Leopold of Habsburg was the most enlightened Grand Duke of Tuscany. Charles Emanuel III of Pied-mont, in concentrating power in his own hands, and in his determina-tion to limit the privileges of the Church, had about him many of the marks of the Enlightened Despot. In Sweden Gustavus III (d. 1792) earned the approval of the *philosophes*, and in Spain Charles III was in some ways the most successful Enlightened Despot of his time.

It is clear from such a list that there was no very precise definition of an Enlightened Despot. The first requirement was that he should be a despot. Mirabeau gave an important clue to contemporary thinking when he once wrote that '*even* enlightened princes some-times allowed their Ministers to influence them'. The use of the word *even* is significant. To Mirabeau an Enlightened Despot was one who handed down laws from the height of his own wisdom and philos-ophy. He was expected to centralise his administration, curb the liberties of his feudal nobility and of the Catholic Church, develop trade and industry, standardise coinage, weights and measures, introduce secular education, encourage the arts and learning by patronage and by the founding of Academies, humanise the law and show concern for the welfare of the peasants. A ruler who pursued any or all of these objectives, might expect to win the approval of the *philosophes*.

In no previous century had the thought of the philosophers been so highly regarded by rulers.[1] The Age of The Enlightenment saw a great extension of humanitarianism and cultural ideals, both as a general possession of society in western Europe, and in a great extension eastwards in Germany, Poland and Russia. There was also a widening and deepening of learning. We might illustrate this from a new approach to the study of history. Historiography took a great step forward in the eighteenth century. The old meandering chronologies would no longer do. Writers began to treat history analytically; that is to say, not as a chain of events, but as a development linked by causes. In history they sought a justification of their philosophy, and consequently they asked new questions of history, of the Middle Ages, of Homer, or the Old Testament. The researches of Professor Butterfield have shown that the 1760s opened a new chapter in the history of historical scholarship, with the birth of the German Historical School. He has shown that the number of predominantly historical periodicals in Germany rose from 3 in 1700 to 131 in 1790, and that between 1769 and 1771 about a thousand writings on history appeared in Germany, four times the number which appeared in France. German universities had a great flowering in the eighteenth century. In 1734 Baron Münchhausen, cousin of the famous storyteller, founded the University of Göttingen under the patronage of the Elector, George II of England. From the start it enjoyed a freedom denied to other universities of the time in Germany, and it had the best library in Germany. The Prussian University of Halle received lustre from its connections with the great names of Leibniz and Christian Wolff, and the University of Jena from its associations with the names of Goethe and Schiller. As in the Middle Ages, the

---

[1] There were of course earlier exceptions to this generalisation. The Medici Lorenzo the Magnificent, for instance, certainly valued the good opinions of the philosophers, and so, in a sense, did the Hohenstaufen Emperor Frederick II in the thirteenth century.

extension of university activities was an important aspect of the growing secularism of the age.

In the eighteenth century the Roman Catholic Church was on the defensive.[1] It was attacked by the *philosophes*, the men of the Enlightenment and by the Enlightened Despots, primarily because it was seen as an obstacle to progress. Instead of Reason and Enlightenment, the Catholic Church seemed to stand for tradition and obscurantism. It was seen also as an obstacle to economic progress, for the most progressive parts of Europe, England and the Dutch, with their merchant fleets, colonies and commerce, were Protestant. The dead hand of the Church seemed to rest upon a too great proportion of the lands of the State; great sums were swallowed up in ecclesiastical revenues which might otherwise enrich the secular ruler. The Church controlled education at a time when it was thought that the benefits of a rational education were boundless. The prime enemy was thought to be the Papacy itself. The Popes indeed were often men of piety and learning. Benedict XIV (1740–58) was a pious and humble man with an engaging sense of humour; Clement XIII (1758–69) was a noted patron of the arts, especially of Raphael Mengs and Piranesi. He completed the Villa Albanesi in Rome, with its great collection of antiquities, and greatly enriched the Capitoline Museum and the Vatican Library. But none of the Popes of the period was able to do more than fight a rearguard action against the enemies of the Church.

The latter regarded the Jesuits as the advance-guard of the Papacy. The Jesuits were attacked by deists, sceptics and philosophers from without the Church, and by Gallicans and Jansenists from within. The Jesuits certainly made mistakes. They were accused of engaging in private trade and of tyrannising over South American natives. Their theology alarmed the Augustinians of the Catholic Church, who thought that they were making too many concessions to the rationalist thought

---

[1] Eighteenth-century Protestantism had some remarkable manifestations of religious enthusiasm: in England the Methodists, the Quakers, the Evangelicals, as well as great churchmen like Butler and Berkeley; in Sweden the Swedenborgians; in Central Europe the Moravians. In the Catholic Church also there were ample examples of religious devotion, for instance in the Jansenism of Port Royal, or in the Quietist movement of Mme. Guyon and Mme. de Maintenon in France, or among the Camisards of the Cévennes (a revivalist movement stamped out by the authorities), and in the lives of men like Fénelon in France or Fabio de Vecchi in Tuscany. Yet it remains true that the Catholic Church was divided and on the defensive.

On this see Palmer: *Catholics and Unbelievers in 18th-century France*.

of the day, while on the other hand the rationalists gave them no credit for their enlightenment. They were hated by the Jansenists, by the *parlements* of France, by Ministers such as Pombal of Portugal, Tanucci of Naples or Choiseul in France. The *philosophes* thought that the suppression of the Jesuits would be the prelude to the real Age of Enlightenment. D'Alembert wrote to Voltaire in 1762:

> I see everything in the rosiest colours at the moment. I can see the Jansenists here dying a peaceful death next year, after having brought about the ruin of the Jesuits by a violent death this year. I see the coming of tolerance, the recall of the Protestants, the marriage of priests, the abolition of the confession, and the unobtrusive extirpation of fanaticism.

In short, once Jansenists and Jesuits had destroyed each other, the way would be prepared for a new era of toleration and the triumph of Reason.

The climax of the movement came with the suppression of the Jesuit Order in 1773. In 1759 the Jesuits were expelled from Portugal, in 1764 from France, and in 1767 from Spain. On the death of Clement XIII in 1769, the election of a new Pope was of such importance that Joseph II and his brother Peter Leopold hastened to Rome incognito, and used their influence for the election of Cardinal Ganganelli as Clement XIV. The new Pope was met with the united pressure of the Catholic monarchs of Europe for the suppression of the Jesuits. He bowed before the storm, and by the Bull *Dominus et Redemptor* (August 1773) the Jesuit Order was suppressed.

The fall of the Jesuits did not lead, as D'Alembert had expected, to the triumph of Reason. In France the fall of the Jesuits was another nail in the coffin of the Monarchy. The Age of Enlightenment culminated, not in the triumph of Reason, but in the French Revolution. It is one of the objects of this book to trace how this came about.

1: The Age of The Enlightenment

The Scientific Revolution

Historians have come to speak of the *Intellectual* or *Scientific Revolution* of the seventeenth century. In general there is a well-advised reluctance to divide history too rigidly into periods, to emphasise separateness rather than continuity and development, but in this case it can hardly be avoided. The element of continuity is certainly there, and in this sense Enlightenment is the consummation of the intellectual, political and economic phenomena known as the Renaissance. But in other ways it is startlingly new. From one point of view some historians are quite right to regard the Renaissance as the beginning of 'modern' thought, but others are equally justified in regarding the Intellectual Revolution of the seventeenth century as its beginning. There are times at which, say, Rabelais or Leonardo da Vinci strike a 'modern' note which would have seemed strange in any earlier period. But it is equally clear that the thought of the age of Bacon, Galileo, Kepler, Descartes and Newton was based upon a new attitude to life and its problems.

In the seventeenth century there emerged a new way of looking at the Universe. As a background to this we must remember that life had become steadily more complicated during the preceding centuries. The growth of industries, trade and material wealth had given men a greater concern with material things. The growing complexity of society had produced lawyers, doctors, administrators, in short an educated secular class. Learning was no longer the exclusive preserve of the Church. The Reformation had broken up Christendom into conflicting sects, and men discovered that in the last resort they must make up their own minds about the conflicting interpretations of religious beliefs and practices. Secular rulers grew in authority as men looked to the State to give relief from feudal disintegration and religious conflicts. All these developments are the necessary background to the new ideas in science and philosophy.

In the seventeenth century the fundamental problem of science was

that of motion.[1] For 500 years European thought about the nature of
the Universe had been dominated by the theories of Aristotle. To
Aristotle the 'natural' state of any body was to be at rest. A body
moved only when there was a mover. Heavy bodies 'naturally' sought
the centre of the Universe (i.e. the centre of the earth), just as 'light'
bodies (such as a flame or a gas) leapt upwards. A stone dropped over
a cliff accelerated in its downward path, perhaps because of a joy it
felt at approaching its natural home. What made a stone continue to
move in any other direction once it had left the hand of the thrower
was a more difficult problem, and was thought to be something to do
with air pressures, or perhaps with moving spirits which guided the
Universe. Aristotle had postulated the need for a Prime Mover of the
Universe, and superstition added the idea of spirits directing natural
phenomena. In the last resort, to any question why things acted in
the way they did it was always possible to give the conclusive answer,
'Because God wills it so'. But since the fourteenth century there had
been growing doubts about Aristotle's interpretation of such matters
as acceleration. The seventeenth century gave the subject of motion
an entirely new interpretation.

The new view was the result of two developments. The first was the
development of the experimental method of science. Experiments had
of course been made in preceding centuries, but the seventeenth
century erected it into a recognised method of thought. At the same
time it is possible to exaggerate its importance at that time. Galileo
did conduct experiments, but it is not true that he dropped weights
off the Tower of Pisa to disprove Aristotle, and very often what he
said in his writings was: 'If you were to conduct such-and-such an
experiment you would find such-and-such a result'; he did not say
that he had attempted it. The most spectacular advances in scientific
thought of the seventeenth century were the result, not so much of
experiment as of the development of mathematics. In this century
arithmetic and algebra took on their modern shape; John Napier
devised logarithms by 1614; Kepler's great work on planetary motion
rested on his study of conic sections; Descartes formulated analytical
geometry, and Leibniz and Newton simultaneously discovered infinitesimal calculus. Experimentation and mathematics, these were to be

[1] The subject of the next few pages is explained more fully in my *Science, Mind and Method*.

the tools of scientific advance. Leonardo da Vinci and Francis Bacon had both conducted experiments, but without mathematics they had not known how to interpret and synthesise their results. The age also made great advances in the instruments with which experiments and observation could be conducted, above all in the development of the telescope and the microscope. With experimentation, improved mathematics and the telescope, it needed only the genius of Galileo, Kepler and Newton to provide a new view of the Universe.

A typical mediaeval view of the Universe, based on Aristotle, and formulated by Dante, was somewhat as follows. The Universe was spherical, and the heavenly bodies were attached to transparent spheres which turned about the centre of the earth. It was a pleasant poetical fancy that they might make heavenly music as they turned. The earth was a sphere with the land, so to speak, uppermost, and the lower regions water. The heavenly bodies were perfect and unchangeable; change and decay belonged only to this world. The four elements of which the Universe was composed were earth, water, air and fire. The whole Universe turned in frictionless motion about the earth once in twenty-four hours. But it had long been recognised that there were defects in this picture of the Universe. In particular it was clear that the paths of the planets did not conform to this pattern. Elaborate theories of epicycles were invented to explain these erratic paths. Finally Copernicus, in his *De Revolutionibus Orbium* (1543), though he retained many of the old ideas, such as the doctrine of the spheres, suggested that it would be preferable to suppose that the sun was the centre of a planetary system and that the earth moved around it. The theory did not cause a great stir, partly because it was not popularised, partly because it was merely stated as a hypothesis, and partly because it left unexplained the principle of motion governing the heavenly bodies. It took a further hundred and fifty years to work out the implications. William Gilbert, about 1600, discovered that a spherical magnet revolved in a magnetic field, and he suggested that the earth was a magnet. In the next thirty years Johann Kepler brought a giant mathematical genius to bear upon the problem, and at last hit upon the laws of planetary motion: that the path of a planet is an ellipse which has the sun at one focus; that the line joining the sun to the planet sweeps out equal areas in equal times; and that the square of the time which any planet takes to complete its orbit is proportional to the cube of its distance from the sun. These laws were a stupendous intellectual achievement. Meanwhile Galileo in 1609, with the use of the telescope, was able for the first time to witness the satellites of Jupiter and the phases of Venus. He showed also from the observation of sun-spots that the sun was revolving. The old ideas of the perfectibility of the spheres was destroyed for ever. Moreover Galileo, unlike his predecessors, blazoned his ideas to the world, in popular works, written in Italian, not Latin. Finally it was left to Isaac Newton in 1665–66, in one of the greatest pieces of discernment in the history of thought, to impose upon the whole subject his laws of motion. He showed that it was mathematically necessary for the paths of planets to be elliptical, and that the planet was drawn towards the sun by a force which varied in inverse proportion to the square of its distance from the sun. He was thus led on to formulate his famous law: 'Every particle in the universe attracts every other particle with a force varying jointly as their masses and the inverse square of their distance apart.'

The New Philosophy

A generation before Newton was born, Francis Bacon, in his *The Advancement of Learning* and the *Novum Organum*, had felt the need for an entirely new approach to learning. He was convinced that men needed to throw off the authority of Aristotle, to reject authority of any kind in the matter of learning, and to adopt the new method of induction and experiment. Aristotle, he wrote, 'corrupted natural philosophy by logic', whereas

> experience is by far the best demonstration, provided it adheres to the experiment actually made.

Once this truth was learnt, Bacon saw an endless vista of progress, wealth and material benefits stretching ahead for mankind. But above all there was the beauty of truth.

> Sight is more excellent and beautiful than the various uses of light; so is the contemplation of things as they are, free from superstition or imposture, error or confusion, much more dignified in itself than all the advantage to be derived from discoveries. . . . Let mankind regain their rights over nature, assigned to them by the gift of God.

The same desire to find an entirely satisfactory starting-point for human thought was expressed by the French mathematician and philosopher René Descartes (1596–1650). Descartes was profoundly influenced by the new scientific discoveries. He was convinced that the whole Universe operated on clear principles of reason. The starting-point was God, and God was pure reason, and His principles were mathematical. The Universe consisted of two elements, Mind and Matter, and he left it as an enigma for the future to decide how two such different elements could operate upon each other. In his little book *Discourse on Method* (1637), rejecting all 'authority' as a basis for thought, he sought for a satisfactory starting-point. The one thing of which he could be certain was that he was a thinking being, possessed of reason capable of comprehending the Universe (*cogito ergo sum*). This is known as the principle of 'Cartesian doubt'. It was often subsequently misunderstood. It did not at all mean that he doubted, say, religious belief, for he was convinced that men knew God by intuition. What he meant was that, starting from this launching-pad, man could comprehend an entirely reasonable Universe. He well knew that men were often deceived in their observations; things were not always what they seemed to be. Certainty could be obtained only by one of two means, either by intuition (as when the Scriptures proclaim 'I *know* that my Redeemer liveth'), or by deduction, and thus he thought the deductive sciences, especially geometry, the highest form of intellectual activity. There are many difficulties in Descartes' thought which it is not possible to raise here. In some ways his immense influence during the following century cut across and impeded the development of empirical thought, but he was one of the great formative influences in the Age of Reason.

The Scientific Revolution of the seventeenth century, which came to a triumphant climax with the publication of Newton's *Principia Mathematica* in 1687, had a profound influence on the thought-world of the Age of The Enlightenment. Aristotle had been dethroned. There had come into being a mechanistic view of the Universe; that is to say, the Universe was now thought of as a gigantic piece of machinery working according to ascertainable laws, and those laws were shown to be mathematical. It was not too much to say that men, by the use of their reason, had penetrated the mind of God, and had found that it was mathematical. The intellectual world of Europe was heady with excitement in the 1680s. From now on it was not a matter of a few geniuses working in isolation. A great popular tide of enthusiasm arose; the new ideas were broadcast, vulgarised, often misunderstood. As early as 1686 Fontenelle, who may be regarded as the first of the *philosophes*, published *The Plurality of Worlds*, the first book of popular science, and set the French world of fashion buzzing with the new ideas. There was nothing in the work of Galileo, Descartes, Kepler or Newton which was necessarily opposed to religion, and most of the great men of science of the seventeenth century were sincere believers. But some members of the Roman Catholic clergy had taken up an attitude of hostility and had made statements which were foolish, or at least ill-advised. There thus began the conflict between the *philosophes* who embraced and popularised the new ideas, and the Catholic Church. Fontenelle's work was tinged with the new scepticism. It was carried further in the writings of Pierre Bayle (1647–1706), a Roman Catholic converted to Protestantism, who for a time was a professor at Sedan. He was a prolific journalist, believing profoundly in freedom of thought and discussion, a convinced Cartesian believing that all ideas must be examined in the light of Reason. In his *Dictionnaire historique et critique* he sought to apply Cartesian methods to history, exposing, as he put it, 'a complete inventory of the various errors perpetrated' by previous writers. In other writings he came to the conclusion that certainty could be arrived at in nothing; that nothing could be known beyond all doubt, that religion and philosophy had nothing to do with each other, that one was simply a matter of belief, the other a matter of reason, and that most of the questions raised by religion were not amenable to a definite answer. Bayle himself was not a sceptic in religion, but his *Dictionnaire* became the handbook of the sceptics of the eighteenth century.

Serious attempts were made in the period to reconcile religion with the new philosophy. Malebranche (1638–1715) was a sincere Catholic and wrote a great work on metaphysics which he called an attempt at 'a liberal Christian philosophy'. One problem which constantly pre-occupied *philosophes* during the eighteenth century was that of miracles: could they be reconciled with the idea of a Universe governed by fixed and mechanical laws? Malebranche rejected the idea, for God was supreme Wisdom; He acted in a general way through laws He had Himself established; it followed therefore that He would not contravene His own laws.

One of the greatest geniuses to attempt the same task was Leibniz (1646–1716). He was the son of a professor of philosophy at the University of Leipzig. He entered the service of the Duke of Brunswick-Lüneburg and acted as his librarian for the rest of his life, with the special task of writing the history of the House of Brunswick. He was a prodigious intellect who tried to take all knowledge into his compass, mathematics, physics, logic, metaphysics, history, law, philology, theology and ethics, and sought to find a new synthesis. He discovered infinitesimal calculus at the same time as Newton. He hoped to see Europe united in a new peace system. He postulated the need for a new European language, clear, precise and definite, suitable to the new philosophy. He hoped to bring about a reunion of Christendom; the differences between the various Churches he thought unimportant compared with the underlying agreement. For this purpose he entered into a famous correspondence with the great Bossuet, Bishop of Meaux. Bossuet was the champion of the Catholic faith and the greatest intellect among the Catholic hierarchy at the time, with an unshakable belief that God revealed truth to man in the Bible. They soon came to an impasse, for Bossuet would not budge from the position that the Catholic Church was infallible and that the decisions of the Council of Trent were valid for all time. The Protestants on their side could not begin by admitting their error at the Reformation. Yet the correspondence continued until 1698, and grew into lengthy treatises, but reconciliation was no nearer at the end than at the beginning. Bossuet stood for dogmatic authority, Leibniz for the right to full and free enquiry.

The Age made great strides in biblical criticism, for it seemed natural that the Bible should be studied as a collection of historical documents if its true significance was to be appreciated. Richard Simon was a priest ordained in 1670 and trained by the Oratorians in Paris. He had a passion for Hebrew and for going back to the sources of things. His purpose was to examine the authenticity of the texts and to bring philology into service. In his great work, *Histoire critique du Vieux Testament* (1678), he wrote:

> I am convinced that we cannot read the Bible intelligently if we have no preliminary acquaintance with textual criticism.

He never for a moment doubted the divine inspiration of the

Scriptures, nor the efficacy of Tradition, but he showed, for instance, that the Pentateuch could not have been written by Moses, as was commonly supposed, but was put together at widely separated dates. His work was placed on the Index and banned in France, but it was published in Amsterdam. Throughout the period the Netherlands were the place of refuge for persecuted intellects, and the source of a great stream of forbidden literature on religion and philosophy.

The new scientific attitude produced a new interest in travel stories of the customs of strange lands, for it was no longer supposed that Christendom contained a monopoly of truth. As early as 1619 an obscure writer named Bergeron declared:

> The exploration of the globe having resulted in discoveries that have destroyed many of the data on which ancient philosophy reposed, a new conception of things will inevitably be required.

In England, when Sir William Temple retired from politics, he busied himself with the moral and political history of China, Peru and Arabia. Great interest was aroused in the Red Indians of North America, and in 1703 an adventurer named Baron de Lahoutan published an account of his travels which painted a picture of the noble savage, and contrasted him with the evils of civilisation. For the first time there was felt the fascination of the mysteries of ancient Egypt. Some scholars looked with a new detachment and much admiration at the religion and culture of the Mohammedans. The Persians were even more popular, thanks to the publicity given them by a traveller named Chardin, who showed them to be an old and cultured people; and above all by Montesquieu. Jesuit missionaries and Dutch, English and French traders brought back wonderful accounts of the Chinese civilisation, and 'chinoiseries' became one of the artistic fashions of the time.

All this had the greatest influence upon the philosophic outlook of Europe. Dogmatism, authority, suppositions of European superiority, were no longer sufficient. The age was passionately interested in the business of living, in ethics and social customs, in law and the rights of property, in philosophy and religion. Jesuit missionaries were astounded to discover that the philosophy of Confucius was very similar to that of Christianity, although Confucius had been born nearly five centuries before Christ. Such facts reinforced the idea that all men participated in some degree in a universal reason which transcended any particular society or religion. Truth could best be arrived at by cool discussion and comparison of social customs. Nothing could be accepted which did not stand up to the test of reason. The same test which Richard Simon applied to biblical criticism was applied to history. The Age swept away a great cloud of myths which engulfed historical facts. Saint-Évremond, in his *Reflexions sur les divers génies du peuple romain*, exposed the legendary character of many of the classical stories still accepted as factual; he wrote:

> There is so much that is real to admire in the Roman people that we do them a disservice in flattering them with fairy-tales.

A study of Egyptian chronology and Chinese claims to antiquity (false as they turned out to be) made it evident that the Jewish chronology by which there was an interval of 4,004 years between the creation of Adam and the birth of Christ must be inaccurate. It is true that Bishop Usher in England and Bishop Bossuet in France produced ingenious arguments to preserve the old order, but they were overborne by the facts.

In religion the new philosophy powerfully reinforced the ideas of Deism, which had begun to emerge in the seventeenth century. Herbert of Cherbury drew up a Deist profession of faith in England as early as 1642; Deism flourished in England after 1660 and powerfully influenced the Continent. The Deists accepted that there was a Supreme Being, but rejected the need for an organised Church, priests, sacraments, rites, or mortification of the flesh. They rejected Revelation as unnecessary, all that man needed was to be guided by his Reason. All men needed to do was to follow their moral instinct, and God would approve. The effect of Deism was really to substitute for the idea of a personal God the idea of a law of nature immanent in all men. In some ways Deism was a reaction from the excessive theological conflicts and ecclesiastical power-politics of the previous 150 years. At best it was imbued with a warm humanitarianism which hated cruelty and tyranny; at worst it descended to a mere materialism. John Toland, an Irishman, was its passionate defender about the turn of the century. Anthony Collins went further and invented the term 'free thinking'. Voltaire was the most famous of all Deists. Deism and free thinking flourished in many of the Lodges of the

Freemasons during the eighteenth century. The London Grand Lodge
of Freemasons was opened in 1717, and that of France in 1725.

The New Political Thought

The intellectual revolution after 1660 was intimately connected with
social development, for the age was marked by the phenomenal rise
of the middle class. The first half of the reign of Louis XIV has
sometimes been regarded as a golden age for the middle class. The
King avoided employing his nobility, except in the army, and promoted men of humble birth; Colbert was the son of a draper, and
Molière, Le Brun and the others were mostly of humble birth.
Financiers and merchants grew wealthy in the new settled conditions,
had their portraits painted, and read the new literary journals. In
England this development was even more marked, in the age of the
coffee house, of Steele and Addison, Swift and Pope. The new science
extended its influence, not only to religion and philosophy, but also
to the business of making money. The science of political economy
was conceived in the pamphlets of Josiah Child, the *Political Arithmetic* of Sir William Petty, and the voluminous scribblings of Daniel
Defoe. It would not however be true to say that the age was more
concerned with making money than with philosophy or religion, for
people passionately devoured essays and dissertations on ethics and
the whole business of living. Among the middle classes there was a
strong revolt against aristocratic excesses, a kind of puritanism, which
was revealed in Jansenism in France, and in Nonconformity in
England. But against this must be set the brilliance of French salons,
where wit and poise were so highly valued, and where science, literature and ethics were the chief subjects of conversation. As an example
of those who were most welcomed there, we may remember Charles
de Saint-Denis, better known as Saint-Évremond, the ideal 'gentleman' of the period, a writer, a dabbler in ethics and politics, an Epi-
curean and cultivated conversationalist, who shone in the salon of
the Duchesse de Mazarin in London (he was an exile from France
under Louis XIV). He enjoyed the pleasures of the table, abhorred
asceticism, believed in moderation in all things, was in love with life,
lived to advanced old age, and was finally buried in Poets' Corner,
Westminster Abbey. Some will think that man could hardly ask for
more.

One can learn a great deal by asking what an age most admired. In the early years of Louis XIV it was the hero, the warrior, the great ruler, such as the King himself, who gave his people security. By the end of the reign the hero-warrior was sneered at in the writings of La Bruyère, Saint-Évremond, Fontenelle and Fénelon, and the new ideal was the 'gentleman' in Saint-Évremond's sense of the word. Later in the eighteenth century it was the middle class with their simple virtues, and finally with Romanticism it was the noble savage, untouched by the corruptions of civilisation. The spirit of the age was critical, often satirical, for the new test of Reason threw much of the old order into a lurid light. There is no more apt example of this than in France, where the heroics of the days of Racine gave place to a new generation of writers in which every one was intensely critical of the régime of the Grand Monarque.

For the political theory of the Divine Right of kings could not stand up to the tests of the Age of Reason. This is not to say that the theory had not served its purpose in the sixteenth and seventeenth centuries. For at that time the Monarchy was the great symbol of the nation, the centralising force against the disintegrating tendencies which tore society apart. Theorists had usually regarded politics as a branch of ethics. If all goodness and legitimate power came from God, it was natural to emphasise that the King ruled by Divine Right, and that therefore resistance to him was a sin against God, as well as a crime against the State. In the first half of his reign Louis XIV gave France internal peace, security and prosperity, and thus justified the theorists. In the later years of his reign the picture changed.

The greatest influences in bringing about the change were, first, the example of the Dutch republic, where a bourgeois society pursued wealth and happiness under the rule of law and in an atmosphere of free speech unknown elsewhere in Europe. The second was the Revolution of 1688 in England, and the third was the work of John Locke. John Locke was one of the great formative influences upon European thought in the eighteenth century. His influence was felt in three distinct ways. In his *Two Treatises of Government* he gave the death-blow to the doctrine of Divine Right. To Locke man was essentially a reasonable being who had entered society for clearly discernible purposes, the chief of which was the protection of his property. The ruler ruled, not by Divine Right, but by virtue of a contract with his people. He was a steward, not a tyrant. The ultimate test of government was the happiness of the subjects; if the ruler ruled well, he deserved to be obeyed; if not, he might be deposed. Locke was no revolutionary; it was no part of his purpose to open a period of political instability. But he did proclaim a new test for good government, namely the happiness of the subjects and the welfare of the State. This was the starting-point of the theory of Enlightened Despotism. The second influence of Locke was to be found in his *Letters concerning Toleration*. These declared that a man's religious beliefs were no concern of the ruler, so long as he was a good citizen. Written within a few years of Louis XIV's Revocation of the Edict of Nantes,[1] it destroyed the intellectual foundations of intolerance, and toleration became one of the most persistent cries of the *philosophes* during the eighteenth century. The third influence was more strictly philosophical. With his *Essay concerning Human Understanding* Locke became the father of modern psychology. The claims which Descartes made for Reason seemed to Locke to be excessive. Man's reason was like a candle to a traveller in a wood on a dark night, feeble and limited, but nonetheless sufficient for his purpose. Man could find his way by its aid in the light of his experiences. For men's ideas were the result of their experiences; the ultimate test of good and bad was the happiness of men. Locke was no materialist; he was a sincere Christian, but his arguments powerfully reinforced Deism and the whole thought of the *philosophes*.

Locke in his political writings drew deeply upon the idea of Natural Law. Natural Law had been an essential part of Stoic thought in the late Roman world, had been Christianised in mediaeval thought, and was given a new lease of life in the seventeenth century in a rather different form. The Universe, as we have seen, was thought of as a mechanism governed by ascertainable laws. Similarly in human affairs, Reason provided a code of conduct both in personal and in social affairs. Natural Law operated throughout humanity, regardless of religion, because all normal men were reasonable beings. Grotius, the Dutch philosopher, in his *De jure belli et pacis* (1624) defined Natural Law, and declared that it operated universally even in war-time. He proposed therefore the European recognition of an inter-

---

[1] See p. 92.

national law which should be operative in the name of humanity, even when nations were at war. The first Chair of Natural and International Law was established at the University of Heidelberg, and was occupied by Samuel Pufendorf (1632–94). Later he became professor at the Swedish University of Lund. In his famous book on *The Law of Nature and Nations* (1672) he called for a great reform of the law according to Reason. The law of nature, he wrote

> is one which is so uniformly adapted to all that is sociable and reasonable in human nature that, unless its dictates were obeyed, it would be impossible for mankind to live together in peace and security.

He believed in the contract between subjects and ruler, but he was reluctant to allow the subject any right of resistance, for the ruler must be expected to know best. But the supreme duty of the ruler still remained the welfare of his subjects. Pufendorf believed in the natural equality of all men, and argued therefore that each man had a social duty to his neighbour; war seemed to him to be an offence against human reason and dignity. There was indeed much that was liberal and civilised in the thought of Pufendorf. Christian Thomasius (1655–1728), professor of law at Leipzig, held much the same views, for which indeed he was driven out of Leipzig, and forced to seek refuge at Halle under the protection of the Elector of Brandenburg (1690). Much influenced by Locke, he was an empiricist who advocated practical reforms in the new spirit. Freedom he regarded as 'the very life of the spirit, without which human reason is as good as dead'. Under the influence of such men, the persecution of witchcraft and the use of torture rapidly declined in Europe. He made the University of Halle a centre of progressive thought, and his writings are known to have greatly impressed the young Frederick the Great.

The *Philosophes*

Once Louis XIV was dead, the new ideas circulated more readily in France, and the Enlightenment advanced apace. In 1721 one of the greatest of the *philosophes* gave his first work to the public. Montesquieu was the son of one of the minor *noblesse d'épée* from the Toulouse area. He inherited large estates from his uncle, together with the title of baron Montesquieu, and, perhaps even more important, he inherited from him the office of president in the *parlement* of

Bordeaux. In 1721 he published (in Amsterdam!) *Lettres Persanes*, which was an enormous success and ran into ten editions in the first year. Two wealthy Persians, Usbek and Rica, travel in Europe in search of the wisdom of the West, and send letters home recounting their findings. As we have seen, the age had great interest in Persia; the *Arabian Nights* had been published in 1704; and Montesquieu took great care to preserve the local colour of the East. The work is full of the new humanism. Institutions are put under searching criticism; tax-farmers, journalists, Jesuits, doctors, the theatre, the French Academy are all satirised. There is a most hostile picture of Louis XIV. Montesquieu subtly discredits monarchy and religion, by making them the subject of debate and comparing them with Persian practices. He was not seeking simply to discredit either of them, but to show how prone they were to abuse. Monarchy tended to degenerate into despotism, or to give way to a republic. He mocked at religious practices which would not stand the test of Reason, such as widow-burning among the Hindus, or the prohibition of pork-eating among the Moslems. The real point he sought to make was that beneath the individual characteristics and disputes in religion there was a solid core of reasonable morality. Montesquieu was the enemy of narrowness and prejudice. In his *L'Esprit des Lois* (1748) he brought the new empirical spirit to bear on social problems, particularly of history and economics. He sought for the laws which governed man in society, and emphasised the importance of geographical conditions in determining men's actions. He considered in a dispassionate spirit the relative merits of different forms of government. Constitutions, he realised, could not be transplanted; they were related to social forces, and he made it his life-work to discover what they were. In Book I.3 he wrote:

> Law in general is human reason, inasmuch as it governs all the inhabitants of the earth; the political and civil laws of each nation ought to be only the particular cases in which human reason is applied. They should be adapted in such a manner to the people for whom they are framed, that it is a great chance if those of one nation suit another. They should be relative to the nature and principle of each government. . . . They should be relative to the climate of each country, to the quality of its soil, to its situation and extent, to the principal occupation of the natives, whether husbandmen, huntsmen, or shepherds: they should have a relation to the degree of liberty which the constitu-

tion will bear; to the religion of the inhabitants, to their inclinations, riches, numbers, commerce, manners and customs.

He considered the republic to be the best form of government, because it was motivated by the classical principle of public virtue. Despotism on the other hand was wholly bad, degrading to human nature, but nonetheless widespread in the world because it was the simplest form of government. Louis XIV, for instance, governed by enslaving his people and excluding the ablest from his service. To Montesquieu, good government was moderate government actuated by considerations of public welfare. He was not writing as a political propagandist, still less as an agitator; he was the philosopher, the dispassionate investigator of the mainsprings of government, analysing the traditions, habits, customs, passions and sentiments he saw about him. Above all, he believed that the State should be governed by just laws, and not merely at the whim of a ruler. Of all the political ideas which Montesquieu transmitted to his age, the most important was that of the rule of law as the prerequisite of good government. He greatly admired the English constitution, without fully understanding it. He described the separation of powers into executive, legislative and judicial, showed how they balanced one another, and especially praised the jury system and the control of the Commons over taxation; but he noticed also the grim realities of political power:

A Minister thinks only how to triumph over his adversary in the House of Commons; and to achieve this end he would sell England and all the powers of the world.

There is much more in Montesquieu than can be included in a brief summary; his was one of the most profound minds of the eighteenth century, and he has left a great mark upon the study of history and sociology. His cool, balanced, contented view of life reflects many of the most admirable characteristics of the Age of Reason. He once wrote, in a passage too good to translate:

Je m'éveille le matin avec une joie secrète; je vois la lumière avec une espèce de ravissement. Tout le reste du jour je suis content.

He moved in the brilliant society of the Paris salons, especially that of Mme. de Lambert; he was the friend of Fontenelle, Voltaire, Diderot and D'Alembert, and he contributed a famous article on 'Taste' to L'Encyclopédie.

B

Voltaire

The central figure of the Age of Enlightenment was Voltaire. His reputation has suffered eclipse: in his day he was thought of as the greatest literary and philosophical figure of the century, and his poetry and dramas were received with delight. Today they are little read except by specialists, and Voltaire has become something of a period piece. Yet of his historical importance there is little doubt. His real name was Arouet, but he preferred the more fanciful name of Voltaire. He was born in 1694, the son of a well-known lawyer, and received the best education of the time at the Jesuit Collège Louis-le-Grand, though in later life he was contemptuous of it. As a young man he moved in the brilliant but corrupt society of the Regency, and began writing verses and plays. A supposed snub to the Duke of Rohan, one of the greatest names in France, earned Voltaire a caning at the hands of the Duke's servants, and a period in the Bastille. It was an insult Voltaire never forgot; he hated the feudal aristocracy, and all his life became a champion of human freedom. On his release he was ordered out of Paris, and took refuge in England (1726–79). The English experience made a deep impression upon him. He was captivated by the philosophy of Locke and Newton, and henceforth became their greatest publicist on the Continent. He was immensely impressed with the atmosphere of intellectual freedom in England, and he learnt, as he said, that the greatest of all blessings was the rule of law, in which a man need not fear arbitrary arrest. From Locke, rather than from Descartes, Voltaire learnt the principle of philosophic doubt as the beginning of wisdom. He became opposed to all dogmatism, even the dogmatism of Diderot's atheism. He venerated the name of Newton, who had given the age a new view of the Universe. He embodied his views on England in his *Lettres sur les Anglais,* in which the superiority of the English over the French system of government was demonstrated, so that the book was banned by the *Parlement* of Paris in 1734. From England too he learnt the principles of Deism.

He returned to Europe as the chief protagonist of the new philosophy of Enlightenment. If one seeks for a single formula which explains the significance of Voltaire, it is that he was a great champion of humanity. His test for all things was the test of Reason. He rejected miracles, because they offended the order of the Universe. He was never tired of pointing out the wars, cruelty and persecutions which had been inflicted on humanity in the name of religion. He jeered at the wealth and power of the Catholic hierarchy. He thought of Jesus Christ as the greatest of the prophets, and wrote 'If you want to imitate Jesus Christ, be martyrs and not executioners!' He was a great exponent of toleration. The ultimate test he applied to an institution was that of the happiness of mankind. 'Virtue,' he wrote, 'consists in doing good to one's fellows, and not in vain practices of mortification.' Injustice and cruelty threw him into a passion; of this nothing is more characteristic than his attitude to the famous Calas case. In 1762 Jean Calas, a sixty-three years' old Huguenot cloth merchant, was tortured and executed at Toulouse, for the supposed murder of his son who may have been contemplating conversion to Roman Catholicism. To this day the facts of the case are in doubt. There may well have been a miscarriage of justice, but, according to the traditions of the time, Calas had a fair trial. But Voltaire was convinced that he had been the victim of religious intolerance, and that Calas' son had in fact committed suicide. Voltaire hated torture and intolerance, and he never let the matter rest until, after a spirited campaign which interested all Europe, Voltaire secured the exoneration of Calas three years later. Similarly, Voltaire never let his age forget the brutal mutilation of the young chevalier de La Barre for impiety. Another example of his humanity, and also of his principle of philosophic doubt, is illustrated by his witty novel, *Candide* (1758). He reacted sharply against the spirit of optimism which was to be found in the attempts of Leibniz and Christian Wolff to combine the new philosophy with the teachings of Christianity. Voltaire twisted Leibniz's philosophy into meaning that this was the best of all possible worlds. In 1755 a great earthquake convulsed Lisbon and killed 50,000 people. All Europe was deeply moved, and Voltaire used the occasion to describe the adventures of Candide, an innocent who stumbles through a world of ignorance, cruelty and violence, until he asks:

If this is the best of all possible worlds, what can the rest be like?

For fifteen years Voltaire lived at the country seat of Madame du Châtelet, and here he wrote his most popular tragedies, and entered into correspondence with Frederick the Great. After the death of his patroness in 1749 he was induced to settle at the Court of Frederick the Great. Frederick admired the philosopher, and wished to learn the art of literary composition in French, while Voltaire was well aware of the significance of having captivated the cleverest prince in Europe. But by 1753 the two had quarrelled, and Voltaire left Berlin, ultimately to settle at Ferney, near Geneva. For the rest of his life he was the philosophic monarch of Europe, and, as one French historian put it, before long King Voltaire became God Voltaire.

Voltaire's political ideas were much less clearly defined than his humanity. His most important political writing was in his *Lettres philosophiques* (1733). He was clearly deeply impressed by the English system of government, with the division of powers, and with the equitability of taxation. He admired the status of the English peasant. Above all he admired a social order based on the rule of law, and one which accorded such high status to the merchant, the scholar and the poet. But he never suggested that France should imitate the English constitution. Indeed he was not interested in any constitution for France. His *Histories*, which are of a high order, of the reigns of Louis XIV, Louis XV and Charles XII of Sweden, revealed how much he admired the power of a great monarch. In so far as he envisaged an ideal form of government, it was that of a philosopher-king, that is to say an Enlightened Despot who ruled according to the principles of Reason and toleration advocated by the *philosophes*. The idea that the common people should participate in government seemed to him fantastic. He once wrote to a friend:

> I think we misunderstand each other on the question of the people, whom you deem worthy of receiving education. I doubt whether this class of citizen will ever have the time or the capacity for education; they will die of hunger before ever becoming philosophers. I deem it essential that the ignorant poor should exist.[1]

But this attitude did not prevent his becoming indignant at the injustice of hanging a servant-girl for stealing handkerchiefs. The historic importance of Voltaire was his undermining the intellectual foundations of the *ancien régime*, his popularisation of philosophic doubt and his proclamation of a new philosophy of humanism. Shortly before his death he declared: 'I die adoring God and detesting superstition.'

[1] To Frederick the Great he wrote: 'I love not the government of the "canaille".'

L'Encyclopédie

Voltaire, by popularising the name of Newton and empirical science in Europe, helped to check the rationalist influence of Descartes. The age became fascinated with the possibilities of science, and its appetite was further whetted by the publication of *L'Encyclopédie* between 1751 and 1772, the greatest literary effort of the *philosophes*, and the mark of the triumph of their teaching.[1] It was edited by the philosopher Diderot and the scientist D'Alembert, and contained articles by a galaxy of great names, Voltaire, Montesquieu, Helvétius, Baron d'Holbach, Rousseau, Duclos and Buffon. It was full of the new science, explaining the new physics, the new cosmology, new techniques, new machinery. It proclaimed the new philosophy of humanism. One French historian has called it 'the balance-sheet of progress accomplished and the promise of future progress'. It made no direct attack either on religion or on politics, but articles were clearly written from the new point of view, and treated the old order with irony or disdain. Fanaticism and superstition were castigated, and the reader will find such statements as: 'Two principal obstacles have for a long time retarded the progress of philosophy—authority and the spirit of system'.[2] Voltaire, in the article on 'Happiness', hinted that virtue was not necessarily ascetic, and he added, with a characteristic jibe: 'Morality can exist without religion, and religion, perhaps often, can exist with immorality'. The article on 'Toleration' speaks with an incisiveness which suggests that public opinion had already been converted. About politics *L'Encyclopédie* mainly repeats the ideas of Montesquieu, or else proclaims the virtues of a philosopher-king.

The real instigator of *L'Encyclopédie* was Diderot, one of the most interesting and important of the *philosophes*, for he, more than any other, formulated the philosophy of materialism. He believed passionately in the possibilities of science. By the study of physics, chemistry,

---

[1] The first two volumes appeared in Paris in June 1751 and January 1752. They were suppressed by an *arrêt du Conseil* in February 1752, as 'tending to destroy the royal authority, to encourage a spirit of independence and revolt . . . and to erect the foundations of error, the corruption of manners, irreligion and impiety'. The sale of the books was forbidden, but no attempt was made to seize those copies already in circulation, and some ministers, like D'Argenson, acted as protectors of the Encyclopedists.

[2] By which was meant Aristotelian philosophy.

biology and the like, man could learn everything, even the true nature of so-called spiritual phenomena. Some of his ideas were set out in his *Pensées sur l'interpretation de la nature*, others lay buried in manuscript form until after the Revolution. Taking his stand firmly on the efficacy of experimental science, he attacked superstition, fanaticism and religion itself. Adapting Locke's famous metaphor, he wrote:

> Having strayed into an immense forest during the night, I have only a small light to guide me. I come across a stranger who says to me: 'My friend, blow out your candle in order the better to find your way.' This stranger is the theologian.

At the same time, Diderot was a man of sentiment, the author of plays, the *Pére de famille* and *Fils natural* which appealed to the heart of the middle classes of the time, and thus made his contribution to the 'comédie larmoyante' which heralded the new Romanticism. It was this aspect of Diderot which so inspired Rousseau. It was Diderot who called for 'War on civilisation and a return to Nature'. In his *Supplément au voyage de Bougainville* he idealised the 'natural' man, living in a state of nature. Civilisation brought corruption, tyranny and warfare. If you wished men to be free you should leave them alone. Morality was a fraud, a means by which a minority of society dominated the majority. But Diderot was no anarchist. His political views are difficult to disentangle. Perhaps it is fairest to say that he saw politics as a dilemma: the essence of politics was power, and power might be used for good or evil. The requisite for a well-governed State was just laws, and he wrote:

> There is no true sovereign, there can be no true legislator, but the people.

But he seems to have meant that their welfare should be the true test of a law, not that they should actively make laws. He was the correspondent of Catherine the Great of Russia; he advised her to set up a Commission to codify the law, and he entered her service as adviser on such matters. Yet in one of his writings he specifically rejects Enlightened Despotism:

> It has sometimes been said that the happiest government was that of the just and enlightened despot: it is a very reckless assertion. It could

easily happen that the will of this absolute master was in contradiction with the will of his subjects. Then, despite all his justice and all his enlightenment, he would be wrong to deprive them of their rights even in their own interests.

Diderot well understood the nature of political power, and his thought looks forward to the liberalism of the nineteenth century, but he must not be expected to produce a clear-cut programme of political reform for Europe.

A shallower thinker, but an important one in view of his influence, was Helvétius,[1] whose best-known work was *De l'Esprit* (1758). He was neither a notable philosopher nor a vigorous stylist, but his book was well received, and was approved by the French king. Starting from the theory of Montesquieu, Helvétius emphasised the influence of environment upon the human mind. Man was a product of his environment; his mind was moulded by manners, customs and above all by education. The mind was actuated by considerations of pleasure and pain, and by nothing else. It was these ideas which were developed later by Jeremy Bentham in England into the principles of Utilitarianism. Helvétius's theory of education also had great influence upon Rousseau, who did not, however, follow him to the conclusions of his materialism.

The ideas of the *philosophes* first became the subject of general discussion in the salons of Paris. At one time in the reign of Louis XIV there had seemed to be only one cultural centre in France, that of Versailles itself, but as in the eighteenth century the aristocracy and the wealthy returned to Paris, they once again established centres of pleasure and refinement. In the days of Fontenelle it was the salon of Mme. de Tencin, and later of Mme. Geoffrin and Mme. du Deffand. Here conversation was gentle and probably literary. The later salons, about the middle of the century, those of Helvétius and Baron d'Holbach, were bolder, and Diderot has left an account of the daring and scintillating subjects discussed. Here the new age of Science was applauded, and religion condemned as outmoded and corrupting. But whether it was the salon of Mlle. de Lespinasse, who was a Deist, or Mme. Necker, who was a Christian, all were agreed on the necessity for the triumph of the new philosophy. After the middle of the century, political and social subjects played a larger

[1] A tax-farmer, and a man of wealth.

part in the discussions. About 1760 a member of the *Académie française*, Lefranc, denounced the 'cynical liberty' which was abroad, and the 'proud philosophy which undermines equally throne and altar'. Yet even the *Académie française* was increasingly invaded by *philosophes*, who accounted for nine of the fourteen elections between 1760 and 1770.

The *philosophes*, if they published or circulated their books in France, still risked imprisonment. Diderot was imprisoned in Vincennes for one of his works. Buffon, a scientist and contributor to *L'Encyclopédie*, had his *Histoire naturelle* publicly burnt for seeming to contradict the Book of Genesis. *L'Encyclopédie* was for a time banned in France, although it circulated all the same. Moreover, books were very expensive (Voltaire's *Siècle de Louis XIV* cost fifteen livres) and could reach only a fortunate minority. Yet books did circulate, and a stream of literature poured from Amsterdam, Geneva and London. Banned books circulated freely at Court, and some of the *philosophes* could count on the patronage of Mme. de Pompadour, or powerful politicians like the Marquis d'Argenson. By 1770 the *philosophes* were becoming bolder in their assertions. Baron d'Holbach, a German who had settled in Paris and who became a kind of host to the encyclopedists, wrote *Le Système de la Nature* and *Le Système Social*, which proclaimed a complete materialism and defended complete liberty of thought. Between 1740 and 1770 there was a great increase in the publication of journals and newspapers, some of them short-lived, but numbering nineteen by 1770, such as the *Journal encyclopedique*, *Journal économique* and *Journal de physique*. The *Mercure* in particular recounted the theories of the *philosophes*. They were expensive, and did not reach more than a few thousand, but, within these limits, disseminated the new ideas. Voltaire was no longer a hunted refugee, but the powerful lord of Ferney, with an enormous income of almost 200,000 livres, the protector of his tenants, the builder of schools, and the object of pilgrimages from all over Europe. Yet it is doubtful whether before 1770 the new ideas of Enlightenment had extended far beyond the intellectuals and a select group of the aristocracy. Voltaire wrote in 1770:

> Go to a small village in the provinces, and rarely will you find one or two books there. . . . Judges, canons, the bishop, the subdélégué . . .

no-one has books, no-one has a cultivated mind; they are no more
advanced than in the twelfth century.

But perhaps such remarks are hardly evidence. After about 1770 a
change set in which represents not so much a triumph of the *philosophes* as a reaction against them. In following through the thought of
the *philosophes* from the Scientific Revolution of the seventeenth
century we have left out of account other tendencies of the thought
of the period. It must not be supposed for instance that the Catholic
Church did not combat the anti-religious tendencies with sound
arguments. Often these arguments were drawn from the philosophers
themselves, for Descartes' clear division of the Universe into Mind
and Matter provided effective arguments against the new materialism.
There was still plenty of evidence of intense religious feeling;
the great mass of the peoples of Europe were sincere Roman
Catholics, Greek Orthodox or Protestants. The increasingly important middle classes were closely connected with the religious revivals
of the time. In France and Italy the Jansenists reacted against the
tendencies of the age; they detested both the Jesuit power within the
Catholic Church, and the teachings of the *philosophes*. In England
Nonconformity flourished; attempts were made by Colley Cibber to
purify the stage; Addison emphasised the importance of the simple
virtues; Richardson's novels gave rise to a new literature of sentiment; and John Wesley made Methodism a new religion of the heart.
In France and Germany there began after 1670 a religious movement
known as Quietism, led by Philip Jacob Speuer in Saxony, and Mme.
Guyon in France. The emphasis was on the need to foster the inner
life by prayer and the avoidance of theological controversy. It
revolted against the rationalist tendencies of the time, and emphasised the sufficiency of love and simplicity of children. The movement
made notable converts in Germany, including the Elector of Brandenburg in 1694, and in France Mme. Guyon won over a number of
great ladies at Court, above all Mme. de Maintenon; but perhaps her
greatest triumph was the conversion of the great Fénelon. In a different field, the painters Greuze and Chardin, with their simple, homely
and often sentimental themes, emphasising the attractiveness of the
peasant life, and Diderot in his plays emphasising the value of the
simple virtues, all in their different ways indicated the coming

Romanticism. And thus the way was prepared for Jean-Jacques Rousseau.

Rousseau

Rousseau was born in Geneva in 1712, the son of a watchmaker. For years he was a wanderer, feckless, irresponsible, immature. But in 1749 he suddenly began pouring forth a number of passionate works which made an immense sensation. The Academy of Dijon offered a prize for an essay which discussed the question: 'Has the progress of science and art contributed to the corruption or to the improvement of morals?' Rousseau won the prize with an essay which argued that society had corrupted the natural man. In 1753 he followed this with a *Discours sur l'origine de l'inégalité parmi les hommes*. Essentially Rousseau's thought ran counter to that of Voltaire, Diderot and the Encyclopedists, who saw in science and knowledge the indispensable condition for man's progress towards happiness. Rousseau did not doubt the achievements of the intellect, but thought that they were far outweighed by the corruption and misery which had come with civilisation. To Rousseau civilisation ran counter to morality. Man was essentially a moral being; he could be happy only when living the moral life, and this could be achieved only in a state of nature. What exactly Rousseau meant by 'a state of nature' can easily be misunderstood. Some critics have jeered at the idea of advocating a return to conditions of caveman savagery. But that is not what Rousseau intended; indeed he explicitly stated that he did not suggest a return to primitive savagery. What he had in mind was a moral rather than an anthropological state, a return to a state of society in which the simple virtues, those of family-life and love of one's neighbour, should be supreme. Rousseau was a sincere Christian, and his idea of a state of nature was a moral concept, roughly the same as the interpretation of the Kingdom of Heaven, given in the Gospels. Rousseau did not suppose that civilisation should be destroyed, but he did urge that it should be reorientated, and this was the theme of his next two works. His essays had already made him famous, but he hated Paris and society, believed that he had not long to live, and was already developing a pathological fear of people which was to obsess him in his later days. It was therefore of infinite relief to him in 1756 to be allowed by Mme. d'Epinay to occupy her house, known as the

Hermitage, in the forest of Montmorency. Only then, he said, did he begin to live. Here he wrote his great romance, *La Nouvelle Héloïse*, in which, in a torrent of tears and sentiment, he painted a picture of the blonde Julie and her search for the true happiness of the simple life. This book was followed rapidly by *Emile* (1762), a study in educational theory. He began by declaring that 'in the natural order men are all equal', and their prime duty was to develop their essential manhood, regardless of the false requirements of civilisation, for 'civilised man is born and dies a slave':

> Fix your eyes on nature, follow the path traced by her. . . . Our passions are the chief means of self-preservation; to try to destroy them is therefore as absurd as it is useless.

To Rousseau's horror, his book was condemned by the *Parlement* of Paris, and he was forced to flee to Switzerland. The *Contrat social* (1762) was also condemned, but attracted much less attention. It was a difficult book, which did not exercise a perceptible influence upon political events until the French Revolution had actually begun. With his flight, Rousseau's health and mind rapidly gave way. His last work was his famous *Confessions*, one of the most moving works of self-revelation in any language. He died in 1778, the same year as Voltaire. By that time there had been six editions of his complete works, and ten of *La Nouvelle Héloïse*, and the cult of Rousseau reached phenomenal proportions as pilgrims filed to the Ile des Peupliers where he was buried. Brissot, Danton and Robespierre were among his devoted disciples. Rousseau's influence upon the French Revolution is beyond the period of this book but his influence before 1789 was of a different order; it was moral, not political. It was due to him more than to any single person that the idea was abroad that men were not evil by nature, but only corrupted by society; that the sentiments of pity, generosity and love could conquer the forces of egotism and cruelty. Kant summed up the matter best when he said that, before he read Rousseau, he supposed that man earned honour by virtue of his knowledge; Rousseau had taught him to honour man for his own sake. The great springtime of idealism which accompanied the French Revolution was in a special way presided over by the spirit of Rousseau. To this theme we shall return in the last chapter of this book.

The Nature of Enlightenment

We may now attempt a summary of the meaning of Enlightenment. In the eighteenth century men liked to think of 1,500 years of 'darkness' giving way to the new age of 'light', the light of Reason, or perhaps of reasonableness, dispersing the darkness of ignorance, authority and superstition. The new Science had shown that many of the former answers to great questions had been wrong; authority in matters of the intellect was shaken; in the long run the only ultimate test of right and wrong must be the individual reason and conscience. The age had to ask anew the old questions: 'What can I know? How ought I to act?' Enlightenment was therefore accompanied by a steady secularisation of thought. This did not necessarily mean a rejection of Christianity, but it did mean a rejection of authority which could not be squared with man's reason and conscience. The thought of the Enlightenment was strongly anti-clerical because the Catholic Church was seen as the great citadel of authority. The Universe was seen to be a mechanical structure moving according to ascertainable laws. Life was reasonable, and none the less enjoyable. The world still contained much wickedness, obscurantism, torture, tyranny, and these things must be eliminated. But with all its imperfections this world was no vale of tears, and happiness was a legitimate object of pursuit. Enlightenment meant humanitarianism. In society the two great enemies were feudal privilege and Catholic intolerance. *Écrasez l'infâme!* Enlightenment was a doctrine of action. It looked to the philosopher-king, the Enlightened Despot, to reform the State, rule by good laws and bring men light and happiness. The great hope for the future was man's increasing power over his environment. The *philosophes* worshipped power, because power could bring practical results. To them the Middle Ages were a period of violence, lawlessness, famine and misery. The eighteenth century looked to the rule of law, the advancement of science, good roads, the arts, to banish human misery. That was why the Lisbon earthquake was such a shock to them; they were suddenly reminded of the uncertainty of life, the injustice which could still accompany human affairs. On the whole, however, it was an age of optimism, although often the optimism of the *philosophes* concealed much agony of heart-rending doubt. The eighteenth century had a comfortable sense of growing mastery over environment. *L'Encyclopédie* was not just, or even primarily, a tirade against the Church—it was full of practical information on the arts and crafts. The material things of life were there to be enjoyed. Economics assumed a new importance, and it is to this subject that we must now turn.

2: The Age of Mercantilism

The Tendency towards Centralisation

The period 1660–1789 was one of remarkable economic progress in Europe. The fact is reflected in the growth of population. Although in the absence of exact statistics it is difficult to be precise, it appears likely that whereas the population of Europe was about 118 millions about 1700, a century later it was 187 millions. The French population increased from about 20 millions in 1660 to 26 millions by 1790; that of Britain from about 5 to 10 millions; that of Spain about the same as Britain's; Poland's increased from 6 million in 1660 to 11 millions at the time of the Partitions; Russia (including annexations) increased from 8 to 30 millions. These increases were often the result of more settled conditions and the growth of economic activity; in many cases they were connected with the growth of State activity in ordering and encouraging production and exchange of goods. But economic development did not proceed at an equal pace all over Europe. There was in fact a sharp line to be drawn between England, the Dutch and France on the one hand, which made rapid economic progress, and the rest of Europe, which moved much more slowly.

All Mercantilists believed it important that every means should be taken to encourage the growth of a vigorous and useful population. Some doubted whether the founding of colonies was a good thing if it deprived the mother country of valuable citizens. It was always the policy of the Hohenzollerns, from the Great Elector to Frederick the Great, to encourage immigrants who could bring in new crafts or settle the land. In France Colbert thought it so important that men should be encouraged to marry young and have large families that in 1666 it was enacted that if they married before the age of twenty they were exempt from *taille* until the age of twenty-five. The same law granted tax exemptions to the father of a family of ten or more children on condition that none of them became priest or nun. A decree of 1669, applying to Canada, imposed fines on fathers who did not marry off their sons before the age of twenty, or their daughters before the age of sixteen. Although many mercantilist writers were concerned at problems of beggary, on the whole they favoured a large pool of cheap labour as needful to a healthy economy.

In 1660 an intelligent statesman, say a Colbert, pondering the problems of wealth and power which faced any State, could not fail to observe two astonishing facts. The first was that the power of the great Spanish Empire, which included Spain, Spanish America, the Netherlands, Franche Comté, Milan and the Two Sicilies, appeared to rest upon the wealth which flowed into Spanish coffers in the form of gold and silver from the New World. The second was that the numerically insignificant Dutch people had achieved boundless wealth and prosperity by foreign trade. The fact was inescapable that the power of a State depended upon its wealth, and the wealth of a State depended upon organisation and foreign trade.

In 1660 the very conception of a 'State' was a new one in many parts of Europe. The Middle Ages, in spite of its theory of universality, was a period in which particularism triumphed. Except in special circumstances, where geography or the existence of a remarkable line of rulers favoured centralisation, as for instance in the States ruled by the Normans, or in Aragon, mediaeval Europe was really a patchwork of autonomous entities, feudal nobility, towns, guilds, which did much as they liked without restraint from a central authority. The very fact that a town was growing wealthy by trade meant that it was little subject to the control of a mediaeval ruler; and, within the town, authority was divided between its powerful gilds. Mediaeval rulers levied tolls, and sometimes directed trade through staples, but there was usually a complete lack of coherent economic policy. Difficulties in the way of mediaeval trade were enormous. Each town might have its own system of weights and measures and a different coinage, while along the main trade routes customs barriers were erected every few miles. In Germany for instance it would be necessary to change currency with every day's journey, and along the Rhine there were no less than sixty customs stations. At the end of the seventeenth century in the Archbishoprics of Mainz and Cologne there were customs barriers about every ten miles. The river Weser had thirty-three customs barriers, one for every ten miles. At the end of the Thirty Years' War it was said that wine and wheat sent from Mannheim to the Dutch frontier trebled in price on the journey. In

1685 it was said that of every sixty planks of timber floated down the Elbe, fifty-four of them went in customs payments, twenty-one of them in customs to Brandenburg alone. There was also a great waste of time. A boat which would normally take eight days to sail from Dresden to Hamburg, took four weeks with delays at the customs houses. There was also the danger of corruption and extortion, for customs officials could demand much what they liked from unfortunate merchants and traders.

In the seventeenth century the idea grew that the way out of the difficulty was by increased action on the part of the central government. In 1604 the privy council of Brandenburg complained that in spite of what they regarded as favourable conditions, especially its good waterways, fewer and fewer merchants appeared to be visiting Brandenburg. The reason, they stated, was that the executive was too weak, and that there was too little internal unity. During the Thirty Years' War conditions became worse for much of Germany. Yet it was apparent that the States which in history had become rich, Venice, Milan, Genoa, Spain, Portugal, Holland, and later France and England, did so because there was a strong central authority, and a good deal of State control, or at least State encouragement. In the seventeenth and eighteenth centuries there was therefore a strong economic incentive towards centralisation, supported by the most progressive and intelligent sections of the community. As early as 1560 a member of the French States General had declared 'We want one religion, one law and one king'. Colbert, in a memorandum to Louis XIV in 1665, spoke of his great project

> to bring the whole of His Majesty's kingdom within the same statutes and within the same system of weights and measures, an undertaking very worthy of our great king. . . . Whatever His Majesty has done so far is nothing in comparison with this work. His Majesty will derive satisfaction from achieving that which hardly any prince before him has ever attempted.

The work of Louis XIV and Colbert will only be understood if it is realised with what sense of creative adventure it was initially undertaken. In Brandenburg too the Hohenzollerns between 1640 and 1740 built their scattered dominions into a centralised State based on economic and military unity. European monarchs became increasingly despotic because there was an overpowering need to check feudal and municipal liberties, and to encourage greater economic activity and create wider economic units. Thus all the more or less 'enlightened' monarchs of the period were mercantilists. The task was a difficult one, for rulers were poor and lacked resources. They had difficulty in achieving administrative uniformity and bringing nobility and towns under their control. In Brandenburg-Prussia towns like Stettin, Stralsund, Königsberg and Magdeburg retained positions of independence almost like that of Imperial cities until the time of the Great Elector and Frederick William I. It is significant that ordinances had been made in the sixteenth century that the Berlin weights and measures should be the regular measures throughout Brandenburg, but these were almost entirely ignored. In the matter of customs the ruler was in a particular dilemma, for although excessive customs duties undoubtedly hampered trade, he was far too dependent upon them for revenues to reduce them. Frederick William I of Prussia attempted to regularise the system, but not to change it, and there is no evidence that any of the Electors of Brandenburg ever abolished a customs house. Indeed, when new territory came under their control, it was more likely that customs dues would be increased and become more oppressive than ever before. If to this is added the difficulties imposed by geography on a country so disunited as Brandenburg-Prussia, it will be seen that commercial expansion was gravely handicapped. So far as customs barriers were concerned, Prussia continued to be a mediaeval country until the great Prussian tariff reform of 1818. In Bavaria in the eighteenth century there were nearly 500 customs barriers. No European ruler could afford to dispense with so valuable a source of revenue.

The Principles of Mercantilism

There never was a complete and coherent theory of Mercantilism, no single and unified body of Mercantilist doctrine. Sir George Clark wrote that

> it was not the same thing for Frenchmen as for Englishmen, not the same for Englishmen as for Dutchmen. It was variously understood and applied by politicians and by merchants. It meant one thing to the apologists of the East India trade and another to the home manufacturers who tried to compete against imported eastern goods.[1]

[1] Clark: *The Seventeenth Century*, 1947, p. 21.

Heckscher asserted that

> the first attempt to portray the workings of economic life as a consistent whole was probably that of the physiocrats, and no mercantilist arrived at such an outlook before their time.[1]

But in spite of such limitations, it is possible to state the general nature of Mercantilism. The German historian Schmoller long ago declared that

> in its innermost kernel it is nothing but State-making. The essence of the system lies not in some doctrine of money, or of the balance of trade; not in tariff barriers, protective duties or navigation laws; but in something far greater, namely in the total transformation of society and its organisation, as well as of the State and its institutions, in the replacing of a local and territorial economic policy by that of the State.[2]

It was a policy pursued by all the more or less despotic governments of the period 1660–1789, in so far as they had a policy at all. All the 'enlightened' governments of the time were much concerned with economic development; it followed that they were opposed to feudal, municipal and gild independence, and to the spirit of particularism. Even in the Dutch Netherlands, which so often seem to provide exceptions to such generalisations, it is probably true that the State was strongest when there was a Stadholder, and declined most rapidly when bourgeois localism triumphed. Richelieu's attacks on feudal independence in France, and upon Huguenot particularism in the towns, had important economic, as well as political, significance. Mercantilism usually placed obstacles in the way of the importation of foreign manufactures, always for revenue purposes, and sometimes for the protection of home industries; often there was prohibition of the export of raw materials; sometimes there were bounties paid on exports; fisheries were encouraged as an important source of trade, and as a breeding-ground for experienced seamen; the possession of colonies was encouraged if they produced raw materials and foodstuffs which could not be produced at home, and colonial trade was strictly reserved for the benefit of the mother-country.

Colbert and French Mercantilism

The most complete Mercantilist of the period was Jean-Baptiste Colbert, who for twenty-two years, until his death in 1683, was the

---

[1] Eli Heckscher: *Mercantilism*, trans. Shapiro, 1935.

[2] Schmoller: *The Mercantile System*, 1884.

chief servant of Louis XIV. He was first and foremost a practical government agent. The purpose of his policy was simply to make France strong, and the key to strength, he held, lay in wealth. Rulers like Louis XIV were not naturally interested in trade, nor had much to do with merchants, but Colbert saw that in the economic activity of a State lay its means to power. Colbert was primarily concerned with power; the object of his efforts was to make Louis XIV supreme in France, and France supreme in Europe. He wrote in 1664:

> Trade is the source of public finance, and public finance is the vital nerve of war.

In terms of wealth and power the greatest enemies of France in Europe were the Dutch, for the Dutch were using their economic power as the carriers of Europe to dominate the Continent. In 1664 he wrote:

> Upon this they base the principal doctrine of their government, knowing full well that if they but have the mastery of trade, their powers will continually wax on land and sea and will make them so mighty that they will be able to set up as arbiters of peace and war in Europe and set bounds, at their pleasure, to the justice and all the plans of princes.

Colbert saw all commercial relations between States as a kind of warfare. In 1670 he wrote to the King:

> It seems as if Your Majesty, having taken in hand the administration of your finances, has undertaken a monetary war against all European States. Your Majesty has already conquered Spain, Italy, Germany, England, and several other countries, and has forced them into great misery and poverty. At their expense Your Majesty has waxed rich and so has acquired the means of carrying out the many great works Your Majesty has undertaken. . . . There remains only Holland, which still struggles with all its great power. . . . Your Majesty has founded Companies (i.e. commercial companies) which attack them everywhere like armies. The manufactures, the shipping canal between the seas[1] and so many other new establishments which Your Majesty sets up are so many reserve corps which your Majesty creates from nothing in order that they may fulfil their duty in this war. . . . This war, which must be waged with might and main, and in which the most powerful republic since the Roman Empire is the price of victory, cannot cease soon, but rather it must engage Your Majesty's chief attention during the whole of your life.

[1] Colbert is referring to the Languedoc Canal, see p. 48.

This was a direct invitation to Louis to engage in war for the destruction of the Dutch, and the motive was the pursuit of power as an end in itself. It is true that when Colbert writes of war he is thinking, not of what today would be called 'hot' war, but of economic rivalry. Some confusion may arise if it is forgotten that Colbert's metaphors were deliberately chosen to appeal to the peculiar predilections of Louis XIV. The King, for instance, would be more interested in the progress of a commercial company if he could be persuaded to think of it as part of his army. But the metaphor did not falsify Colbert's real intentions. He certainly welcomed the war of 1672 against the Dutch. When later he attacked Louvois' war expenditure, it was not because he disapproved of the objects of the war, but because he thought that excessive military expenditure was weakening the economic strength of the State. To Colbert, the strength of a country lay in its finances; the more money there was in a country, the easier it was for people to pay taxes; the more money there was in the Treasury, the stronger the ruler. He wrote:

> I believe this principle will be readily agreed to, that it is only the abundance of money in a State which makes the difference in its greatness and power.

It follows that the object of the State should be to attract money into the country, and where possible to prevent its export. The latter will also have the effect of correspondingly weakening one's neighbours. The policy must therefore be to encourage exports and reduce imports, and to increase the economic self-sufficiency of the State. Colbert's attitude may be illustrated by his difference in approach to French trade with Cadiz and with the Levant. The Cadiz trade gave France a favourable balance of trade, and a share in Spanish bullion from the New World, and thus should be encouraged. But trade between Marseilles and the Levant had an unfavourable balance, involved the export of bullion, and therefore came in for severe criticism, as did also the trade of the East India Company. These trading activities, he argued, could be justified only if French merchants exported goods, not bullion.

Colbert's attitude to trade was based on a faulty theory, but one which led to practical developments. He believed that the amount of trade in the world was fixed, so that one country could expand its trade only at the expense of another. In a famous report to the King, he wrote that Europe's trade was carried in 20,000 ships, a number which could hardly be increased, and that the Dutch had about 15,000 of them, the English 3,000 to 4,000, and the French 500 or 600. These proportions represented therefore the extent of the participation of these nations in European trade. If we think of European trade as a cake, the question was how large a slice France could gain. Trade therefore was a form of warfare. Colbert wrote to the King:

> Commerce causes a perpetual combat in peace and war among the nations of Europe, as to who shall win most of it.

At that time the Dutch were in possession of three-quarters of the cake, and therefore were the principal enemies of France ('mortal enemies' he called them). Colbert wrote that Louis XIV 'has undertaken a war of money against all the States of Europe'. He regarded commercial companies as armies attacking Dutch ascendancy. Commerce was to him a form of warfare, and when actual war began in 1672, he strongly supported it. For the resistance of the Dutch, he thought, would be shortlived, and the conquest of the Netherlands, and the incorporation into France of Dutch wealth and commercial power, would be of enormous benefit to France.

French commercial expansion under Colbert was very different in character from that of the English or Dutch, where the initiative came from enterprising individuals, at best encouraged by the central government. In France Colbert thought of the initiative as coming mainly from the State, that is from Colbert himself. In 1664 he persuaded the King to establish a new royal council, the Council of Commerce, presided over by the King himself, to direct commercial activity. After 1669 it declined in importance, because Colbert preferred to work through the Council of Finance, and it disappeared in 1676. A new Council of Commerce, however, emerged in 1700, which lasted until the Revolution. Its business was to assist commerce, to establish a new code of commercial law and business practice, fix rates of interest, encourage the formation of companies and increase the freedom of internal trade. To Colbert it seemed that the secret of Dutch success lay in great monopoly companies, such as the East India Company. He studied in detail the accounts of the Dutch East

India Company, and saw with amazement that in 1664 they possessed property worth 800,000,000 livres. In 1664 the French East India Company was founded, and in the same year the West India Company; in 1665 the Albouzême Company (for trade with Algiers and Morocco); in 1669 the Company of the North (for trade with the Baltic) and in 1670 the Levant Company. There were also several attempts at an Africa Company to develop the slave trade. They were all largely State enterprises. A large proportion of the capital was put up by the King himself. Private citizens were very reluctant to invest, and all sorts of government pressure was put upon local authorities to raise the necessary capital. Directors of companies were strictly controlled, and their position was more like that of civil servants than merchants. Thus in 1664 Colbert persuaded Louis XIV to write to the financial officers in Bourges to persuade them to subscribe to the new East India Company. Intendants brought heavy pressure in their provinces; magistrates and other officials were expected to invest, and those who did not were penalised. The King himself put up sometimes one-tenth and sometimes one-quarter of the capital, and in addition guaranteed investors against losses. In spite of all this, the Company of the North, after four years of vigorous propaganda, could extort investments of only 5 million livres from the public, and more than half the total share capital was owned by the State. Merchants often regarded the Companies with active hostility, for they were monopolistic, oppressive and minutely controlled by Colbert. Colbert always believed that the central government knew best, that State interest was paramount, and that he could ride roughshod over local interests and prejudices.

It is difficult therefore to assess the degree of success of Colbert's commercial policy. Eli Heckscher, when he came to examine Colbert's achievements, came to the conclusion that merchants in the time of Louis XIV showed 'less spontaneity than in the time of Henry IV, Richelieu and Mazarin', though he left open the question whether too much State control 'had acted as a deterrent upon private enterprise or not'. It is certainly true that few of Colbert's Companies were for long a financial success, and few of them survived him. Heckscher showed that 'French mercantilism failed to pave the way towards any vigorous development of companies with corporative capital'. Yet Colbert's achievements were substantial, and it is debatable how far

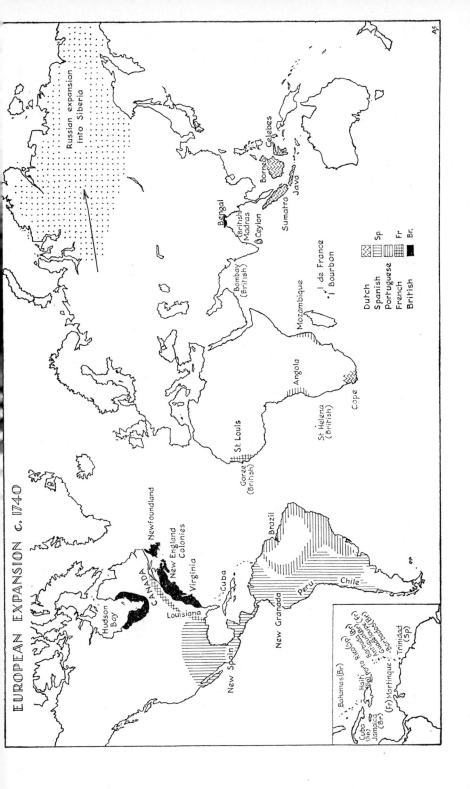

EUROPEAN EXPANSION c. 1740

Russian expansion into Siberia

Bengal
British
Madras
Ceylon
Bombay
(British)
Sumatra
Borneo
Celebes
Java

I de France
I Bourbon

Mozambique

Angola

St. Louis

Gorée
(British)

St. Helena
(British)

Cape

Dutch   Sp.
Spanish
Portuguese
French   Fr.
British   Br.

Hudson Bay
CANADA
Newfoundland
New England Colonies
Virginia
Louisiana
New Spain
Cuba
New Granada
Peru
Chile
Brazil

Bahamas (Br.)
Cuba (Sp.)
Jamaica (Br.)
Haiti (Sp.)
Puerto Rico (Sp.)
Guadeloupe (Fr.)
Antigua (Br.)
Martinique (Fr.)
Trinidad (Sp.)

45

the failure of France to continue his work in the eighteenth century should be blamed on Colbert. The East India Company was not at first a financial success; between 1675 and 1684 its receipts of nearly 4½ million livres were insufficient to cover expenditure. But the profits of the Company were substantial in the eighteenth century, and whereas in 1664 the India trade was a monopoly of the Dutch, English and Portuguese, by 1683 the French had two stations at Surat and Pondicherry, and in the time of Dupleix provided a formidable challenge to the British. Similarly, when the West India Company was founded, French trade with the fourteen French West Indian islands was almost entirely in the hands of the Dutch. The Dutch carried slaves to the islands and exchanged them for sugar, cotton, tobacco and indigo which they carried to France, the whole trade engaging some 200 ships. Colbert found the usual difficulties in launching his Company. Capital was hard to find, and Dutch hostility was great. His decree excluding Dutch ships from the West Indian islands in 1664, before his Company was strong enough to take over, left the islands to starve, and the sugar crops to waste. War also meant heavy losses of shipping, and the Company had constantly to be propped up by Treasury grants. Eventually Colbert had to abandon the Company's monopoly and allow private traders to operate. The Company itself went bankrupt and was wound up in 1674. Yet the monopoly of the Dutch was broken, and by 1674 a hundred French ships a year were going to the West Indies. The Company of the North was ruined by the wars of the 1670s, was partly liquidated in 1677, but dragged on a shadowy existence until 1689. Yet French Baltic trade had begun, and it played its part in strengthening Louis XIV's relations with Sweden. The Levant Company was a complete failure, but the Africa Company had in the 1680s an annual trade worth 1½ million livres, and gave the French a firm foothold in Goree in West Africa. The conclusion therefore would seem to be that Colbert's Companies, with all their failures, did lay the basis for a French commercial and colonial empire in the eighteenth century, and did greatly stimulate French overseas trade.

Colbert also wished to stimulate the internal trade of France. Here the greatest obstacles were the internal customs barriers; there were more customs houses on the Loire than on the Rhine. In his report of 1663, Colbert emphasised his determination to abolish them, but this statement must be clearly understood, for he seems to have been referring, not to the customs houses which yielded valuable sums to the Treasury, but to illegal ones which had grown up for the benefit of privileged individuals. In this he seems completely to have failed. Thus in 1682, as an encouragement to road-building, all land-owners were granted the right to tax vehicles passing along roads through their estates. As for the customs levied by the Crown, they were far too important a source of revenue for Colbert ever to attempt to abolish them, though he was well aware of their hampering effect, and he would have abolished them if he had had the power. After his death conditions became worse. In 1697 the intendant of Languedoc reported that the Rhône was so encumbered with royal and private customs stations that ships were held up at almost every reach. In Poitou there were more than a hundred road and river customs houses in the hands of private landowners alone. As Louis' wars towards the end of the reign increased the need for revenue, internal customs were doubled. Even before this a consignment of grain which had to travel 250 miles would double in price. In 1701 there were thirty customs stations in the 600 kilometres between Roanne and Nantes, and conditions were no better than they had been in 1664, when it had been declared that:

> freedom of trade is so restricted among our own subjects of the same province that they cannot supply one another with fruit and food or with the products which they themselves produce, or trade with their neighbours, without paying the aforesaid customs.

So far was Colbert from contemplating internal free trade that in some ways he strengthened the old system. Most of France north of the provinces of Poitou, Bourdonnais and Burgundy was known as 'les cinq grosses fermes', because their customs and other revenues were organised into five tax-farms. In addition to countless internal dues, 'les cinq grosses fermes' imposed customs duties on the rest of France as if it had been a foreign country. In 1664 Colbert established a unified and single customs system to govern trade relations between 'les cinq grosses fermes' and the rest of France, and thus simpli-fied, though it helped to perpetuate, the evil system. It is only fair to say, however, that where Colbert failed to carry reform, so did all other Ministers down to the French Revolution. A good plan of reform was at last worked out by the Physiocrats in the 1780s, but by then the Government was quite incapable of carrying it out, and the whole system was finally swept away by the Constituent Assembly.

Part of the money from the excessive customs was spent on the provision of a greatly improved system of transport. Colbert began a programme of road-building which was continued in the eighteenth century, and gave France a system of highways which was the wonder of Europe. Intendants were made responsible for the main roads and the expenses were borne by the King. But in the seventeenth century waterways were even more important than roads, and Colbert began a great programme of improvement of the navigability of some twenty-five of the chief rivers. Still more remarkable was his achievement in canal-building. The Loire and the Seine were connected by the Orleans Canal in 1679. But the canal which gave him special pride was the Languedoc Canal, which connected the Atlantic with the Mediterranean. Built by Pierre-Paul Riquet in 1666 and not completed until 1681, it was 175 miles long and contained 65 locks, at a cost of 17 million livres, a remarkable piece of engineering which would greatly have reduced the cost of transport if the tolls had not been so high.[1]

It was typical of the extreme particularism of mediaeval Europe that there was, in France, as elsewhere, the greatest confusion in weights and measures, and the difficulty of achieving uniformity was great. The measure for liquids in Paris was the *muid*, in Orleans the *queue*, in Burgundy the *feuillette*, in Poitou the *pipe*, in Bordeaux the *tonneau*. Even where a measure had the same name in two places there was no guarantee that it was really the same. The difficulties which this created for commercial transactions can be imagined. There was, for instance, ample room for corruption. The tax-collector might collect payments in kind with a large measure, keep his accounts in a small measure, and appropriate the difference. In coinage France was more fortunate; there was already a unified coinage system by the reign of Louis XIV. Colbert did not attempt a single system of weights and measures, but issued countless regulations governing the size and quality of manufactures. No eighteenth-

[1] Arthur Young was very impressed with the sight of the canal in 1787, and commented, 'Here Louis XIV thou art truly great!'

century government went much further, and one of the *cahiers* of 1789 declared:

> If only we had a single weight and a single measure in the whole kingdom! Oh, for what a number of years we have longed for this and how many lawsuits and arguments it would prevent!

Again it was left to the French Revolution to carry the reform which Colbert never felt strong enough even seriously to contemplate.

By the customs reform of 1664 Colbert aimed at standardisation and administrative efficiency, with some 580 articles paying specific single duties. The customs reform of 1667 was more frankly protectionist, and raised the import duty on 57 articles and the export duties on four. This was part of a tariff war against foreign manufactures, a proclamation of economic nationalism, and a blow struck in the bitter economic struggle with the Dutch. A tariff war followed, in which in 1671 the French excluded Dutch herrings and the Dutch replied by excluding French brandy. The war of 1672 had, among others, strong economic motives. Colbert was jubilant, and wrote that the annexation of Dutch wealth was the most desirable of all things. But he miscalculated. He thought that the war would last six weeks; instead it lasted six years, and the Dutch were not conquered. Finally in the Treaty of Nijmegen in 1678, the Dutch insisted upon the abrogation of the tariff of 1667, in so far as it discriminated against the Dutch. Economic nationalism was thus a powerful factor making for war in the period, and the idea that Colbert was a man of commerce and peace, opposed to wars because of their expense, is wide of the mark. Colbert often complained of the cost of wars, but he saw them as steps to the increasing power and grandeur of Louis XIV.

Colbert provided not only the financial means to war, but in one respect clearly forged the instruments of war. For he was the creator of the French navy. But he saw it not merely as an instrument of war, but also as the means of protecting commerce, and defending colonies and trading stations throughout the world. In 1661 the French navy consisted of eighteen vessels, some of them quite unseaworthy, and cost only about 300,000 livres a year. Colbert spent, on average, 10 million livres a year on the fleet. He developed a prosperous shipbuilding industry, and the manufacture of naval supplies which previously had been imported. In twenty years he built up a fleet of 200 ships of all types, with some 30,000 trained officers and men, capable for a time of threatening the combined Anglo-Dutch fleets, the two greatest fleets in the world, during the War of the League of Augsburg. Colbert was passionately interested in his fleet (in the work of which he was ably assisted by his son Seignelay), and it was always a matter of great regret to him that he failed to interest the King in its progress. Not until 1680 did Louis even visit a port, and he never understood, as Colbert did, the uses to which a fleet might be put in war. In the age of Mercantilism the growth of naval power and overseas trade was intimately connected, and in this Colbert's work was of the greatest importance.

In the pursuit of self-sufficiency it was an essential part of Colbert's work to encourage French industry. In 1661 he calculated that whereas France annually imported some 25 million livres' worth of manufactures, she exported not much more than half that value, and thus had an unfavourable balance of trade. Colbert's attempts to regulate and develop industry were all part of the attempt to central-ise and unify the State, and his measures were so detailed, and so widely publicised, that they became the model for all such legislation throughout Europe in the following century. He sought to regulate industry on a national basis. Some such control was certainly neces-sary to counteract the chronic particularism and obscurantism of local industries. Many industries were organised in particular towns in gilds known as *jurandes*, in which their members were bound by oath, with full powers to make by-laws and regulate the industry throughout a particular town, and impose detailed regulations on their journeymen and apprentices. Contrary to general belief, these *jurandes* were mostly not of mediaeval origin, but had proliferated rapidly in the seventeenth century. Poitiers, for instance, which had about fifteen gilds in 1400, had thirty-five by 1708. Some towns, like Lyon, resisted the growth of powerful gilds until at least the six-teenth century. It is sometimes supposed that Colbert's policy was opposed to the gilds, but this was not so. In fact his aim was to extend the operation of gilds over the countless small producers, and impose upon them a uniformity in every detail of organisation and production. Strictly this was not a new policy. Since the sixteenth century the French monarchy had encouraged the gilds and had given them privileges, with the object of achieving greater uniformity of workmanship and a greater guarantee of quality. In 1581, for instance, to encourage the spread of craftsmanship throughout the country, masters of a gild in Paris or Lyon were permitted to practise their craft anywhere in the country. Gilds were unpopular with many workmen, and it was a recurrent difficulty to force craftsmen to join them. Many gilds therefore grew in the seventeenth century because of the active encouragement of the central government. In Paris, for instance, there were 60 gilds in 1673, but 129 gilds in 1683. Colbert sought to work through the gilds and to control them in all details. In this he worked mainly through the Intendants, but also through inspectors of manufactures, an office he developed in 1669, with the widest powers of control in their area. These inspectors were virtually Colbert's eyes and ears in the provinces. They were widely hated, but were often men of great ability and devotion. Nowhere in Europe was industry more thoroughly organised than in the France of Louis XIV.

Colbert issued a huge number of *règlements* with the object of unifying industry throughout the country, especially in textiles. Looms were to be of a certain size, wool of a certain weight, cloth of a certain width. In 1669 it was decreed that only masters of gilds could produce cloth of any kind, thus compelling producers to be members of gilds. The *règlements* continued to be issued after Colbert's death, and those for the period 1666–1730 are contained in seven quarto volumes. The dyeing regulations alone ran into 317 articles. Contravention of any of the rules could incur a fine of 100 livres. Gilds must inspect each operation and affix a mark accordingly. Fine cloth carried a disc with the arms of the King, and the words 'Louis XIV, Restaurateur des Arts et du Commerce'. Many of Colbert's *règlements* were in the best interests of the industry, and were made only after consultations with the best workmen. Still, they were constantly disregarded, for few workmen could read; gild officials, and even government inspectors, were often careless. Even so, such a rigid system pressed heavily on new ideas and improvements; colour-printing of textiles instead of dyeing, for instance, was for a long time forbidden (to the great benefit of English cotton printers). Gilds were often rigidly exclusive; between 1684 and 1706 the Lyon silk industry refused to take any new apprentice who was not the son of a master of the gild. Gilds were also constantly at expensive litigation in an attempt to retain their exclusivism as well as their standards, and in this they could usually rely upon the good will of the *parlements*. Gilds were also increasingly subjected to unnecessary expenditure at the hands of an impecunious government. There was a growing practice of purchasing the right of mastership of a gild, not from the gild itself, but from the King. One of the great curses of the *ancien régime* was the sale of offices, and even the creation of offices for the sole purpose of raising money by sale. In the second half of the reign of Louis XIV at least 10,000 such offices were created; it was by such means that the Grand Monarque was able to make ends meet. The practice pressed heavily up on the gilds, as indeed upon the whole administrative system. They were forced to appoint 'auditors' or 'greffiers', to pay heavy fines from time to time as means of purchasing the continuance of their privileges. These evil practices did not begin with Louis XIV, and they continued throughout the eighteenth century. The result was a clogging of the administrative system, until it ground almost to a standstill; and most of the gilds were heavily in debt when Turgot unsuccessfully attempted to abolish them in 1776.

Colbert succeeded in powerfully stimulating large-scale industry in France, especially in textiles. In 1661 France was importing some 5 million livres of woollen fabrics; Colbert set out to make her self-sufficient. His methods of encouragement were various: there were tariffs on imports, bounties on exports, periods of tax exemption for new industries, special privileges for skilled foreigners who came into France and set up new industries, and free loans of capital. The most famous of the immigrants was Van Robais, a Dutchman whom Colbert persuaded to come in with fifty Dutch workers in 1665. He received letters patent from the King, and was given a monopoly and other privileges at Abbeville, where he set up his works. By 1680 Van Robais had 80 looms and 1,690 workers engaged in the production of fine cloth. It is significant that in spite of his Protestantism, he survived the Revocation of the Edict of Nantes, and his works were still prosperous at the time of the Revolution. Similarly, two Dutchmen, Massieu and Jemblin, settled at Caen and began the manufacture of fine cloth, and other manufactures were established at Louviers, Elbeuf, Fécamp, Sedan, Dieppe, Rouen, Paris, Troyes, Meaux and Senlis. A contemporary in 1727 described Van Robais' factory with admiration. It was a large factory surrounded by a high wall and a moat, and with keepers in royal livery guarding the entrances. Other manufacturers often preferred the 'putting-out' system, but many of them (*maîtres marchands-fabriquants*) had as many as a thousand employees. The most progressive trades in the eighteenth century were the luxury trades, and silks, hosiery, lace and tapestry were in great demand. The silk industry had been introduced from Italy in the sixteenth century, but it remained small until encouraged by Colbert, not only at Lyon, but also at Virieu, Pelussin, La Rivière, Nîmes, Tours, Toulouse and Saint-Étienne. The stocking industry expanded at Paris, Lyon and Nîmes, and the linen industry at Auxerre, Toulouse, Poitou and elsewhere. In 1661 the best lace still came from Venice, and France imported a million livres' worth a year. In 1665 Colbert established a monopoly company for the manufacture of French point at Arras, Reims, Alençon and elsewhere, and although in some places there was failure, in others there was moderate success. There was also a rapid growth of sugar-refining, soap, paper, glass and porcelain industries. But the centre and show-piece of Colbert's efforts was the Gobelin works which, together with the Savonnerie and Beauvais factories, produced the *décor* for the Grand Monarque at Versailles. Colbert spent hundreds of thousands of livres in support of the Gobelins, and millions of livres on their products, all to the glorification of the royal palaces. Skilled workers of all kinds were gathered there, painters, sculptors, goldsmiths, cabinet-makers and Flemish tapestry-makers, and were highly paid. Orders for the royal palaces were the life-blood of the industry, but French gobelins, furniture, fine silks, brocades, hosiery, ribbons, lace with gold and silver threads, mirrors and porcelain were purchased with envy and admiration by the princes of Europe. They made France the artistic dictator of Europe; every petty prince longed to have a miniature gobelin factory for the imitation of French designs. The artistic aspect of the Grand Siècle, and the luxury industries associated with them, acted as a great civilising influence upon Europe, and were clearly the product of State enterprise. Perhaps they constitute Louis XIV's greatest claim to the gratitude of posterity.

Heckscher called Louis XIV's creation of these luxury industries 'the most powerful, most typical and most purposeful achievement of mercantilism', and this is true. Yet Colbert's efforts did not win industrial supremacy for France. There were strict limits to what could be achieved by State control. Much of French industry always remained outside gild control, and nonetheless expanded and flourished. The French iron industry received much less help from Colbert than did the luxury trades, yet expanded and produced goods of excellent quality. These facts suggest that the greater freedom of the English system was preferable. Perhaps there was too exclusive a concentration upon the luxury trades. Moreover, State control of industry could be stifling, and its fiscal demands ruinous. The general tendency of the eighteenth century was towards greater freedom in economic matters: Colbert certainly paid too little attention to agriculture. Even without a Colbert there would have been a great economic expansion consequent upon the greater peace and security which Louis XIV's reign brought to France. Yet his achievements were great. He created the luxury industries, and the vigorous State activity during the reign gave a powerful stimulus to economic development throughout France. He created the navy and mercantile marine, and pointed the way to overseas and colonial expansion. The impression remains that he provided France with a tremendous opportunity which was never adequately pursued after his death. The fact is that in 1683 France was the leading industrial nation in the world; her wealth and volume of trade continued for the next two generations to be the greatest in the world. Colbert's work, with all its shortcomings, represents the greatest attempt to reform the French State before the Revolution. His powers were limited; one notes, for instance, his failure to institute an adequate reform of French finances, which might have changed the whole course of eighteenth-century history. Perhaps there was a paradox in Colbert's Mercantilism, for it needed peace in which to produce its greatest results, yet by its very nature it helped to produce wars, which often ruined his companies and placed intolerable burdens on State finances. Colbert did not merely tolerate Louis XIV's wars; he actively promoted them. His work remains, however, the greatest piece of State planning in the age of Mercantilism.

The Netherlands

In the middle of the seventeenth century the Dutch were by far the greatest mercantile people in Europe, and the Mercantilists of France,

England, Prussia and Russia all gave particular attention to Dutch methods in their search for the principles which led to State wealth. The Dutch were the most hated, yet the most admired and envied, people in Europe. Yet in many ways their Mercantilism was quite different from that of most European countries, where the key to economic organisation was centralisation and State action.

The Netherlands were a federal Republic consisting of Holland, Utrecht, Guelderland, Zeeland, Friesland, Groningen and Overijssel. The Republic had a national foreign policy, a national army, even a national navy, but strictly no national administration. So loose was the federal system that the miracle is that it worked at all. That it did so was due partly to the predominant position of the province of Holland, which was vastly more wealthy than the others, and partly to the semi-monarchical position of the House of Orange, which from time to time stepped in to rescue the Republic in its hours of danger. The Republic was really an oligarchy of some 10,000 persons, wealthy burghers, who sought to keep all power in their own hands. They were hard-headed men of business, clear-sighted and free from corruption. Each province and each city was jealous of its autonomy. There was not even a single continuous foreign ministry. All common problems were dealt with by the States General, which consisted, not of representatives of the provinces, but merely of delegates who reported back to, and carried out the instructions of, the provincial assemblies. The provinces were always afraid the States General would gain too much power. In times of crisis the system was too cumbrous, and it was then that the province of Holland or the House of Orange tended to take over. Then the Grand Pensionary of Holland, and Oldenbarnevelt or a John De Witt, then stood forth as virtual head of the Republic, and was opposed by the House of Orange. Each province had a Stadholder who was in theory merely the servant of the assembly, and might be a different man in each province. If in moments of crisis the provinces chose the same Stadholder, and if he happened to be a member of the House of Orange, he was for the time being virtually a monarch, addressed as 'Your Highness'. In this way Prince Maurice saved the Republic at the time of the Thirty Years' War. But the republican tradition was strong, and when the crisis passed it reasserted itself.

The strength of the Netherlands lay in its commerce and its sea-
C

power. Amsterdam in 1660 was the richest city in Europe, with a population of 100,000 (the total population of the Netherlands was no more than 1½ millions). The origins of their economic strength are probably to be found in the Baltic trade, which the Dutch were already beginning to dominate in the sixteenth century, and in the profitable herring trade. Europe became increasingly dependent upon the Dutch for Baltic wheat and for fish. They early acquired superior seamanship; they designed a new, long, narrow ship of about 300 tons, called a *fluit*, which was superior for mercantile needs to any other ship at the time. They built up capital resources from their trade which were ploughed back into further ventures. Thousands of merchants and industrialists, driven by the Spaniards from Antwerp, Brussels and Ghent, settled in Holland and brought their capital and their skills with them. It was superiority in capital resources and skill which gave the Dutch their supremacy in the seventeenth century. By offering better terms, they drove foreign competitors from the carrying trade of Europe. In the middle of the seventeenth century the Dutch carried most of British trade with Germany; they dominated French overseas trade; they supplied Spain and Portugal with foodstuffs; they supplied Italy with wheat, and they had extensive trade with the Levant. In the seventeenth century they began to build up a spectacular colonial empire. The first Dutch ships reached the Far East in 1595; the Dutch East India Company was launched in 1602, and there followed a great outburst of activity in China, Japan, Indo-China, India, Arabia and South America. The Dutch were interested in trade, not empire; difficulties were great and profits not always high. In forty years they discovered Hudson Bay, founded New Amsterdam, named Cape Horn and Staten Island, founded Capetown and Batavia, discovered Tasmania and New Zealand and explored the Pacific.

All this was achieved with the minimum of organisation, and very little centralisation. Commercial ventures were not great State enterprises, as with Colbert, but largely private ventures, virtually partnerships between merchants and ship-owners. There were times, however, when the difficulties and dangers of an enterprise required greater co-operation, and then what were known as *Directions* were formed, when a board of seven or eight merchants were appointed to organise convoys, appoint consuls and so forth, and for this purpose they were empowered to levy taxes and exercise some control. But they did not organise the trade itself, which was still left to the partners in the venture. The East India Company went further. The formidable difficulties in the way of Far Eastern trade required stronger and more permanent organisation, and so did the West Indian trade, which was the monopoly of the West India Company. These did approximate to State ventures; the Government contributed a large proportion of the capital and the Companies were subject to the authority of the States General. The East India Company soon acquired the greatest importance; trading in its shares led to the rise of the Amsterdam stock exchange. It was the Company which attracted the attention of foreigners, and was the model for Colbert's monopoly companies. Its spectacular achievements concealed the fact that most of the Dutch trading ventures in the seventeenth century, which accounted for most of their wealth, were undertaken with very different organisation.

The Dutch East India Company acquired its special organisation and powers because it was necessary to fight and destroy the great State enterprises of Spain and Portugal. Its Charter gave it the widest powers. It had the monopoly of trade east of the Cape of Good Hope; it could build forts and raise troops. It was organised into six chambers on a local basis, one each in Amsterdam, Zeeland, Delft, Rotterdam, Hoorn and Enkhuizen. Each contributed to the Company's capital and to each enterprise in fixed proportions, and profits were distributed accordingly. The chambers in fact were the shareholders, but their powers were small. The dividends were decided by a common assembly known as the Seventeen Masters, which in fact was always dominated by Amsterdam which contributed by far the largest proportion of capital. The Seventeen Masters were accountable to no one, and thus we come near to the reasons for Dutch success. For they combined a powerful instinct for local particularism with a still more powerful instinct for oligarchical control. The Dutch were the greatest bourgeois people in Europe.

.   .   .   .   .

The Dutch and Colbert provided Europe with the greatest object-lessons in the nature and advantages of Mercantilism. The Hohenzollerns applied the lessons in Prussia; Peter the Great applied them in Russia. In most German States the geographical unit was too small for much to be attempted or achieved. The Habsburg Charles VI, with his Ostend and Trieste Companies, tried to bring some of the life-blood of trade to his impoverished dominions. Maria Theresa and Joseph II were fully alive to the economic problems of their time. In Sweden there was a tradition of State enterprise dating from Gustavus Adolphus, to which the eighteenth century added little. England prospered in its own special version of Mercantilism. In Spain, as we shall see, men of ideas were more interested in economic development than in any other aspect of Enlightenment. Almost everywhere in Europe where progress was to be recorded, there was a new interest in material things, in economic development and the good things of life. In this, as in so many ways, Bacon had indicated the future when he wrote:

> No man, by taking care (as the Scripture saith), can add a cubit to his stature in this little model of a man's body: But in the great frame of Kingdom and Commonwealths it is the power of Princes or Estates to add amplitude and greatness to their Kingdoms. For by introducing such ordinances, constitutions and customs as we have now touched, they may sow greatness to their posterity and succession. But these things are commonly not observed, but left to take their chance.

3: The Age of Baroque and Rococo

Artistically speaking, the period covered by this book may be said to fall into two periods, roughly coincident with the reigns of Louis XIV and Louis XV. If we are thinking of Europe as a whole the first for convenience is termed the Age of the Baroque, and the second the Age of Rococo. If we are thinking specifically of France the terms 'Louis Quatorze' and 'Louis Quinze' are sometimes more convenient. In 1660 in artistic matters France was still in a sense provincial, for Italy and the Netherlands were the mainsprings of artistic inspiration. In the eighteenth century, except in music, France was the artistic centre of Europe.

It is first necessary to attempt an explanation of the term 'baroque'. First, however, a word of warning: it has no precise meaning, such as a scientific term has. It is a label used for convenience, and sometimes is used so vaguely as to cease to be meaningful. When we speak of the Age of the Baroque we may simply mean the period of about a hundred and forty years from about 1568 (the year Il Gesù was started in Rome). But this would include, for instance, the great Dutch painters, like Vermeer, and much classical building in France, neither of which can be regarded as 'baroque' at all. For this reason some art critics urge that the term should be reserved strictly for use in architecture and sculpture, where it can be given more precise definition. Yet this too is unsatisfactory, for the architecture and sculpture of the period are closely related in spirit to much of the literature, painting, and indeed the whole philosophy of life of the seventeenth century. It is best then to continue to use the word in a wider context, but also to recognise that there is much in the artistic development of seventeenth-century Europe which sprang from sources other than the Baroque.

Both 'baroque' and 'rococo' began as terms of abuse. The former may have come from the Portuguese 'barroco', an irregular pearl, or (as Italian scholars prefer) from 'baroco', a term used in Scholastic philosophy, here adapted to mean the rejection of logic, and thus to describe art which was ornate and hyperbolic. Baroque art used to be thought of as the decadent dissolution of Renaissance art, and Ruskin once said that it was 'impossible for false taste and base feeling to sink lower'. This view is now rejected by most art historians, and Baroque art is seen as an intensely vigorous and fertile creation of a vibrant civilisation. Perhaps its starting-point was the great Catholic Counter-Reformation. From the Council of Trent (1545–63) the Catholic Church launched a great spiritual and doctrinal revival. A new emphasis was laid on the sacraments, on the power of the clergy, on the doctrine of Transubstantiation, and on the cult of the Virgin and the Saints. There began a great period of church building, associated with the new Jesuit Order. There was a vast upsurge of religious feeling which found expression in the dramatic and the arts were summoned to the service of religion. Michelangelo had pointed the way to the exploration of architectural space, and this was now exploited to the full. Anything was attempted if it would create surprise and dramatic intensity. Straight lines were replaced by curves, there was a constant bulging and recession of masses; columns twisted and curved upwards, pediments were broken dramatically, cornices projected daringly; cupolas opened the way into heaven itself; there was cunning use of chiaroscuro, so that shadows and brilliant light amazed the observer; everywhere there was fantasy. Architect, painter and sculptor combined to create surprise, drama and spectacle. Clouds rent asunder the very walls, and angels invaded the very church and the hearts of the faithful. Cupolas revealed the saints riding upwards towards the central light to the very gates of heaven. The mood was ecstatic, and not easy for the northern mind to appreciate, for the home of Baroque is in southern Europe and Germany.

Baroque art was characterised by restlessness, instability, mobility. Both the Baroque and the Rococo were fascinated with the problem of time. They were conscious of the significance of the fleeting moment, and constantly warned man of how little time he had in this world of change and decay. Nothing is more characteristic of the Baroque than the violent contrast to be found in the tombs of popes or potentates, where the figure above kneels in prayer in the full regalia of his office, while, below, the stone lid of the coffin has slipped aside to reveal the naked and emaciated corpse, the helpless victim of corruption. Pre-occupation with the fleeting moment is seen throughout Baroque art. It is seen in the dramatic twists and contortions (called *contrapposto*) of the human figure in sculpture and painting, the massive limbs, the swelling muscles, the significant glance, as some hero struggles against the enemy and braces himself for the final thrust which will give him victory. It is seen in the frequent use of the images of water and cloud, cascades and fountains; indeed it has been said that 'water in movement leads us straight to the heart of Baroque'. Baroque made Rome a city of fountains. No age, also, has paid more attention to the impermanent arts, to great fêtes, vast spectacles, firework displays, masques, which lasted for a few hours, or at most a few weeks, and then disappeared for ever. Whether in Montaigne, or Pascal, or Bernini, or Watteau, there is a vision of an impermanent world, of the ebb and flow of the inner life of man, and a sense of the transitoriness of things.

Baroque art is also concerned with the greatness of man, a glorious expression of his power and a hymn to the magnitude of his achievements. It was heroic art, glorifying the great man, and the office which he held. Sixtus V (1585–90) was the most prolific of all the 'building popes'. It was he who built in Rome the Ponte Sisto, the Corso, the Piazza del Popolo, the Vatican, the Quirinal Palace; he continued the building of St. Peter's and planned Santa Maria Maggiore. He planned fine piazzas, set up ancient obelisks, surmounting them with a triumphant Cross. He crowned the Trajan and Antonine columns with statues of St. Peter and St. Paul, to indicate the defeat of Paganism. His work was continued by Pope Paul V (1605–21), who employed the architect Carlo Maderna (1556–1629) to lengthen the nave of St. Peter's and to build a façade from which the Pope could give his blessing '*urbi et orbi*'. It was a significant development indicative of the new prestige and power of the Papacy. The way was thus prepared for the great figure of Bernini (1598–1680), and it may be said that Bernini *is* Baroque.[1]

Bernini always felt that his real genius lay in painting. He was certainly a superb portraitist, but few of his paintings have survived, and his fame rests mainly on his work as architect and sculptor. He was a man of exuberant and restless energy and fertile imagination, capable of any amount of work, and with an unsurpassed

[1] See Plates 4, 5 and 6.

facility in handling marble. He was fortunate in living at a time when there was a lavish patronage of art without parallel in history. His early sculpture, such as his 'David' (1623) and 'Apollo and Daphne' (1622–24), were in the classical tradition, yet in their movement and tension, their attempt to catch the fleeting moment of change, opened a new age in sculpture. He also produced some splendid portrait busts, full of vigour and vitality, some of them real psychological studies. In some ways his earlier portraits are better than his later ones, partly because he was so overworked, and partly because he was later more concerned with conveying the majesty or grandeur of his subject than with making a real psychological study. In 1623 he entered the service of Pope Urban VIII, and served succeeding popes for the rest of his life. His greatest achievements are connected with St. Peter's; the grandest of all is the laying out of St. Peter's square, with its great double colonnade, symbolising the arms of Mother Church welcoming the faithful. He built the baldachino over the tomb of St. Peter, with its great, black, convoluted columns, and the high altar, an amazing creation symbolising the power of the Holy Spirit. He built the giant tombs of Urban VIII, in which the Pope is giving his blessing while the figures of Justice and Charity look on, and Death writes Urban's name in a large book; and of Alexander VIII, in which the Pope kneels in prayer, while a skeleton emerges from the grave holding an hour-glass. In the Vatican, at the head of the Scala Regia, Bernini erected a magnificent equestrian statue of Constantine the Great. Again it attempts to capture the dramatic moment; it is the moment at which Constantine saw the Cross in the Heavens, the moment of his conversion. The horse rears wildly; an enormous wind sweeps the drapery behind, and the observer is made to participate in the intensity of the occasion.

The supreme example of Baroque statuary is to be found in Bernini's 'Ecstasy of St. Teresa' in the Cornaro Chapel in the Church of Santa Maria della Vittoria, in Rome. There is a great light from heaven; an angel is about to plunge the fiery dart into the heart of St. Teresa, the symbol of her mystic union with Christ. Eight members of the Cornaro family sit in little 'theatre boxes' watching the miracle. The subject is a fantastically difficult one, for ecstasy is a transitory phase, and how is it possible to capture it in stone? Bernini's work has been bitterly criticised for its sensuality, yet as an expression of the religious fervour of the age it is superb, and the angel is a lovely creation, though some observers are troubled by its mischievous grin.

Much less popular and prolific, but equally a master of the Baroque was Borromini (1599–1667). His subtle genius makes him the connoisseur's architect. He was immensely original in all he did; he ignored rules, or more often stood them on their head to show that the opposite was possible. His best work is to be seen in the Church of Sant'Agnese in the Piazza Navona, his San Carlo alle Quattro Fontane, and in the dome and lantern of La Sapienza, all in Rome.

For much of Europe the seventeenth century was a period of wars, famine and devastation, in which there were two great centres of hope, the Church and the Monarchy. Both employed Baroque art to exalt their power. The Church sought, by spectacle, colour, drama, to warm the hearts and increase the faith of the people; the Monarchy sought to overawe its enemies and establish its power by a display of magnificence. There was also the insatiable love of pleasure. The age had a passion for theatricals and music, and of these too Italy was the true home. The Medici had instituted spectacular displays in Florence; Venice and Rome had had their carnivals for centuries; Italy was the home of the Commedia dell'Arte. In music the seventeenth century saw important developments. Orchestras became larger and more professional, music more chromatic. Instruments were perfected, especially the organ and the violin, so that the finest violins ever made were those of Niccolo Amati (1596–1684) and his pupil Antonio Stradivari (1644–1737), both of Cremona. The clavichord and harpsichord were developed, until they gave place to the piano about 1711. But the seventeenth century preferred the sound of the human voice to that of any instrument, and the characteristic musical forms of the Baroque period were the oratorio and the opera. Opera was created by Monteverdi (1567–1643), Cavalli (1600–73), Cesti (1620–99) and Carissimi (1604–74); in the last 60 years of the century over 700 operas were produced in Italy. It was an art form which gave full scope to the voluptuousness and sensuousness of seventeenth-century Italian society. The French came to it more slowly. It was really introduced by Mazarin, himself an Italian, who had a great love for the Italian theatre, and brought Italian actors and musicians to Paris. In 1647 he had them perform *Orfeo*, a grand opera by Luigi Rossi, with superb scenery and effects. The first French opera was produced in 1659, also under his patronage, and thereafter opera became popular in France. The young Louis XIV had a passion for the theatre and grand spectacles, in which he himself would sometimes take part. In 1655, for instance, a combination of opera and ballet called *The Nuptials of Thetis and Peleus* was performed with Louis XIV playing the part of Apollo, accompanied by the most astonishing effects by which characters rode down from heaven on clouds, palaces arose and mountains moved. Louis XIV's favourite musician was Jean-Baptiste Lully (1633–87), and accordingly he built up a virtual monopoly of music at the Court of Versailles. He wrote operas, and played an important part in the development of the orchestra.

Italian opera spread rapidly throughout Europe. Vienna took to it much more readily than Paris, and Cavalli and Cesti were both for a time enticed from Venice to Vienna. By the 1670s German operas were being performed in Hamburg and Dresden. In England Henry Purcell (1658–95) wrote the finest opera of the century, *Dido and Aeneas*. A number of Italian operas were performed in England in the early years of Queen Anne. In 1710 Frederic Handel (1685–1759) came to live in England, but, apart from this and *The Beggar's Opera*, England made little contribution to music during the century.

Church music was an integral part of the organised religion, and this led to the development of the organ, viols and the Oratorio. The greatest composer of church music of the century before Bach was Heinrich Schütz (1585–1673) for sixty years Kapellmeister at Dresden. He is the great musical link between Palestrina and Bach and Handel. The organ first reached a high degree of development under Dietrich Buxtehude (1637–1707), at Lübeck, where for a time Bach was his pupil. Johann Sebastian Bach (1685–1750) was born into a north German Protestant society in which music was an essential part, not only of life at Court, but also of civic affairs and church services. He spent much of his life training choirs, and his compositions include much organ and church music. His 'Mass in B Minor' is one of the supreme works of man. He wrote chorales, cantatas, preludes, fugues, and brought the suite to perfection.

To return to the subject of architecture; the Baroque style became dominant in Bohemia, southern Germany, Poland, Austria and Hungary. Wallenstein was one of the first to introduce the new style from Italy in the palaces he had built in Bohemia. In his ornate Palace in Prague the ballroom was decorated with the apotheosis of Mars, with Wallenstein himself as Mars. The Czech spirit, with its exuberance and its sadness, found the Baroque congenial, and there arose in Bohemia a great outburst of religious and aristocratic art. The Jesuits celebrated their return by building the Church of San Salvador in Prague. Italian artists and builders were used, and some designs were simply copied from Rome. The Archbishop of Prague commissioned the building of the Church of St. Francis of Assisi, almost in the style of Bramante. Such building was part of the great effort made to reclaim the Czech peasant for Roman Catholicism, and the movement had a national flavour, for at the head of the list of saints glorified by Czech Baroque was St. Wenceslas.

In Vienna Leopold I was the first Emperor who could afford to build extensively. He built the Am Hof church, and the beautiful abbey of Klosternemburg, dedicated to St. Leopold. The Emperor sought to give his Court the same brilliance which attached to that of Versailles. He was passionately fond of opera, which were accordingly produced in profusion during his reign. His nobility vied with each other in the building of magnificent palaces, the Prince of Liechtenstein setting the pace, and Prince Eugène following suit. Soon all the great noble families had splendid town palaces as well as country houses, the Schwarzenburg, Lobkowicz, Dietrichstein and Esterhazy palaces were the settings for a constant round of receptions, theatricals and concerts. Society here, as elsewhere in Europe, was intensely aristocratic, and Imperial power rested heavily on the good will of the Austrian and Hungarian nobility. The greatest German architects of the period left their mark in Vienna. Fischer von Erlach had spent twenty years in Rome before he became Inspector of Buildings to the Emperor Joseph I. He built the winter palace for Prince Eugène as well as two fine churches in Salzburg for the Prince Elector. Above all, he built the palace of Schönbrunn for the Habsburgs in Vienna. Lukas von Hildebrandt built Prince Eugène's summer palace in Vienna, the Belvedere. The inspiration for Austrian, as for Czech, Baroque came directly from Italy, though the motive for building lies rather in Versailles.

In Spain the predominance of the Jesuits during the seventeenth century led to the building of the most heavily ornamented Baroque churches. The most characteristic architects were José de Churri-guera (1655–1725) and his sons, whose churches were loaded with the decoration of fruit, garlands, flowers, twisted pillars, mock-draperies and scrollwork. Much eighteenth-century building seemed inspired by the decorations of the theatre, and indulged in a riot of gold and marble. Even more riotous was the Jesuit architecture in Latin America, which groaned beneath its surging decoration, and was often reminiscent of Hindu building. In Portugal the finest Baroque architect was Minho-Douro, in the second half of the eighteenth century, a more restrained artist than his Spanish neighbours. Perhaps the most congenial art to Spain was that of sculpture, in which every-thing was done to create dramatic surprise. Wooden figures, luridly painted, in the death agony, with gaping, bloody wounds and emaci-ated bodies, sought to arouse the emotions of the faithful.

The greatest artistic achievements of Spain were in painting. When our period opens in 1660 three great Spanish painters, Ribera (d. 1652), Zurbarin (d. 1664) and Vélasquez (d. 1660) had just died. Ribera painted dramatic works in the manner of Caravaggio; Zur-barin painted deeply-felt religious works with the simplicity of mediaeval painting; Vélasquez was a great realist painter, and the creator of the loveliest nude painting in Spanish art. Murillo (1617–82) painted sweet and rather sentimental pictures of the Virgin. The only eighteenth-century Spanish painter of the first rank was Goya (1746–1828), who said that his only masters were Vélasquez, Rem-brandt and Nature. His was a great reaction against decorative art. As he grew older, and became very deaf, a bitterness entered his soul, and he made savage attacks on human stupidity in his caricatures. Much of his art was a nightmare of horrors, concerned with corpses, hangings, rapes and starvation. His 'Nude Maja' was a piece of unabashed sexuality. Some of his portraits are very fine, with an amazing realism, even when they were royal portraits. His portraits of the Spanish royal family are a dreadful record of decadence. He portrayed his hatred of religious intolerance, and also the horrors of 'The Third of May 1808.' Goya was not part of any general European movement in art; like Rembrandt and Vélasquez, he stood alone.

There was much in European art in the seventeenth century which resisted the influence of the Baroque. Nicolas Poussin (1594–1665), for instance, who spent almost all his artistic life in Rome, ignored

Baroque fashion. His inspiration was always classical antiquity, and the designs of Raphael and Titian. He sought the perfect repose of studied composition; his art speaks to the intellect, not to the passions. Claude Lorrain (1600–82) was the unsurpassed painter of landscape, the master of light and colour. Figures were introduced to provide an excuse for the painting, but there is no doubt that his main interest was in the study of light, in the luminosity of the sunset playing upon the sea. Both as a colourist and as a draughtsman he is unsurpassed in the history of European art. His subjects are classical or biblical, but treated with a new romanticism.

Dutch painting also owed little or nothing to Baroque influences, but sprang from the soil and the sturdy middle-class life of the Dutch people. Hobbema (1638–1709) and Jacob van Ruisdael (1628–82) painted landscapes with superb cloud effects. Paulus Potter (1625–54) painted farm animals and simple peasant scenes. Jan Vermeer (1632–75) painted the streets and houses of Dutch towns with great technical perfection, and Pieter de Hooch (1629–83) painted interiors with a delightful sense of texture, composition and light and shade. Incomparably the greatest painter of the period was Rembrandt (1606–69). He had studied Italian art, although he never left Holland. His sense of drama, and his preoccupation with problems of light and shade have led some art historians to term his work 'baroque', but Rembrandt is too great an artist to wear any label. His greatest work was in profound psychological studies—he painted more than sixty self-portraits—reflecting his humanity and his intense poetic imagination. In England there was little which can be termed Baroque. The inspiration of Inigo Jones (1573–1652) was entirely Palladian. Some of Sir Christopher Wren's churches show Roman influence, but the spirit of St. Paul's is not Baroque. The dramatic conception of Blenheim and Castle Howard (Hawksmoor and Vanbrugh) justifies their being regarded as 'restrained baroque', but with William Kent (1684–1748) Palladian influences triumphed, and John Wood at Bath and Robert Adam built in the classical spirit.

The central artistic event of the second half of the seventeenth century was the building of Versailles. Louis XIII had built a château there in what appeared to be a most unpromising place; Saint-Simon called it 'of all places the saddest and most barren, with no view, no water and no wood, for it is all shifting sand and marsh'. Louis XIV's first intention was to use Versailles as a 'maison de plaisance' for himself and his friends, away from the Court of St. Germain. In 1668 he began his additions, when the old buildings were encased by the 'Château Neuf'. Large spaces were laid out for *carrousels* and tournaments; also a grotto and a menagerie, where animals could be inspected, and plays be performed in the open air. Le Vau was the architect; splendid gardens were laid out by Le Nôtre and Le Bouteaux, and interior decoration was entrusted to Le Brun. It was decided to make the whole palace an allegory, representing the year, personifying the seasons of spring, summer, autumn and winter, with full classical allusion, and over all would reign the sun-god, Apollo, Louis XIV himself. Louis' appetite for building grew with time. In 1669 he began the Trianon de Porcelaine as a private retreat for himself and Mme. de Montespan, with superb gardens of jasmine, jonquils and wallflowers. For the retirement of Mme. de Montespan and her children Louis employed a young architect, Jules-Hardouin Mansart, to build the Château de Clagny, one of the most beautiful buildings in France. Le Nôtre laid out its magnificent gardens, with fine trees and shady walks. Louis XIV was so pleased with it that he appointed Mansart to the post of First Architect, and henceforth he was in charge of the final enlargements at Versailles. But Mme. de Montespan occupied Clagny only about a year, and when she lost the King's favour she retired to a convent. By 1775 Clagny was in very bad repair and was demolished.

By 1678 Louis was at the height of his military glory. Versaille had come to be an essential part of his political system, and was too small for his purpose; thus there began the final enlargements. Mansart built the magnificent Galerie des Glaces, and Le Brun supervised its decoration; it was completed in 1684. It was a great hall with windows on one side, and mirrors reflecting the windows on the other. Tables between the mirrors were of solid silver and exquisite workmanship, and the ceiling was a riotous profusion of allegorical figures. The Galerie was large enough to accommodate the entire Court, which assembled several times a week under the eye of the King. But the magnificence was short-lived. In 1689 Louis had the silver tables melted down to help pay for the war. He himself in his later years tired of the ceremony of Versailles, and Saint-Simon has left a grim picture of the painted sadness of the Court in Louis' last days, something of which the modern visitor to Versailles shares. At this time also the Princes' Wing was built for the Princes of the Royal Blood, the Grand Appartement, and the stables which led the Elector of Hanover to comment that he was not so well housed as the horses of the King of France. Some of Louis XIV's buildings sprang from his love of hunting. Marly, begun in 1679, was a hermitage in the grand style, with twelve apartments, and twenty-four pavilions, set in magnificent woodlands. Also, when the Porcelain Trianon was pulled down in 1687, Louis erected the Trianon de Marbre, as a private retreat. On summer mornings the King would leave Versailles early with a few special friends to go to Trianon to hunt. The evenings would be spent in listening to the music of Lully, or in a trip on the lake in gondolas. It was a very special honour to be invited to the Trianon.

In the France of the age of Louis XIV one must distinguish between official art and that which was independent of the Court. To discuss official art first, the 'Style Louis Quatorze' may be said to have been created by Charles Le Brun (1619–90). Le Brun studied with the French painter Simon Vouet, and then in Rome, and was a Court painter to Louis XIII before he was nineteen. He was employed by Fouquet at Vaux, and showed himself astonishingly inventive as a director of décor of every kind, from tapestries to spectacular fêtes. In 1662 he became Principal Painter to the King: he loved power, and used skilful stratagems to win and retain the patronage of Colbert. With the latter's aid he became virtual dictator of the arts. He built up the Gobelin factory as a major art industry, and employed a whole army of craftsmen, painters, sculptors, silversmiths, to create the tapestries, furniture, silverware, statuary and fountains, which were needed at Versailles. For twenty years he had absolute sway; painters and sculptors simply worked according to his plans. He imposed therefore a grandiose consistency of style. His natural instinct was severely classical, and classical themes and allegories were repeated *ad nauseam*; but he never for a moment forgot that his prime function was to glorify the Grand Monarque, Apollo, the Sun-King, and this brought with it the need for some of the exuberance of the Baroque. It was inevitable that much of this official art should be repetitive, vapid, mere decoration, for Le Roi Soleil did not want an art of ideas, but glorification and adornment. If we look at some of

Le Brun's early painting, such as 'The Death of Cato' (1660), we see that he was capable of vigorous work. His 'Allegory of the Capture of Ghent by Louis XIV in 1678', in which Louis is represented as Jupiter, is grossly inferior. Paintings such as Van der Meulen's 'The Siege of Luxembourg 1684', or Coypel's 'Louis XIV receiving the Persian Ambassador' glorify the Monarch, but are artistically feeble. Most of the paintings and busts of Louis XIV tell the same story, and that is very little. All this was not the fault of Le Brun. No one could find sufficient poetry in homage to the glory of the Sun-King to produce a life-time of great art. Yet Le Brun's achievement is astonishing. He achieved what he was commissioned to do: he created the décor of the Grand Monarque, and made Versailles in some ways the cultural centre and envy of Europe. He himself was eulogised in verse and prose; but he made enemies. He sorely missed his patron Colbert, who died in 1683; Louvois was his enemy, and the King was preoccupied with other matters. Finally in 1688 he withdrew from Court, with a very comfortable fortune, to make way for the seventy-eight-year-old Mignard, and died two years later. By now the Gobelin factory was at a standstill because of the ruin of the country's finances, and many of the superb pieces of gold and silver work which he had designed were melted down. Le Brun was not a great artist in the sense that Poussin or Claude were, but as the creator of the formal magnificence of an age he is unsurpassed.

The power of Versailles should not be allowed to conceal the fact that there was much vigorous French art which existed quite independent of the Court. In the first half of the seventeenth century painters like Simon Vouet (1590–1649), Georges de La Tour (1593–1652) and the Le Nain brothers were fascinated with the problems of chiaroscuro which Caravaggio had posed in Italy. Philippe de Champaigne (1602–74) was deeply influenced by Jansenism, and painted splendid portraits in a cold and severe style, for numerous bourgeois patrons. Portrait-painting was in fact one of the most distinctive arts in seventeenth-century France. Not only was there an insatiable demand for portraits at Court, but there was a growing demand among the sturdy middle class of the provinces. The most baroque of French portrait-painters were Rigaud (1659–1743) and Largillière (1656–1746). Rigaud was for years official Court painter to the Regent Orleans and Louis XV. He painted in the most voluptuous and official style some 2,000 portraits, including five Kings, while some of his unofficial portraits achieve an intimate naturalism and remarkable likeness. While Rigaud worked for the Court, Largillière painted the rich Parisian bourgeoisie with a fluent richness, saturated with colour. Indeed he may be said to provide a bridge between the formal Age of Louis Quatorze, and the more varied and natural style of the Age of the Rococo. Paris was no longer dominated by Versailles, but lived a vigorous life of its own. The same transition is seen in the still-lifes and hunting scenes of Desportes (1661–1743). He was appointed Painter of the Hunt to Louis XIV and Louis XV, and prepared many of his hunting scenes directly from nature. He loved painting rich and luxuriant still life, full of precious objects indicative of a life of taste and luxury.

Portraits in the age of Louis XIV tended to be formal, haughty, with splendid costumes and official poses. In the reign of Louis XV, the Age of the Rococo, there is a change. Versailles is no longer the whole of France, the Monarchy no longer subsumes the nation. Portraits become human, witty, casual, simple, graceful, rather than grand. Largillière and La Tour (1704–88) set a new fashion. There is a new cult of charm and beauty; portraits radiate at best an elegance and distinction, though sometimes no more than a pleasing prettiness. But all emphasise the pleasures of life, the love of flowers, music, springtime, dancing. It is an aristocratic art, where everything is given over to the pursuit of love and beauty. The fact that it is aristocratic does not mean that the middle class are excluded. They too have their portraits painted in aristocratic poses, while the aristocrats had themselves painted in the clothes of the bourgeoisie. The Queen of France, Maria Leszczynska, was painted by Nattier in the town garb of any bourgeoise. Mme. Vigée-Lebrun repeatedly painted Marie-Antoinette in simple, domestic poses. Indeed the history of eighteenth-century art makes quite clear the new importance of the middle class, especially if they are men of culture, above all men of letters. Especially interesting in this connection is the Swiss painter Graff, who painted 1,200 portraits of the great men of the German Enlightenment, including Herder, Wieland, Lessing and Schiller.

There was a significant change too in the symbolism of painting. In the age of Louis XIV the favourite classical subjects were Apollo, the sun-god, representing the King of France, Jupiter representing the Emperor, Minerva the arts, and Parnassus the Court. Art had a strongly didactic purpose, and there was a frequent emphasis upon classical or Christian virtues. The eighteenth century was less austere; the favourite classical themes became Venus, goddess of love and beauty, Pan, who presided over Arcadia with his nymphs and satyrs, Diana, goddess of the moon and of the chase, and Cupid, son of Venus and god of love. Love is a constant theme, treated idyllically, as a matter of sweet dalliance. Louis XV had a whole series of tapestries completed in 1757 under the title of 'Les Amours des Dieux'. Painting became sensuous, luxurious and often frivolous. Tiepolo continued to paint Olympian scenes in the grand manner, such as his frescoes for the palace of Würzburg, some of the most important of the century, but they are in the Baroque rather than the new Rococo style.

The world of Rococo is the world of Arcadia, presided over by Pan and his pipes, where the time is spent in hunting, dancing or making love. It is a world of bucolic peace and erotic yearnings, a world to which the eighteenth century loved to escape. It is the world above all of Watteau (1684–1721), Boucher (1703–70) and Fragonard (1732–1806). Watteau created an ideal world of grace, charm, coquetry and beauty, set against a background of nature which the Goncourts described as

amorous woods, meadows overflowing with music, echoing groves and overarching branches hung with baskets of flowers; solitary places, remote from the jealousy of the world, refreshed by springs and inhabited by marble statues, by naiads dappled with the trembling shadows of leaves.... Gardens overgrown with bramble and rose bushes.... It is a bucolic theatre with a green drop-curtain and flowers for foot-lights; the Comédie-Française has mounted the stage and the Commedia dell'arte trips lightly across it.

It was a fragile world of delicate females, silken dresses, provocative coiffures, glitter, charm and exquisite enjoyment, the quintessence of a great civilisation, in which there is always the hint of melancholy as we are reminded of the fragility of all beauty. The eighteenth century always referred to the island of Cythera as the symbol of the world of love, and Watteau's painting, 'Embarkation for Cythera', shows the lovers of his ideal world about to leave for the magic island.

Boucher was a protégé of Mme. de Pompadour; his art was light, sensuous, luxurious, frivolous. All his life he sought to capture the pleasures of youth. Subjects such as 'Mars and Venus surprised by Vulcan' were congenial to him. His portraits of Mme. de Pompadour, such as that in the National Gallery of Scotland and in the Wallace Collection, are exquisite reminders of the grace and charm of that remarkable woman.

The Goncourts wrote:

> The last century had no poets . . . poetry in the noblest and profound sense of the term, poetry which is a creation through imagery . . . such poetry was unknown to eighteenth-century France; her two poets, the only two, were painters: Watteau and Fragonard.

Fragonard was a fine draughtsman and portrait-painter who delighted in the voluptuous and pretty scenes which were popular at Court. His pictures are full of vivacity, exuberance and sense of colour. His best known picture, 'The Swing', in the Wallace Collection, in spite of its absurdities, is full of the poetry of which the Goncourts wrote.

After the death of Louis XIV interest was no longer exclusively fixed on the Court. The Regent Orleans preferred Paris to Versailles. The great *hôtels*, or town houses of the nobility and the big city financiers, resumed the importance they had had in the days before Louis XIV. The salons became the centres of the social graces, centres for the discussion of literature, philosophy or merely of gossip, where wit and intellect came to be prized above rubies. Louis XV returned to Versailles, and he retained much of the ceremonial of his predecessor, but life at Court became less burdensome. He himself liked nothing better than to escape to his private apartments, or to some château. The exquisite hand of Mme. de Pompadour was seen in the furnishings of the royal apartments. In this period, France became unquestionably the artistic leader of Europe. The ornamentation which is especially associated with the Rococo, shell forms, ovals, 'rocaille' asymmetrical designs, were developed in France by, say, Meissonier or Boffand, and were soon imitated all over Europe. German princes great and small built their own versions of Versailles, as did the Elector of Bavaria at Munich, and in the Amalienburg. Fine tapestries were imported from Gobelin or Beauvais; costumes were of the finest silks, brocades, damasks; furniture was elegant, in exotic woods, and with copious gold leaf, or lacquered. The most elaborate table-ware was developed, tureens, dishes, ice-buckets, wine-coolers, tea- and coffee-sets, snuff-boxes, powder bowls, in fine gold, silver, lacquer or the favourite porcelain. Porcelain was held in high regard, and many princes had their private porcelain factories. In a word, the Age of Rococo saw the art of gracious living carried to the highest point it ever reached in the history of Europe. There was truth in Talleyrand's remark that those who had not lived in the *ancien régime* had not experienced the full delights of life.

In the art of such painters as Watteau, Boucher, Chardin, La Tour, Greuze and Fragonard we see the princes, nobility and *grandes dames* of the *ancien régime*, the splendours of Versailles, and the new honour paid to Philosophy and Science. It was a fragile world, and one which was to disappear in 1789. Only Fragonard and Greuze lived on into the world of revolution, and Greuze died in poverty and Fragonard died a forgotten figure. 1789 ended an artistic period in European artistic history.

4: The Monarchy of Louis XIV

The New Monarchy

Louis XIV's earliest memory was of his mother, Anne of Austria, coming from the death-bed of Louis XIII and kneeling before him as the King. Two days later he entered Paris in magnificence; the city magistrates knelt before him at the Porte Saint-Honoré, the crowds shouting 'Long Live the King'. Two days later the child was carried in the arms of the captain-general of the *parlement* and seated on the throne while the Chancellor knelt before him. At the early age of five Louis XIV began his reign of seventy-two years.

Louis' formal education was shamefully neglected, for Mazarin was too mean to spend money on education, or even to dress him well, but he did teach the boy the rudiments of statecraft and carefully prepare him as his successor. Statecraft, after all, was not to be learnt from books. It is certain that the event which first left a deep impression upon Louis was the Fronde (1649–53). The Fronde was an uneasy alliance between the nobility and the *parlement* to wrest from the Crown the political power which it had gathered under Richelieu. It was thus the last great outburst of feudal reaction in France in the seventeenth century. In 1651 the King, Mazarin and the Court found themselves blockaded in the Louvre, and one night the mob invaded the King's bedroom. The thirteen-year-old boy pretended to be asleep, and they left without damage. But Louis had been terrified; he never forgot the humiliation, and all his life he disliked Paris and the *canaille*. Here perhaps was the genesis of the idea of Versailles, and also of his suspicion of the nobility and the *parlement*, who were behind the Fronde. He saw the difficulty Mazarin had with the powerful Condé family, the hostile Mme. de Chevreuse, and Henri IV's grandson the Duc de Beaufort, the prime movers in the Fronde. He saw also the skill with which Mazarin overcame them. On the collapse of the Fronde in October 1652 Louis rode amidst wild enthusiasm into Paris, the symbol of peace and order. But he continued the obedient pupil of Mazarin so long as the Cardinal lived. He attended the camp of the great Turenne in his campaigns against the Spaniards, and he saw Mazarin's life-work completed when by the Peace of the Pyrenees in 1659 France gained Artois, Roussillon and parts of Flanders.

When Mazarin died in 1661, Louis at once took over the Government. There was no successor to Mazarin; Louis never had a Prime Minister and he never employed a churchman. Louis was twenty-three, handsome, dignified, reserved, calm, courteous and majestic. Mazarin had done his work well; Louis had learnt how to handle men. Six years before, for instance, Mazarin had shown him how to overawe the *parlement*. Louis was always susceptible to the delights of Court life, and when this had appeared dangerous, Mazarin had hurried him off to the more bracing atmosphere of camp. Now Louis looked every inch a king. Bolingbroke once wrote of him: 'If he was not the greatest king, he was the best actor of majesty, at least, that ever filled the throne.' All his life he was immensely industrious; what could be done by meticulous effort, Louis would do. He was a master of detail; what he lacked was the broadest view of statesmanship. He was a great egotist, as all despots must be, but he loved flattery too much, and as time passed he came to be surrounded by time-servers who gave him only the advice he wished to hear. It is significant that the great success of the early part of his reign was in large measure due to men who had been trained under Mazarin. But Louis possessed an utter belief in himself. Even in the great days of Colbert and Louvois, Louis was convinced that all the great achievements were his own doing. He had a simple belief in the divine origin of kingship, and a conviction that God would always give him success. If he did not say 'L'Etat, c'est moi', he certainly believed it. For Louis there was never a moment when he ceased to be the King. His human failing was that 'il ne peut pas se passer des femmes', but at least it could be said that, except for Mme. de Maintenon, he never allowed his favourites to influence politics. To himself he was, quite simply, God's representative on earth, and this gave him a deep sense of responsibility. He wrote in his *Memoirs*:

> As [the King] is of a rank superior to all other men, he sees things more perfectly than they do, and he ought to trust rather to the inner light than to information which reaches him from outside.... Occupying, so to speak, the place of God, we seem to be sharers of His knowledge as well as of His authority.

He was genuinely interested in the welfare of his subjects; he had a strong sense of justice and an excellent memory, and was accustomed to hear all petitions personally. We shall not get the work and achievements of Louis XIV into perspective if we do not see them as the completion of the work of Henry IV, Richelieu and Mazarin. The fundamental theme of government in seventeenth-century France was the defeat of the forces of feudal disintegration, and the achievement of State absolutism. In judging of the reign of Louis XIV historians have perhaps paid too much attention to the later years of failure. It is natural that they should seek the seeds of the French Revolution laid in this reign; but this must not blur the great achievements of the first half of the reign. Louis XIV was then no tyrant imposing a despotism upon an unwilling France, but a life-giver bringing peace and prosperity to a land torn by feudal and sectional disintegration.[1] There was a glorious springtime of achievement about the period of the building of Versailles and its early years, which the later gloom ought not to mar. His governmental system and his reforms were on the whole according to the needs of the time. Perhaps their chief defect was that they did not go far enough; a new financial system, for instance, might have made the French Revolution unnecessary. Also it must be remembered that in one sense the French Revolution completed the work of Louis XIV, for Napoleon's system of government was nearer the intentions of Louis XIV's government than Louis himself had been able to achieve.

His Ministers

In the first half of his reign Louis XIV was well served by his Ministers, Colbert, Le Tellier, Louvois, Vauban. It is not true that he was dominated by them, that he was some puppet actuated by his

[1] It was this aspect of Louis XIV which so impressed early historians of the reign. Paul Pelisson (1624–93) was deeply impressed with the order and progress achieved, and referred to his government as 'nature mastered by art'. Voltaire thought the age of Louis XIV greater than the ages of Alexander, Augustus or the Renaissance because 'human reason in general was brought to perfection'. In this he was thinking of the triumph of the philosophy of Enlightenment which indeed owed little to Louis, but also of the civilising influence which France exerted throughout Europe. Guizot admired the administrative achievements of the reign, and wrote of it as 'the first government that presented itself to the eyes of Europe as a power sure of its position, which had not to dispute its existence with internal enemies', and he regarded it as a most progressive government: 'There have, in fact, existed very few governments of such an innovating spirit.'

Ministers. His policy was always his own; his Ministers were no more than the chief servants of the Crown. His chief delight was in military affairs, and in his *Mémoires* he posed as a great general. It is true that he took immense pains with the details of a campaign, and pored for hours over plans of Netherlands forts, but he never had the makings of a general. He fondly supposed that he could conduct a campaign from Versailles, and his interference with his generals sometimes cost France heavily. For their part the generals played the charade of deference to the new Caesar, and did their best with what freedom of action was left to them. Fortunately for them, Louis soon tired of the hardships of camp life, and took to being present only at the actual fall of a citadel. Then having staged a magnificent entry into the fallen city, he returned to Versailles.

He took the closest interest in foreign affairs, and was an able director of policy. Of all the aspects of French government, the most perfectly conducted was diplomacy. For years Louis and his servants, Lionne, Servien, Gremonville and the others, divided Europe with a mixture of bribery and intimidation, setting one country against another, and gradually reducing them to dependence upon France. At home Louis was able to leave administration in the capable hands of Colbert. Matters of trade and finance did not much interest him, and Colbert had an uphill task to gain his attention for the fleet, the mercantile marine or colonies. But he appreciated Colbert's work, and was always a most generous master. He fully understood the importance of giving his Monarchy a suitable décor, and Colbert was virtually the artistic dictator of France. So long as Louis had such able servants as Colbert, such able diplomats as Lionne, and such fine soldiers as Turenne and Condé, all went well. There was a grand simplicity about Louis's purpose of government. Inside France and abroad the object was always the same, the glory of the Monarchy. His ambassadors demanded precedence throughout Europe, just as the King's administrators demanded obedience inside France. At the top of a giant pyramid of power there was Louis himself, the symbol of power, justice and mercy, and the fountain-head of the arts, culture and prosperity.

When Mazarin died, Louis's chief ministers were: Sequier, the Chancellor, an old man of little ability; Le Tellier, an able administrator, much concerned with his own interests; Lionne, the acting

Secretary of State for Foreign Affairs, and, above all, Fouquet, the Superintendent of Finances. Fouquet, according to the standards of the century, was an able and reasonably honest public servant. That French finances were in the utmost confusion was not Fouquet's fault; he simply continued a system he had inherited. He fully expected to succeed Mazarin as the King's chief Minister. But at his first Council meeting, Louis declared: 'In future I shall be my own prime minister (*premier ministre*)', and he at once set the young Colbert on to watch Fouquet. The chief names among Louis' Ministers were to a remarkable degree drawn from a small family group and its satellites, a fact often concealed by the fact that they acquired titles and therefore different names. Louvois was the son of Le Tellier, and Seignelay was the son of Colbert, and so forth. Colbert's father was a draper and his uncle was one of Mazarin's bankers. Moreover, a cousin had married Le Tellier. Using these connections, Colbert secured a post with Le Tellier in the 1640s (he was born in 1619), and from 1651 onwards had been one of Mazarin's most trusted agents. He was a prodigious worker, who lived only to further the interests of his master, at first Mazarin, and later Louis XIV. In a quiet, mole-like way he gathered information against Fouquet. For a time Louis hesitated to act, for Fouquet was a powerful Minister. Fouquet, for his part, was busy drawing up a great plan of financial reform, which Colbert afterwards carried out. Finally in August 1661 he gave a splendid fête at his magnificent château at Vaux which the King attended. If it was intended to impress the King with the power of his Minister it was a singularly foolish move. In September Louis had him arrested. A special Court (*chambre de justice*) was set up to try him. It met for three years; most of the charges of treason were absurd, and those of corruption did not show that Fouquet had been any more corrupt than Mazarin. Eventually, on the King's orders, Fouquet was sentenced to perpetual imprisonment. It was an act of great injustice, but Louis felt it necessary to assert his supremacy over his Ministers from the beginning.

Colbert

Colbert stepped into Fouquet's shoes. The office of Superintendent of Finances was discontinued, but Colbert in 1665 became Controller-General of Finances, and also Minister of Buildings (1664), of

Commerce (1665) and of the Navy (1669). In fact he dealt with almost all aspects of government except the army (Louvois' preserve) and foreign affairs. In everything he acted as the mere agent of the King. The two worked well together, for Colbert was the perfect courtier, and Louis was a kindly and generous master to a Minister he trusted. At one moment Colbert would be issuing orders for the governance of a province, the next he would be pursuing the King's lost swans, buying toys for the Dauphin, or arranging foster-parents for the royal bastards. Colbert never for a moment forgot his essential purpose, which was to glorify the Monarchy, for Louis *was* France. Colbert was the perfect civil servant, cold, hard, remote, but devoted, efficient, indefatigable.

The most urgently needed reforms were in finance. In 1661 the receipts of taxation were about 80 million livres, of which only 31 millions reached the Treasury. As there was an expenditure of 54 millions, there was an annual deficit of 22 millions. Six years later it was a different picture. Colbert had increased the receipts to 61 millions, reduced the expenditure to somewhat over 32 millions, and thus had an annual surplus of over 29 millions. This was done mainly by good management. The Chambre de Justice, set up in 1661 to try Fouquet, sat until 1669, and found some 4,000 financiers guilty of peculation, and recovered in all some 100 millions of livres for the Crown. He sharply reduced the rates of interest on the *rentes*, or government loans, thus infuriating the financiers of Paris. He obtained better terms from the tax-farmers, improved the book-keeping system and kept a close check on the whole administration. With the system of taxation he was never able to carry a fundamental reform, and this was an important defect in his work. We have seen, in considering Colbert as a Mercantilist[1] that he was quite unable to sweep away internal customs duties; they were too important a part of the revenues. All he could do was to try to limit the number of *illegal* customs houses which landowners had erected. Similarly, with direct taxes, he could tinker with the old system, but not replace it. The chief direct tax was the *taille*, a grossly inequitable tax from which the nobility and clergy were exempt. The sum required by the Treasury was apportioned out among the provinces, the richest provinces usually finding means of securing a light assessment,

[1] See p. 46.

so that the poorest provinces carried an unduly large share of the tax. Each province apportioned its assessment among the villages. In the village a communal council appointed a collector and assessor, and the richest farmer usually found means to get a moderate assessment, so that the burden fell heaviest upon the unfortunate peasant. In the *pays d'État* (that is, the provinces where the local Estates survived) conditions were a good deal easier than in the *pays d'Election* (where they had disappeared). Because of the exemptions and the high cost of collection (for the *taille* was not farmed), Colbert's policy was to rely less upon the *taille* and more upon indirect taxes from which there were no exemptions. He also tried to reduce the cost of collection, and in 1680 on one occasion he had as many as 400 collectors in prison for corruption in the *généralité* of Tours alone. The *Gabelle* or salt-tax pressed heavily on the peasant, and the *aides* or customs on almost every article of consumption hampered trade and made prices high. After his death a further personal tax was invented, the *Capitation*, or poll tax. In addition, the peasantry were subject to the *Corvée* in the *pays d'Elections* though not the *pays d'État* (where labour services were employed to build and maintain roads and bridges). Colbert was highly efficient in raising money by new means. A government monopoly of tobacco (which has continued ever since) helped to pay for the Dutch War in 1674. The postal service was made a government monopoly and was worth a million a year. Colbert found that under Louis's predecessors much of the royal domain had been alienated, and the remainder yielded a mere 80,000 livres a year. He used the Chambre de Justice to reclaim much of it, and by 1682 it was yielding $5\frac{1}{2}$ million livres a year. By such means Colbert was able to achieve an annual surplus until Louis began his wars. Then there was an annual deficit, but so long as Colbert lived the finances were sound.

An important aspect of Colbert's general policy of centralisation was his law reforms. In 1665 he set up a Council of Justice, and there followed a number of new law codes. In 1667 a Civil Ordinance dealt with procedure in civil cases, in 1669 a similar Ordinance dealt with criminal procedure. In 1673 there was issued a new Commercial Law, in 1681 a new Admiralty Law, and finally, after Colbert's death, a *Code Noir*, affording some legal protection to slaves. Wherever possible, Colbert limited the judicial powers of local authorities and strengthened the powers of the Intendants. Colbert hated the survival of local and feudal jurisdictions, and few of them survived the encroachments of the central authority. The great exceptions to this were the *parlements* of France. They were the royal courts of law, the last relics of the mediaeval French constitution. There were thirteen *parlements* in France, but the *parlement* of Paris was incomparably the most important. Its prestige rested upon the part which it had played in the history of France since the Middle Ages. One writer in 1701 declared that it had been the *parlement* which had saved France from being dismembered like Italy and Germany. Altogether there were some eleven hundred members of the *parlements* of France, and they constituted the most powerful corporation in France. They were known as the *noblesse de robe*; they were immensely wealthy, completely secure in their office, and, in moments of weakness on the part of the Monarchy, could be an effective threat to royal power. The root cause of the trouble was the practice of selling offices, which had grown up to relieve the Monarchy of its pressing financial difficulties. An office, for instance, with an annual salary of 5,000 livres might be sold for 50,000 livres, so that for the first ten years the Government could show a profit, but thereafter was in fact paying interest on the initial 'loan'. Moreover, the office would be for life, perhaps for three lives, and thus the practice created a perpetually increasing problem for the future. Sometimes offices were created simply for the purpose of raising money by their sale, regardless of the consequences for the future. To this problem we shall return. Colbert repeatedly sought to bring down the price of offices, and would have wished to abolish the practice altogether, but he was never able to do so. In his time the office of President of the Paris *parlement* was worth half a million livres, so that the man who bought it had to be very rich. His salary was small by comparison, but the social prestige was immense. He was received in his official capacity with the firing of cannon, like a prince. The *parlements* did not give much trouble during Louis XIV's reign, but remained to be a most important problem to his successors.

We have seen already the general principles of Colbert's commercial policy, and how the main object was the use of State action to bring about economic expansion, because only prosperous subjects could ensure a wealthy monarch, and wealth was the indispensable condition for power. The same principle of centralisation was seen in the administrative system. The King was assisted by four Secretaries of State, the Chancellor and the Controller-General. Under the King there was the *Conseil d'État*, the supreme executive, legislative and judicial body. It was divided into some six Councils, the *Conseil d'en haut*, dealing with important matters of policy, the *Conseil des Dépêches*, dealing with internal affairs and routine foreign affairs, the *Conseil des Finances*, which included also trade and agriculture, the *Conseil privé*, the Court of Appeal, and the *Conseil de la Guerre*. In 1700 a permanent *Conseil du Commerce* was added. But these separate bodies were of little real importance, for whether they met, what they discussed, and who attended them depended entirely on the will of the King. At times other Councils were set up for particular purposes. It must not be thought that government was crystallised into departments and other institutions as it is today. Colbert's special position rested on the trust the King placed in him and the numerous offices he held. A Minister ceased to be a Minister when the King ceased to summon him to conference. Every decision in government was, in theory at least, the King's. Under the Controller-General the most distinctive instruments of government were the thirty-two Intendants, one to each of the Provinces.[1] The office was a creation of Richelieu. Intendants were men of middle-class origin, able administrators, tirelessly devoted to the service of the Central Government, and directly answerable to the Controller-General for all their actions, just as their subordinates, *subdélégués*, inspectors, and the like, were answerable only to them. The Intendants were the chief administrative reasons for the success of the centralisation of Louis XIV. He drew both his Ministers and his administrators from a narrow circle and class, avoiding the employment in high places of either members of the nobility or clergy. By such means he brought the French Monarchy to the peak of its power. In the first half of his reign at least he was served loyally and unquestioningly.

Versailles

The Palace of Versailles, which began, as we have seen[2] as a retreat

---

[1] Governors of provinces, who were nobles, did indeed remain, and received large salaries and much honour, but they could take no active step in government without the consent of the Intendant.

[2] See pp. 67–8.

for himself and his friends, soon became an essential part of his system of Monarchy. No nobleman who did not attend at Versailles could hope for any royal favour; should such a one be proposed for any appointment, Louis would cut short the suggestion with: 'He is a man I never see'.[1] The lesser nobility, who did not attend at Versailles, sank into provincial insignificance. The greater nobility who did attend at Versailles were all dwarfs at the disposal of the Great Man. The Duc de Saint-Simon, one of the great names in France, describes in his *Memoirs* his fury at being kept waiting for an audience while the King was closeted with his architect, a man of low birth! At Versailles the nobles were expected to keep up an extravagant equipage which they could often ill-afford, for few of them were really rich. To be exiled from Court or to live on one's estates were dreadful forms of deprivation. At Court, although there were no important political appointments to be had, there were many Court appointments, and perhaps a command in the army or a benefice in the Church for one's sons: all were in the gift of the King. Louis kept his nobility entirely dependent upon himself for favours. When Versailles was completed there was held a 'jour d'Appartement' three times a week in the Grand Appartement (including the Galerie des Glaces), where the whole Court assembled for four hours of gaming, dancing, music and refreshment in the most sumptuous rooms in all Europe. The two ceremonies of the 'lever' and 'coucher' were daily of the deepest significance, when the nobility vied with each other for the honour of holding the candle or the royal nightshirt. Louis was a good judge of human nature; these may have been tedious, but were not pointless, ceremonies. In its early days Versailles must have been a place of great beauty and gaiety. Louis loved music, and was himself a pleasant performer. His gardens showed considerable taste, and he knew enough of the arts to appreciate the music of Lully, the comedies of Molière and the tragedies of Racine. He ennobled

[1] This was Saint-Simon's picture of the King at Versailles: 'He saw and noticed everybody; not one escaped him, not even those who hoped to remain unnoticed. He marked well all absentees from the Court, found out the reason for their absence, and never lost an opportunity of acting towards them as the occasion might seem to justify. With some of the courtiers (the most distinguished) it was a demerit not to make the Court their ordinary abode; with others it was a fault to come but rarely; for those who never or scarcely ever came it was certain disgrace. When their names were in any way mentioned, "I do not know them," the King would haughtily reply, or "They are people I never see".'

Mansart, Le Nôtre and Le Brun for their work in creating Versailles, and extended his patronage to all the arts.

Colbert was, as we have seen, virtually his Minister of Fine Arts. Not only did he appoint Le Brun as artistic director at Versailles, but he employed Charles Perrault, a versatile young author, to be a kind of patronage secretary. He regimented the French Academy, which was slowly producing the French Dictionary, insisted that they met daily, and even installed a clock by which they could keep time. Many famous names gathered at Versailles in receipt of royal patronage. Corneille was always ill at ease at Court, and Molière perhaps endured Versailles rather than enjoyed it, but Boileau, the great name in prose, the Dr. Johnson of the period, lived all his life in Paris or Versailles, and was entirely happy there. He found Louis an appreciative master, with his kindly words, 'Remember, I have always an hour a week for you when you care to come.' Racine was the poet laureate of the Court, and for twelve years, as official historian, he recorded Louis XIV's victories. His early plays were much appreciated at Court, but after 1677 he wrote no plays for an interval of thirteen years. His last play *Athalie* was a study between the forces of stability and instability in society, and it appears probable that he already felt the disintegration which threatened the despotism of Louis XIV. It was characteristic of Colbert that he should seek to gather all artists into their respective corporations. The literary *Académie française* had been established by Richelieu. Colbert organised a similar Academy of Painting and Sculpture with Le Brun as director. In 1666 he established the French Academy in Rome, and in 1671 he established an Academy of Architecture at the Palais Royal. Great sums of money were spent during the reign on building and decorating palaces, and a readily recognisable artistic style emerged, which is frankly dull and insipid. Yet at the time it all served to increase the wonder of the age at the Monarchy of Louis XIV. There was sound policy behind the expenditure of many millions of livres on the glorification of the Grand Monarque.

Louvois

Colbert provided the money and the décor for Louis's greatness; Louvois provided the military power. Indeed Louvois helped to transform the art of war in the seventeenth century, and in this respect deserves comparison with Gustavus Adolphus, Wallenstein and Marlborough. Michel Le Tellier and his son Louvois were successively Secretary of State for War from 1643 until 1691 and during that time the army entirely changed its character. In 1643 the army was little better than a rabble, undisciplined, ill-fed and badly paid, living by loot and terrorising the countryside wherever it happened to be. Officers bought their commissions and sold them again when they retired. Having paid a large sum for a commission (a command in the Guards might cost several thousand livres) an officer felt justified in recouping himself by all means in his power. The army was not recruited by the State, but by captains who contracted for their regiments with the Government. Habitually he declared that his numbers were much greater than they were, and pocketed the pay of his mythical men. The result was that no general knew the real size of his army. Other practices were the sale of troops' equipment, systematic looting of provinces and corrupt government contracts. Le Tellier began a change when he introduced *intendants de l'armée*, who, with wide powers, carried out systematic inspections. In 1661 Louis XIV took into his own hands the granting of the higher commissions. Up to the rank of colonel, commissions were still bought and sold (ensign, lieutenant, captain and colonel), and Louvois was not strong enough to end the practice. Instead he created two more ranks, lieutenant-colonel and major. These could not be bought, and gradually the lieutenant-colonel replaced the colonel in importance on active service. By systematic inspection he made the deliberate undermanning of regiments a dangerous practice liable to severe punishments. Louvois gradually introduced the wearing of uniforms, though only for officers. He overhauled the almost entirely neglected subject of training, especially of officers, and appointed Martinet Inspector of Infantry, and Fourilles Inspector of Cavalry. The former has added a word to our language to indicate military discipline and precision. He established cadet companies for young officers, and a reserve system whereby old soldiers could speedily be recalled. He attempted to raise the quality of recruits, which had too often been the dregs of society, though with limited success. He saw to it that officers and men were regularly paid, and this did something to prevent the wholesale desertions which afflicted all armies in the seventeenth century. Louis XIV showed genuine interest in the welfare of his troops. In 1674 the Hôtel des Invalides was established for ex-soldiers. Louis sometimes paid pensions to soldiers' widows. Field hospitals were for the first time provided. One of the greatest problems facing seventeenth-century armies was that of supplies: troops were always in danger of outrunning supplies, and were constantly at the mercy of fraudulent contractors. There is a recorded incident in 1675 in which the French were defeated in the Saar because they were unable to use their artillery because the contractor had hired out the horses to local farmers for the day! Louvois made full use of the *intendants de l'armée* as administrative officers, and developed the magazine. Louis XIV is himself said to have invented a portable field oven for the use of his troops. In weapons the *fusil* slowly replaced the musket, and the bayonet (invented by Vauban as a weapon of attack rather than defence) replaced the pike. The cavalry were still thought of as the main instrument of attack, and for this purpose the sabre slowly replaced the sword. Louvois' reforms made the French army the finest in Europe. He himself was a passionate advocate of war, and he has thus been called Louis XIV's evil genius, ever tempting him on to further war. He died in 1691.

Religious Policy

After the fierce sixteenth-century Wars of Religion in France, and the Thirty Years' War in Germany, in which neither Catholic nor Protestant gained an unqualified victory, religious issues played a less decisive part in European affairs than they had done before. This was partly due to the triumph of monarchical absolutism, but also to a change in the intellectual climate of the age. As we have seen already the scientific revolution in thought and the growth of the philosophy of Enlightenment induced the idea that the old theological issues, and the Catholic–Protestant controversies, were outmoded. But religious issues remained, particularly in the relations of Church and State. The Catholic Church remained a powerful corporation, retaining the devotion of the great majority of the subjects of France, Spain, Portugal, Italy, Poland, southern Germany and the Habsburg dominions. Louis XIV was a powerful monarch; the whole trend of his policy was towards centralisation and monarchical absolutism, and he himself claimed an authority based upon Divine Right. It was

D

natural therefore that he should seek to exercise considerable influence over the Church.

In this he was aided by the tradition of Gallicanism in France. Gallicanism was a vague word which served to express a French nationalistic suspicion of too much power exercised by the popes of Rome. Sometimes it took the form of claiming that the Council of the Church was superior to the popes, at others that the King had as much to say as the Pope in the selection of bishops, at others that bishops were autonomous in their dioceses, and not subject to the control of Rome. It was usually the case that the Sorbonne (the faculty of theology of the University of Paris), the *parlement*, some of the bishops, and also the General Assembly of the Church (which met every five years to vote a *don gratuit* to the Crown) could be relied upon to support Gallican 'liberties', and thus Louis XIV would have powerful allies in France for any step he took to increase his authority over the Church. But there were also powerful forces on the other side. The theory which upheld the independence of the Church and the authority of Rome is known as Ultramontanism, and was held strongly by the Jesuits and the *dévot* party. These argued that the Church represented the Kingdom of God upon earth and therefore must be independent of the secular power. At this the reader might logically suppose that it followed that Louis XIV would be a Gallican and therefore anti-Jesuit. But this was not so. For Louis was, according to his lights, a sincerely religious man, and a strictly orthodox son of the Church. Moreover, in all matters other than Gallican, the Jesuits were devoted supporters of monarchical power. Louis was much influenced by his confessors, who argued that authority was single and indivisible; that the Church and Monarchy were twin supports for each other, and that the greatest evil was what the twentieth century might call deviationism. In particular they convinced Louis that there were two enemies who should be exterminated, first, the Jansenists, and second, the Huguenots, Louis' Protestant subjects (for how could Louis claim to have established a centralised and unified State so long as an important number of his subjects refused to follow his religious lead?).

It is difficult to explain the nature of Jansenism in a short space, for its roots go far back into mediaeval theology. Theologians had always had difficulty in reconciling the two doctrinal ideas, of the omnipotence of God and the freedom of man in some way to achieve his own salvation. St. Augustine of Hippo, in emphasising the omnipotence of God, had emphasised also the utter sinfulness of man. Salvation therefore was a divine mystery, the result of the direct intervention of God through the instrument of His Grace. In the course of the sixteenth century Jesuit philosophers had emphasised rather the doctrine of Works as the means of achieving salvation, and this had been the theme of the writings of the Jesuit Molina in 1588. The opponents of the Jesuits, especially the Spanish Dominicans, feared that Molina exalted the liberty of man to the detriment of the omnipotence of God, and a determined struggle took place between the Jesuits and the Sorbonne, in which Antoine Arnauld père was the advocate for the University (1594–1619). His daughter became the saintly Mère Angélique, who began the reform of the famous convent of Port-Royal in 1608, and his son Antoine became one of the leading French Jansenists. Jansen (1585–1638) was a professor at the University of Louvain, and later bishop of Ypres, and he wrote his famous *Augustinus* in reply to Molina. It re-emphasised the teaching of St. Augustine in the matter of Grace, and was published two years after his death. It was closely followed by a powerful book from Antoine Arnauld, *De la Frequente Communion*, accusing the Jesuits of laxist views. The Jesuits carried the controversy to Rome, and in 1653 Pope Innocent X condemned the Five Propositions in the *Augustinus* which were held to be heresy. By this time Jansenism had acquired a good deal of support in France, where it was argued that, though the Five Propositions were certainly heresy, Jansen had never held them. (So far it might be said that Arnauld and a few nuns at Port-Royal were defying the authority of the Church, but in 1656 they received powerful aid from Blaise Pascal, the mathematician and philosopher and a figure of European stature. In his famous *Provincial Letters* he defended Arnauld, and with merciless logic attacked the Jesuit doctrine of Grace and their whole attitude to morality. By this time four bishops had joined the movement.)

This was the situation when Louis XIV took over the business of government in 1661. His knowledge of theology was rudimentary; to him the Jansenists were troublesome deviationists who must be suppressed. His position was soon complicated by the fact that in the following year he was in conflict with the Pope in a quite different matter. In 1662 his swaggering and foolish ambassador in Rome, the Duc de Créqui, had clashed with the Pope's Corsican Guard. Louis demanded the fullest apology from the Pope, and the dismissal of the Papal Corsican Guard, and, to enforce his demand, he seized the papal territory of Avignon.[1] Eventually the Pope had to make an abject submission, and even erect a monument in Rome to the French triumph (1664). The whole incident was an indication of Louis XIV's intentions to assert his primacy in Europe.

In the following year Louis applied to the Pope for a formulary which all the French clergy should accept, and which would thus end the Jansenist heresy. Pope Alexander seized the opportunity to reassert his influence in France, and complied. The four bishops refused to accept the formulary until 1668, but then a 'Peace of the Church' was formally announced. Port-Royal had submitted, and was left in peace for another decade.

In 1673 there arose a further cause of conflict. Since A.D. 511 the Kings of France, it was said, had had the right to the *régale temporelle*, or revenues, of most of the bishoprics of France during a vacancy, but this did not apply to four particular bishoprics. In 1673 Louis announced that he was extending the right to all bishoprics, and also extending the royal rights of patronage in the bishoprics during the vacancy. It was not that Louis was anxious for the money; it was the prestige and powers of patronage with which he was concerned. Two of the bishops who protested were Jansenists. In 1676 the new Pope, Innocent XI, was pro-Jansenist, and took a strong line of opposition to Louis's policy. Time was on the Pope's side, for without his approval, no new bishop could be legally inducted in France, and Louis feared the consequences of an alliance between the Pope and French Jansenists. The position was complicated by the fact that France had never fully recognised the decisions of the Council of Trent: only its doctrinal findings had been approved. Relations between the State and the clergy were therefore still governed by the Concordat of 1516. Jansenists had always defended the privileges and prerogatives of the bishops, and Louis' policy now was forcing them into alliance with the Ultramontanes. Innocent XI himself said that

---

[1] Louis XIV always demanded precedence for his ambassadors in foreign capitals. Where this was refused, as in Vienna where the Emperor accorded precedence to Spain, Louis XIV refused to appoint an ambassador, but merely a resident minister. Appointment as ambassador was one of those open to the *noblesse d'épée*.

there were no longer any Jansenists in France, meaning that they were pillars of orthodoxy; and his secretary defined a Jansenist as 'a man of outstanding piety and goodness and an enemy of the Jesuits'.[1] Louis decided to use the power of Gallicanism in France to obtain his way. In 1682 he held a carefully packed Assembly of the French Clergy, which proceeded to carry the famous Four Articles:

1. that the King was not subject to the ecclesiastical power in temporal matters;
2. that the General Council of the Church was superior to the Pope;
3. that the Pope could not modify the canon law or customs of the Gallican Church;
4. that Papal definitions of faith were not 'irreformable' by the Council of the Church.

The Pope strongly condemned the actions of the French Assembly, and refused to institute any of Louis' nominees to bishoprics during the next eleven years, by which time there were thirty-five bishops awaiting institution, and the French Church was in considerable chaos. The Jansenists in France had been forced into an alliance with the Pope and the Ultramontanes against the Monarchy.

In 1688 conflict between Louis and the Pope reached a new height when the Pope refused to receive a new French ambassador; and when the latter forced his way into Rome, the Pope secretly excommunicated Louis himself. Louis for his part again seized Avignon. But this conflict could not continue. Louis was about to fight the War of the League of Augsburg, and needed the goodwill of the ecclesiastical princes of Germany. Negotiations were opened; they were long-drawn-out and not completed until two new Popes had been elected (Alexander VIII and Innocent XII). Finally in 1692–93 it was agreed that the Pope would accept the thirty-five bishops who awaited institution; Louis restored Avignon and recalled the offending ambassador. The Four Articles were not withdrawn, but Louis ceased to require that they be taught in seminaries. The King retained the *régale temporelle*, and the subject on patronage was allowed to lapse. On the whole it was a victory for the King.

Meanwhile Louis XIV had sought to prove himself a good son of

[1] 'vir eximiae pietatis ac virtutis inimicus Jesuitarum.'

the Church by his policy towards the Huguenots. The Edict of Nantes of 1598 had granted the Huguenots freedom of worship, and had left them in some ways a powerful State within a State. Richelieu had deprived the Huguenots of their fortifications, so that they were no longer a danger to the State. As time passed the Huguenots lost their militancy; they were mostly prosperous middle-class merchants, industrialists and officials, vieing with each other in their excess of loyalty to the Monarchy. Some, like Turenne, Ruvigny, Schomberg, were among the most distinguished names in France. But, as a minority, they were intensely unpopular, and to Louis it was represented that the continuance of the Huguenots was an insult to royal authority, and a destruction of the principle of national unity. It was also represented to him that the Huguenots were being converted apace to Catholicism, and that it would require only a policy of steady pressure to extinguish Protestantism altogether in France. At first Louis decided to respect the Edict of Nantes, but to 'interpret' it as narrowly as possible. For instance, since the Edict of Nantes made no reference to churches built after 1598, it was decreed in 1669 that all such churches should be demolished. It was hoped that such pressure would induce Huguenots to accept conversion. Certain professions, such as those of midwife, were closed to Huguenots, and it became increasingly difficult for them to secure justice in the Courts. Sums of money were set aside as inducements to conversion. After 1679 the pace of the repression was quickened, and in 1681 the Intendant of Poitou hit upon the policy of the dragonnades, the quartering of dragoons upon the Huguenots. This was accompanied by much brutality; the dragoons acted as seventeenth-century soldiers acted whenever they had the chance, and when the Huguenots resisted they were beaten. Huguenot emigration had begun as early as 1666, and now was speeded up. Finally in 1685, by the Edict of Fontainebleau, all the privileges of the Edict of Nantes were cancelled; the Huguenot churches were demolished, and the practice of their religion was forbidden. Louis' prime motive had been that which governed the reign as a whole; namely to complete the centralisation of the French Monarchy. An additional motive was to be able to pose as the greatest protector of Catholicism in Europe. It was an act which was immensely popular in France, but it has earned the almost unanimous condemnation of historians. For it deprived

France of some 800,000 of her most valuable citizens, whose skills strengthened France's neighbours, the Dutch, the English and the Brandenburgers in particular. The French army lost 600 officers and 12,000 good troops; the French navy lost 9,000 sailors. Many of these were to give a good account of themselves fighting against France in the following years. The moral effect upon Europe was immense. Protestant Europe interpreted the events as Louis XIV's declaration of war upon Protestantism. In England the events in France helped to hasten the decision to bring about the Revolution of 1688. The League of Augsburg was perceptibly strengthened. In France the violence and persecution coarsened religious life and did great harm to the Catholic Church. So far as one can see, the Revocation of the Edict of Nantes brought many disadvantages, but not a single advantage to France. Louis himself seems to have realised something of this, for on his deathbed he was at pains to excuse his actions. Nor was Protestantism fully crushed in France; it lay dormant for a time, but revived, and was openly followed in the remoter parts of southern France, for instance in the *généralité* of Toulouse, during the eighteenth century.

A word here may be said about the character of the French clergy in the reign of Louis XIV; on the whole the standard was high. Most of the higher clergy had sprung from the nobility, but some, like bishop Bossuet, the greatest ecclesiastical intellect in France, were of middle class origin. The Church was certainly regarded as a means of livelihood for the younger sons of the nobility, but once they entered the Church they often proved to be able administrators, if not inspired pastors, while some, like the bishop of Bayeux who died in 1715, or the bishop of Beauvais who died in 1713, lived lives of great saintliness. Convents were the normal destination for some of the younger daughters of the nobility, for they could not be spared dowries. The Duke of Beauvilliers made eight of his eleven daughters nuns. Most convents were in reality places of elegant retreat rather than places of great piety, but Angélique Arnauld, who became abbess of Port-Royal at the age of eleven, became a saintly person and a great reformer, and her house was a model of devotion and learning.

To return to the Jansenists in France. Their numbers had steadily increased; they had distinguished writers, Antoine Arnauld, Nicole, Pasquier Quesnel, author of *Reflexions morales*; and they had support in high places, Cardinal Noailles, Archbishop of Paris, bishop Bossuet, and the poet Racine. To suppress the Jansenists the King needed the support of the Pope. The election of an anti-Jansenist Pope, Clement XI in 1700 provided the opportunity. In 1709, on Louis XIV's insistence, the Pope agreed to suppress the convent of Port-Royal. French troops forcibly distributed the inmates throughout France, and the buildings were demolished. Louis regarded this as an achievement comparable to the Revocation of the Edict of Nantes; the unity of his kingdom had been vindicated.

The most important Jansenist book of the time was Quesnel's *Reflexions morales*. Quesnel had had to flee from France, for a time was imprisoned in the Spanish Netherlands, and eventually escaped to Holland. He repeatedly defended the orthodoxy of his book, which had been approved by Bossuet himself, and finally, in 1712, aged nearly eighty, he appealed to the Pope himself. The Pope's reply was the Bull *Unigenitus* (1713), which condemned one-hundred-and-one propositions in Quesnel's book. The Bull was accepted by an assembly of French bishops. Eight of them, with Noailles at their head, wished to appeal to the Pope to modify it, but the King forbade their protest and banished them to their dioceses by *lettres de cachet*. But the *parlement* of Paris stoutly refused to register the Bull, in spite of royal threats, until Louis XIV held a *lit de justice*. Before the matter could be settled, Louis XIV died (September 1715). *Unigenitus* aroused all the Gallican susceptibilities. The French Church was split into those who accepted the Bull and those who rejected it, and the issue now broadened out into a great conflict between rival parties within the Church. The consequences in the reign of Louis XV were considerable.

Although there was some lack of consistency about it, Louis XIV's religious policy was governed by the same considerations of State policy and centralisation which governed his policy in other directions. To him it was inconceivable that loyal subjects could hold religious views different from his own. But before we condemn this attitude too readily, we should recall how frequently religious divisions had been the cause of bloody conflicts in both France and Germany during the previous century. To Louis, religious conformity meant peace as well as unity. Protestant Europe however interpreted it as virtually a declaration of war.

Foreign Policy: The Policy of Prestige

Lord Acton wrote that the two fundamental facts governing the position of France in Europe in the time of Louis XIV were, 'the break-up of the imperial power in Germany after the Thirty Years' War, so that France was bordered by small states incapable of self-defence', and the decay of Spain. Cardinals Richelieu and Mazarin, by the Treaties of Westphalia (1648) and the Pyrenees (1659), had given France the basis for a dominating position in Europe. During the Thirty Years' War France had fished in the troubled waters of the Holy Roman Empire, had posed as the champion of German Protestantism against the Habsburg power, and by the Treaty of Westphalia had annexed part of Alsace, together with the bishoprics of Metz, Toul and Verdun. By the Treaty of the Pyrenees France annexed Artois, Roussillon and Cerdagne. Richelieu had shown what could be achieved by French gold, as well as by French arms, in winning allies. The military power of Spain had collapsed on the field of Rocroi (1643), and thereafter Spain was in a deplorable condition of weakness. The States of the Holy Roman Empire were exhausted and divided. France was by far the strongest and most united Power in Europe, and it was inevitable that Louis XIV should seek to assert his power wherever he felt that prestige required it. His foreign Minister was Lionne, but Louis XIV directed foreign affairs personally, and Lionne was never much more than his chief executive.

For it was prestige, the love of glory, which was the principal motive of his foreign policy. If Louis was the supreme power within France, and if France was the strongest Monarchy in Europe, his first requirement was that Europe should recognise the fact. Thus in 1661 he inflicted a humiliation upon Spain by forcing her to grant precedence to the French ambassador in London. We have seen already how he inflicted a similar humiliation on the Papacy in 1662 over the affair of the duc de Créqui. He forced the pleasure-loving Duke of Lorraine to do homage to him for the duchy of Bar. In 1662 he purchased from England the port of Dunkirk. He soon took measure of the unprincipled Charles II of England, and later applied French gold both to the English king and to English politicians, in order to keep England a client State. He found it equally easy to buy German princes. He supported Portugal in its war against Spain. In all these ways he made his power felt in the first years of his reign. The death of Philip IV of Spain in 1665 provided further opportunities.

The War of Devolution and the First Dutch War

Philip IV had had two daughters by his first marriage, of whom the elder was now Queen of France, and one son by his second marriage. This son succeeded to the throne of Spain as Charles II (the unfortunate Charles the Sufferer). But in parts of the Spanish Netherlands, including Brabant, the Law of Devolution governed the rights of inheritance, whereby the heirs of the first marriage took precedence over those of the second. By this law Louis XIV laid claim to the territory in the name of his wife. She had in fact renounced her claims upon her marriage, on the payment of her dowry, but as her dowry had never been paid, Louis declared the renunciation invalid. The fallacy of the French claim in any case was to suppose that the law governing rights of property applied to rights of sovereignty. But it was precisely as pieces of property that Louis did regard his lands, and in any case, the legal niceties were less important than the facts of French power.

Louis' diplomacy prepared the way carefully. An alliance with Portugal weakened Spain. The Emperor Leopold I was neutralised by French alliances with German princes, purchased, as those with the Electors of Mainz and Cologne, with French gold. In 1663–64 he concluded treaties with Sweden, Brandenburg and Saxony. He was in touch with the Magyars, who were in revolt against the Emperor. He could also count on the Emperor's desire to share in the Spanish spoils. The Dutch presented a more difficult problem. They were traditionally French allies, but must be expected to oppose a French domination of the Netherlands. But between 1665–67 they were at war with England, and Louis hoped that they might agree to some partition of the Netherlands. French gold might secure England's neutrality. When all was ready, in 1667, Louis XIV invaded the Netherlands without a declaration of war; he simply announced to Spain that he was taking possession of his wife's inheritance.

Turenne marched into the Spanish Netherlands with 50,000 men. The Spanish Governor, with only 20,000 men, offered little resistance, and one by one Charleroi, Tournai, Douai, Courtrai and Oudenarde were occupied almost without firing a shot. Only Lille put up a resistance of seventeen days. John de Witt, the Grand Pensionary of Holland, was in a pitiable dilemma. He was loath to end the traditional alliance with France, yet he could not stand by and see France absorb the Spanish Netherlands. He attempted to negotiate a settlement with France, but was repulsed. An alternative policy was alliance with England against French pretensions, but he was under no illusions about the reliability of any treaty with Charles II. Eventually in January 1668 an Anglo-Dutch treaty was negotiated by Sir William Temple, which Sweden later joined to form the Triple Alliance: the three Powers were to offer mediation to France and Spain.[1] In the seventeenth century winter campaigns were almost unknown, but in the winter of 1667–68 the French under Condé suddenly invaded the Spanish province of Franche Comté, and occupied it within a fortnight (February 1668), for Spanish power was as feeble there as it had been in the Netherlands. In face, however, of the Triple Alliance, and the prevaricating attitude of the Emperor, Louis had to decide between peace and a general war. He decided that he was not ready for general war, and that he could gain most of his ends by negotiation. By the Treaty of Aix-la-Chapelle (May 1668) Louis surrendered Franche Comté, but retained his conquests in the Netherlands, Lille, Tournai, Charleroi, Douai, Oudenarde, Armentières and Courtrai. Vauban was already employed on their fortification, and France now had a defensible frontier. Louis XIV wished, by a show of moderation, to disarm the hostility of Europe, but his anger against the little Dutch Republic for thwarting his plans knew no bounds. Colbert was feeding him with the facts and figures of Dutch wealth and commercial supremacy, and in 1667 had clapped a heavy tariff on Dutch trade. If the Dutch Republic could be extinguished and annexed to France, the wealth, and therefore the power, of France would be immeasurably increased. Colbert had already begun a commercial war against the Dutch, and Louis now detested the Dutch both for their Republicanism and their Protestantism. He thought that their extinction would be no difficult matter, for the Triple Alliance was short-lived. In 1670, by the secret Treaty of Dover, Louis secured English adherence to the plan to

---

[1] Lord Acton wrote: 'The Triple Alliance was the earliest of that series of coalitions which ended by getting the better of the power of Louis XIV, and is therefore a landmark in history.' It was, however, of very short duration.

destroy the Dutch, and the neutrality of Sweden was obtained by the payment of an annual subsidy. The neutrality of the Emperor was also obtained (1671). The Elector of Cologne and the Bishop of Münster were French allies; the Palatinate and Brunswick were friendly territories, and only Brandenburg was an ally of the Dutch. When in 1672 the Dutch placed an embargo on French imports, this was the signal for war.

It was a fundamental change in French policy. Since Richelieu, France had posed as the ally of the Protestant States against the overweening power of the Emperor. Now France was attacking a Protestant Power and threatening the independence of the Rhineland and north Germany. In 1670, on a flimsy pretext, Louis occupied the duchies of Lorraine and Bar. Germany reacted sharply against the new threat in the course of the next few years. Moreover, Napoleon called the Dutch War of 1672 'a new era in warfare'. The army of Louvois and Turenne was in fine form; the French infantry was the best in Europe; Vauban had organised a body of engineers who would reduce siege warfare to a science; Turenne and Condé were magnificent commanders. In May 1672 the French army of 100,000 men advanced against the isolated Dutch Republic, defended by an army of only 30,000, and with widespread disaffection and defeatism in the country. While the French marched down the Meuse and Rhine and occupied Nijmegen, the armies of the archbishop of Cologne and the bishop of Münster occupied Overijssel and part of Groningen. A determined push from the French must have extinguished the Republic. But instead Louis listened to Louvois and wasted time reducing the Yssel forts, thus giving the Dutch time (June 1672) to open the dykes and save Amsterdam. William III had been appointed captain-general, though with limited powers. John de Witt had entirely failed to gain reasonable terms from France, and in August he and his brother were assassinated by an infuriated mob. Louis's best policy would have been to make a speedy peace with the Dutch and proceed to the subjugation of the whole of the Spanish Netherlands, but he repeatedly threw away his opportunities, through inexperience and vainglory. So contemptuous was he of the Dutch that he released 20,000 prisoners, who promptly became the nucleus of a new army. The summer of 1672 passed, and with it the French opportunity to crush the Dutch.

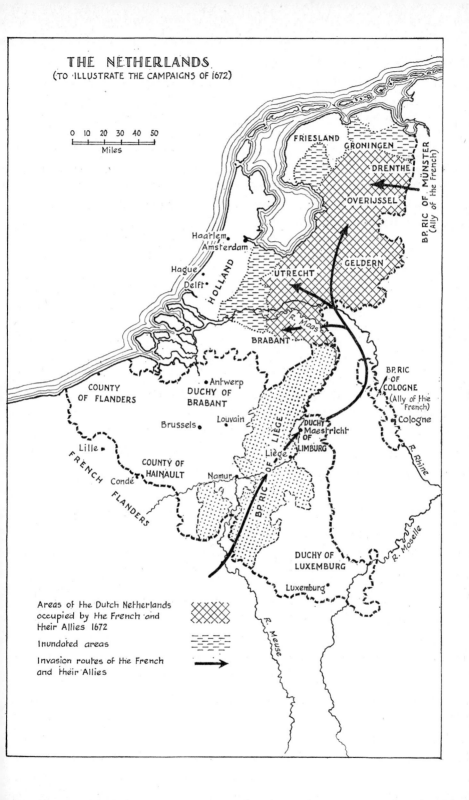

THE NETHERLANDS
(TO ILLUSTRATE THE CAMPAIGNS OF 1672)

0 10 20 30 40 50
Miles

FRIESLAND
GRONINGEN
DRENTHE
OVERIJSSEL
BP.RIC OF MÜNSTER (Ally of the French)

Haarlem
Amsterdam
Hague
Delft
HOLLAND
UTRECHT
GELDERN

BRABANT
R. Maas

BP.RIC OF COLOGNE (Ally of the French)
Cologne

Antwerp
DUCHY OF BRABANT
COUNTY OF FLANDERS

Brussels
Louvain
LIÈGE
DUCHY OF LIMBURG
Maestricht

Lille
FRENCH FLANDERS
Condé
COUNTY OF HAINAULT
Namur
Liège
BP. RIC OF LIÈGE

R. Rhine

DUCHY OF LUXEMBURG
Luxemburg

R. Moselle

R. Meuse

Areas of the Dutch Netherlands occupied by the French and their Allies 1672

Inundated areas

Invasion routes of the French and their Allies

In 1673–74 the Emperor and Spain entered the war in alliance with the Dutch, occupied Bonn, and forced Cologne and Munster to desert the French. Vauban besieged and took Maestricht, but in other respects the French were forced on to the defensive. England made peace with the Dutch in 1674. The Emperor was successful in rallying a German coalition of the Palatinate, Saxony, Brunswick and Brandenburg against the French. The only remaining French ally was Sweden, which promptly attacked Brandenburg and was defeated at the Battle of Fehrbellin in June 1675. The chief success of France in 1674 was Turenne's famous march to Belfort in December to repel an Allied army threatening to invade France. It was his last great achievement; his death in battle in 1675 was a disaster for France. Condé's health was also broken, and France never again in Louis' reign had two such generals. The following years were indecisive and largely taken up with negotiations, though in 1677 Vauban besieged and took Cambrai, and Louis XIV's brother, the Duke of Orleans, defeated William of Orange at the Battle of Cassel; and in 1678 the French took Ghent and Ypres. Finally by the Peace of Nijmegen (1678–89—actually it was a series of treaties which France made with each of her opponents separately), France gained from Spain Franche-Comté, Cambrai, Bouchain, Valenciennes, Aire, St. Omer, Ypres, Cassel, Charlemont and Dinan, but restored Courtrai, Oudenarde, Charleroi, Ghent and Limburg. France thus obtained a strong line of defence from Dunkirk to the Meuse. French gains were at the expense of Spain. The Dutch not only survived, but were even able to insist that Colbert's hostile tariffs of 1664 and 1667 should be suspended. Louis had not extinguished the Dutch, but in all other ways his success had been considerable. It is possible to argue that in 1678–79 he stood at the height of his power, for his army was at a peak of power, the European alliance against him quickly dissolved, the Spanish power was shown to be defunct, and he had won for France a strong frontier. Looking back on his achievement late in life, he declared:

> Ambition and glory are always pardonable in a prince, and especially in a young prince so well treated by fortune as I was.

Reunion and the Truce of Ratisbon

Having achieved much by war, Louis XIV now sought to extend his dominion by other means. In 1680 he put into operation an idea which may have originated with Louvois, and was known as the *Réunions*. Judicial Chambers of Reunion were set up at four centres in eastern France, at Metz, Breisach, Tournay and Besançon, to look into the rights of the French King in Alsace, Lorraine, Bar, Flanders and Franche Comté. In fairness to Louis it must be recognised that the whole area was a maze of conflicting jurisdictions in which the rights of France and the Empire were ill-defined. The Treaty of Westphalia, for instance, had given France sovereignty over Alsace, saving the rights of the 'immediate' nobles and of the Imperial towns. Many princelings found that in fact they were subject neither to the King of France nor to the Emperor. The Chambers of Reunion now simply declared that they were subject to the King of France. The bishoprics of Metz, Toul and Verdun were declared entirely within French jurisdiction. Areas which previously had belonged to other rulers were now declared to be French territory. Thus Saarbruck was taken from the Elector of Trier and declared French, and Vauban proceeded to build the fortress of Saarlouis to defend it. Wildentz was taken from the Elector Palatine, and Deux-Ponts from the King of Sweden. In 1680 French sovereignty was declared throughout Alsace with the exception of Strassburg and Muhlhausen, and in the following year Louis received with elaborate ceremony the homage of all nobles and towns. Strassburg was indeed the ultimate object of Louis' policy of Reunion; it was one of the greatest fortresses in Europe, and it would certainly fall to Louis if the Emperor did not intervene. But in 1679, at the instance of Louis XIV, the Emperor withdrew his troops from the city, for he was deeply involved in eastern Europe. In 1681 Louvois occupied the city without resistance, and on September 27th Louis XIV made a splendid entry to the sound of cannon, trumpets and bells, and attended a solemn Te Deum in the cathedral. On the same day the fortress of Casale was also occupied. There remained one other great fortress which Louis desired, that of Luxemburg, which Spain refused to surrender. Its turn must be next, unless Europe prevented it.

There was not a great deal that Europe could do, for the Emperor was engaged in mortal combat with the Turks, who in 1683 laid siege to Vienna. In the Rhineland the three electoral archbishops (Mainz, Cologne and Trier) were still in French pay. But German opinion was turning against France; the Dutch were alarmed at the French advance, and in England it was doubtful how long Charles II could resist the demands of the Whigs that he should abandon his neutrality. When Louis began the siege of Luxemburg in November 1681, Charles II urged him to desist. It was always Louis XIV's way, after a period of advance, to draw back as opposition mounted, in order to prepare the ground more thoroughly by diplomatic means. In 1682 therefore he abandoned the siege of Luxemburg. But in 1683, with incredible folly, Spain declared war on France, though without money or arms it is difficult to see what Spain could hope to achieve. The French, for their part, occupied Courtrai, and in June 1684 took the fortress of Luxemburg.

At the same time, Louis XIV could not be indifferent to the events in eastern Europe. There was gradually evolving an 'Eastern' foreign policy for France, which in theory was simple enough, but in practice was difficult to pursue. Since the days of Gustavus Adolphus and Richelieu it was clear that a Franco-Swedish alliance could benefit both countries. A Polish alliance was more difficult, for Poland and Sweden might well be enemies, and Poland was not always prepared to aid France against the Emperor. In the 1670s, for instance, Louis XIV tried in vain to win the alliance of John Sobieski: the latter preferred to aid the Emperor against the Turk. The easiest ally to win against the Emperor was the Turk, but here Louis' policy was equivocal. As the Most Christian King, he could hardly openly support the infidel against the Emperor. There were times also when he dreamed of emulating his great namesake and predecessor St. Louis in putting himself at the head of a European crusade against the Turks, which would wrest from the Emperor the leadership of Europe. There was also the question of French ascendancy in the Mediterranean. With the decline of Spanish power, French naval supremacy in the Mediterranean seemed challenged only by the Republics of Venice and Genoa, and the Barbary Corsairs; for England's challenge came only with the reign of William III. Louis' relations with Genoa and Venice were always strained, and in 1683 he sent a successful naval expedition against the Corsairs of Algiers and Tripoli, which destroyed their bases and liberated numerous Christian slaves to the annoyance of the Sultan. In the same year the Turks were hammering at the very gates of Vienna. Louis XIV did nothing to aid them, and indeed announced that if Vienna fell, he would march to the salvation of Christendom. If the Emperor Leopold died, Louis was determined to seek the Imperial Crown, and in this he appeared likely to succeed, for with the three Electoral Archbishoprics and Brandenburg, Louis had a majority of the Electors in his pay. But Vienna did not fall, and the saviour of Europe was not Louis XIV, but the Habsburgs and John Sobieski of Poland.

All these issues complicated Louis's position in 1683–84. The most immediate issue was whether the Emperor and Diet of the Holy Roman Empire would accept the changes of sovereignty consequent upon the *Réunions*. These had indeed already been effected by the might of French power, but it was important to Louis that the appearance of legality should be preserved throughout. At this point, in 1684, the Dutch proposed that there should be a general truce between the Powers for twenty years, during which the Diet could examine the *Réunions* pending a permanent peace. Louis accepted this, and the Truce of Ratisbon was concluded in August.

The League of Augsburg

The great German historian Von Ranke regarded the Truce of Ratisbon as the peak of Louis XIV's power. The work of Colbert, Turenne, Condé and Louvois was all but done (the first three were dead, and Louvois died in 1691). French military and naval power were the terror of Europe. Versailles was all but finished; Louis XIV was the admiration of his subjects and the envy of Europe. Yet in some ways the Truce of Ratisbon was a serious error, for it left open for twenty years questions which Louis would have done well to settle in 1684. In the interim his enemies had time to gather, and it is possible that Louis was never quite so strong again as he was in 1684. In some ways his own attitude coarsened; he still pursued *la gloire*, but more recklessly. His suppression of the Huguenots in 1685 struck fear into the heart of Protestant Europe. Two questions now obsessed European statesmen: first, what would happen when the Truce of Ratisbon expired, unless Europe was united enough to resist further French pretensions? Second, what would be the fate of the Spanish Empire on the death of Charles the Sufferer? Charles II of Spain was a poor, misshapen creature, without an heir, and expected to die at any time. It was to guard against the dangers of these questions that the secret

League of Augsburg was formed in 1686 between the Emperor, the Dutch, Spain, Sweden, the Palatinate, Saxony, Bavaria and Savoy, and the Pope Innocent XI gave it his adherence. No one saw the menace of Louis XIV more clearly than William of Orange, Stadholder of Holland. He saw equally clearly how weak the League of Augsburg would be if put to the test, unless it had a stronger focal point, for the Emperor was still at war with the Turks. That focal point could only be himself, but merely as Stadholder of Holland the weight he carried would be limited. As King of England as well, he could play the part of a keystone to the whole alliance. For years he had followed events in England with the closest attention, and watched with increasing anxiety the way in which Charles II and James II allowed themselves to be mere clients of France. The Revolution of 1688 changed the balance of power of Europe. For the time being Louis XIV's political skill seems to have deserted him. He knew of the League of Augsburg, but hesitated to smash it in 1686 before it grew to strength. He failed to prevent William of Orange from reaching England in 1688, partly because Louis' attentions were elsewhere, partly because he could not believe that William would attempt so audacious a move, and partly also because he felt that, should the unlikely happen, William would be probably bogged down in an English civil war which could only strengthen Louis' position in Europe.

Faced with the League of Augsburg, Louis could direct his attack in one of two directions, either against the Emperor on the Rhine, or against the Dutch in the Netherlands. Gifted with hindsight, historians have pointed out that if Louis had chosen the latter, William of Orange might have been so deeply involved that it would have been impossible to leave for England at the critical moment. But, in the light of the facts of the time, Louis chose the first course. The occasion was the death of the archbishop of Cologne. Louis at once nominated his own puppet as the archbishop's successor, William of Fürstenberg. The Emperor naturally refused to accept him, and French troops occupied Cologne. They went further, and occupied the Palatinate, which was a member of the League. Louis' policy was, by an overwhelming show of force on the Rhine, to overawe the Emperor and force him to a speedy settlement. But on the day that Louis' troops occupied Philippsburg, the gateway to Germany,

William of Orange set sail for England, and the League of Augsburg changed its character. Louis' move had failed, and in 1689 he ordered the withdrawal from the Palatinate, but not before the countryside was ravaged, Heidelberg was burnt and its magnificent castle left in ruins. These acts were intended to overawe Europe, and to indicate what would happen to countries which joined in alliance against France, but they were a grave miscalculation. They tarnished the figure of Louis XIV as the most civilised king in Europe; they destroyed his moral claim to candidature for the Holy Roman Empire; and they aroused in Germany a hatred which was long remembered. When, nearly two centuries later, Von Ranke witnessed the defeat of France by Prussia in 1870, he remembered Heidelberg, and declared that it was Louis XIV who was being defeated at Sedan. Louis XIV later understood the error that had been made and in his *Mémoires* placed the blame for the barbarity upon Louvois.

The War of the League of Augsburg opened the long period of Anglo-French rivalry which continued until 1815. For the first time France was called upon to fight a maritime war against the two leading naval powers, the Dutch and England. Colbert had created French naval power, and his work was continued by his son Seignelay as Minister of Marine, who however died in 1690. Louvois died in 1691 and was succeeded by his incompetent son Barbézieux. France's most brilliant surviving general, Luxemburg, died in 1695, and thereafter, though some of them, like Vendôme (1654–1712) and Boufflers (1644–1711), were able generals, some like Villeroi (1641–1730) were incompetent, and none achieved the brilliance of the days of Turenne. Louis' most immediate task was to save the situation for James II in Ireland. In 1690 some 6,000 men under Count Lauzen were sent to Ireland, and the French admiral Tourville defeated the English admiral Torrington off Beachy Head in July 1690. If France could achieve command of the Channel, it would be a serious matter for England. But in July James was defeated at the Battle of the Boyne and fled to France. Moreover, the French seemed incapable of making decisive use of their naval power to effect an invasion of England, and finally their defeat at the Battle of La Hogue in May 1692 destroyed their hopes of achieving naval supremacy. They were still capable of inflicting considerable damage upon the English mercantile marine in the following years, and the subject of the invasion of England was again mooted in 1696, but the English Jacobites failed to rise, and the opportunity, if one existed, passed.

In Europe there were three theatres of war, on the Rhine, in the Low Countries and in Italy. On the Rhine the campaigns were poorly directed, indecisive and of little importance. In the Netherlands the war took the form of a series of sieges. Vauban had constructed for France a strong defensive frontier, and beyond that the French advanced against the great fortresses defended by the Allies. Both sides were anxious, according to the theory of the time, to avoid pitched battles, for armies were difficult to raise, and it was thought preferable to engage in scientific manoeuvrings, like some giant game of chess, by which fortresses could be isolated and then made to surrender. Thus the French took Mons in 1690, and Namur in 1692. William III sustained a dogged resistance against superior French forces. In 1693 he prevented Louis from taking Liège, though he was himself defeated at Neerwinden, and in 1695 he won his only major victory in Europe by the recapture of Namur. Meanwhile in Italy, during 1692–93 the French had overrun most of Piedmont, and in 1696 Victor Amadeus of Savoy, making a virtue of necessity, deserted the Allies, and made an alliance with France, thus releasing 30,000 French troops who might be transferred to the Netherlands. But by this time both sides were anxious for peace, and at the Congress of Ryswick, 1697, terms were easily arrived at. Louis XIV retained Landau and Alsace, including Strassburg, but apart from these, surrendered all his conquests since 1678, including Luxemburg, Cologne, the Palatinate and even Lorraine, which the French had claimed the right to garrison since the time of Richelieu. Louis also recognised William III as King of England, and agreed to the Dutch fortifying and garrisoning the Barrier Fortresses (e.g. Ypres and Namur) against France. Louis XIV's moderation was the result of a recognition of France's inability to reach a decisive victory in a short space of time. And time had become important. The health of Charles II of Spain was reported to be more precarious than ever. The whole question of the fate of the Spanish Empire was the main political issue of the time. It was important to Louis that when the time came for Charles II to die, he should not himself be faced with a hostile European alliance. The League of Augsburg must be dissolved, and this could be purchased by a peace settlement in which Louis had again displayed to Europe his essential moderation. In this he succeeded. England and the Dutch were weary of war, and the Emperor was still (until the Treaty of Carlowitz, 1699) at war with the Turks. As soon as the Treaty of Ryswick was signed, the League fell to pieces, and Louis was left free to pursue his Spanish policy.

The Partition Treaties

In this period Louis XIV showed great diplomatic skill. The Comte D'Harcourt was sent as ambassador to Madrid in 1698, and he succeeded in building up a strong pro-French party to offset the pro-Habsburg party which previously had been uppermost. There were three possible claimants to the Spanish inheritance upon the death of Charles II:

1. Louis XIV claimed it for the Dauphin of France, as the son of Maria Theresa, eldest daughter of Philip IV of Spain. She had in fact renounced her claims on marriage as soon as her dowry was paid, but as her dowry had never been paid, Louis regarded the renunciation as invalid.

2. The Emperor Leopold claimed the inheritance for his son, the Archduke Charles, first through his mother, the sister of Philip IV, and also through his first wife, the younger daughter of Philip IV, and neither of these ladies had ever renounced their claims. Spanish public opinion preferred the Habsburg claim, as inaugurating a return to the great days of the Emperor Charles V.

3. The third candidate was the son of the Elector of Bavaria, who was the great-grandson of Philip IV of Spain, through his mother, the daughter of the Emperor Leopold I. As his candidature did not involve a major change in the balance of power in Europe, there was much to be said in favour of his claim.

No one was more alive to the dangers of the Spanish question than William III of England. His personal interest in it was threefold: first, as Stadholder of Holland, he wished to prevent the Spanish Netherlands from falling into French hands; second, as King of England, he wished to protect the Atlantic and Mediterranean trade routes, and to prevent the union of French and Spanish economic, naval and colonial power; third, in both capacities he wished to prevent, if possible, the onset of a general European war, for both England and the Dutch were war-weary. Thus in 1698 he sent Portland to open negotiations with Louis XIV, and Louis subsequently sent Tallard to continue the talks in London. The result was the First Partition Treaty of October 1698: the Electoral Prince of Bavaria was to inherit Spain, the Netherlands and the Indies; the French claim was to be satisfied by the Duke of Anjou receiving the Two Sicilies and the Tuscan Ports; and the Habsburg claim was to be satisfied by the Archduke Charles receiving Milan. From the point of view of the balance of power in Europe, it was a good settlement, and it will be noted that it safeguarded the special interests with which William was concerned, except in one respect, namely that French power in the Two Sicilies would give France control of the Mediterranean, and would threaten British trade with the Levant. This was the occasion for repeated attacks on the settlement in England. But William's task had been difficult, and had been made much harder by the insistence of the Tories that the English army be cut to 7,000 men in 1698, thus making it impossible that he should negotiate from strength. Other defects of the Treaty were that the Emperor was not a party to it, and that the terms were extremely unpopular in Spain. In any case, in January 1699 the Electoral Prince died, and negotiations had to begin over again. This time it was much more difficult to arrive at a settlement, and negotiations dragged on over fifteen months. Finally, by the Second Partition Treaty (May 1700), it was agreed that the Archduke Charles should inherit Spain, the Netherlands and the Indies, and the Duke of Anjou would be compensated by receiving the Two Sicilies, the Tuscan ports and the Milanese, but the Emperor was to be persuaded to exchange Lorraine for the Milanese. There was little enthusiasm for this Treaty anywhere in Europe, for it represented a considerable increase in the power of France, already the strongest Power in Europe. The Emperor, in spite of the Archduke Charles' share, refused to be a party to the agreement. Spanish public opinion was infuriated at this apparently cynical proposal for a partition of the Spanish Empire. The Queen of Spain was so enraged at the news of it that she smashed all the furniture in her room. The Pro-French party in Madrid at once gained the upper hand, and in October 1700 the dying Charles II was persuaded to make a final Will leaving the whole inheritance to the French candidate, the Duke of Anjou, on the grounds that France alone would be strong enough to prevent the partition of the Spanish Empire. A month later Charles II died. On November 10th 1700 there took place a famous meeting of the *Conseil d'en haut* at Versailles. The question was, should the King uphold the Second Partition Treaty, or should he accept the Will of Charles II? Pontchartrain, the Controller-General expressed no opinion; Beauvilliers, the President, was for the Partition Treaty on the grounds that the alternative was a general war, which France could not afford; Torcy, the Foreign Minister, was for the Will. Then the Dauphin spoke heatedly in favour of the just claims of his son under the Will. Louis XIV withdrew without expressing a decision, but next day he announced the acceptance of the Will. On November 16th Louis introduced Philip of Anjou to his Court with the words, 'Gentlemen, there is the King of Spain', and the Spanish Ambassador murmured, to the alarm of Europe, 'Il n'y a plus de Pyrénées!' To William III Louis penned a long letter, pointing out the cruel dilemma in which he had found himself, having to decide between the Treaty and the Will. He argued that the Partition Treaty might still have brought about a war, for the Emperor had refused to accept it. He promised that the thrones of France and Spain should never be united, and thus urged that France would be weaker by accepting the Will than by accepting the Partition Treaty. These arguments were, up to a point, sound and genuine. The Emperor had not accepted the Partition Treaty, and the last wishes of Charles II, as a Monarch by Divine Right, must needs be respected. But if Philip of Anjou had succeeded peacefully to the Spanish throne, it was too much to suppose that his Kingdom would not have been taken over (as indeed it was during the subsequent war) by French administrators. The acceptance of the Will could only be interpreted by Europe as a final bid on the part of the Grand Monarque to dominate Europe.

The War of the Spanish Succession

Still, the acceptance of the Will did not at once mean war. England and the Dutch had disliked the Second Partition Treaty, and some politicians in both countries thought the Will preferable. The Emperor was hostile, but, without the help of the English and the Dutch, he could have done little. That war came was largely the fault of the aggressive and clumsy policy of the French King during the next few months. A period in which he had shown careful concern for the susceptibilities of Europe might have avoided war. Instead he acted as if he were already the master of Europe. In December 1700 he publicly reserved the rights of Philip V of Spain to the French throne, in contradiction to his promise in his letter to William III. In 1701 he seized the Dutch Barrier Fortresses Namur, Mons, Luxemburg, and the others, in the name of his grandson, on the grounds that henceforth it was nonsense to suppose that Spanish dominions needed protection against the danger of French attack. In reality, Louis was convinced that war was inevitable, and therefore determined to make himself master of these fortresses before hostilities began. In these circumstances, William III and Marlborough were able to conclude the Grand Alliance between England, the Dutch and the Emperor in September 1701. At this point James II of England died in exile, and Louis XIV, against the advice of his Ministers and with an act of recklessness for which he had to pay dearly, at once recognised the Old Pretender as James III of England. No act could have been better calculated to unite English public opinion on the need for war as this insult from the French King.

Agreement between the Allies on the objects of the war was not easy to obtain, for while the Emperor wanted the whole Spanish inheritance for Charles of Habsburg, Heinsius, Grand Pensionary of Holland was interested only in France not having the Netherlands, and England was primarily interested in the fate of the Mediterranean, the Atlantic trade routes and the Indies, and in the withdrawal of the French from the Barrier Fortresses. Finally it was agreed that Philip of Anjou should have Spain and the Indies, and the Emperor was to have Milan, Naples, Sicily, the Spanish Mediterranean islands, the Low Countries and Luxemburg. Thus the separate interests of the Allies were safeguarded. Prussia was brought into the alliance by the recognition of the elevation of the Elector Frederick III to the rank of King. Marlborough also signed a treaty with Charles XII of Sweden whereby Sweden promised neutrality; and with Denmark for troops in return for subsidies. In February 1702 William III fell from his horse, and a fortnight later he was dead. He, more than anyone else, had been the architect of the resistance to the growing power of France; his final achievement had been the Grand Alliance; the conduct of the war now devolved upon his Commander-in-Chief, the earl of Marl-borough. Apart from him, the most important man in the Alliance was Heinsius, the Grand Pensionary of Holland, perhaps the greatest statesman in Europe, and an inveterate enemy of France. The League of Augsburg had been quite incapable of defeating the French, and France was stronger in 1701 than a decade earlier, for Spain was now an ally; the Dutch Barrier Fortresses were in French hands, and Portugal, Savoy, Cologne and Bavaria were French allies. By occupying Cologne Louis could make himself master of the Rhine, and his alliance with Bavaria was a grave threat to the Emperor. Throughout the war France largely controlled Spain, and had always the advantage of internal lines of communication. On the other hand, the command of the sea lay always with England and the Dutch. England had a fleet of over 200 ships, and the Dutch agreed to provide three ships for every five English. The French fleet num-bered about half the combined Anglo-Dutch strength. It was never a serious threat to the Channel, but it did try to control the Mediter-ranean. It was always an essential part of Marlborough's strategy to command the Mediterranean and the Atlantic sea routes, at the same time making the main military effort in the Netherlands. He was handicapped by having to serve two masters, the English and the Dutch, but if the Dutch were difficult masters,[1] their war effort was heroic, for this small country of less than 3 million people succeeded year after year in putting armies of 120,000 men into the field against France, as well as maintaining a first-class fleet at sea. England's war effort also, thanks to Marlborough, Godolphin and their Whig allies, was far greater than had ever been made before. Almost overnight England found herself one of the leading military Powers in Europe.

The war opened in Italy in 1701. The French alliance with Savoy gave them free access to Milan, which was occupied at the outset. But brilliant manoeuvring on the part of the Austrian general, Prince Eugène of Savoy, kept the French on the defensive, and in February 1702 Prince Eugène succeeded in surprising the incompetent general Villeroi at Cremona, and capturing him and his entire staff. This had

---

[1] The Dutch forbade Marlborough to fight any action without their express consent. Their policy was that no battle should be fought if it could possibly be avoided. Marl-borough on the other hand always sought decisive solutions to any military situation.

much to do with persuading Victor Amadeus of Savoy in 1703 to desert France and join the Allies.[1] North of the Alps there were two main theatres of operations, in the Netherlands, where Marlborough was in command, and on the Rhine, where the Margrave of Baden, the leading general of the Empire, had constructed the strong defensive lines of Stollhofen between Fort Louis and the Black Forest. The French began the war in control of the Meuse, the Scheldt and much of the Rhine, and between Antwerp and Namur Vauban had constructed the 'Lines of Brabant'. Because of his orders, Marlborough had to confine himself to manoeuvring the French out of their positions without fighting a pitched battle. During 1702 he manoeuvred them out of the line of the Meuse, and in October captured the great fortress of Liege. He was thus able to occupy the Archbishopric of Cologne and the Bishopric of Liege, and control the navigation of the Rhine and the Meuse. It must be remembered that rivers were the highways of those days, and vitally important to the needs of any army. Early in 1703 he extended his control as far as Bonn.

During 1703 it was the French strategy to hold Marlborough in the Netherlands while the main drive was to be against the Emperor. Tallard was to hold the Margrave of Baden behind his Lines, while Villars pushed into Germany from Alsace to join up with the Elector of Bavaria, and Vendôme attacked Austria through the Tyrol from Italy. This was very largely achieved during the year, for the Emperor was hampered by a serious rising in Hungary, stirred up by French gold, and Marlborough was not allowed to change the balance of power by a major victory. In 1704 the fate of the Empire would be decided, for unless effective help could be brought to the Emperor, he must needs be overwhelmed by Franco-Bavarian power. In May 1704 the French joined up with the Bavarians; Vendôme was instructed to launch an offensive from Italy, and Villeroi was instructed to remain on the defensive in the Netherlands. Marlborough was prepared for the situation. He had obtained English orders for the use of his troops outside the Netherlands, and he tricked the Dutch into supposing that he was moving his army only to the Moselle. In May 1704 he moved his army down the Rhine. By June he was at Philippsburg,

---

[1] The instinct for survival made it necessary for the Dukes of Savoy to pursue a perilous foreign policy, poised as they were between the Habsburg and Bourbon Powers. Victor Amadeus changed sides in spite of the fact that his eldest daughter had married the Duke of Burgundy, and a younger one had married Philip of Anjou.

where for the first time he met Prince Eugène, thus beginning a unique partnership between the two greatest soldiers in western Europe. In July he seized Donauworth, thus securing a bridgehead over the Rhine, and for the next month his troops devastated Bavaria. The French general Tallard hastened to join up with the Elector of Bavaria, making a combined army of about 60,000 men. Marlborough and Eugène had about 56,000, and in fact that was roughly the size of each side in the Battle of Blenheim, which was fought on August 13th 1704. Marlborough's brilliant attacks routed the enemy, who fled and were relentlessly pursued by the Allied cavalry. Tallard was captured, and there were some 11,000 French prisoners and as many casualties. The Allies had about the same number of casualties. Some 16,000 French soldiers straggled back into France, all that remained of three great armies. Marlborough, in a single day, had risen to the foremost rank of generals. Sir Winston Churchill wrote that Blenheim 'changed the political axis of the world', for if the battle had been lost the Sun-King would have dominated Europe, the Elector of Bavaria would have supplanted the House of Habsburg in the Imperial Crown, with Munich instead of Vienna as the capital, and both capitals would have been mere satellites of France. As it was, for the rest of the war, Louis XIV could fight only to retain what he had already had, and to stave off defeat.

Marlborough saw that it was now possible completely to defeat France. His plan for 1705 was a combined attack down the Moselle to Metz as a first step on the road to Paris. But the plan failed through lack of co-operation among the Allies and above all through lack of manpower. Instead therefore he returned to the Netherlands, where again the Dutch prohibition on a pitched battle doomed him to indecisive manoeuvring. In 1706, however, Marlborough fought his most brilliant campaign. Louis XIV put 40,000 men under Villars to hold the Margrave of Baden on the Upper Rhine, and 60,000 men under Villeroy to attack Marlborough in Brabant, with a further 25,000 in reserve. At last the Allies had to fight. The result was the great battle of Ramillies, in which in four hours the French army was shattered and their baggage and artillery captured. The battle gave Marlborough the Netherlands, for barely 15,000 of the French army remained. Villeroi had to abandon the whole of Spanish Flanders and fall back to Courtrai. Antwerp surrendered without firing a shot.

The battle had the greatest consequences in Italy, for Louis XIV had been about to crush the Duke of Savoy, and Vendôme, who had been on the brink of final victory in Italy, was now called away to take over the northern command. Prince Eugène seized the opportunity to attack Vendôme's successor Marsin, force him to raise the siege of Turin, and eventually to fall back towards France (during which Marsin was killed) and abandon the whole Italian theatre of operations to the triumphant Eugène.

Meanwhile, the Allies had been led into a full-scale war in Spain. We have seen that in their original war plans it had been agreed that Philip of Anjou should have the Spanish Crown; there was therefore no initial reason for a campaign in Spain. But two considerations changed the situation. The first was the extreme concern of English politicians for the safety of Atlantic and Mediterranean trade routes, which made them increasingly hostile to the idea of the French Prince on the Spanish throne. The second was the adherence of the King of Portugal to the Allies (1703), on condition that the Archduke Charles should fight in Spain, and that no peace should be made until Philip V surrendered Spain. This amounted to a serious enlargement of the war aims of the Allies, and committed them to a war in Spain. It is doubtful whether the Portuguese alliance was worth so high a price. Marlborough, for instance, was always convinced that the Allies could use their power more effectively elsewhere. But he was a strong supporter of a Mediterranean strategy, which could seriously limit French activities in Italy, as well as protect maritime trade routes to the Levant. This necessitated an efficient naval base for the British fleet. Admiral Rooke seized Gibraltar in 1704, and Louis XIV at once realised its significance and ordered its recapture. A stiff naval battle was fought off Malaga in August 1704, but the British retained Gibraltar, and never again during this war did the French fleet challenge the British in a general action. There was already an Allied army in Portugal under the command of the Earl of Galway, one of William III's generals, a Huguenot refugee and a fine soldier. In 1705 a second army was sent under the command of the Earl of Peterborough, a restless and quarrelsome character, and it was decided to launch an attack on Barcelona, for it was thought that the cause of Charles of Habsburg would be most popular in Catalonia. Barcelona was captured, and soon 'Charles III' found himself master of eastern Spain. In England the Spanish campaigns received a quite exaggerated importance, far surpassing that of the Netherlands. In 1706 it was decided to make a three-pronged attack on Madrid, Galway advancing from Portugal, Charles III from Barcelona and Peterborough from Valencia. As they approached Madrid, the French under Marshal Berwick fell back from the city, and Charles III was proclaimed King. But the Allies were heavily outnumbered by the French, and guerilla risings against them broke out in their rear. By August they had begun their retreat to the coast, and Berwick re-occupied Madrid. Dissensions were rife among the Allies; Peterborough in particular had shown himself to be completely unreliable. Galway was heavily defeated by Berwick at the Battle of Almanza in 1707, and thereafter the Spanish campaign petered out, though for some time 'Charles III' retained Barcelona.[1] In August 1708 the British occupied the island of Sardinia, and General Stanhope also seized Minorca, thus giving Britain a first-class naval base at Port Mahon, capable of covering both Barcelona and Toulon. Gibraltar and Minorca were the only two permanent Allied gains from the unfortunate Spanish campaigns, and both could have been achieved without any expensive operations on the mainland.

By 1708, with both the Italian and the Spanish campaigns virtually at an end, the war concentrated once more on the Netherlands. The French captured Ghent and Bruges, but were completely defeated at the Battle of Oudenarde, and Marlborough went on to capture the great fortress of Lille. French resources were strained to their limits. Moreover, the winter of 1708–9 was one of the hardest on record, and it was followed by a great famine which swept through France. Louis XIV sent his Foreign Minister Torcy to seek peace from the Dutch. From a reasonable point of view there was everything to be said for a general peace settlement in 1709. Louis XIV was prepared to accept reasonable terms from the Allies. The degree of co-operation between the Allies was not such as to justify confidence in a long-continued war. But the peace offer broke on two obstacles. The first was the conviction of the Whig Ministers in England that it would be unsafe to make peace so long as Philip V continued to be King of Spain; or, in the cry of the time, 'No peace without Spain!' The

---

[1] General Stanhope re-occupied Madrid for a short time in 1710, but this was no more than a flash in the pan.

second was the misapprehension of the Emperor that Louis XIV was completely defeated, and that if the Allies held out for high stakes the Habsburgs might obtain the whole Spanish inheritance. Eugène wrote to the Emperor in May 1709:

> All the facts go to show that France is quite unable to prolong the war, and we can therefore, if we wish, obtain everything we ask for. We have only to hold together and preserve a good understanding among ourselves.

When the *Conseil d'en haut* met at Versailles to consider the Allied peace terms, Louis was prepared to accept all the terms except Art. XXXVII which demanded that Philip V, his grandson, should be deposed, if necessary with French aid. The King could only reject the offer.[1]

The war now changed its character. It had begun in order to prevent French domination of Europe; it now became a war to bring about an Allied domination of France and Spain. Louis XIV was able to appeal to the patriotic instincts of France, and there was a rallying for a final stand. In September 1709 there was the appalling slaughter of the Battle of Malplaquet, when the Allies lost 24,000 men and the French about half the number, and Marlborough proceeded to take Mons. In 1710 the Tories returned to power in England, bent on making peace. Moreover, in 1711 the Emperor Leopold died of smallpox, and this changed the whole European situation, for Charles III of Spain now became the Emperor Charles VI, though this in no way diminished his determination to be King of Spain as well. During 1711 Marlborough smashed through the final ('Ne Plus Ultra') lines of defence which the French commander Villars had constructed. But in December the Tories persuaded the Queen to dismiss Marlborough from all his offices. Secret peace negotiations had already been opened between St. John (soon to be Viscount Bolingbroke), the new Tory Minister, and Louis XIV, without reference to the Allies, and terms were soon agreed to, which only then were communicated to the Dutch and other Allies. The Emperor refused to accept them, and continued the war against France on his own, only to be soundly

---

[1] An interesting fact is that Marlborough thought that one of the clauses of the peace should have been the proviso that the French King should summon the States General, 'which I think is more likely to give quiet to Christendom than the tearing provinces from them for the enriching of others'. It is interesting to speculate what might have been the result of such a proviso.

beaten in Alsace. Meanwhile a Congress at Utrecht had worked out the terms of peace, which were signed in 1713. The Emperor delayed the making of peace until 1714, when he accepted terms agreed to at Rastadt and Baden. In all some eleven separate treaties were signed.

The Spanish Empire was partitioned. Philip V retained Spain and the Indies, upon his explicit renunciation of his claims to the French throne. The Emperor received the Netherlands, Milan, Naples, Mantua, and Sardinia, but the Dutch received the right to garrison the Barrier Fortresses against France: Ypres, Ghent, Tournai, Mons, Charleroi, Namur, Furnes and Menin. Savoy was strengthened by the rectification of her frontiers, and also by the acquisition of the island of Sicily. England received Gibraltar and Minorca, and also the colonial possessions of Newfoundland, Hudson's Bay, Nova Scotia and St. Kitts, and Spain granted the right of *Asiento* in her American Empire, by which Britain could supply 4,800 negroes a year. France retained Alsace, including Strassburg, agreed to demolish the fortifications of Dunkirk, and recognised the deposition of James II and the rights of the Hanoverian Succession in England.

In general the Peace of 1713-14 was one of the most successful settlements following a great war in European history. One of the main reasons for this was that strictly France was not defeated and was not humiliated. The French candidate retained the Spanish throne, and France suffered no loss of territory. It certainly seemed a misfortune to Spain that her Empire should have been so ruthlessly dismembered, but the extent of the Spanish dominions far exceeded the capacity of Spain to rule them, and the division was in the interests of European stability. The great acquisition of territory by the Habsburgs had not been justified by the contributions of the Emperor to the war effort, which, in fact, apart from the achievements of Prince Eugene in Italy, had been small. It was in fact just because the Habsburg power could no longer threaten Europe that Britain and the Dutch were so ready to see these territories go to the Emperor. The Habsburgs, in short, became the great counter-weight to French power in western Europe. The Dutch secured in the Netherlands a neighbour they did not fear, and also the right to maintain an advanced line of defence in the Barrier Fortresses. England secured modest maritime and colonial benefits, and also the recognition of the Hanoverian Succession. This was a considerable concession from

Louis XIV, for it represented a breach of the principle of the Divine Right of Monarchy. So did Philip V's renunciation of his claims to the French throne, and it remained a question whether in fact a Prince could by any renunciation slough off his responsibilities to God in this way.

The Last Years of Louis XIV

The last years of the reign were saddened not only by military failure, but also by the deaths in the royal family.[1] The Dauphin, 'Monseigneur', died in April 1711, on the same day as the Emperor. He was

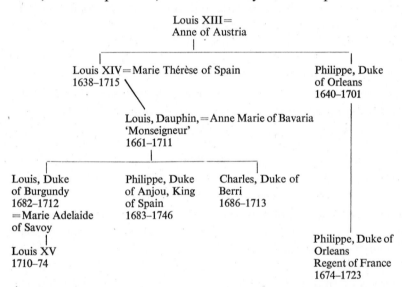

Louis XIII = Anne of Austria

Louis XIV = Marie Thérèse of Spain
1638–1715

Philippe, Duke of Orleans
1640–1701

Louis, Dauphin, = Anne Marie of Bavaria
'Monseigneur'
1661–1711

Louis, Duke of Burgundy
1682–1712
= Marie Adelaide of Savoy

Philippe, Duke of Anjou, King of Spain
1683–1746

Charles, Duke of Berri
1686–1713

Louis XV
1710–74

Philippe, Duke of Orleans
Regent of France
1674–1723

a shadowy figure who had been allowed to play little part in the events of the reign. In February Monseigneur's eldest son, the Duke of Burgundy died, a few days after his wife, the charming Marie Adelaide of Savoy, and a few days before his infant son. There was a panic at Court, for poison was suspected, and wild rumour whispered that the Duke of Orleans, who dabbled in alchemy and chemistry, was responsible. Finally, in May 1714, Monseigneur's youngest son, the Duke of Berri, died after a hunting accident. These deaths put the succession in jeopardy, for there remained now, in direct succession

[1] Voltaire wrote: 'These years of desolation left such a deep impression on people's hearts that during the minority of Louis XV I have met many people who could not speak of the late king's bereavement without tears in their eyes.'

from Louis, only Philip V of Spain and the Duke of Burgundy's infant son, the future Louis XV. After these the succession would pass to the Duke of Orleans. Louis XIV hastily legitimised the royal bastards, especially his favourite, the Duke of Maine, but he could not change the rights of succession. He did, however, deposit a Will with the *parlement* of Paris seeking to limit the power of the Regent Orleans by imposing upon him a Council of Regency composed of the royal bastards.

The round of ceremonies at Versailles continued, though they had lost the gaiety of their early days. Louis spent most of his time with Mme. de Maintenon, whom he had secretly married after the death of the Queen in 1683. She was of humble birth, had married an aged poet named Scarron, and, when he died, she had become governess to Louis' children by Mme. de Montespan. She was a woman of piety and refinement, and the King came to prefer the simple domesticity of her rooms to the grandeur of the Court. She was a close friend of Fénelon, and had procured for him the bishopric of Cambrai. She was devoted to Bossuet, and to Noailles, archbishop of Paris. But, apart possibly from religious affairs, her influence on Louis XIV in political matters has been much exaggerated.

Louis XIV died in September 1715, having reigned for seventy-two years. During the second half of his reign the criticisms of intellectuals had grown. Jean de la Bruyère (1645–96) in his essays wrote some effective satires on life at Court. The Duc de Saint-Simon, in his *Mémoires* has left a grim, though jaundiced view of the emptiness and pomp of Versailles. Above all, Fénelon (1651–1715), once tutor to Louis XIV's grandson, in 1694 penned a letter to Louis XIV which he never delivered, but which was a terrible condemnation of the reign. By misgovernment, he declared,

your people, whom you should love as your children, and who have been until now so passionate for you, die of starvation. The cultivation of the soil is almost abandoned; towns and countryside are depopulated, handicrafts languish, and no longer maintain its craftsmen. Commerce is annihilated. In consequence, you have destroyed half the real forces within your State, in order to win vain conquests without.

It is an amazing letter, and is so fraught with prescience that it has sometimes been thought to be a forgery. It cannot, however, be said that Fénelon spoke for France, for Louis XIV throughout his reign

E

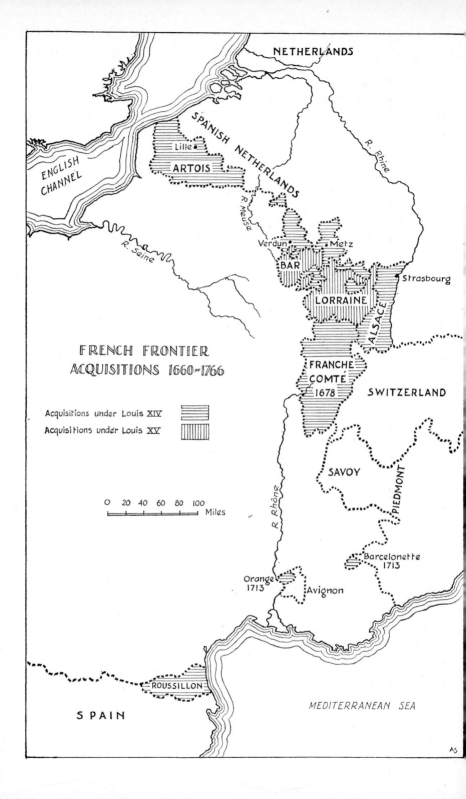

NETHERLANDS

ENGLISH CHANNEL

SPANISH NETHERLANDS

Lille

ARTOIS

R. Meuse

R. Seine

R. Rhine

Verdun   Metz

BAR

Strasbourg

LORRAINE

ALSACE

FRENCH FRONTIER
ACQUISITIONS 1660~1766

Acquisitions under Louis XIV
Acquisitions under Louis XV

FRANCHE
COMTE
1678

SWITZERLAND

0   20 40 60 80 100
                          Miles

SAVOY

PIEDMONT

R. Rhône

Barcelonette
1713

Orange
1713

Avignon

ROUSSILLON

MEDITERRANEAN SEA

SPAIN

AS

was a popular king.[1] The despotism he had established was still young, and to outward appearances efficient. He had given France a unity essential to it, yet his despotism was limited by custom and tradition, and had the marks of a highly civilised society. In some respects the defect of his despotism was that he had not gone far enough in the direction of change. In Europe the position he had achieved was unique. Some of the errors of his policy Louis himself recognised. His final advice to his grandson was:

> Try to keep peace with your neighbours: I have been too fond of war; do not imitate me in that, nor in my too great expenditure.

Estimate of the Reign

Under Louis XIV the French Monarchy reached its highest peak; the forces of centralisation triumphed over feudal and sectional interests. The strangle-hold of the nobility and powerful corporations over the provinces was broken; the nobles were left their privileges and induced to become the adornments of Court, but their political power had ceased to exist. The States General had ceased to meet since 1614; the power of the *parlement* was for the time being curbed; administration was in the hands of the Central Government and the Intendants. The Monarchy was exalted until 'the royal throne' became 'the throne of God himself'. France was the greatest military power in Europe; her frontiers were carried forward until the independence of Europe appeared to be in jeopardy. France was also the cultural centre of Europe, setting the pattern for architecture, and also for the whole décor of monarchy. French wines, French costumes, French cookery, French literature, French philosophy, dominated the European cultural scene. What the Monarchy of Louis XIV had achieved is best recognised when one compares the France of, say, the 1670s with the days of anarchy a century earlier, in the time of the Duke of Guise, Coligny and Constable Montmorency.

Behind this front of power and achievement there were grave weaknesses. The Monarchy never solved the financial problem; the tax system was inadequate. The exemption of the nobility from direct taxation, the privileged position of the *pays d'État*, and a clumsy and

---

[1] Although it could be argued that the Revocation of the Edict of Nantes was equivalent to a declaration of war upon nearly a million of his subjects, and it was followed by the revolt of the Camisards in the Cevennes.

expensive system of tax collection meant that the Treasury received far less than it might have done. The result was that the unprivileged classes bore a heavy burden of taxation without corresponding benefit to the State. Trade was hampered by burdensome customs dues. The whole financial system was clogged by corruption. Sully, Richelieu, Mazarin, Fouquet, all amassed great fortunes. So did Colbert, Le Tellier and Lionne, though not by means then thought to be particularly corrupt. There was much fraudulent tax-farming and government contracting. Every military campaign saw colossal wastage, though probably less than in most other European armies. The sale of offices was an iniquitous system from which no French government before 1789 could free itself. In the first half of the seventeenth century there were times when one-third of the total revenues came from this practice. The sale of an office for ready money simply created a problem for the future, and in addition increased administrative inefficiency and the spirit of corruption. It is not too much to say that the practice was ruinous to sound finance and administration. New taxes were created to pay for the offices, and new offices created to pay for the old.

Absolute Monarchy in France appears to have succeeded for a combination of different reasons. There was first in the seventeenth century a great deal of public support for greater centralisation, which would give internal peace, security and prosperity, and this need was well satisfied by the work of Colbert. Colbert's work gave a great stimulus to economic life and overseas trade and colonies. But secondly Absolutism succeeded by what might be regarded as a giant piece of bribery; by the purchase of the acquiescence of the nobility, and privileged and wealthy classes, by tax exemptions, social privileges and a disastrous system of the purchase of offices. The very conditions of French despotism therefore doomed it to a system of social injustice and chronically unsound finance, and it was upon these rocks that the French Monarchy finally foundered.

The absolute Monarchy of Louis XIV was the greatest Europe had seen since the fall of the Roman Empire, but it was not a totalitarian government. The privileges of rival bodies were curbed for the time being, but not abolished. The Catholic Church remained a powerful and privileged body; gilds, now that they were brought in to serve Colbert's system, increased rather than diminished in power. The *parlements* were politically quiescent, but still remained in their own eyes the guardians of the constitution of France. The nobility were masters of their estates, and the purchasers of offices had freehold rights which no French king dared ignore. Indeed, what seems most strange at first sight to the modern student, accustomed to twentieth-century totalitarianism, is the way in which the French Monarchy was tender to antiquarian survivals, until eventually it found itself under Louis XVI powerless to carry even the most needful reforms.

Louis' wars placed a great strain upon France. Undoubtedly the French peasant often lived in conditions of misery. La Bruyère wrote of them as 'savage animals. . . . They retire at night into caves, where they live on black bread, water and roots'. In periods of famine they starved in great numbers. But for the unfortunate peasant this had always been his condition in history, and it is doubtful whether he was worse off in Louis XIV's reign than he had been at any former time. What is certain is that with the growth of humanitarianism in the Age of Enlightenment his condition was certainly thought to be far less *tolerable* than in earlier periods. Wars also put a great strain upon French finances, and increased the importance of the class of wealthy bankers and contractors. The Monarchy found it increasingly necessary to have good relations with the moneyed interests. The latter for their part grew in social prestige, often married their daughters to the impoverished nobility, purchased great offices for themselves, and thus established a powerful social interest upon which the Government became increasingly dependent. As French society proliferated in complexity, wealth and ideas, it outgrew the monolithic form of government which Louis XIV had laid upon it. Long before Louis XIV died, the intelligentsia of France had become restive. Under his successors it was not that the French despotism was oppressive, but that because of its inner contradictions it failed to provide adequate government.

5: The Rise of Russia

Geography and Origins

No one today will doubt the importance of knowing something of Russian history, yet it is difficult for the westerner to feel that he really understands Russian development. For one thing, it is more difficult to gain access to the sources; translations are often non-existent or inadequate; there are few memoir writers or eye-witness accounts during the seventeenth and eighteenth centuries, and those which exist are strangely idiosyncratic. It is therefore difficult to penetrate to the Russian mind beneath. Yet the attempt must be made, for Russian history, although in one sense a series of violent convulsions, is nevertheless all of a piece, and there has been a strong current of continuity running through it.

Russian history has been profoundly influenced by geography. Today the Russian Empire covers 8·6 million miles, or about one-sixth of the world's land surface. It is really one gigantic plain which runs continuously from Germany and Poland across Siberia to the Pacific, for the Ural mountains never presented any real barrier to expansion. When a boundary with the West was needed, it had often to be provided by a river, such as the Dnieper or the Dniester. The climate of most of the area is severe, with long frozen winters and icy Arctic winds, followed by very hot summers. The vast expanse of Siberia was too grim a country to do more than support sparse groups of hunters and trappers. The struggle for life was too hard for social or political development to proceed beyond the most rudimentary stage. Thus the great areas of the north and of Siberia presented no obstacles to Russian expansion other than those of nature itself. Conversely, once expansion began, it could be continued only by a centralised despotism. The conditions which in Europe made for small States and diverse characteristics were entirely absent in Russia.

Geography also determined that Russia should be mainly a land-locked country. The Arctic seas were frozen for much of the year. The early Russian State was cut off from the Baltic by Swedish, Lithuanian, Polish and Teutonic powers, and from the Black Sea by Tatar and Turkish powers. It was inevitable that in the seventeenth and eighteenth centuries the Baltic and the Black Sea should determine the directions of Russian expansion. But that would be only when a Russian State had already become powerful enough to challenge her western neighbours. Before that could occur there were centuries of development which had gone on almost unimpeded by, and in isolation from the West, in the vast, ill-populated area between the Dnieper and the Urals.

Geographically Russia may be thought of as falling into four areas. In the north, tundra; then, proceeding southwards, the great forests in which Russia has always had such boundless wealth; then the great plains of the Russian steppe; and finally the rich 'black soil' area of the south, stretching into the Ukraine. Russia is not richly endowed with first-rate agricultural land, and the 'black soil' area is only about one-tenth of the whole. But Russia is rich in mineral resources, and these, especially in the Urals, were already being worked in the seventeenth century.

The origins of Russia are a vexed question which need not concern us here. In the ninth century A.D. there grew up an important city at Kiev. Archaeology shows that it was one of the oldest settlements in Russia, and its importance from the ninth to the twelfth century lay in its position on the trade route from the Baltic to Byzantium. The origins of Kiev were certainly closely connected with the outward thrust of the Scandinavians who in the West are known as Vikings, or Normans. Oleg was a historical ruler in Kiev in 882, and he and his successor made both war and trade treaties with Byzantium. It was a warrior kingdom which expanded rapidly in all directions; or perhaps not so much a kingdom as a loose confederation of warrior chieftains. In 1015 its ruler adopted Christianity, and thenceforward Kiev entered into close cultural relations with Byzantium. In fact in the eleventh century Kiev was little more than a cultural outpost of the Eastern Roman Empire. The economic links continued also, for all the northern trade of Byzantium passed through Kiev, and in addition there was an exchange of Kievan furs, hides and agricultural produce for the exotic products of Byzantium. Kiev also exported grain northwards in return for timber and furs. By the eleventh century agriculture was organised on an extensive scale; there was a powerful aristocracy dominating the land; peasants were mere labourers and tax-payers, and slavery was a normal feature of life. The Prince was often not much more than a *primus inter pares*, and had to act in all important affairs only with the consent of a *Duma* (or council) of the boyars (aristocracy). The Greek Orthodox Church played a most important part. It was a highly formal and ritualistic religion; a religion of saints and monasteries. Its priests were an important and privileged class in society. Its Metropolitan, usually a Greek, was appointed by the Patriarch of Byzantium. The Church was an autonomous society, largely independent of the secular authorities, wielding jurisdiction, not only over the clergy, but over all in any way connected with the Church; and rich in lands with which it was endowed by the faithful. Above all, the Church was a civilising influence, bringing to Kiev all the elements of Byzantine culture which it thought fit to imitate. It brought with it a written language, for St. Cyril and St. Methodius, two missionaries sent out to convert the Slavs in the second half of the ninth century, devised the Cyrillic alphabet, and henceforth Russia had two languages, Church Slavonic and Old Russian. The Church brought also new developments in architecture, consequent upon the use of stone instead of wood for churches. The great Cathedral of St. Sophia in Kiev, built in the first half of the eleventh century, was an early example of Kievan architecture.

Importance of the Tatar Invasions

Gradually as Kiev expanded, especially towards the north and east, there was a differentiation of peoples, and there emerged the divisions into Great Russians, Ukrainians and White Russians. Kiev was never a united or a centralised state, and there were constant divisions and internal weakness. It was therefore no match for the mighty power which attacked and overwhelmed it in the thirteenth century. The Tatars came from Mongolia. They were a warrior people, suddenly galvanised into unity in the second half of the twelfth century by a great leader, Jenghiz Khan. In five years he overran China, and then turned westwards. His successors conquered Russia 1237–40, and for a time ruled a mighty Empire stretching from Poland to the Pacific. Batu, grandson of Jenghiz Khan, established himself on the Volga and his dominions became differentiated under the title of the Golden Horde. Russian princes paid tribute and homage to him. The Tatar invasion was accompanied by devastation and massacre. Towns were sacked, whole populations were carried off into slavery. The connection with Byzantium was for a time severed. Kiev never recovered from the blow, and ceased for ever to be the centre of the cultural or political life of Russia. Yet the Tatar conquest did not mean the entire extinction or disruption of the Russian way of life. The Golden Horde was primarily concerned with the extortion of heavy taxes and, provided these were paid, it was content to leave the Russians to their own way of life. The real importance of the Tatar domination lies in the changes it brought about in the political organisation of the Russian peoples.

There was little that the conquered peoples could learn directly from the Tatars, for they had little to offer, either of culture or social organisation. They were a warlike and nomadic people, held together for a time by military discipline, but from 1380 onwards rapidly disintegrating into insignificance. Their firmest hold was always over southern Russia, and hence the destruction of the influence of Kiev. Further north, however, the relationship between Tatar and Russian prince was more strictly that between suzerain and vassal. The authority of the Russian prince was enhanced by the necessity for the collection of tribute to pay to the Tatar. It is significant that the Russian word for coin comes from the Mongolian. And as Tatar power declined, the northern princedoms were the first to establish virtual autonomy.

As Kiev declined, so Novgorod arose. Novgorod was an important city on the great trade route from north to south. In the thirteenth century, at the very time that the Tatars were conquering Kiev (1240), Alexander Nevski, the hero-ruler of Novgorod, was, like some early Peter the Great, defeating the Swedes and the Teutonic Knights, and making a bid for domination of the Baltic. It is quite wrong to think of Peter the Great's later conquest as an entirely new development in Russian history. In fact, as Riasanovsky shows, Novgorod fought the Swedes no less than twenty-six times between the twelfth and the fifteenth centuries. What was new about Peter's conquest was the permanence of his success.

Novgorod in some ways resembled the great trading cities of the

Hanseatic League, or of Italy. It traded in furs, wax and honey, in exchange for fish, manufactures and luxuries from the Baltic ports. Its markets were thronged with foreign merchants. By the late thirteenth century it was increasingly ousted as a trading centre by the cities of the Hanseatic League, and finally in 1471 it was conquered by Ivan III of Moscow. Culturally Novgorod was always an offshoot of Kiev. Its government was oligarchical, never despotic, always much more concerned with trade than with territorial expansion. Although for over two centuries it was by far the most important Russian city, it never attempted to unify Russia. That task was left to Moscow.

The Rise of Moscow

During the century following the Tatar conquest of Kiev, the area between the Dnieper and the Volga was divided into numerous small and shadowy princedoms, all subject to the Tatar overlord. The Prince of Moscow was the first to overthrow Tatar domination. This was the achievement of Ivan the Great (1462–1505), a man of remarkable statesmanship and vision, one of the truly great rulers of history. He established the Muscovite despotism, conquered Novgorod, and extended his dominions north and west, until they were four times his original inheritance. He claimed to be the true heir to Kiev, and finally in 1480 made good his claim by renouncing his allegiance to the Golden Horde. Thus was established a Muscovite despotism, such as had no counterpart in the history of Kiev. Tatar domination had taught the Russians military organisation and the necessity for centralised despotism, for no other form of government could throw off the Tatar yoke or achieve territorial expansion. In 1472 Ivan the Great married the Byzantine princess Sophia Paleologue, niece of the last Byzantine Emperor, and thus he became the heir to the Byzantine imperial tradition. He adopted the new title of Tsar; he surrounded himself with Byzantine ceremonial; and adopted the two-headed eagle as his symbol. Most of the legends concerning the nature and origins of Muscovite power, such as its supposed descent from the Emperor Constantine, dates from this reign. It was in a sense a theocratic monarchy, a mixture of Roman, Old Testament and Byzantine ideas. The new title of *Tsar* was derived from *Caesar*, and was used in Church-Slavonic to translate the Greek *Basileus*, the word used to denote both the Byzantine Emperor and the kings of the Old Testament. The Tsar's power derived directly from God; he was answerable to no man. The land of Russia was his; all his subjects were his tenants and his servants. Even without them he would still be Tsar of Russia, but without him there would be no Russia.

The new Imperial power (as we may term it, for the West always translated *Tsar* as Emperor) had many advantages. It was a centralised despotism, resting squarely upon the great landowners and the Orthodox Church. Moscow occupied an advantageous central position on trade routes, within easy reach of the great rivers, the Volga, Don and Dnieper. It was fortunate in a succession of strong rulers to succeed Ivan the Great. There was a stready drive to expansion, sometimes by conquest, sometimes by agreement; and always there was the drive to agricultural extension and settlement. There was a growth of great estates as new lands were taken over. The peasants sank further to the status of serfs; the gentry, growing prosperous with expanding agriculture, supported the Tsars in their despotism and in their conquests. To understand further developments we should look more closely at the position of these gentry, or boyars.

The boyars were one of the pillars upon which the Muscovite power rested. They had once been a nobility of service, but by the sixteenth century they held their estates by right of *votchina*, or free hereditary succession. In the days following the decline of Kiev, when there were numerous princes, a boyar could attach himself to any prince, and could leave his service when it pleased him. He was master of his estates, collected taxes, administered justice, and governed his peasants so that they were virtually in the position of serfs. The latter were obliged to pay to his lord both *barshchina*, or labour services, and *obrok*, or rent in money or kind. But a peasant could still leave his lord legally once a year, and many peasants had no lord at all. By tradition the prince was dependent upon his boyars for military service, and without their active support he could do little. But this feudal dependence accorded ill with the new spirit of Muscovite despotism, and thus in the sixteenth century there emerged a new tenure of landholding, the *pomestie*, a system by which estates were granted by the Tsar on condition of public service. This was a most significant development. The fifteenth and sixteenth centuries saw the steady increase in the powers and independence of the gentry in Poland and Lithuania, and the consequent diminution of the powers of the ruler. This process was checked in Muscovite Russia, and still further by Peter the Great, and although the gentry had a certain triumph in eighteenth-century Russia, it was not at the expense of the despotism. Peter the Great was not the first Russian ruler to seek to turn his nobility into the servants of the Crown. It was the objective which lay behind the *oprichnina* of Ivan the Terrible (1533–84).

Ivan the Terrible

This indeed was not the only point of striking similarity between Ivan the Terrible and Peter the Great. Both seized power at a very early age in order to put an end to a period of misgovernment and anarchy. Both sought to stamp out corruption; both instituted army reforms and began notable periods of foreign war; both sought to establish a new service nobility. Both realised the backwardness of their dominions compared with the West. In 1547, as in 1697, the Tsar of Russia sent an invitation to western specialists to enter his service, and some doctors, craftsmen and technicians did attempt to reach Russia, but were turned back at Lübeck. For years the rulers of the Baltic states sought to impose an iron curtain between Russia and the West. Then in 1554 the Englishman Chancellor, who had set out with Willoughby to find a North-East Passage, found his way to Moscow through Archangel. He was well received, and returned to England with strange stories of the exotic and semi-oriental despotism of the Russian Tsar. Thereafter an important trade route was opened with Russia through Archangel; English merchants were given favourable terms, and western ideas and skills began to reach Moscow.

Like Peter the Great, Ivan the Terrible sought to carry out an internal revolution by violent means. On every side he found his power thwarted by a turbulent and quarrelsome boyar class. In 1553 he carried out a purge among the boyars in his service, and in 1564 he created a new administration which was to function side by side with the old. It was called the *oprichnina* (*oprich* means 'apart'). Eventually it covered one-third of Russia, and was staffed by a new service nobility devoted to the Tsar. For a time Russia had two administrative systems, the old boyar administration (*zemshchina*) and the new *oprichnina*. Once the *oprichnina* was established, the Tsar used it to destroy the boyars, and there followed a period of terror and devastation. In 1572 he put an end to the *oprichnina*, but the reign of terror went on. Again like Peter the Great, Ivan killed his son and heir in wrath. He rapidly became metally deranged, and died in 1584.

Ivan the Terrible's reign was certainly one of terror. Yet there was method in his madness. Boyar power was feudal and anarchic; it stood in the way of centralised despotism, and had to be broken. Many were executed, and their lands transferred to the new service nobility. It is possible even that the horrors of his reign have been exaggerated, for those who left accounts of them, especially the clergy, were those who suffered at the Tsar's hands. The title of 'the Terrible' is not an accurate translation of the Russian epithet, which might more accurately be rendered as 'Mighty', and there is clear evidence that at times Ivan was popular with many of his people. Much of his work was permanent. Although he failed in his incessant wars with the Poles and Swedes, yet it was in his reign that Russia extended its power across the Urals into Siberia. Russia, once a small region of the Upper Volga, had become a great country extending from the Arctic to the Caspian Sea. So vast an area required a large service nobility, and Ivan had gone far to provide one. As old boyar lands were confiscated, as new lands were acquired, they were granted as *pomestia*, or service estates. Men recruited for military service, which was virtually for life, were granted shares of the new lands. There was no shortage of land, the difficulty was to ensure that peasants remained to work the land; and thus it was that serfdom spread, and the condition of peasants worsened. For the peasants sought to escape to the freer lands of Kazan or Astrakhan, and thus had to be tied to the soil in the service of their masters, in the same way as their masters were to be tied to the service of the Tsar. Centralisation therefore was pursued in Russia at a heavy price of social upheaval and discontent.

The Time of Troubles

This found its expression in the so-called Time of Troubles (1598–1613), when the reigning Muscovite family died out, and there followed a period of turmoil and disputed succession, accompanied by drought and famine, in which thousands died, boyar independence reasserted itself, and the central government came near to disintegration after the death of Boris Godunov in 1605. The Poles took advantage of the turmoil to capture Smolensk, and for a time were in possession of Moscow, while the Swedes occupied Novgorod. Not until 1613 was order restored, when a *Zemski Sobor* (or estates general, representing the Church, gentry, townspeople and some peasants) elected Michael Romanov as Tsar, thus establishing the dynasty which was to continue until 1917.

The Time of Troubles is important for the understanding of the problems of the Muscovite state. It was primarily a revolt of the old boyar class against the new autocracy of the Tsars. They deeply resented the rise of an upstart nobility of service, and hence laid absurd emphasis on the claims of precedence and ancestral dignity. Kliuchevsky quotes an example of a man flogged to death during the Time of Troubles because he had given undue deference to a man who was not of noble rank. The boyar demands were that the Tsar should rule with the aid of a boyar *Duma*, or council, and in important matters, in consultation with the whole *Zemski Sobor*. They sought the recognition of all their privileges, and protection of private property from confiscation, except with the approval of the *Duma*. For a time they appeared to have succeeded, for Michael Romanov appeared willing to rule in close co-operation with the *Zemski Sobor* and the boyar *Duma*. The Time of Troubles had caused immense havoc and slaughter, and a contemporary monk wrote that 'men did forbear to plough and to sow and to reap, because the sword did ever lie over them'. Taxation was a crushing burden which pressed especially heavily on towns. It was indeed the government's preoccupation with taxation, and with the problems of law and order, which goes far to explain the advance of serfdom in the seventeenth century. For the landlord was responsible for the collection of the taxes of his serfs, and also for their good behaviour, and so long as these two functions were fulfilled, the Tsar's government had little further concern for the welfare of the peasant. It is significant that the General Law Code which Michael Romanov issued in 1646,[1] though careful to guard the interests of the Treasury and the landowner, made no attempt to define

---

[1] The first attempt to codify the law since 1550, and one which was not superseded until the codification of Nicholas I in 1835.

accurately the status of serfdom nor the limits of seigneurial authority. But the taxes which could be extorted from the land were strictly limited, and about one-half the total revenues came from customs and excise and pressed heavily, almost beyond the point of endurance, on the feeble mercantile class. About one-half of the total expenditure was on maintaining a large rabble of an army of about 70,000 men, with which the Romanovs kept up a series of unsuccessful wars against Poland, Sweden and Turkey.

The most important direction of expansion under the early Romanovs was into the Ukraine, which came under Muscovite jurisdiction in 1654. The Ukraine had formerly been under Lithuanian and Polish authority. It was peopled by a restive and turbulent people, the famous Cossacks. The Cossacks were originally Russians of the steppe who had been driven hither and thither by the Tatar invaders; the very name of Cossack came from the Tatar word for horseman. They were a liberty-loving and egalitarian people who lived by hunting, fishing, tending flocks and herds, or by freebooting and marauding in frontier regions. They were bold spirits, resentful of authority. In 1654 they revolted against Polish rule, and decided to accept the authority of Moscow on condition that they were granted full autonomy (a choice determined by the fact that the Cossacks were Greek Orthodox, while Poland was predominately Roman Catholic). But their rights to autonomy were soon disregarded, and during the seventeenth and eighteenth centuries they were steadily subjected to the burdens of the Russian State and the extension of serfdom.[1] From time to time they revolted, and were always a problem to the Tsarist government. But they played an important part in Russian history. They were fine fighters, and their regiments were a valuable addition to the Russian military system.[2] Moreover, the Cossacks were more familiar with the ideas of the West, and some of them were among Peter the Great's leading supporters in his work of reform.

Muscovite Absolutism and the Beginnings of Change

The seventeenth century was a great period of change in Russian history. The period of boyar reaction during the Time of Troubles failed;

---

[1] This aspect of Russian rule was not unwelcome to them, for they were the overlords who had always relied on the services of the peasants.

[2] In 1914 the Don Cossacks still supplied 150,000 cavalry to the Russian army.

the centralised despotism of Russian Tsardom marched on. The ever-extending frontiers[1] laid increasing importance on the *voievodi*, or military governors, who were appointed solely by the central government. Moreover, under Michael Romanov the system of provincial *voievodi* was extended to the whole country, with the consequent limitation of the local powers of the gentry. The *Zemski Sobor*, or 'Council of all the Land', representing 'all ranks of men', failed to survive. It had played an important part during the Time of Troubles in making and unmaking Tsarist pretenders, but after 1654 it was hardly summoned, and important matters were decided by the Tsar in consultation with either the Boyar *Duma* or the Holy Synod of the Church. The last time the *Zemski Sobor* met was in 1698, when Peter the Great used it to sit in judgment upon the Regent Sophia. It had served its purpose in helping to make Tsarist absolutism; thereafter it ceased to exist.

The Muscovite absolutism operated through an ever-growing bureaucracy. In the seventeenth century there emerged some fifty *prikazy* or government departments, some concerned with aspects of government, and others concerned with particular provinces, such as Kazan or Astrakhan. The system was hand-to-mouth, repetitive and inefficient, and hence Peter the Great's attempts to reform it. War has always been a parent of change in Russia, and it was so in the seventeenth century. Constant conflicts with the Poles and Swedes brought home to the Russians their military inferiority. By 1630 for the first time the Russian army was being trained by westerners, often Scotsmen, and learning something of the techniques of firearms. In 1634 a Scotsman, Colonel Leslie, was ordered to purchase 10,000 muskets from Sweden, and other military equipment from Holland. But this proved to be too expensive, and foreigners were brought in to mine and smelt metals and to build factories. Cannons and church bells were being cast in Moscow as early as the reign of Michael Romanov. As we have seen, Ivan the Terrible had welcomed foreigners, and a so-called German Quarter sprang up in Moscow (all westerners being known as Germans), which by the middle of the seventeenth century numbered several thousands, and included four Lutheran and Reformed Churches and a German school. They

---

[1] During the first half of the seventeenth century Russia extended a further 3,000 miles across Siberia to the Pacific.

brought in western skills and techniques, western clothes, customs and habits of thought. The Tsar and boyars began to ride in stately German coaches; stone replaced wood as the materials for the mansions of the gentry. A German troupe entertained the Tsar with plays in the western manner; the Tsar Alexis patronised German music, and some of his Court abandoned the inconvenient Russian clothes for the corselet or breastplate of the Germans. Books began to be translated into Russian; in 1649 three monks were appointed to make the first translation of the Bible from the Greek into Russian. The first schools were opened for the sons of gentry, and thus, as Kliuchevsky comments somewhat disapprovingly, 'Russia, beginning with foreign officers and German artillerymen, ended with German ballet and the Latin Grammar.'

All this could not occur without inflicting a great shock to the Russian way of life. Muscovite Russia had been largely cut off from the West. European visitors were struck by the strange and barbaric customs of the Tsar's Court. Its culture was based on the ritualistic and conservative traditions of the Russian Orthodox Church. Isolated, ignorant, deeply self-satisfied, the Russian Church had come to differ from the Greek Orthodox Church in important respects. Their liturgy included notable textual errors; they made the sign of the Cross with two fingers instead of three; they used six wafers instead of five in the Mass, they wrote the name of Jesus as *Issus*. Nikon, a product of this era of change, the son of a peasant, had won the confidence of the Tsar Alexis, and became Patriarch in 1652. He was a man of great force of character, and at once instituted reforms throughout the Church, correcting texts and ceremonies, and beginning the unprecedented custom of preaching sermons. He readily employed foreign scholars whenever he could find them, and did all he could to favour the new ideas of the West. The horror with which these innovations were received by many of the clergy may be dimly imagined. There was the deepest fear of new ideas, a simple belief that no change could be an improvement, a deep suspicion that these changes were in some way a conspiracy by the Roman Church to undermine the Russian Church. Unfortunately for Nikon also, he dabbled too much in politics, and he was deposed by the Council of the Church in 1667. But it was a triumph for him that the same Council approved the reforms he had instituted in the Church. Still, the reforms brought about a schism in the Church. The Old Believers (*Raskolniki*) broke away and refused to accept any of the innovations. They were fiercely persecuted; their leader Avvakum was burnt at the stake in 1682, and in twenty years some 20,000 of them were burnt alive, sometimes whole congregations at a time. Yet the Old Believers continued, and still had millions of followers in 1917. The importance of the Great Schism, as it is called, has been variously interpreted by Russian historians. Some have seen it simply as the revolt of ignorance and fanaticism against change. Kliuchevsky saw it as a nationalist revolt, the culmination of intellectual tendencies which had been gathering since the reign of Ivan the Terrible. For at that time the monk Philotheiss had concocted the idea that Moscow was the Third Rome. Two previous Romes had fallen (Rome and Byzantium), 'the third one, our Moscow still stands, and a fourth one shall there never be'. To those brought up in this faith, the idea that the Russian Church was ignorant and provincial was a great shock. Riasanovsky sees the movement as 'in an important sense the opposite of the Reformation', and also as a revolt against the growing oppression and centralisation of Tsarist government. Both views contain truth. It was important also as dividing and weakening the Church at a critical time, and thus making it easier for Peter the Great to carry his reforms.

By the second half of the seventeenth century there were between fifteen and twenty thousand Europeans in Russia, organising the army, developing trade, mines, manufactures, practising medicine. The first postal service since the time of the Tatars was instituted in 1664. Men were smoking tobacco, taking snuff, trimming their beards and wearing western clothes. In some ways the leader of these was the Tsar Alexis, (1629–76) father of Peter the Great. Although brought up in traditional Russian ways, his mind was open to the ideas of the West, and he was fiercely intolerant of the obscurantism of the Old Believers. He might have anticipated many of the reforms of his son if he had not been dogged by ill health, and forced to rely too much on inferior counsellors. Kliuchevsky writes of him the 'he was the best type of Russian; indeed I see in him the finest figure which ancient Russia ever produced'. Even more far-sighted was his Chancellor Nastchokin, who did not, indeed, adopt western dress, but in other matters had a mind receptive of western ideas, and spent much time planning reforms in government and administration, which did not however come to much, though they were often the same as Peter later attempted. Another example was Prince V. Galizin, an aristocrat of learning, who could speak Latin and Polish fluently, and who possessed a fine house furnished in the western style, with the best library in Russia. Not the least interesting of his plans was for the abolition of serfdom. But for the fact that he was a friend of the Regent Sophia, and thus fell with her, he might have been an invaluable ally of Peter the Great in his work of reform. '

Peter the Great

All that has been written in this chapter so far has been a necessary preliminary to the understanding of the work and importance of Peter the Great. It should now be clear that, as Sumner once wrote, 'the thunderstorm had been slowly working up, growling and flickering on the horizon, long before it burst with Peter'.

Peter was born in 1672, the son of the Tsar Alexis by his second wife, Natalia. Four years later Alexis died and was succeeded by his eldest son Theodore, who himself died without heir in 1682. There was in Russia no longer a fixed law of succession, and Peter was at once proclaimed Tsar in place of his elder half-brother Ivan, who was sickly. But then a revolt led by Alexis's eldest daughter led to a massacre, which Peter witnessed, and Ivan and Peter were made joint Tsars, with Sophia as Regent for the two boys. Sophia ruled Russia from 1682–89, while Peter's mother Natalia took the boy away to the safety of Preobrazhensky. There he was left largely to his own devices. He was fascinated with all foreign weapons of war, and gathered round him a crowd of adventurers, soldiers of fortune, any who could instruct or amuse him. He raised regiments of youths and trained them himself with the aid of foreign experts. They were a curious crowd. There was Alexander Menshikov, formerly a pastry-cook's boy, quite uneducated so that he never learnt to read or write, yet he became the constant companion of the Tsar. There was the Dutchman Timmerman, who taught Peter mathematics, and Patrick Gordon, a Scottish soldier of fortune, and Franz Lefort, a Genevan adventurer. They were an illiterate, riotous and barbarous crowd, but they taught Peter much. Peter appeared to show no interest whatever in government. He preferred to haunt the German Quarter of Moscow, where life was a riotous mixture of barbarism and western ways. He lived the life of a wandering student, doing military exercises, trying experiments, building ships, and indulging in fierce horseplay and drunken orgies. Of formal education he had little. Kliuchevsky, who examined Peter's papers, pronounced his Russian grammar atrocious, his mathematics shaky and inaccurate, and his attempts to write pidgin German in Russian characters laughable. From this rude life he was suddenly shaken when in 1689 his half-sister Sophia plotted to destroy him. Peter was warned, fled in terror in the middle of the night, rallied his supporters at a nearby monastery, forced Sophia to surrender, banished her to a convent, executed some of her Ministers, and thus at the age of seventeen found himself the effective ruler of Russia. Still however he took no part in government. His mother Natalia became Regent; the old régime went on as before, the last few years, as it happened of the old Muscovite order. Not until 1694, when Natalia died, and Peter was twenty-two, did he take over the burden of government.

Peter the Great is one of the most extraordinary and dramatic characters in history, in every respect wrought in enormous proportions. He was nearly seven feet tall, with enormous physical strength, so that he could bend nails and horse-shoes with his hands. Swarthy in complexion, with fierce black eyes, and later in life with nervous twitches and grimaces and rounded shoulders, he was driven on all his life with a restless energy which meant that he could never be still. He was perpetually at work, boat-building, copper-engraving, turning in ivory, dissecting corpses, extracting the teeth of his unfortunate courtiers, writing despatches and memoranda often for fourteen hours a day. Everything he undertook he did with a passionate violence. He would write fifty letters at a sitting; at the receipt of good news he would caper and sing at the top of his voice. He drank deeply, made passionate love, was blasphemous, indulged in coarse practical jokes. His temper was uncontrollable. He habitually thrashed his servants; he once knocked down the Dutch Resident, and on other occasions he slew three monks and mutilated two women who had annoyed him. He was no theorist or visionary about government. Kliuchevsky writes:

> If Peter was not sleeping, travelling, feasting or inspecting, he was busy making something. Whenever he could, he used his hands, which were never free from callouses.

At his death all his dwellings were full of model boats, chairs, crockery, snuff-boxes, all of which he had made himself. Kliuchevsky continues:

> He was more a man of action than a thinker. .... He had no coherent political understanding, but only a vague, confused notion that he had unlimited power. He knew neither moral nor political restraints and lacked the most elementary political and social principles.

His mind was essentially utilitarian. He seemed to know instinctively the direction Russian development should take. Ideas were not at this moment the greatest need, they were already plentiful in seventeenth-century Russia. What was needed was action, and in this Peter was pre-eminent. He did not set out to effect some pre-conceived plan or theory. He faced the urgent and practical problems of the Russian State and dealt with them as they arose.

Peter the Great and the West

Instinctively Peter turned towards the sea. One of his first acts as Tsar was to build a dockyard at Archangel, and to construct there a ship with his own hands. He had inherited a policy of good relations with Poland, and this enabled him to concentrate an attack upon the Turks. He constructed a fleet inland, besieged Azov by land and sea, and captured it in July 1696. In 1697 he set out for western Europe. One purpose was to attempt to form a European alliance against the Turks. But there was a deeper purpose which arose from the instinctive realisation of the backwardness of Russia in face of the potential enemies, the Turks and the Swedes. He travelled incognito as Peter Mikhailov. He wanted to prise open the secrets of the West in the field of technology. He studied gunnery at Königsberg, and then moved on to Holland, where he was feasted by the Electors of Hanover and Brandenberg (who were shocked at his atrocious table-manners). He worked as a carpenter in the shipyards of Saardam and Amsterdam, where he helped to build a frigate in nine weeks. He visited factories, workshops, hospitals; he attended the anatomy lectures of the famous Dr. Ruisch. Then he moved to England, in 1698, and settled at King's Wharf, Deptford. He helped to cast cannon at Woolwich, and was delighted to witness a mock naval battle which William III provided in his honour off the Isle of Wight. He lived riotously in a house rented from the diarist Evelyn, smashed much of the furniture, used the pictures for target-practice, and finally left Evelyn with claims against the Government of over £300. In May 1698, having heard of the revolt of the Streltsy Guard, he hurried away to Vienna. He had been able to recruit some 900 Dutch craftsmen, and he had acquired a wealth of practical knowledge.

The Streltsy Guard had played a turbulent part in making and unmaking Tsars during the Time of Troubles, and were a symbol of the old order. The revolt was suppressed long before Peter reached Russia, but that did not prevent him from further mass executions and the suppression of the Streltsy. It enabled Peter to begin with a flood of new regulations. Foreign dress became compulsory and beards had to be trimmed; a new calendar was adopted, with the years counted from the birth of Christ instead of the creation of the world, and the year to begin in January instead of September. At a stroke the year 7207 gave place to the year 1700. The change was deeply resented, and was thought to be blasphemous, for would God have created the world in the middle of winter? Peter opened the first apothecary's shop in 1700. He encouraged the smoking of tobacco. He abolished the seclusion of women, and gradually in the course of his reign he insisted that women should attend assemblies or salons, as they did in France. For the first time women began to wear hooped skirts. All this was part of an attempted moral reformation. Peter sought to jolt Muscovite Russia out of its backwardness, boorishness and ignorance. The novelty of the changes has sometimes been exaggerated. Most of the nobility had been well prepared for them during the previous decades and welcomed them. It was among the Old Believers and many of the common people that fear and resentment were most marked.

The Swedish War

Peter had little time or inclination for peaceful reform. His eyes were on the Baltic, and the moment seemed ripe for action, for a mere boy was on the throne of Sweden. In 1699 Peter made alliance with the Poles and Danes against the Swedes. He hastily made peace with the Turks by the Peace of Carlowitz, gaining Azov, but leaving the main objective of the Crimea and the Black Sea unachieved. Thus he abandoned his years of preparation in the south in order to achieve,

as he thought, an easy victory in the north. On the day he made peace
with the Turks he declared war on the Swedes It was a great blunder.
He himself later admitted that he had made no preparations in the
north. He did not expect Charles XII to be a military genius. As a result his army of 35,000 was routed, all its artillery, and most of its
senior officers, were captured by the eighteen-year-old Swedish king.[1]
Luckily for Peter, Charles XII turned away for a seven-year campaign
in Poland. Peter threw himself into a feverish attempt to recreate an
army, and an administration capable of bearing the burdens of a long
war against one of the foremost military Powers in Europe. It was
inevitable that all Peter's reforms should be practical, utilitarian,
hand-to-mouth. To see his reforms in perspective it must be remembered that Peter was at war for almost the whole of his reign; the
Swedish war alone occupied twenty years, and only one year of his
entire reign was free from war (1724). This imposed such a burden on
so primitive a State that his prime concerns were always practical considerations of recruitment, training, taxation and the like. One of his
first acts after Narva was to melt down the church bells to cast cannon. Even in 1706, after six years of preparation, Peter's army was
again cut to pieces by Charles XII at Grodno, with the loss of over a
hundred cannon. But in 1709 Charles XII played into his hand, and
Peter showed his superiority as a strategist. The Swedish legend of invincibility was broken for ever on the field of Poltava. Peter was so
excited at his victory that he failed to pursue and destroy the Swedish
remnants, and that night he feasted the captured Swedish generals,
and called them his teachers in the art of war. It was true, and Peter
had learnt the lesson well. He had shown that in generalship, discipline
and military efficiency Russia was now comparable with the West.
Moreover, Peter had conquered the Baltic provinces of Livonia,
Estonia and Karelia, and although the Swedish War dragged on until
the Treaty of Nystad of 1721, it ended in complete victory for Russia.
Russia was now the dominant Power in the Baltic. During the war
Peter had become deeply involved in European affairs. Attacks on
Swedish Pomerania brought Russian troops to the Elbe. Peter signed
alliances with Prussia and Hanover in 1710, and with France in 1717.
But the West grew fearful of the Russian rise to power. Britain feared
for her Baltic trade. Prussia and Hanover resented the Russian

[1] Near Narva.

intrusion into German affairs. For the first time the Russian threat to Polish independence became apparent. To Europe it was clear by 1721 that a new colossus had arisen in the east, with incalculable consequences for the future.

Peter's Reforms

From 1700 onwards the prime purpose of government was to provide an army, and this resolved itself rapidly into a financial and administrative problem. His first army was little better than a rabble. The Streltsy revolt had in a sense been suppressed too thoroughly, and there were too few seasoned troops. It took years to produce a real army. In 1705 a form of conscription was introduced on the basis of one recruit to every twenty tax-paying households, yielding an army of about 150,000 men in five years. By the end of the reign there was an army of about 200,000 men, and in addition about 100,000 Cossacks and other irregulars. Peter also in the course of his reign built up a Baltic fleet of 48 ships of the line, together with some 800 galleys. The expense was enormous, and swallowed up some two-thirds of the budget. New military training was introduced. By 1709 Russia was manufacturing most of its weapons, and had an effective artillery. The Russians were probably the first to use the bayonet as a weapon of attack, for formerly it was regarded as a weapon of defence.

The need to officer so large an army, and to administer a government of increasing complexity, raised the whole question of service to the State. We have seen that old boyar independence had been seriously challenged by Ivan the Terrible and his *oprichnina*; and from that time, in spite of a short period of resurgence during the Time of Troubles, may be dated the decline of the boyars. With the expansion of Russia in the seventeenth century a new service nobility became increasingly evident. In face of the new threat one of the last lines of boyar defence was the *mestnichestvo*, a complicated system of precedence by which no boyar could take a commission or office of lower rank than any of his ancestors, nor serve under anyone who ranked lower in the table of precedence. This fantastic, and grossly inefficient system (which was not without parallels elsewhere in Europe in the eighteenth century) was abolished in 1682, and this greatly simplified Peter's work. Peter the Great laid a new emphasis on a nobility of service, or *dvorianstvo*. A command in the army, or service at Court carried with it the rank and privilege of nobility. At Court there was a whole hierarchy of nobility. In peacetime they made up the Tsar's retinue and administration; in war they were formed into a regiment and sent to the front. In return for their services they received land and serfs. Peter's needs were such that he tried to conscript the sons of the nobility and train them as soldiers, naval officers or administrators, and there were heavy punishments for evasion of service or default. In 1714, for instance, Peter decreed that all the sons of noblemen were to be compulsorily educated between the ages of ten and fifteen, and none was to marry until he had achieved a proficiency in mathematics! But there were few schools, and such decrees were generally disregarded. At the age of fifteen the sons of nobility were to join the Guards as privates, and were given six months' leave every two years to tend to their estates. Those unfit for military service were sent to administrative duties. Peter was prepared to ennoble any man of humble birth who rose to important positions in the army or the administration, and to this end he drew up his famous Table of Ranks in 1722. This consisted of three parallel columns, Civil, Military and Court; in each column there were fourteen ranks. Hereditary nobility was of no assistance, and when a man passed beyond the first six ranks he became ennobled. This must indeed be regarded more as an indication of Peter's intentions than an actual achievement, for three years later, before the system could have had more than a transitory effect, Peter was dead. But it was another nail in the coffin of old boyar independence. Moreover, the new service estates were not surrendered when service ceased, but became hereditary, so that they were *votchina* rather than *pomestie*. Peter gave away in his reign over $1\frac{1}{2}$ million acres in such estates, and in future there was in practice only one tenure of estates, that of *votchina*, or hereditary possession. Still, Peter had attempted to return to the old and almost forgotten principle by which the nobility were primarily servants of the State, and thus he was ready to regard the peasants as serfs of the nobility. The census figures of 1718 showed some 5 million serfs in Russia, but as in some districts the gentry concealed the existence of half their serfs, it is certain that the number was appreciably greater.

The expenses of war placed a formidable burden on so primitive a government. Expenditure exceeded receipts, and it was necessary that Peter should extort the maximum of taxation. For this purpose, about

1708, he divided the country into eight provinces,[1] and distributed his army throughout the country in 126 centres, where they could serve both recruiting and tax-collecting purposes. They inflicted the greatest hardship on the country by their extortions, which, Kliuchevsky asserts, were worse than anything known during the Tatar occupation. The census of 1718 was also for tax purposes, and was followed by a poll-tax on all peasants. Since the landlord was responsible for the payment of the poll-tax, it was simpler for the Government to regard all his peasants as serfs, and thus at one stroke the rural peasantry were reduced to the condition of serfdom. It was not, however, a simplification which Peter had begun; it had been the whole tendency of governments for the previous 150 years. Peter was not unaware of the burdens and brutalities of serfdom, and in one or two respects his attitude may be termed enlightened. For instance, he urged that no serf should be sold if this meant being parted from his family; and he was quite ready to ennoble a serf who had risen to a command in the army. But, like Frederick the Great in a similar situation, his attitude was in the last resort determined by the exigencies of the time, and considerations of power.

In Holland, France and England Peter the Great had learnt the basic principles of Mercantilism. He saw that the wealth of the mercantile nations was closely connected with trade, self-sufficiency and technical development. He saw that Russia was rich in natural resources, and he sought to develop them by State action. But Russia was backward and lethargic; progress was possible only if planned and directed by himself. His subjects were simple and wayward children, hating change; they must be stirred, by force if necessary, from their lethargy. Some industries, particularly the iron industry, had begun under his predecessors; Peter carried this much further. The first objective was to satisfy the needs of war, but after 1709 there was increasing emphasis on peaceful industries. In 1695 there were about twenty industrial enterprises in Russia; in Peter's reign two hundred were established. Nearly one-half were State enterprises, the remainder were established by private individuals. Peter greatly extended the iron industry, especially in the Urals; he created the textile, china and glass industries around Moscow. Many of these industries were started by the several thousand foreign craftsmen he brought

---

[1] Eventually increased to twenty.

into Russia. The Russians themselves were extremely ignorant, and Peter had to send abroad to learn even how to make brooms and boxes. In 1719 he founded a College of Manufactures. He sought to raise the low status of industrial workers, and in 1721 he granted industrialists the rights of nobility, and was always ready to provide them with a compulsory labour force. He freely granted monopolies, and imposed the most minute State regulations. There was much that must be accounted failure and disappointment. Russians were reluctant to invest money in industry, preferring to invest it in London or Amsterdam (Prince Menshikov himself was said to have had a million roubles in London). Some industries lost money and failed (e.g. silk). Yet much was achieved. Textiles made real progress, though Russia was far from being self-sufficient. There were four important iron centres, in the Urals, at Tula, Olonetz and at St. Petersburg, and Tula supplied the entire army with armaments. By 1718 Russian foundries were smelting 105,000 tons of iron. Communications were always a great problem, for roads were so bad that it took five weeks to go from St. Petersburg to Moscow. Peter's main attempt to deal with transport problems was to link the main rivers by canals. In this he employed tens of thousands of men, and thousands perished during the projects, but only one of his six great canals was completed, when St. Petersburg was linked to the Volga by canal in 1732. The attempt to link the Volga to the Don was abandoned after the loss of Azov. In road-building he was even less successful, but he established caravan routes by which, for instance, he imported Hungarian wines, which were sold as a State monopoly. He introduced the vine into the Don area; in 1712 he established the first breeding studs, and greatly extended sheep-rearing in the south. One of his clearest achievements was in the growth of foreign trade. In the Baltic Peter acquired seven ports, two of which, Cronstadt and St. Petersburg, he built himself. He successfully diverted trade from Archangel to St. Petersburg, and at the end of his reign 240 foreign ships a year were reaching St. Petersburg, and over 900 foreign ships were reaching Russia's Baltic ports. This trade was mainly passive, for Peter failed to establish a mercantile marine; but at the end of his reign exports were worth nearly $2\frac{1}{2}$ million roubles, and imports somewhat over $1\frac{1}{2}$ million.

Trade was developed in order that it might be taxed. Kliuchevsky wrote that 'new taxes were poured on to the taxpayers like water from a watering-can'. Everything was taxed: horse-collars, corners of rooms, Old Believers, beards (at the rate of 50 roubles a year) and almost every article of purchase. Many of the latter, such as salt, tobacco, pitch, coffins, were State monopolies, and were sold at excessive prices. By the end of his reign Peter's budget was about three times its size at the beginning, and totalled over 8½ million roubles, of which 4½ millions came from the poll-tax on 5½ million serfs and town-dwellers, and the remainder from customs and excise. Seventy-five per cent. of the budget went on military expenditure. The burden on the country was oppressive, and was accompanied by wholesale corruption by administrators and tax-collectors, so that it was said that only thirty per cent. of the revenues collected ever reached the Treasury. There was a heavy price to be paid for the creation of Russia as a great Power.

Such administrative changes as Peter instituted before 1710 were merely of fiscal significance, but in the later part of his reign his reforms became more fundamental and extensive. Thus in the first decade the number of his decrees was about 500, and in the rest of his reign over 3,600. In 1711, when Peter was about to leave for the Turkish War, he issued a *ukase* (decree) establishing a Senate. The idea and title were borrowed from Sweden. Its function was the supervision of the whole administrative system in the absence of the Tsar, although foreign affairs and war were beyond its competence. Need for some such body had been felt during the previous decade, because in the absence of the Tsar at the wars there had been no effective central government at all. Gradually the Senate extended its authority over taxation, police, justice, trade and religion, and had power to issue *ukases*. But it was never an efficient body; the Dutch Resident commented in 1714: 'The great drawback is that all business is made over to the Senate which never decides anything.' One of its first acts was to appoint *fiscals* in each town (an idea again borrowed from Sweden) whose function was to ferret out tax evasion and corruption. In 1715 Peter sent a group to Sweden to study the collegiate system of organising a government department, for the Russian system of fifty *prikazy* was hopelessly inefficient. In 1718 he established nine Colleges, for Foreign Affairs, Finance, Justice, Audit, Army, Navy, Commerce, Industry and Expenditure. Each College consisted of ten members and a President (often they were foreigners) responsible to the Senate, which thus, in the absence of the Tsar, was the effective ruler of the country and the Supreme Court of Appeal. It was the business of the Senate to carry out all the orders of the Tsar, and in 1722 he created the office of Procurator-General to act as 'our eye and mandatory in affairs of State', in fact to keep a watchful eye on the efficiency of the Senate. The control of the Senate over the provinces was made more complete when these large and unwieldy units were sub-divided into fifty administrative units, each under a *voevoda*, or governor, appointed by the central government.

The effect of all these changes was to transform the character of Russian government. The *Zemski Sobor* and the *boyar Duma* ceased to exist; the old boyar class were ousted from their position of pre-eminence. Russia was now ruled by a form of government imitated from Sweden, by a bureaucracy staffed from all classes, old boyars, new men of service, favourites, adventurers, foreigners. His reforms failed to arouse a national enthusiasm or co-operation; on all sides he met corruption and lethargy. Sometimes an institution broke down for lack of men capable of working it. Kliuchevsky commented: 'Peter created institutions in the same way that a thrifty mother makes clothes which are far too big, and will fit her children only when they grow up.' The question remains whether they were the right clothes, and whether in fact Russia grew to wear them.

Before we attempt to answer that question we must indicate other ways in which Peter was an innovator. He was certainly an innovator in education. He had neither the time nor the resources to attempt a national system of elementary education. It is often said that he tried to establish the teaching of engineering, navigation, surgery, mathematics before many people could read or write. In 1714 he tried to make education compulsory for the sons of gentry and bureaucrats, but by 1719 only one provincial school had been provided. His Academy of Sciences, established in 1724 at St. Petersburg, had hardly any pupils. In one respect, however, his Academy made notable progress, in cartography. Peter was extremely interested in the development of Asia; he himself marched into Transcaucasia in a war against Persia. He sent out explorers to find the best routes to India; he probed the North-East Passage, and sent out Bering who discovered the Bering Straits shortly after Peter's death.

Peter was conscious of the ignorance, independence and wealth of the Russian Church. When in 1700 the Patriarch died, he abolished his authority. The last independence of the Church disappeared when the Senate in 1711 was given jurisdiction over the Church, and treated it as a government department. One Russian historian wrote: 'The Abbot flogged his monks, the Bishop flogged his Abbots, the Government knouted the Bishop.' Finally in 1721 Peter transferred authority over the Church to a Holy Synod, which ranked equal to the Senate and took precedence over other bodies. It was one of Peter's innovations which lasted intact until 1917.

Few of Peter's achievements were more spectacular than the building of St. Petersburg. This he began as early as 1703, at which date he could certainly not be sure that his Baltic conquests would be permanent. No doubt his first intention was to construct a fortress at a strategic place, and only later did the idea of a new capital emerge. It was a most unpropitious site, set amidst swamps, so that the city had to be built on piles at an enormous cost of life and effort. Peter himself worked on the site and lived in a simple hut. It is not clear that, say, Riga would not have served him strategically and commercially as well; but Peter was determined on a city of his own. His instinct was right to turn his back on Moscow, to emphasise that Russia now had 'a window on the West'. In this, as in so many other things, Peter acted with the unerring instinct of a genius, and perhaps in his mind there was the desire to build a city which would look like Amsterdam. Henceforth in the eighteenth century Russia had two capitals, the solemn and religious city of Moscow, and, in contrast, the gayer, cosmopolitan St. Petersburg, with its French theatre and Italian opera; the one Muscovite in its traditions, the other western, commercial and progressive.

Estimate of the Reign

There is no doubt that Peter the Great had tremendous impact upon Russia. Muscovite Russia gave place to Petrine Russia, and the latter may be said to have continued until 1917. This is not to say that there was not continuity also between Muscovite and Petrine Russia. We have seen that there were many points of similarity between the position and aspirations of Ivan the Terrible and Peter the Great. The Russian drive towards the Baltic was a Russian aspiration long before the time of Peter the Great. The decline of the boyars dates from Ivan the Terrible, and was merely completed by Peter the Great. Peter did not initiate serfdom, though undoubtedly he made it more burdensome. Westernisation had begun to influence Russia long before Peter was born. But none of these points in any way diminishes the magnitude of Peter's achievement. He immensely speeded up a process which had already begun; he turned a trickle into a torrent. It might also be true to say that he turned what was a slow and unconscious development into an urgent and conscious one. Riasanovsky makes the point that Peter touched the people at every point: if they used the calendar, it was Peter's, if they wore western clothes it was Peter's innovation and the cloth was manufactured in Peter's factories; if they read, the new simplified script was introduced by Peter; if they read newspapers, Peter introduced them; if they ate potatoes, Peter introduced them; if they drank wine, Peter introduced the vine; if they went to school, schools were begun by Peter; if they travelled abroad, Peter first taught them to do so. When Peter died, his favourite ecclesiastic, Feofan Prokopovich, Archbishop of Novgorod, who had been in the vanguard of Peter's ecclesiatical reforms, and had himself suggested the establishment of the Holy Synod, preached the funeral oration, in which he declared that Peter had 'raised Russia as from the dead', and praised him as a Samson, a mighty man of arms, a Japhet who had created a navy, a Moses among law-givers, and as a Solomon among the wise. On the other hand, by many he was execrated as an Anti-Christ, a 'bloodsucker' who had battened on his people, and for long there was circulated a wood-cut jeering at his funeral under the title of 'The mice bury the cat'. For 150 years Russians were divided in their interpretation of his reign, the Slavophils glorifying the character of Muscovite Russia which Peter had destroyed, the westernisers lauding his work as the beginning of progress. The truth lies somewhere in between, and may perhaps be resolved into component parts.

First, inevitability. The Slavophils were wrong when they idealised Muscovy. If Russia was to develop it could only be along western lines. Kliuchevsky was bitter at the way in which Peter's policy divided Russia into a small élite of westernised, and a great mass of untouched peasantry. But there was no other way in which the change could be effected. All innovations must start as minority innovations.

Second, its incompleteness. It was impossible that even a Peter the Great could be completely successful in so gigantic a task in so short a time. Yet the achievement was real. There is little doubt about the essentially western character of the Russian aristocracy and intelligentsia by the end of the eighteenth century. There is even less doubt about the importance of the part played by Russia in Europe in the century after Poltava.

Finally, the cost. Peter's system meant serfdom, forced labour, oppressive taxation, the knout, and military service often for life. He did not originate any of these, but they were an integral part of his system. State power has often been erected on the sufferings of the people, yet at the same time it has been the prime condition for economic and cultural progress. And so it was with Russia.

6: The Swedish Meteor

The Rise of Sweden

The Swedish meteor first flashed into the European sky in 1630. Two years later the hero-king Gustavus Adolphus perished on the field of Lützen, but his policy of expansion was continued, first by the able Minister Oxenstierna and then by the soldier-king Charles X (1654–60). By the Peace of Westphalia (1648) Sweden gained western Pomerania, Bremen, Verden and Wismar. By the Treaties of Copenhagen (with Denmark) and Oliva (with Poland, both 1660) Sweden annexed Blekinge, Schonen and Bohuslän, and thus made the Sound the boundary between Sweden and Denmark; and the Polish king renounced all claims to the throne of Sweden. It was the zenith of Swedish power in the Baltic.

The Swedish Empire, however, always rested on insecure foundations. It was created by its exceptional line of soldier-kings at a time when Europe was weak and divided. It gained much from its alliance with France. But Sweden was a poor country; much of the land was virgin forest and uninhabited; the total population of the Swedish Empire, including the German provinces, was only 3 millions, of whom less than half were Swedes. Economically it could survive only if it could control the trade of the Baltic in corn and naval stores and thus maintain a strong army and fleet on the proceeds of customs duties. But this it never effectively achieved, and even at the height of the Swedish power only 10 per cent. of the ships engaged in the Baltic trade were Swedish, while 65 per cent. were Dutch. The Baltic and German provinces were impossible to defend against a strong continental Power such as Russia or Prussia, once the Great Elector and Peter the Great had begun their work. Moreover, Swedish kings learnt to love war too much, and the ambitions of Charles XII strained the resources of the Empire beyond endurance, and led to the final collapse of Swedish power.

The growth of Swedish power in the seventeenth century was accompanied by an important internal political revolution which

F

brought Sweden into line with the centralised monarchies of France, Prussia and Russia. When Gustavus Adolphus died in 1632 he left as his successor a four-years' old daughter, Christina, with his friend Oxenstierna as chief Minister. In 1634 the latter established a 'Form of Government' by which he virtually converted the Government into an oligarchy controlled by the great nobility. This system continued unchanged under Charles X, who himself died leaving Charles XI, a child of four as heir. The nobility at once set aside the King's Will, set up a Council entirely composed of great nobles, and continued to dominate the Government during the twelve years of the King's minority. But in 1672 Charles XI became of age, and in the same year Sweden entered into an alliance with France in return for large subsidies and a promise of the independence of the Duke of Holstein-Gottorp from Denmark. The first results were disastrous, for in 1675 the Swedes were defeated by Brandenburg at Fehrbellin, and Denmark attacked the Duke of Holstein-Gottorp and forced him to cede his lands to Denmark. Brandenburg occupied Pomerania, Hanover occupied Bremen and Verden and Denmark occupied Wismar. But then Charles XI launched a counter-offensive, defeated the Danes at Lund, and the intervention of French diplomacy secured Sweden the return of most of her losses in the general peace of 1679.

The war had shown how insecure were the foundations of the Swedish Empire. It revealed also the faults in the Swedish form of government, and Charles XI devoted the rest of his reign to an internal reconstruction which was in many ways similar to that of the Great Elector in Brandenburg-Prussia. The war enabled him to become a despot. In his reforms he could count upon the hostility which existed between the great nobility, who had tended to dominate government since the death of Gustavus Adolphus, and the lesser landlords, townsfolk, Church and peasants. There had long been a demand for 'reduktion', or a resumption of Crown lands which had passed into the hands of the nobility, and to this was now added the demand for an enquiry into maladministration during the period of Regency. These demands were voiced by the Lower Estates of the Riksdag of 1680, in which the desire for political stability and general hostility to the great nobility were the governing motives. Charles XI took full advantage of this, and the Estates proceeded to declare that the King was bound neither by the written constitution of the Form of Government, nor by the Council, nor indeed by any constitutional law of any kind. In 1682 he secured their consent to the resumption of the Crown lands. This, together with the fines levied on those brought to trial for maladministration, and the economies effected by wise administration, left the Monarchy in a sound financial position, and after 1686 he practically ceased to summon the Estates at all. Finally the Estates of 1693 declared him

> absolute sovereign King, responsible to no-one on earth, but with power and might at his command to rule and govern the realm as a Christian monarch.

The establishment of absolutism was accompanied by a social revolution. In 1680 the nobility owned 72 per cent. of the land, much of it in the hands of a few powerful families such as the Oxenstiernas and the Brahes. By 1700 they possessed only about 33 per cent., about the same proportion as was possessed by the Crown and the same also as that divided into peasant-proprietorships. Thus the predominance of the nobility was broken, the royal finances were secured and an independent peasantry safeguarded. The nobility no longer monopolised the higher offices of State, though they retained considerable importance in social, political and military affairs. With his revenues assured, the King built up a standing army, but for the rest of his reign saw to it that peace was maintained. These were years of consolidation and prosperity for Sweden. There was a flourishing Baltic trade in wheat and naval stores; Swedish iron exports doubled in twenty years. When Charles XI died in 1697 he left an absolutism which rested on the support of the great majority of his Swedish subjects, without an internal opposition anywhere except in the Livonian Diet, where the German nobility resisted his absolutism. He left a fine standing army which, with skilled leadership, was strong enough to have defended the Empire against its external enemies. The mistake of Charles XII was to turn it into an instrument for further expansion.

Charles XII

In an age of remarkable monarchs Charles XII seized the imagination of Europe. From the earliest age he had been trained in the art of war. He was a prodigious horseman; no ruler since Attila spent so much of his life on horseback. He came to the throne at the age of fifteen and a half, and he reigned for twenty-one years and one day. He was proclaimed absolute monarch by the Riksdag, which never again met during his reign. The rest of his life was spent in the business of war. The death of his father had encouraged Denmark, Saxony, Poland and Russia to form an alliance for the destruction of the Swedish Empire, and in February 1700 the Poles attacked Swedish Livonia, and at the same time the Danes attacked Holstein. In April Charles XII gathered the flower of his army, and left Stockholm, which he was never to see again.

Charles XI had built up a fine fleet, and naval base at Karlskrona, and for the first time the Swedish fleet outnumbered the Danish. Moreover, the Swedes could also rely on the aid of the Anglo-Dutch fleet. Thus Charles XII landed his army before Copenhagen and forced Denmark to make peace. He then switched his attacking force to Estonia, where the Russians were devastating the countryside, and in November routed the Russians in the Battle of Narva, inflicted heavy losses and captured all the Russian artillery. At the age of eighteen Charles had won his first great battle. At this point he would have done well to have made peace, but he had learnt to love war. He wintered in Estonia until the spring of 1701. The question was whether he should pursue the Russians or invade Poland. It is sometimes said that if he had chosen the former rather than the latter the course of history might have been different, but there is little to justify this view. Russia would have been nearly as difficult a nut to crack in 1701 as it proved to be in 1709, and in 1701 Poland appeared to be the most formidable of Sweden's enemies. It was a mistake, however, to set as his objective, not merely the defeat of Poland, but the deposition of its king Augustus II.

It is true that Poland was in the greatest confusion, and Charles hoped that the Poles would depose the Saxon kings. He occupied Warsaw, and defeated Augustus at Kliszow, a hundred miles southwest of the capital. Augustus fled to Cracow, which Charles captured in July 1702 shortly after his escape. Everywhere the Swedish troops appeared to be invincible, and as they could live comfortably off the land, Charles was in no hurry to leave. In 1704, with Swedish troops standing by, a small group of Polish nobles proclaimed Charles XII's candidate Stanislas Leszczynski King of Poland. In 1706 Charles invaded Saxony itself, a step he could take only because the Habsburg

Emperor was too deeply involved with Louis XIV to be likely to interfere. In September 1706 Swedish troops rode into Leipzig, and two
days later Charles XII and Augustus made peace, the latter resigning
the Polish crown.

Charles XII with an army of 43,000 men now turned against the
Russians, who had advanced as far as Warsaw. At his approach the
Russians fell back, and Charles advanced to Grodno and Minsk, beyond which the Russians made a stand at Holovzin. There in July
1708, in what he always regarded the most skilful of his victories,
Charles routed the Russians. From there he advanced to Moghilev, at
which point his supply problem for the first time became acute. Supplies were not reaching him, the weather was bad, and the Russians
had devastated the countryside. In the summer of 1708 he reached
Tatarsk to find the Russians barring his way. Without supplies,
Charles determined to turn southwards instead of pressing on to
Moscow. He hoped to reach the wheat-lands of the Ukraine; he hoped
the Cossacks of the Ukraine would rise against the Russians and become his allies; and beyond he might expect the support of the Turks
against the Russians. But the march now became one of dreadful
hardship. The abnormally severe weather during the summer of 1708
had greatly increased his difficulties; his troops were exhausted, and
after eight years of campaigning they longed for home. By December
1708 there had set in one of the most bitter-cold winters in history,
and men were frozen to death along the route. In February 1709 there
followed torrential rains. Charles XII had been wounded and was in
great pain. Finally the two sides closed near the town of Poltava, some
22,000 Swedes facing 45,000 Russians. Charles was too ill to command during the battle, and the command passed to his ablest general
Rehnsköld. At the Battle of Poltava (July 28 1709) the Swedes were
routed with the loss of some 7,000 men and 3,000 prisoners. Charles
fled into Turkish territory, and thereupon the remainder of his army,
some 14,000 men, surrendered to the Russians. He remained in Turkish territory for five years, while Peter the Great completed the conquest of the Baltic provinces. Stanislas was driven from Poland, and
Augustus resumed his Polish crown. Even now Charles failed to seek
peace. In 1714 he made his way through Imperial territory to Stralsund, but it was at once attacked by the Danes and Prussians and
captured, and Charles escaped into Sweden. Even now he thought

only of new armies and the continuance of war. Contemporaries came to believe that he was possessed by madness or the devil. Years of campaigning had brutalised him, and he came to be hated by his people, who for years had suffered from famine, high taxes and misgovernment. With the aid of the ingenious Baron von Görtz, a German adventurer, he sought allies, and in 1716 attempted an attack upon Norway; it failed, and two years later he was preparing for a second invasion when he was killed by a stray bullet. He left his Empire in ruins, and three years later by the Treaty of Nystad Russia annexed the Baltic provinces of Sweden. All that remained to Sweden of the former Empire were Finland and part of Pomerania.[1]

The Eighteenth Century

With the Empire there ended also royal absolutism. The Council resumed its old status; the Riksdag which elected Ulrica Eleanora (Charles' youngest sister) Queen, also established a new constitution. There was a general reaction against bureaucratic absolutism. When Frederick I (Ulrica Eleanora's husband) was elected king he was little more than the presiding member of the Council. But it was not simply a return to the domination of the great nobility. The lesser gentry, and even the peasants, asserted themselves. Aristocratic privilege was increasingly questioned; there was a steady increase of peasant proprietorship, and Swedish economic life rapidly revived. The leading figure of the new régime was Arvid Horn, President of the Chancery, and leader of the party known as the Caps. He was opposed by the Hats, who looked back with nostalgia to the days of Swedish greatness, and wanted a policy of hostility to Russia and alliance with France. When Horn was driven from office in 1738 government became parliamentary, with power centring in the Riksdag. In 1756 the King lost the use of the veto, and the Estates of the Riksdag developed the theory that they were the sovereign Estates of the realm. But this growth of parliamentary freedom was accompanied by a good deal of political confusion, and an unsuccessful foreign policy, and finally, after the reigns of two singularly feeble kings, Gustav III in 1772 carried out a brilliant *coup d'état*. The Riksdag was adjourned, and

---

[1] Ranke's comment on Charles XII is still the best: 'He reminds us of one of those Vikings who, after ravaging the shores of the Baltic, at last bring down upon themselves the reaction of fate, retire to the north, and disappear.'

people looked to the new king to put an end to party strife and economic disorder. Voltaire sang the praises of a new Enlightened Despot. In fact Gustav III simply returned to the form of government of Gustavus Adolphus, which had been a government by councils. At heart he preferred to rely on the aristocracy as his great predecessor had done, but this did not save him from assassination at the hands of a group of aristocratic conspirators in 1792. His government was superficially 'enlightened' and he abolished torture, established freedom of the press and was a patron of letters, with a passion for the theatre and opera. But above all his reign was in line with the prevailing tendency towards regalism which marked so many of the European monarchies of the later eighteenth century.

7: The Rise of Prussia

The Great Elector

In 1640, when the Great Elector came to the throne at the age of twenty there was little to indicate the future greatness of Brandenburg-Prussia. The Mark of Brandenburg had been established by the Emperor Otto I about 950 A.D. as a stage in the Teutonic conquest of the Slaves. By the fourteenth century there were three Marks, Old Mark, west of the Elbe, Middle Mark between the Elbe and the Oder, and New Mark across the Oder. In 1417, in a famous ceremony in the market-place of Constance, the Emperor Sigismund invested the Burgrave of Brandenburg with the dignity of Elector in return for his oath of allegiance. In 1591 John Sigismund of Brandenburg married the eldest daughter of the Duke of Prussia, who was without male heir. She was also the heiress to the last Duke of Cleves and Jülich, who died in 1609. In this way the Elector of Brandenburg acquired the duchy of Cleves and the counties of Mark and Ravensberg, and also the duchy of East Prussia, for which, however, he had to do homage to the King of Poland.

East Prussia was a most important acquisition. It had belonged originally to the Teutonic knights, who had conquered it from the pagan Prussians, and established there a strong ecclesiastical principality which they ruled much more effectively than was usual anywhere in Germany at the time. The land was systematically colonised in the thirteenth and fourteenth centuries, serfdom was introduced, and the Grand Master, with his seat at Marienbad, was one of the most effective of mediaeval rulers. But in the fifteenth century his power declined; the Teutonic Order was much weakened by war; the Junker class grew powerful on the corn trade, and finally, with the Reformation, the Teutonic Order was dissolved (1525). The last Grand Master of the Order, Albert of Hohenzollern, became the first Duke of Prussia, and continued as the liegeman of the King of Poland, and with much less hold over his Junker nobility. Still, to the Hohenzollerns of Brandenburg, the acquisition of East Prussia was of great importance. It gave them extensive territory outside the Holy Roman Empire, although this brought its attendant dangers, for Brandenburg could not escape being drawn into the conflicts for power between Poland and Sweden. The same was true in the West, for Cleves, Mark and Ravensberg would probably involve the Elector in any wars concerning the Dutch. Moreover, by the Peace of Westphalia (1648) the Elector, with French help, obtained in addition the secularised bishoprics of Cammin, Halberstadt and Minden, and reversion of the rich archbishopric of Magdeburg, in western Germany, together with the eastern half of Pomerania. The Elector of Brandenburg now had extensive, though very scattered possessions; he ruled more territory than any other north German prince, but there was nothing in common between the fragments except the historical accident of having the same ruler. They were not in any sense a State. Neither in history, social structure, institutions nor law was there apparently a basis for political unity and power. Each province had its own Estates, representing the nobility and the towns, and there was little the Elector could do without their consent. There was no common tradition, no common law, no common administration, and the Elector had no army and no money (except from his private estates, and the subsidies he could extort from France) but such as the Estates voted him. It was difficult to impose a common foreign policy on such scattered dominions, for why should the Estates of Cleves support the Elector's wars in East Prussia? In a general war it was impossible to defend his lands, and thus when Frederick William, known to history as the Great Elector, came to the throne in 1640 he found much of his inheritance devastated and occupied by foreign armies, especially Swedish.[1] The wonder was that in the next forty years he was able to lay the foundations of Hohenzollern despotism.

Frederick William had been carefully educated; he spoke five languages fluently, and the early influences of his life were of the greatest importance in the formation of his later policy. As a boy he greatly admired his uncle, the great Swedish hero, Gustavus Adolphus,

[1] When a boy, he had had to hide in the forest of Letzlingen to escape invading troops. In 1640 he wrote:

On the one hand I have the King of Sweden, on the other the Emperor: here I stand between the two, awaiting what they will do to me, whether they will leave me my own, or whether they will take it away.

and from Sweden he learnt much of the organisation of government. Even more important, he spent four years in the Netherlands and eventually married the granddaughter of William the Silent. We have already seen that in matters of economics, commerce and finance the Dutch were in some ways the instructors of Europe. The young Frederick William was deeply impressed with the wealth of the Dutch, and later modelled his economic policy upon their example.

In 1640 his inheritance was a sad one. Brandenburg was one of the most backward areas of the Empire. Its population was scanty, its soil poor, sandy and often waterlogged. Cut off from the sea, and far from the trade routes of Europe, it seemed ill-favoured indeed. The Elector was little more than a *primus inter pares* among his nobility; he was simply the largest landowner among them. His lands had been devastated by foreign armies. It is true that his father, George William, and his able Minister Count Schwarzenberg, had seized the opportunity of the war to raise taxes without the consent of the Estates, and to set up a war council (*Kriegsrat*) to transact all government, replacing the old privy council and consisting mainly of foreigners or commoners. But the nobles had resisted, and one of the first acts of the Great Elector was to dissolve the war council, and restore the privy council and Junkers to favour. Frederick William saw from the beginning that the key to all power lay in finance, and he attempted to introduce from the Netherlands an excise tax which, not being subject to the vote of the Estates, nor liable to exemptions, would greatly enhance the Elector's independence. But the Junkers would have none of it, and finally by the Recess of 1653 the Estates forced the Elector to confirm all the privileges of the Brandenburg nobility. In return for this apparent surrender, the Elector was granted 530,000 thalers, payable over six years. With this he was able to raise a small standing army, the first step on the road to independence from the Estates.

What gave the Great Elector his chance was the Northern War of 1655–60 between Poland and Sweden. There were at this stage two great objects of his foreign policy, first to obtain East Prussia in full sovereignty by throwing off Polish overlordship, and second to obtain western Pomerania. Eastern Pomerania, which he had gained at Westphalia, was poor territory, and without a port; western Pomerania was rich, and contained Stettin, a good port controlling the mouth of the Oder, Brandenburg's natural outlet to the sea. At first the Great

Elector allied with Sweden against Poland, and when Poland was defeated he allied with Poland against Sweden. In return Poland renounced suzerainty over East Prussia, and Frederick William for the first time became an independent sovereign.[1] He also conquered West Pomerania, but had to return it to Sweden in 1660. Meanwhile the war had forced him to collect taxes and impose a limited excise, without the consent of the Estates. The burden fell particularly on the towns, and was so great that commerce was crushed, and the towns deserted. In 1662 the town of Spandau petitioned the Elector that before the wars it had 400 burghers, and now less than 80 remained. By overburdening the towns, the Elector could leave the exemptions of the nobility intact, and thus buy their acquiescence to his policy. With the money he raised his standing army, and with his army he could now crush the resistance of the Estates. If to this we add the misery engendered by the war, and serious outbreaks of plague, in which thousands died, the plight of the Elector's subjects may be imagined.

The strongest resistance to Frederick William's policy came from East Prussia and the town of Königsberg. The new excise, from which the nobles were exempt, isolated the towns and divided the possible resistance to the Elector. Neither Junkers nor towns could now appeal to the Polish overlord. The leader of the resistance, Hieronymous Roth, a burgher of Königsberg, was arrested and imprisoned for the rest of his life, and the opposition collapsed. The East Prussian Diet of 1661–63 granted the excise for three years, and thus the Elector gained his way as he had done in Brandenburg. In 1674, when war against Louis XIV necessitated further heavy taxes in East Prussia, resistance broke out again from both burghers and nobles, but it was crushed. Municipal liberties were at an end, and between 1677 and 1679 the Prussian Estates paid more than 4 million thalers in taxation. The whole country was in a terrible plight; the peasants were reduced to eating chaff, but to the protests the Elector replied that his demands were dictated by military necessity, and must be met.

In his western provinces, such as Cleves and Mark, the story was somewhat different, though the outcome much the same. In the west the nobility were less dominant and towns more important; there

---

[1] This was not simply a matter of prestige. Hitherto the East Prussian Estates had been able to appeal to the King of Poland against any administrative or legislative order of the Elector.

were no labour services and many peasants were entirely free. The Elector was more tolerant of defeat here than in the east. In 1643 the Estates of Cleves appealed to the Aulic Council and obtained a decision in their favour. Nine times Frederick William attempted to introduce his excise there, but he always failed. Both the Estates and municipal councils retained some of their independence, though by the Recess of 1660 the power of the former was much curtailed. Yet the Elector succeeded in extorting heavy taxes to meet his war needs.

The creation of a standing army in Brandenburg necessitated a government department to organise and victual it. Thus arose the famous *Generalkriegskommissariat*, responsible for collecting money and billeting troops. Brandenburg alone, with a population of only 270,000 people, paid 264,000 thalers in taxes in 1662, and 400,000 thalers by 1680. In East Prussia the same functions were fulfilled by the *Kriegskammer*. In these institutions historians have seen the beginnings of the Prussian bureaucracy which was the foundation of Prussian despotism. With the complexities of war the old Privy Council lost its control over military and financial affairs, which passed to the *Generalkriegskommissariat*. Gradually the maintenance of the army became the prime purpose of the State. In fact it was the means of creating the State. For in 1640 there was no unified State, but a number of Estates. It was the work of the Great Elector to create a single State, with a single administration, headed by a despot. At his accession there was no standing army: in 1688 there was an army of 30,000 men. Professor Carsten, the leading authority on the subject, has written that 'The Prussian bureaucracy developed out of the military Commissariats'.

Between 1650 and 1680, whether in Brandenburg, East Prussia or the western provinces it was the same story. The Elector had established a source of revenue, namely the excise, independent of the control of the Estates, and henceforth had little reason to summon the latter. He had established a standing army, and the beginnings of a bureaucracy, which could provide military power and administrative uniformity independent of the local Estates. In the course of his reign Frederick William increased his revenues from 1 to 3 million thalers, which represented a rate of taxation twice as heavy as that which fell upon France at the height of Louis XIV's power. Nor were the Prussian nobility exempt from many taxes as they were in France. But as they retained to the full their local privileges and powers over their serfs, they acquiesced in the political revolution they witnessed. Many of them found new opportunities for employment as officers in the new army, or as bureaucrats in the new administrative service. Thus gradually an *ésprit de corps* was built up among the Junker class upon which the Great Elector's successors were to draw heavily. Moreover, there was a steady extension of governmental activity. The *General-kriegskommissariat* at first was concerned only with the raising and equipping of the army, but this required greater and greater control over taxation and expenditure, and gradually it became concerned with any aspect of government the Elector chose to entrust to it. Thus, for instance, it was a short step from the collection of taxes to the encouragement of trade and industries upon which the new excise depended. The Great Elector regarded economic expansion, very much as Colbert did, as a State activity, and very little was left to private initiative. But in this he was faced with a dilemma, for taxation fell particularly heavily upon the towns, and he was in danger of encouraging industry one moment and taxing it out of existence the next. It is often said that he was a good mercantilist, but it was impossible to pursue a clear economic policy in territories so scattered. The ideal of self-sufficiency made nonsense in territories the size of Cleves and Berg, and moreover, the Elector was too dependent upon internal tolls to abolish them. But he did encourage new industries. Although a devout Calvinist, he accepted the principle of toleration, and in 1671 issued a charter permitting Jews to settle in Brandenburg. Few German princes could do without their Jewish financiers and advisers. Prussia also took full advantage of the exodus of Huguenots from France, and in the last twenty years of the seventeenth century some 20,000 immigrants settled in Brandenburg. New industries were started, woollens, cottons, linen, velvet, lace, even silk, soap, paper and iron goods. He also encouraged colonists from the Netherlands with their skills in agriculture, drainage and canal construction. One of his proudest achievements was the Frederick William Canal through Berlin, which linked the Elbe and Oder rivers, and enabled vessels from Breslau and Hamburg to reach the capital. This waterway attracted much of the trade of Poland, Silesia and Saxony which previously had had to take overland routes, and Berlin grew as Frankfurt-on-Oder declined.

The Great Elector had learnt from the Dutch the importance of overseas trade; indeed he was the only Hohenzollern to be interested in the sea before the Kaiser William II. Hence his ambition to extend his coastline in Pomerania, which was thwarted by France in 1679. In 1682 he founded an Africa Company, first near Königsberg, and later at Emden, and in 1683 the first station was established on the Gold Coast. He also bought nine men-of-war from the Dutch to protect the trade. He also attempted an East India Company. But Brandenburg had little capital, no suitable ports, and little interest or skill in naval enterprises, and after his death the Companies collapsed, and Frederick William I sold what was left of the enterprise to the Dutch.

No country in Europe had greater difficulties in hitting upon a satisfactory foreign policy than Brandenburg-Prussia in the time of the Great Elector. The complexity of the European situation, and the weakness of the Electorate, did not permit him to pursue either a consistent or a glorious objection. By the Treaty of Westphalia he had gained much; the annexation of eastern Pomerania, the bishoprics of Halberstadt and Minden and the reversion of Magdeburg. In 1660 he won the independence of East Prussia from Polish sovereignty. Thereafter he was mainly concerned with the rising power of France. His family connections and his religion drew him towards a Dutch alliance and thus into opposition against France, as did also his hostility to Sweden and his desire to annex Swedish Pomerania. Yet even when he defeated the Swedes at Fehrbellin in 1675 he failed to gain Pomerania, for the French insisted upon its return to the Swedes as the price of peace in 1679. He turned therefore to a policy of dependence upon French subsidies, which assisted his exchequer at the price of an inglorious neutrality in Europe. Yet he was increasingly alarmed at the growth of French power, and especially at the threat to Protestantism implied in the Revocation of the Edict of Nantes (1685). Thus he joined the League of Augsburg in 1686,[1] and just before his death was chiefly concerned with Louis XIV's threat to William of Orange. French gold had aided him in building up his army, although this source should not be overestimated, for at no time did it account for more than one-tenth of the budget. The Great Elector drew his strength from his own resources. His was a policy dictated by *raison*

---

[1] When Ranke came to examine the alliance with Austria which the Great Elector signed in 1686 he was amazed that he could have signed so un-advantageous a treaty.

d'état and the weakness of his State. Attempts to reveal the Great Elector as a 'good German', anxious to free the Fatherland from the French menace, have entirely failed; the underlying idea is anachronistic. His Political Testament of 1667 advised his successor to seek to hold the balance between the powers of Habsburg and Bourbon, and this objective was always present in his mind.

Personally the Great Elector was a simple man who liked nothing better than working in his own garden, although he was attracted also to the ceremony which Louis XIV was making the indispensable mark of sovereignty. By nature he was kindly and considerate, meticulous and industrious, but he became hardened by difficulties and dangers, and in later life was much given to violence. Perhaps the mainspring of his life was his Calvinist religion, by which he was convinced of the direct protection and guidance he received from God in all he did. He had great respect for learning, founded the University of Duisburg and the Berlin Library, and was a patron of Pufendorf. In his reign the first bookshop was opened in Berlin, a town which grew from a mere 7,000 to 20,000 during his reign, and for the first time students were encouraged to study abroad. Above all, he was the founder of the Prussian despotism, the superstructure of which was erected by his grandson Frederick William I.

Frederick I

The Great Elector was succeeded by his son the Elector Frederick III (1688–1713). A weak and somewhat deformed man, he nonetheless won the affection of his people as did no other Hohenzollern. In foreign affairs he anchored Prussia to the Habsburg alliance in return for the Imperial consent to the conversion of Prussia into a kingdom. Accordingly in 1701, with great ceremony, the Elector Frederick III crowned himself King Frederick I.[1] This has often been regarded as meagre reward for Prussia's services to the Habsburgs, but in the eyes of the Europe of the time it was a considerable achievement, and a recognition of the fact that Prussia was now the strongest State in North Germany. Much of the reign was spent at war, for Prussia took full part in the War of the League of Augsburg and the War of the Spanish Succession. There were no appreciable territorial gains, but there was a beginning of the military tradition which was so

[1] He was to be King *in* Prussia, but Elector in the Holy Roman Empire.

characteristic a mark of eighteenth-century Prussia. There were also heavy financial burdens and administrative difficulties with which Frederick was quite unable to cope and which he left to his successor. In cultural matters the reign marks an important stage in Prussian development. Frederick loved the show and splendour of monarchy. He not only prided himself on having fine troops; he also built beautiful palaces and surrounded himself with elaborate ceremony. He loved to sit on his throne in full regalia, surrounded by the Margraves his brothers, the knights of the Order of the Black Eagle (which he founded), chamberlains, privy councillors and generals. His bodyguard had splendid uniforms of white satin edged with gold lace. Dinner was announced by twenty-four trumpeters; his servants wore blue liveries trimmed with gold lace, and there was an orchestra and even the traditional jester. Potsdam had been built by the Great Elector; Frederick I built a new palace in Berlin, and also Charlottenburg as a palace for his Queen, Sophie Charlotte. She was a remarkable woman, deeply imbued with the new spirit of the Enlightenment, and delighting in religious and philosophical discussions. She was much impressed by Bayle's *Dictionnaire*, and was the patron and close friend of the great Leibniz. She loved to listen to discussions on the differences between the Protestant and Catholic viewpoints, on Natural Law, or the new science. The two great trends of the time, Pietism and Natural Law, tended to centre in the University of Halle which Frederick I founded in 1692. At its opening Paul von Fuchs had asked: 'Where do you find a nation which has become mighty without science?' By now Prussia had four universities, at Königsberg, Frankfurt-on-Oder, Duisburg and Halle, and in 1700 Leibniz, an indefatigable worker in philosophy, science and mathematics, persuaded the King to found an Academy of Sciences on the model of the London Royal Society. Samuel Pufendorf, the great philosopher of Natural Law, and his disciple Christian Thomasius, both enjoyed royal patronage at Halle. Frederick I welcomed as immigrants both craftsmen and scholars, and among the latter were Jacob Lenfant, historian of the Council of Trent, Isaac de Beausobre, translator of the New Testament, Vignoles, the student of Biblical exigesis, and Philip Speuer, the leading Pietist of his day. It was in this reign that many of the ideas which later influenced Frederick the Great found their way into the hitherto intellectually starved lands of Prussia.

Frederick William I

Frederick William I (1713–40) was a ruler of very different calibre. His father had left him an enormous deficit; he had been exasperated by the waste, confusion and futility of much that he had witnessed of his father's reign, and he determined to prevent their recurrence in his own. He was convinced that it was not by ceremony or display that a king became powerful, but by the size of his army. He dispensed with Court ceremony, dismissed great numbers of Court officials and cut the salaries of those who remained. He dismissed all artists and architects, and his Master of Ceremonies, Besser, soon found he had nothing to do, and eventually found more active employment in Saxony. All this was a blow to the luxury trades which had been growing up in Berlin, but they were speedily converted to supplying the needs of the army. He was passionately devoted to his army. As Crown Prince he had had his own battalion of hand-picked recruits, which later became the nucleus for his famous Potsdam regiment. In his first year he raised seven new regiments, and to all his troops he showed, as he said, 'a fatherly care', although this did not mean that discipline was not brutally severe. At his accession Prussia had a standing army of 45,000 men; he almost doubled it in the course of his reign. He had a passion for enormously tall men for his Potsdam Guards, and was prepared to pay absurd sums to procure them. Often his agents abroad kidnapped them and smuggled them into Brandenburg; Hanover in particular suffered severely from this practice.

With all his military preparations, he was a man of peace. He had seen too much of the wastage of war during his father's reign, and he sought to further his ends by diplomacy rather than force. But his approach to diplomacy was naïve and amateurish, and he was often the dupe of foreign diplomats. He had a simple faith in the need for the continuance of the Habsburg alliance. His only excursion into war was in 1715 when Charles XII returned from Turkey, bent as ever on the continuance of war, and occupied Stralsund. Frederick William at once attacked, drove out the Swedes and occupied Stralsund. In 1720 he signed a Peace with Sweden by which Prussia annexed the port of Stettin and Pomeranian territory west of the river Oder. He continued his predecessor's policy of close relations with the Dutch and with England, and this was strengthened when the Hanoverians succeeded to the English throne, for Frederick William's mother was George I's sister, and Frederick William married George I's daughter. The two families would meet together at Göhrde or Herrenhausen (the gardens of which were said to be the finest in Europe) when George I was in Germany. It was at the latter in 1725 that George I's Minister Lord Townshend persuaded Frederick William to desert for the moment his alliance with the Emperor and join the League of Hanover.[1] But Frederick William was always ill at ease with this new departure, and in 1728 the Habsburg envoy Seckendorf found it easy to persuade the King to return to the fold ('I am far more of an imperialist than of a Hanoverian') when by the Treaty of Berlin Frederick William recognised the Pragmatic Sanction in return for a Habsburg promise to support Prussia's claim to Berg.[2] In this way Frederick William helped to bolster the illusion of Habsburg strength in Europe and to conceal the strength of his own kingdom.

The genius of Frederick William I lay, not in foreign, but in domestic affairs. His political theory was simple. In the first letter he wrote after his accession he declared:

> Tell the Prince of Anhalt that I am the finance minister and the field marshal of the King of Prussia; this will uphold the King of Prussia as he should be upheld.

In short, the road to Prussian power lay through a strong army and healthy finances. He was convinced of the need to supervise every detail of government himself, for Ministers were rogues or incompetent or both. He had studied carefully the Dutch system of government. He had been deeply impressed by the duties of a monarch as portrayed in Fénelon's *Télemaque*. If he drove his subjects hard, it was at least true that he drove himself still harder; in everything the test was the same: what were the needs of Prussian power? At all times he was the supreme ruler, quite capable of laying about him with his cane on the back of some offending Minister, some judge who had been too lenient, some postmaster who neglected his duties, or some Berliner who made a nuisance of himself in the streets. All governmental orders

---

[1] See p. 278.

[2] The Jülich-Berg Question was a vexed one which had continued since 1609. In 1624 the Elector of Brandenburg had received Cleves, Mark and Ravensberg as his share of the inheritance, and now that the House of Neuburg was facing extinction, Frederick William claimed Jülich and Berg as well. The Habsburgs did not keep their promise, and Berg became Prussian only in 1814.

emanated from the King himself, and to carry out his orders he devised the most efficient bureaucratic machine in Europe. Instead of the French ministerial system he preferred the Swedish collegiate organisation. In 1723 he established a General Directory of four departments, each responsible for certain provinces, consisting of a ministerial chief and four or five assistants. Its business was simply to carry out the orders the King had framed, and never to frame policy itself. It was especially concerned with the collection of taxes, the provisioning of the army and the administration of the royal estates. The latter constituted about one-third of the kingdom and largely paid for the army. The King formulated a policy, and then left it to the General Directory to work out the details. The system worked well during the years of peace under Frederick William I, but later under Frederick the Great the business of government so increased that the Directory was often overwhelmed, and Frederick became increasingly dissatisfied with it.

Under the General Directory were the seventeen provincial chambers (*Kriegs-und-Domänen-Kammern*) and these were the most successful instruments of the Prussian bureaucracy. Although strictly subordinate to the General Directory, and often operating under the eye of the King himself, these provincial chambers were the real governors of the country. Their prime function was to collect revenues, encourage agriculture, establish colonies, reclaim wastes and swamps, and foster new industries. In fact there was no aspect of provincial life which did not at some time come within their authority. A provincial chamber consisted of a president, two directors and some fifteen or twenty members together with numerous junior officials, and all decisions were taken collectively. All careers were open to talent, and an industrious junior could rise to the highest positions. Originality and initiative were not required; the indispensable requisite was absolute obedience. To make assurances of bureaucratic efficiency doubly sure, the General Directory and every provincial chamber contained a special royal agent, or *fiscal*, to keep a close watch on the interests of the Monarch. In addition, the King required secret reports annually on all bureaucrats, and an official suspected of corruption or inefficiency might find himself in the Spandau prison without ever being faced with the charges against him. On the whole the system worked with amazing efficiency and honesty. The entire kingdom was administered by only about 14,000 civil servants (less than one-tenth the proportion of the population a twentieth-century State would think necessary), and it was they who provided Frederick the Great with the money and supplies necessary for his wars, supported a first-rate army, established some 300,000 colonists on the land, developed mining in Westphalia, the fisheries in Ostfriesland, the industrial re-adjustments in Silesia after its conquest, and agriculture everywhere. Civil servants were poorly paid, but were highly trained and singularly honest. Many of them were university graduates[1] and had gone through a long course of practical training on the royal domains and farms. Frederick William I was the architect of a system which in the main continued until 1806. The strength of the Prussian State lay in the fusion of the economic and military power of its Junkers with the efficiency of its bureaucracy. Frederick William I regarded his nobility with some suspicion, and often preferred to employ commoners or foreigners. Frederick the Great also employed foreigners when it suited him, but in general he relied heavily upon his nobility, and thus he drew closer the bonds between the Monarchy and the Prussian Junkers.

The two servants upon whom Frederick William most relied were, significantly, his commander-in-chief, Prince Leopold of Anhalt-Dessau ('Old Dessauer') and his Minister, Field-Marshal von Grumbkow. Samuel Cocceji became Minister of Justice and began tentative steps to humanise the law, but few other names are worth remembering during the reign, for policy was always that of the King. He continued his predecessor's policy of religious toleration. He greatly favoured the spread of a practical education, and in the course of his reign established over a thousand schools for the sons of peasants. In spite of the burdens of taxation, town life grew, and Berlin increased to nearly 70,000 people. Frederick William was a ceaseless worker, his only relaxations being a wild boar hunt, and the discussion of the events of the day with his intimates amidst clouds of smoke in his 'tobacco parliaments'. It was in these that much of the hatred against his eldest son was fomented.

The future Frederick the Great was born in 1712, and his early education was entrusted to his father's old governess, Mme. de Rocoulles,

---

[1] Frederick William I was the first European monarch to establish University Chairs of Economics—at Halle and Frankfurt.

a Huguenot refugee from whom he learnt to speak French better than German. The King minutely organised the boy's day from 6 a.m. to 10.30 p.m., and the boy had learnt all the fifty-four movements of the Prussian drill by the time he was five. Frederick said that he owed his real education to his tutor, Duhan de Jandun, who, contrary to the King's strict orders, introduced him to classical and French authors. Frederick William had a deep suspicion and hatred of ideas which were alien to him. Frederick once described to Henri de Catt the violence to which he was habitually subjected:

> I was still a child, learning a little Latin, and was declining *mensa*, *dominus*, *ardor* with my master, when suddenly my father entered the room. "What are you doing there?"—"Papa, I am declining *mensa*", I said in a childish voice which should have touched him. "Ah, rogue, Latin to my son! Get out of my sight", and he gave him a volley of kicks and blows with his stick, accompanying him in this cruel manner into the inner room. Frightened . . . and shivering with fear, I hid under the table thinking that I should there be in safety. . . . He took me by the hair, pulled me from under the table, and dragged me thus into the middle of the room, finishing by smacking my face several times: "If I catch you again at your *mensa*, I will let you know what is what."

By the time Frederick was fourteen the King was treating him with the greatest hostility. Frederick had begun to show a preference for French ideas and affectations which his father detested, and this in preference to military training, although Frederick's interest in the army was always real and genuine. Again, Frederick William was pathologically suspicious of all those about him, and he was convinced that the Queen's circle at Monbijou, including Frederick and his sister Wilhelmine, were in an English conspiracy against him. The King's leanings towards England ceased when his hated rival and boyhood enemy, George II came to the throne. He refused a double marriage of Frederick and Wilhelmine to Princess Amelia and the Prince of Wales, children of George II, and was convinced that the latter was plotting against him. He was furious when he learnt that George II had paid the Crown Prince's debts. There were also those in the King's tobacco parliament, not least Grumbkow, who thought it in their own interests to spread all the rumours and suspicions in their power against the Crown Prince, and it was easy to enflame the King with jealousy against 'the Rising Sun' as he called the Crown Prince. His taunts to his son became unbearable:

> Had I been treated in this way by my father, I would have put a bullet through my head, but you have not it in you even to do that.

Frederick wrote to his mother:

> I am driven to extremity. I have too much honour to endure such treatment, and I am resolved to end it one way or another.

In 1730 Frederick William thrashed his son in full view of all the guests at a great reception given by the King of Saxony. It was the last straw, and Frederick had determined to escape to France. The plans were laid in co-operation with his friend the young lieutenant von Katte, but they miscarried, and when the King learnt of it his wrath was uncontrollable. He had Frederick and Katte court-martialled. The court-martial, much embarrassed, replied that they were incompetent to try the Crown Prince, and Katte was sentenced to life imprisonment. The King instructed them to sentence Katte to death, and he had the sentence carried out before Frederick's eyes. Frederick fainted at the sight, and for a time was in delirium. When he recovered he thought his execution was to follow. In fairness to the King, it must be said that he was much concerned lest clemency to his son should be interpreted as weakness which would destroy the royal authority. His principle, he said, should be 'Fiat iustitia et pereat mundus'. But the Emperor appealed for mercy, and eventually Frederick William pardoned his son, and sent him to Küstrin to work in the provincial chamber. In 1733 Frederick married, and was then given a residence at Rheinsberg, near Ruppin. He would have no relations with his wife, but at Rheinsberg (completed 1736) he began the only period of happiness he had known, surrounded by his friends, playing his flute, composing music and poetry, and reading French literature and the philosophy of the Enlightenment. In 1736 he began his famous correspondence with Voltaire. Voltaire's was already the greatest contemporary name in literature, and Frederick sought to learn from him the art of perfect composition in French. All his life he was an inveterate scribbler of verse, and these he sent to the unfortunate Voltaire to correct. Voltaire, for his part, was flattered to have gained as a disciple one who would soon be a powerful monarch. He therefore replied with fulsome flattery as to his wisdom, and tactful criticisms as to his prosody, at the same time encouraging him in his Enlightenment:

> One of the greatest boons to mankind will be to overthrow superstition and fanaticism, to prevent those in authority persecuting others who think differently. Assuredly philosophers will never disturb States: why then disturb philosophers? You see, worthy heir of the spirit of Marcus Aurelius, with what freedom I speak to you.

The relationship continued on this footing until Frederick came to the throne; it was never quite the same after that. In 1750 Frederick at last persuaded Voltaire to go to live in Prussia, but by this time neither trusted the other (with good reason, for Voltaire was in the pay of the French government, and Frederick wanted Voltaire only for his learning). A quarrel developed in 1752, and in the following year Voltaire left Prussia; the correspondence was resumed in 1757 and continued until Voltaire's death in 1778. But long before then Frederick habitually spoke of him as an immoral rogue who could not be trusted.

Frederick William I ordered his end as he had ordered everything else during his reign. He laid down minute instructions for his funeral, and had his coffin placed ready beside his bed. He gathered the Court for hymn-singing, and when they sang 'Naked I came into this world, naked I shall leave it', he interjected—'That isn't true, I shall have my uniform on.' And thus, having ordered everything to his wishes, and having been reconciled to his son, he died on June 1st 1740. Frederick was for a time overcome with genuine grief. He had had a real affection for his turbulent father, and years later came to appreciate his work more fully: he declared to de Catt:

> What a terrible man, but what a just man, and intelligent and fitted for State affairs! You have no idea of the thorough order he put into all branches of the government. There never was a prince more capable than he of entering into the smallest details, and he entered into them, he used to say, to bring all parts of the State to the greatest degree of perfection. It is therefore through his care, his indefatigable labour, his great and admirable economy, and that severe discipline he brought into the army which he created, that it has been possible for me to do what I have done to the present.

This was true. Frederick William left his son an overflowing Treasury, an annual revenue of 7 million thalers, flourishing industry, and an

army of over 80,000 men. Frederick wrote to Voltaire that the Lithuanian province of East Prussia was, by colonisation 'entirely the
creation of the King my father. Now the richest and most prosperous
of our provinces, Lithuania, at the beginning of the present century
was a desert.' It then had a population of half a million. Frederick
indeed owed an enormous amount to his father. He inherited from
him a flourishing State, the finest army in Europe, and an administrative system which in the main continued unchanged during Frederick's
reign. Frederick's achievement was to display the new Prussian
strength to the world.

Frederick the Great

The first acts of the new reign were largely in accordance with the new
ideas of the Enlightenment. Frederick abolished torture, ended the
practice of public penance for unmarried mothers, curbed cruelty in
the army, abolished press censorship, limited the hunting privileges of
the Crown and nobility in the interests of the peasantry, re-established
the Academy of Berlin[1] and recalled the philosopher Christian Wolff
to his Chair at Halle. Even more remarkable was the publication in
September 1740 of his pamphlet 'Anti-machiavel', which, although
anonymous, was soon known to be from his pen.

> Machiavelli maintains that, in this wicked and degenerate world, it is
> certain ruin to be strictly honest: For my part, I affirm that, in order
> to be safe, it is necessary to be virtuous. Men are commonly neither
> wholly good nor wholly bad; but both good and bad. . . . But without
> supposing all the world to be wicked, how could Machiavelli have
> supported his detestable maxims?

It has always seemed strange that this attack on Machiavelli should
have come from the man who three months later launched an unpro-
voked attack upon Silesia, and it has been variously explained away
either by regarding the 'Anti-machiavel' as merely a juvenile work of
little importance once the writer had become king, or by regarding
Frederick's enlightenment as no more than skin deep, a mere affecta-
tion which it was fashionable to assume but which had no relevance
to practical politics. Neither interpretation will quite do. The 'Anti-

---

[1] Maupertuis, who had led a French expedition to test whether the earth was an
oblate spheroid, became its President, and soon its virtual dictator. Voltaire's satire on
him led to the famous quarrel with Frederick the Great.

machiavel' was certainly a juvenile work, containing little deep thought, yet it touched on problems which concerned Frederick all his life. Nor is it true to say that Frederick's enlightenment was merely skin-deep. He was profoundly influenced by the ideas of the new philosophy, but what he had to discover, and what the *philosophes* did not tell him, was how the new ideas could be reconciled with the practical problems of political power. He embraced the new trust in human reason; he accepted the new ideal of 'humanity'; he believed that it was the business of the State (i.e. the Ruler) to provide for the happiness of the people. He did not believe that the State existed for the gratification of the ruler; instead the ruler must regard himself as 'the first servant of the State'. He wrote that the ruler must look upon his subjects not merely as his equals, but in certain respects his masters. Thus in 1757 he instructed his Ministers:

> If it should be my fate to be taken prisoner, then I forbid anyone to have the smallest concern for my person, or to pay the slightest attention to anything I might write from my place of confinement. . . . I shall sacrifice myself to the State, and everyone must then obey my brother.

In his *Essay on the Forms of Government* he wrote:

> Men granted pre-eminence to one of their equals in expectation that he should do them certain services. These services consisted in the maintenance of the laws; a strict execution of justice; an employment of his whole powers; to prevent any corruption of manners; and to defend the State against its enemies. It is the duty of this magistrate to pay attention to agriculture; it should be his care that provisions for the nation should be in abundance, and that commerce and industry should be abundant. He is a perpetual sentinel. . . . Princes and monarchs are not invested with supreme authority that they may, with impunity, riot in debauchery and voluptuousness. . . . The sovereign represents the State; he and his people represent but one body which can only be happy as far as united by concord. The prince is to the nation he governs what the head is to the man; it is his duty to see, think and act for the whole community.

Throughout his life Frederick sought for the answers to questions of religion, morality and power which puzzled him. Above all he turned to French literature for guidance. He never welded the results of his reading into a coherent philosophy. At one moment in conversation to Henri de Catt he would proclaim the supremacy of a moral order, and at another deny it:

> Do you believe that, if when walking in my garden at Sans Souci I tread on an ant-hill, I think even that there in my road are little beings who are running about worrying themselves?... No, my friend, unburden yourself of this self-esteem, which misleads you by presenting heaven to you as being ceaselessly occupied with your preservation, and get this well into your head, that nature does not concern itself about individuals, but only about the species: the latter must not perish.

But that Frederick was deeply concerned with the moral nature of government is illustrated in a remarkable way by his reading. Of all writers the one he most admired was Racine; he would read his tragedies over and over again, and much of them he learnt by heart. And of all Racine his favourite passage, and one over which he would weep, was that from *Britannicus*, in which the ruler is faced with the choice between governing well and governing ill:

> And, Sire, is it not enough for your desires
> That the public weal should be one of the blessings of your reign?
> It is for you to choose, you still are master of your fate.
> Virtuous hitherto, you can be virtuous always.
> The way is plainly traced, nothing more holds you back.
> You have only to march forward from virtue to virtue.
> But if you follow the precepts of your flatterers
> You will need, Sire, to run from one wrong to another,
> To sustain the rigours of your rule by yet more cruelty,
> And wash your bloodstained arms in yet more blood.
> Britannicus, by his death, will excite the fervour of his friends,
> Ready as they are to take up his cause,
> These avengers will find new supporters
> Who, even after their death, will have successors.
> You are lighting a fire which will never go out.
> Feared by the whole universe, you will need to fear all,
> Always to punish, always to fear for your projects,
> And reckon all your subjects as your foes.
> Ah! Sire, does the happy experience
> Of your early years make you hate your innocence?
> Have you in mind the happiness which marked them?
> In what peace of mind, of Heaven you spent them?
> What joy to think and say to yourself
> "Everywhere, at this moment, I am blessed and loved."[1]

[1] Translation by courtesy of F. H. Voigt.

Frederick, with all his approval of the *philosophes*, had never entirely lost his early belief in Predestination. He believed in a moral order the contravention of which brought inevitable retribution, and he had seen the misery brought by the ravages of war. The problem of 'Britannicus' was his own, and the mention of 'his early years' reduced him to tears. Once when Catt referred to the glories of war, Frederick replied:

> Ah, deuce take it, a fine glory indeed, of burned villages, towns in ashes, thousands of suffering men, as many massacred, horrors on all sides, and finally finishing oneself off; speak no more of it; my hair stands on end at the thought of it.

With Frederick the problem always remained the same: how to recon-cile the pursuit of power with the requirements of morality.

The first act of the new reign was when Frederick made clear to his Ministers that his authority was supreme, that they had no share in determining policy. The district of Herstal had refused allegiance to Prussia and declared for the Bishop of Liège. Without so much as warning his Ministers, Frederick sent his troops to occupy the Bishopric, and extracted a war indemnity. He then sold Herstal to the Bishop for 240,000 thalers, double the sum his father had thought it was worth. It was a warning to Europe. In October 1740 the Emperor Charles VI died, and Frederick at once determined to profit by it. He wrote to Voltaire:

> His death alters all my pacific ideas and I think that next June it will be rather a matter of gunpowder. . . . Now is the moment for a com-plete change in the old System of Europe.

Brandenburg had had long-standing and reputable claims to three areas in Silesia, namely Wohlau, Brieg and Jägendorf; and Ludewig, professor at Halle, had compiled voluminous proof of the rights to the whole of Silesia in the event of the failure of the male line of the Habsburgs. But none of this justified a sudden attack. In December 1740 the Prussian army marched into Silesia, and on January 3rd Frederick entered Breslau in triumph.

There is little doubt that his chief concern here was to cut a figure in Europe. To appreciate this we must recall two facts. First, Frederick William had made the name of Prussia a laughing-stock in

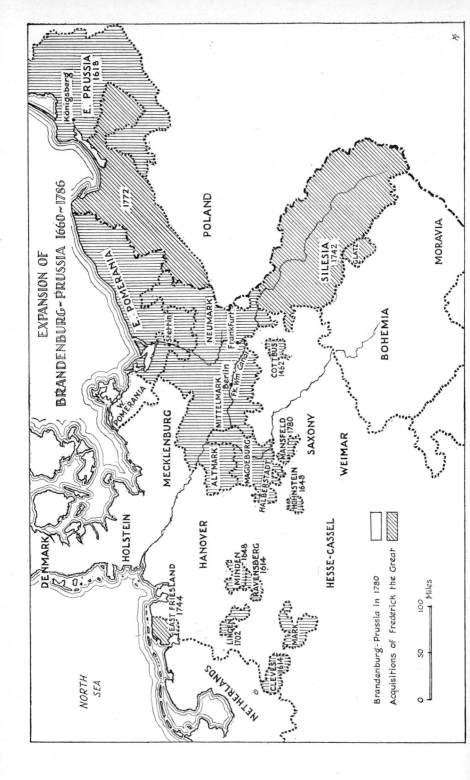

EXPANSION OF
BRANDENBURG~PRUSSIA 1660~1786

NORTH SEA

DENMARK

HOLSTEIN

MECKLENBURG

W. POMERANIA

E. POMERANIA

Stettin

NEUMARK

Frankfurt

MITTELMARK

Berlin

Fk.Wm.Canal

COTTBUS
1621

ALTMARK

MAGDEBURG

MANSFELD
1780

HALBERSTADT

HOHNSTEIN
1648

SAXONY

WEIMAR

BOHEMIA

MORAVIA

POLAND

1772

E. PRUSSIA
1618

Königsberg

SILESIA
1742

GLATZ

HANOVER

EAST FRIESLAND
1744

LINGEN
1702

MINDEN
1648

RAVENSBERG
1614

MARK

CLEVES
1614

NETHERLANDS

HESSE-CASSEL

☐ Brandenburg-Prussia in 1780
▨ Acquisitions of Frederick the Great

0   50   100
Miles

Europe. He well knew his own incompetence in handling foreign affairs; he once admitted: 'I was not cut out for higher statecraft: in this I am no use to man or beast.' Foreign diplomats, particularly Austrian, had been able to make him dance to their tune, and only recently they had coolly broken their promises about Jülich-Berg. The second fact is a still more personal one. Frederick had been bullied and even thrashed before the very eyes of Europe. It was a most natural reaction now to show Europe that he was not the *petit-maître* his father had always declared him to be, and to assert the power which his father had built up but never dared to display in a European conflict. It is significant that he instructed his special envoy to Versailles, Colonel von Camas, to represent him there as a hot-head of great vanity, eager for action, and capable of setting all Europe alight. At this moment Frederick undoubtedly enjoyed power for its own sake. The death of the Emperor, aged only fifty-five, at this very time seemed an invitation from destiny. Frederick did not calculate the consequences; he had not even made careful military preparations; he simply invaded Silesia.

This is the governing event of the reign of Frederick the Great, and we should therefore consider its significance further. It is the most conspicuous instance in modern history of a second-rate State turning itself in the eyes of Europe into a 'great Power' by a piece of naked aggression. In fact, the spade-work for this had, as we have seen, been done by Frederick's predecessors since 1640, but to Europe it appeared that there had come about a sudden change in the balance of power. Essentially it was a reckless act, a complete denial of the moral principles he had advocated in the 'Anti-machiavel'. The cynic might say that it was worse than a sin, it was a blunder, for Prussia was completely isolated, without allies, and without diplomatic preparation, and it plunged Prussia into a period of conflict lasting twenty-three years, in which only the super-human endurance of King and people prevented catastrophe. His advisers, General von Schwerin and Foreign Minister von Podewils, tried in vain to dissuade him, but he alone determined policy. In its radical breach with the European order it is perhaps the central event of eighteenth-century international affairs, and it prepared the way for the partitions of Poland. Its best justification is that it succeeded in its objective of making Prussia a great Power.

To the moral issue raised by the invasion Frederick returned when he came to write his *Histoire de mon temps*, 1740–45:

> Posterity, perhaps, will see with surprise, in these memoirs, a recital of treaties concluded and broken. Numerous as such examples are, example would not justify the author of this work, if he had not better reasons to excuse his conduct. The interest of State ought to serve as the rule to the monarch. . . . To me it appears evident that a private person ought to be scrupulously tenacious of his promise, even though he should have made it inconsiderately. If he is injured he can have recourse to the protection of the laws. . . . But where is the tribunal that can redress a monarch's wrongs, should another monarch forfeit his engagement?

In short, *raison d'état* is the only safe guide for the Monarch; which was what Machiavelli had taught. With all his genuine concern for the welfare of his subjects, Frederick plunged into years of war in pursuit of *raison d'état*, and thus rendered himself one of the greatest Machiavellians in modern history. With all his apologies for making war it is clear that he intended history to judge him upon his achievement in war, for of the 539 pages of the first volume of his *Memoirs*, only a few pages are devoted to internal reforms; the remainder are devoted to his military and diplomatic achievements.[1]

Frederick's administrative system was essentially that inherited from his father, but there were some changes. The collegiate system worked less successfully as government became more intricate, and from time to time Frederick withdrew particular matters from the jurisdiction of the General Directory and placed them under particular Ministries. Commerce was so dealt with in 1741, as was Silesia in 1742 and the army in 1746. A characteristic incident occurred in 1765, when the King demanded that the revenues be increased by 2 million thalers. The General Directory declared it to be impossible as the country was already exhausted. In anger the King introduced the French system of customs administration (*Régie*) under a tax-farmer De Launay, who duly delivered the increased revenues, and Frederick was encouraged to extend the experiment to mining (under the expert Heinitz) and finance and banking (under Schulenburg). Frederick dealt less and less with the General Directory collectively, and more with individual Ministers, and thus prepared the way for its final disappearance in 1806.

[1] For the wars, see Chapter 11.

Another change which came over the administration was its growing dependence on the Junkers. Under the Great Elector most civil servants were nobles, though many were immigrants, and some were commoners, mostly lawyers. Under Frederick I many able bourgeoisie, merchants for example, could rise to high office (the merchant Krautt, the richest man in Berlin, was a Minister and died in 1723; Danckelmann, another Minister, was of low birth). Frederick William I mistrusted the nobility, who had seemed to threaten the power of the Monarchy, and he preferred to promote men of humble origin who were devoted to him. In fact his reign has been called 'the golden age of the able commoner'. His policy succeeded, for during his reign there was a marked rise of bureaucratic standards, and most of his secretaries and councillors were commoners, although the nobility continued to play their part in the command of the army. In 1737 of the 118 councillors and secretaries of the central administration only 36 were nobles. But in the provincial chambers the Junkers always retained their predominance. Under Frederick the Great the Junkers consolidated their position. They retained to the full their authority over their serfs, they dominated the provincial chambers, they provided almost all the army officers above the rank of captain, and Frederick preferred nobles for all appointments about him. In this way he sought to build up an *ésprit de corps* among the nobility which would be a powerful buttress to the State.

This was one of the reasons why Frederick the Great made no attempt to relieve the burdens of serfdom in his dominions, in spite of his agreement with the views of the Enlightenment upon it. In his *Essays on the Forms of Government* he wrote:

> Serfdom, of all conditions, is the most unhappy, and that at which humanity most revolts. Certainly no man was born to be the slave of his equal. . . . (Yet) whoever should suddenly desire to abolish this abominable administration would entirely overthrow the mode of managing estates, and must be obliged, in part, to indemnify the nobility for the losses their rents must suffer.

It would have involved a social revolution he would not undertake.

One of the most distinguished men of the period was Samuel von Cocceji (1679–1755), a great scholar and lawyer, formerly professor of law at Frankfurt whose father had been ennobled. He became

Minister of Justice in 1727, and in 1737 began the reform of the corrupt judicial system. But he was hated by the old Junkers, and was dismissed in 1739. He won the favour of Frederick the Great, and was reinstated in 1746 with the title of Lord Chancellor. He was trusted by the King more than any other Minister, except perhaps De Launay, and for nine years he attempted the reform and codification of the law. His object was to give a single law for the whole State, and provide a legal system which was independent of the executive. He did nothing to undermine Junker privileges, indeed he reinforced them. But many of his ideas were inspired by the concept of Natural Law, and Frederick had a passionate desire to see that justice was done. There was the famous case, of which all Europe knew, of miller Arnold, whose interests were protected by the King against what he thought was a conspiracy of the nobility to deprive him of his rights.[1] One of his favourite stories was of the woman who asked the King of Epirus, when he refused to listen to her complaints, 'What, then, was the King for, if he would not do her right?'

Once Frederick was dead, Cocceji's work became part of the process by which Prussia was converted from a personal despotism into a legal absolutism; one might speak of a 'constitutional absolutism'. Thus, for instance, in 1770 Frederick was able to enforce a strict educational qualification for the civil service, and this, together with the growing complexity of the State, made appointments far less a matter of personal choice by the sovereign. This tendency was carried further by the General Legal Code of 1794 which, although it reserved all rights for the nobility, put the King under the law, and protected the bureaucracy from the arbitrary actions of the Crown. In this way it was seen, once the dynamic hand of Frederick the Great had been removed, that Prussian government had subtly changed its character. Professor Kraus, Kant's colleague at Königsberg, summed it up in 1799 when he wrote:

> The Prussian State, far from being an unlimited monarchy, is but a thinly-veiled aristocracy. This aristocracy rules the country in undisguised form as a bureaucracy.

So long as he lived, however, Frederick maintained the closest per-

---

[1] On the other hand a judge who stood in the way of what the King thought to be justice was instantly dismissed and imprisoned.

sonal control over policy. Mirabeau has left a clear picture of Frederick's system:

> The king of Prussia rose at five o'clock in the morning[1] and then worked for two or three hours, not with his ministers, but with his secretaries. The difference is immense. Ministers have authority and opinions, and exert influence upon the purposes even of enlightened princes, while they direct those of ordinary sovereigns. The secretaries of the king of Prussia were only scribes (*Schreiber*). . . . Had any of them been so rash as to express his opinion regarding the matters on which he was reporting, the king would have thought that the man had lost his mind.

The weakness of the system, Mirabeau saw, was that it depended upon the continuance of one great man:

> The mistakes of kings must be included when one reckons the strength of states. The Prussian monarchy is so constituted that it can support no calamity whatever, not even the one which is inevitable in the long run—a government without ability. . . . One man, even the best of men, cannot do everything.

But so long as Frederick lived he personally supervised the development of his lands. He continued the colonisation of waste lands, and wrote with pride in his *Memoirs* of the drainage of the marshes along the Oder from Swinemunde to Küstrin, and the establishment of 2,000 families, and from Schwedt to Stettin where a further 1,200 families were settled. New industries were established in a number of towns, velours at Berlin and Potsdam, sugar refineries, leather, silks elsewhere. In fifteen years he doubled the yield of the customs. But during the Seven Years' War his lands were terribly devastated by invading armies. He himself described the scene:

> To have an idea of the general upheaval of the country, to show the desolation and discouragement of subjects, it is necessary to imagine whole countries ravaged, in which one could scarcely discover traces of former habitations, towns ruined completely, others half burnt, 13,000 houses of which not even the vestiges remained, lands not sown, inhabitants destitute of food, farmers lacking 60,000 horses for labour, and in the provinces a decrease of 500,000 people compared with the year 1756, which is considerable in a population of 4,500,000 souls. The nobility and peasantry had been pillaged, ransomed, foraged by so many different armies that only life and miserable rage to cover their nakedness remained to them.

[1] 4 a.m. was nearer the truth.

G

The King provided funds to rebuild towns and villages, issued grain from the reserves for seed-planting, requisitioned horses for agricultural work, discharged some areas from the obligation to pay taxes for from six months to two years. He did everything possible to start new industries, and by 1773 there were 264 new factories of various kinds in operation, including tobacco and porcelain. A further 3,500 families were settled in the Netze–Warthe area, and 2,000 more near Magdeburg. Silesian industries were encouraged, and there was a re-distribution of land by the partition of many of the great estates of the nobility (who now lost their tax exemption). In this way some 213 new villages were established. Much of this was done under the personal eye of the King, who toured his lands talking to farmers, enquiring into their crops and herds, comparing new production figures with the old, urging on this farmer that his cows needed rock salt, noting that such-and-such village lacked building materials, or that such an industry was languishing. The strictest principles of self-sufficiency were enforced, and the export of raw materials such as wool was forbidden. In his *Memoirs* Frederick proudly claimed that between 1740 and 1779 the total population of his dominions increased by 1,100,000,[1] and he added:

> The king could not, with all these expenses, maintain the ostentation so common in great Courts: he lived as a private person in order not to shirk his chief duties.

This was true in many ways. He dressed simply, often carelessly, in clothes heavy with snuff, so that the English envoy found it difficult to approach him without sneezing. His bedroom was as simple as a barrack-room. James Harris wrote in his *Diary* that it was notorious how little the King paid his courtiers, and how little he spent on entertainment:

> On these occasions he suffers no-one to interfere, but orders every-thing, down to the quantity of candles, himself. . . . All the apart-ments, except those immediately dedicated to supper or cards, were lighted by one single candle. The supper itself was badly served, and without dessert—the wines bad, and the quantity of them stinted.

But on the other hand, Harris commented on the expenditure on building, for instance:

[1] It is probable that this was a considerable under-estimate.

the sum of money[1] sunk in erecting the Château Neuf, near Sans Souci, where every room is furnished in the most expensive manner, and that not in taste, but with loads of gilding, and tawdry furniture.

The truth is that Frederick the Great was an artist in kingship. He was the first to give embodiment to the new idea of Enlightened Despotism, that is, to abandon the idea that the Monarch's authority rested simply on custom or divine right, and to base it squarely on the utilitarian idea of service to the happiness of his people.[2] It is often said that the object was to make absolutism respectable, that this was in fact the age of 'repentent absolutism'. Frederick certainly seized the imagination of Europe. The *philosophes* lauded him as one of themselves;[3] other rulers attempted to imitate him. Dr. Johnson was greatly attracted by his personality. He referred to him as 'an honest fellow', thought him the only great king in Europe, and commented that under such a despot a man might be appointed to an office simply because he was the fittest for it, an occurrence which was never found in England. To the Habsburgs, on the other hand, 'Old Fritz' was always the very devil incarnate.

In the Europe of the years after 1763 Frederick was aware of two things above all, the desperate need of Prussia for peace, and the enormous power of Russia in eastern Europe. Both considerations led directly to the Russo-Prussian alliance of 1764, which secured him against Russian attack, at the price of the possibility that Prussia must aid Catherine in her expansionist policy. The skill with which Frederick avoided this danger is described in a later chapter.[4] The Partition of Poland of 1772 was a master-stroke of Frederickian diplomacy, whereby he united the two main portions of his dominions by the annexation of West Prussia, and at the same time diverted Russia from the dismemberment of the Ottoman Empire. Thereafter the Prussian alliance had served Catherine's purpose, and she drew closer

[1] Two million thalers. His annual budget usually showed a 2 million thalers' surplus and when he died he left a treasure of 51 millions.

[2] The imagination of Europe was often illuminated by anecdotes of the great man. One of the neatest stories told against him was of a conversation with the English envoy Sir Andrew Mitchell, after the news of the fall of Quebec. Frederick asked 'Est-ce vra, qu'à la fin vous avez pris Quebec?' 'Oui, Sire,' said Sir Andrew, 'par l'aide de Dieu.' 'Comment,' dit le Roi, 'Le bon Dieu est-il aussi de vos alliés?' 'Oui, Sire, et c'est le seul à qui nous ne payions pas de subsides.'

[3] On the other hand, Frederick detested Diderot and Baron d'Holbach.

[4] See Chapter 12.

to Austria in preparation for a final onslaught on the Turk. Frederick was isolated in Europe, but Joseph II played directly into his hand, and by raising the Bavarian Question[1] enabled the Prussian King to put himself at the head of the German princes in resistance to Habsburg aggression in the Empire, although at the price of making Catherine II the arbiter of Germany.

At the time of his death in 1786 Frederick had long been a legendary figure in Europe. In his last years he was, however, filled with foreboding for the future of Prussia. He had only contempt for his heir and successor, his nephew, Frederick William (II), and in his *Considerations on the Political State of Europe* written four years before his death, he expressed the fear that Prussia faced early disaster. Any final estimate of Frederick's system must take into account the fate of Prussia on the field of Jena in 1806. By 1786 it had outlived its usefulness, and could not work in the absence of a superman. Twenty-one years later Stein instituted a new period of administrative reform. Historians have sometimes treated that fact as proving the 'barrenness' of Frederick's system. Yet it was that system which had, in less than half a century, made Prussia a great Power.

[1] See Chapter 8.

8: The Habsburg Empire

The Holy Roman Empire

In an age of growing State absolutism the Holy Roman Empire was increasingly an anachronism. In the Middle Ages the Holy Roman Emperor had stood at the apex of temporal power, and the Empire was still in the eighteenth century the most remarkable mediaeval survival. It consisted of well over 300 separate States; there were over 200 ruling princes, some ruling more than one State; there were 51 Free Towns, and in addition nearly 1,500 Free Knights, a special mediaeval curiosity, each ruling a tiny State with an average of 300 subjects and an annual income of about £160 sterling. The largest States of the Empire were, first, the Habsburg Monarchy, with a population of about 10 millions inside the Empire, and about 12 or 14 millions outside it; second, Prussia, with a population at the end of Frederick the Great's reign of $5\frac{1}{2}$ millions; then Bavaria and Saxony each with 2 millions, and Hanover with 900,000. Some rulers were therefore of European stature, while the great majority were politically insignificant. Moreover, some German rulers had important possessions outside the Empire. More than half the area of the Habsburg Monarchy lay outside the Empire; Prussia possessed East Prussia; the Elector of Hanover was King of England; the Elector of Saxony was King of Poland; the Duke of Holstein was also King of Denmark. It was difficult for the Emperor to avoid being in some way involved in almost any political development anywhere in Europe. Even the exact extent of the Empire was in doubt. The Emperor claimed the suzerainty of seventy-five principalities in Italy, but they were not represented in the Diet; the Duke of Savoy was represented in the Diet, but Piedmont was not a part of the Empire. The Austrian Netherlands were regarded by the Habsburgs as part of the Empire, but do not appear to have been subject to Imperial contributions.

The constitution of the Empire made sense in the mediaeval context, when the relationship between overlord and vassal was the usual order of Europe, but became much less real in the new age of State absolutism. In theory the Emperor, as Emperor, could take no important political step without the consent of the Diet of the Empire, but in practice his power was considerable because the Emperor was also the ruler of the Habsburg lands. He was elected by the Electoral College, and since 1437 it had been customary to elect the ruler of Austria as Emperor, because he alone had sufficient power to make the power of the Emperor effective. On the one occasion in the eighteenth century when an Emperor was elected who was not a Habsburg (Charles VII of Bavaria), the experiment was too unhappy to be repeated. The Diet of the Empire consisted of three Colleges, that of the Electors, that of the Princes and that of the Free Towns. In the eighteenth century there were nine Electors. The College of Princes numbered a hundred votes, some princes having merely fractions of votes. There were fifty-one Free Towns. Each College voted separately, and in political matters the large States had decisions all their own way. Certain general tendencies could be discerned in the divisions in the Diet. For instance, many were Protestant versus Catholic divisions. By the Principle of Parity, laid down in 1648, neither religion was permitted to impose an advantage upon the other by a majority vote: in the case of a division of votes along Protestant–Catholic lines, the question had to be solved by agreement. There was little or no feeling of national solidarity; the Electoral Archbishop of Cologne, for instance, for years voted according to the wishes of the King of France. The attitude of Princes towards the Habsburgs tended to differ according to geographical position and the strength of the State. Thus the geographical position of their territory made it natural for the Bavarian Elector to be anti-Habsburg and often pro-French. On the other hand the small States of the Empire looked to the Habsburgs to protect them from being swallowed up by their more powerful neighbours. A special example of this was provided by the Free Knights. They were subject to the Emperor alone, and had no seats in the Diet. They were entirely dependent upon the Emperor, and the continued existence of the Reich, for their survival as independent entities. They were anachronistic, but by no means without their use, for, with their tiny territories and their small incomes, they were readily encouraged into the service of the Emperor, or some other reigning prince, and provided many of the soldiers, statesmen or bureaucrats of the time. Perhaps the most famous of them was Baron Stein, the great reformer in Prussia.

The Diet had once met whenever summoned by the Emperor, and had been the occasion for a great assembly of princes; but since 1681 it had sat permanently, and had thus become a diplomatic congress. Many of its proceedings were infinitely tedious, time-wasting and devoid of real political significance. Months were sometimes wasted in disputes about the merest questions of etiquette and precedence. Even when a decision was taken the Diet lacked an executive body for enforcement. In the case of war each circle of the Empire was supposed to provide a regular quota of troops for an Imperial army. But these were usually slow in forthcoming, and often arrived too late in the year to be of any use. (It was said, with a bad pun, that they were August's rather than Augustus's troops.) In the great crises of the century, in the wars against Louis XIV, or in 1733 or in 1740, it was apparent what little effective strength or unity the Empire had.

Yet it would be wrong entirely to dismiss the Empire as an anachronistic absurdity. It could not always control the actions of its more powerful members, but it did have some success in imposing law and peace on its smaller members. Without some such organisation it would have been impossible for 300 States to have lived in peace. Its greatest service was to keep alive the idea of the rule of law and of the overriding sanctity of constitutional agreements. Historians are contemptuous of the attempts of rulers to justify aggression by fictitious legalistic claims. But these claims were not always fictitious, and in any case they paid lip-service to a civilised code of conduct among States. There were two supreme Courts in the Empire; legal disputes might be taken either to the *Reichskammergericht*, which at first met at Speyer, and after 1684 at Wetzlar; or to the *Reichshofrat*, or Aulic Council, which was appointed by the Emperor himself, and sat in Vienna. The Emperor was regarded as the fountainhead of justice, and in theory anyone in the Empire could appeal to his Court. It is true that the *Reichskammergericht*, which was paid for by the Electors, was always underpaid, and heavily in arrears with work, yet both Courts did good work in revealing grave errors of justice in the legal decisions of particular States. The most important aspect of their work was the support which they gave to Estates in resisting encroachments on the part of rulers. We have seen already that the

Estates of Cleves successfully appealed to Vienna against the attempts of the Elector of Brandenburg to oppose an excise without their consent. The Duke of Mecklenburg-Schwerin in 1725 similarly attempted to tax without the consent of his Estates. They appealed to the *Reichskammergericht*, which supported them, and when the Duke refused to submit he was deposed by the Emperor (1728), the Elector of Hanover acting as executor of the Emperor's decision. This was not the only ruler to be deposed by legal process during the period, and others were imprisoned for the misgovernment of their subjects. Even the Emperor himself could feel the force of the hostile opinion of States, as Joseph II was to learn to his cost in the case of the Bavarian Succession.

The prevailing atmosphere of the Reich was undoubtedly static, and little conducive to the growth of a vigorous economic life. Since the great days of the Hanseatic League and the House of Fugger, Germany had become an economic backwater, remote from the Atlantic trade routes, and too divided to foster an active economy. In the eighteenth century Hamburg was still a highly prosperous city, with an extensive trade with England and France; Leipzig was an important centre of trade with eastern Europe, and Frankfurt was a financial centre. Vienna was by far the largest city in the Empire, with a population of a little over a quarter of a million; Berlin came next with about 100,000, and Hamburg not far behind. But many towns with important names numbered only a few thousand, and few reached 30,000. There were many reasons for this economic backwardness. Germany had been dreadfully devastated during the Thirty Years' War; whole areas had been depopulated, and did not again reach their former population figures for more than a century. Trade, industry and agriculture were shattered. This was one of the potent reasons for the rise of absolute rulers, for it needed strong governments to repair the devastations. But these governments were poor, and the cost of government was high. On an average, half of the expenses might be borne by the princely demesnes, but the other half must be raised either from a land tax or from a tax on trade. It was natural that both ruler and Estates should favour the latter; the Elector of Brandenburg had pointed the way, and thus industry and trade became hampered by excessive customs and excise dues, which pressed with stifling effect upon town life. Every petty frontier tended to have its custom barriers. Few rulers could afford to spend money or effort upon roads, and *corvées* were unpopular and inefficient. The best transport was by river, and the main arteries of the Empire were the Rhine, Danube, Oder, Elbe and Weser. Yet even in this the Reich was unfortunate; at the beginning of the eighteenth century the mouths of these rivers tended to be in the hands of foreigners, the Dutch, the Swedes and the Turks. Banking and credit were ill-developed; the Germans as yet lacked the capitalist spirit, and much of their trade and banking were in the hands of the Dutch, or Huguenots or Jews. In most towns gilds fostered a narrow and exclusive attitude.

But it would be quite wrong to paint too black a picture. In comparison with the economic development of the Dutch or English or French, Germany was behindhand. But the Germans had their own way of life, deeply rooted in past history, which had much to commend it. Goethe, in his *Dichtung und Wahrheit* gives us a vivid and nostalgic picture of the Frankfort of his boyhood, about 1750:

'Best of all I loved to walk along the great bridge over the Maine. . . . Generally I extended my walk through Sachsenhausen, and for a farthing was ferried pleasantly across the river. I was then on this side of the stream, and would stroll along to the wine-market, and admire the mechanism of the cranes when goods were unloaded. But it was particularly entertaining to watch the arrival of the market-boats, from which such various cargoes, and sometimes such extraordinary figures were seem to disembark. On entering the city, the Saalhof, which at least stood on the spot where the castle of the Emperor Charlemagne and his successors was reported to have been, was invariably greeted with profound reverence. It was pleasant to lose oneself in the old trading town, particularly on market days, among the crowd collected about the Church of St. Bartholomew. From the earliest times, throngs of buyers and sellers had gathered there, and the place being thus occupied, it was not easy in later days to bring about a more cheerful and roomy arrangement. . . . But what chiefly attracted the child's attention were the many little towns within the town, the fortresses within the fortress; viz., the walled monastic enclosures, and several other buildings dating from earlier times, and more or less like castles —such as the Nuremberg Court, the Compostella, the Braunfels, . . . and several strongholds transformed in modern times into dwellings and warehouses. . . . Everything pointed to a period long past and full of disturbances . . . gates and towers, defining the bounds of the old city—then farther off, other gates, towers, walls, bridges, ramparts, moats, with which the new city was encompassed. . . . A certain love of antiquity was thus implanted in the boy. . . . Passing from the ornamental pleasure-gardens of the rich to the orchards of the citizen, kept for the sake of their produce—thence to the factories, bleaching-grounds, and similar industries . . . a little world lay within the limits of the city. . . .

We listened to many a legend of Charlemagne. But our interest in History did not begin till Rudolph of Habsburg, who by his heroism put an end to a time of such dire confusion. Charles IV also attracted our notice. We had already heard of the Golden Bull, and the Code of Criminal Justice. . . . We heard Maximilian praised as a friend both to mankind, and to the townsfolk his subjects, and were told of the prophecy that he would be the last Emperor belonging to a German house. This unhappily came to pass, as after his death the choice lay between the King of Spain, afterwards Charles V, and the King of France, Francis I. With some anxiety the narrator added that a similar prophecy was again current, for there was room left for the portrait of only one more Emperor.

It was a traditional way of life, but civilised and comfortable for such middle class families as those of Goethe. Indeed the Rhineland, Saxony, Silesia and Bohemia were prosperous and progressive. Hamburg was a rich mercantile city, exporting the manufactures of Silesia, especially linens, and itself manufacturing velvets, silks and brocades, refining sugar and tanning hides. The Bank of Hamburg was founded in 1619, and ranked second only to that of Amsterdam. But the typical industrial organisation was that of the small-scale workshop and the exclusive gilds reminiscent of Wagner's *Die Meistersingers.*

The prevailing spirit of Germany was aristocratic, not mercantile or industrial. There were wealthy merchants, and others who became so as a result of the wars; but as a class they were not honoured; they lacked status, and on the whole the towns tended to lose ground in the preservation of their privileges in the face of the growing pretensions of the rulers. Germany lacked a single centre; there were instead several hundred miniature centres, the Courts of the many rulers. There the tone was aristocratic, and strongly cosmopolitan, for the lesser nobility had to become soldiers or administrators, and often went from Court to Court. Men of learning and culture were highly honoured, even when of middle class origin, but merchants much less so. The tradesmen who provided for the needs of the Courts lived simple lives, and were often deeply influenced by the religious influences of Pietism.

The princes, who on the whole have had less than their deserts from the hands of historians, tended to be ostentatious and to live well above their means. Some were undoubtedly bad. The Margrave Charles Frederick William of Ansbach, who died in 1769, was an atrocious ruler, and his successor cared so little for his inheritance that he sold it to Prussia, and retired to England to enjoy the proceeds. Some rulers had more important territories elsewhere (the Landgrave Frederick I, for instance, was also King of Sweden) and preferred to live there, to the neglect of their German territories. Many German princes made a comfortable income by hiring out their subjects as mercenaries to more powerful monarchs (as the rulers of Hesse habitually did to the Kings of England). But many German princes were excellent rulers, deeply influenced by the spirit of paternalism and Enlightenment. Ernest the Pious, Duke of Saxe-Gotha (d. 1675) was genuinely concerned for the welfare of his people, and was a great pioneer of education. His successors, however, were too often extravagant and oppressive. Henrietta Caroline of Hesse-Darmstadt, and Prince Frederick Franz of Dessau were most enlightened rulers, beloved of their subjects. Duke Frederick I of Mecklenburg (d. 1785) and his successor were both excellent rulers. When a ruler was accused of extravagance, it was usually because he was aping the ways of Versailles. In this way many of them were noted patrons of the arts. The Landgrave Charles of Hesse (d. 1730) established a splendid Court, insisted on religious toleration, and engaged in an extensive programme of building. The Elector Charles Lewis of the Palatinate (d. 1680) did much to build up Mannheim into a commercial centre, patronised the University of Heidelberg, and was an enthusiastic friend to the philosophers Pufendorf and Spinoza. Frederick II of Hesse Cassel (d. 1785) kept a splendid Court, and surrounded himself with scholars and artists. Of most of the Archiepiscopal rulers of Germany not much good can be said, but even among them there were exceptions. The Archbishop–Electors of Cologne were on the whole bad rulers, but then in 1761 Maria Theresa secured the election of her son Max Franz, and he proved to be a model prince of the Enlightenment. The Archbishop of Salzburg, Count Colloredo, was so far a disciple of the Enlightenment that he had the busts of Voltaire and Rousseau in his study, and instituted reforms in the Church not unlike those of Joseph II in Austria, although music-lovers will not forgive him for his treatment of Mozart.

Many of these small Courts were to be swallowed up in the mael-strom of the Napoleonic Wars, and were to receive scanty attention from the German historians of the nineteenth century. They seemed to mean little in an age of power politics and nation-states. But in fact they played a notable part in the eighteenth-century process of En-lightenment. To understand this, perhaps the best way is to look more closely at a single famous example, that of the tiny State of Weimar. Thuringia had been subjected to constant subdivisions among branches of the ruling families, and in the eighteenth century there were no less than thirty princedoms in the area. Weimar consisted of the duchies of Weimar, Eisenach and Jena, and the bailiwick of Ilme-nau, each with separate laws and traditions. The total area was about 700 square miles, and the population was a little over 100,000. Weimar itself, the centre of government, was a town, of five or six thousand inhabitants, with narrow streets and its houses clustered round the ducal Schloss. It was a market town, the home of the Court and a considerable number of gentry; most of the other inhabitants were servants, shop-keepers and journeymen.

There was nothing remarkable about Weimar before the second half of the eighteenth century, although J. S. Bach had been *Hof-musikus* to its Duke Johann Ernst; the dukes had tended to spend their slender revenues on a toy army and on hunting. In 1756 the sixteen-years-old Anna Amalia of Brunswick married Ernst August Konstantin of Weimar. Her father, Duke Karl I of Brunswick and Lunëburg (d. 1780), was a great patron of the arts and learning, and nearly ruined his State in building up a royal library and art gallery. Anna Amalia was therefore a woman of culture. In 1758 her husband died, and for the next nineteen years she was regent for her son Karl August. During that period she made Weimar into a centre of the arts. Weimar was very poor, and heavily hit by the Seven Years' War, so she had to proceed cautiously. But she established the first Court theatre for the performance of German plays. At this time comic operas were becoming the rage, and in 1766 the first permanent theatre was opened in Leipzig, and Anna Amalia encouraged a musi-cian named Wolf to attempt the same operas in Weimar. In 1772 she appointed Wieland to be tutor to her son. Wieland while in Weimar founded the literary periodical *Der deutsche Merkur* which flourished for forty years, and left a notable mark on German literary development. In 1775 Anna Amalia's son, Karl August, came of age, and one of his first acts was to invite Goethe to Weimar. Goethe was twenty-six, already famous by the publication of his *Sorrows of Werther*. After the middle class atmosphere of Frankfort, Goethe found the aristocratic atmosphere of Weimar stimulating. It is sometimes thought strange that he should have been content with the confined atmosphere of a petty German State, but in fact it accorded well with his mental development. For Goethe was concerned with the spiritual development of man, which could best be observed in the ordered peace of Weimar. He wrote, in some notes, with what satisfaction he observed enlightenment spreading among the smaller rulers of Germany, their growing concern for the welfare of their subjects and the rule of law and economic prosperity. This, he thought, was more fruitful in small States than in great ones, because the latter were inevitably preoccupied with the problems of power. Goethe became the close friend and intimate of the Duke (to the indignation of the courtiers, for was not Goethe merely of middle class birth?). They rode together, they arranged amateur theatricals, and, as Goethe recorded, the two sat up far into the night discussing art, nature and science. Goethe became the unofficial *maître de plaisirs*, organising plays, writing articles and poems for Anna Amalia's private Court magazine, and also studying botany, mineralogy and anatomy and collecting the drawings of Dürer. It was this life of the mind and the spirit which most interested German Enlightenment in the period. He also became a member of the Privy Council, and interested himself in some road-building. But nothing could be done to give much stimulus to economic life in so small and scattered a dominion.

Rapidly the fame of Weimar spread. In 1783 the philosopher Herder arrived to be head of the clergy in Weimar, and to carry on his important studies in the philosophy of history. In 1788 Wieland formed in Weimar his 'Order of Cosmopolitans', a society to spread enlightened liberalism and the love of humanity. Herder had great faith in the power of education, and spent much time in drawing up plans for education in Weimar, with secondary schools teaching both the classics and modern subjects like history, geography and mathematics. Not much came of these plans, but they throw light on the ideals of German Enlightenment. Goethe was especially interested in the University of Jena, of which he had great hopes as an intellectual centre for Germany. Jena was a small, walled town of about 4,000 inhabitants, yet for the twenty years after about 1785 it had its greatest days of intellectual eminence. Reinhold was professor of philosophy, and Schmidt of theology. Fichte succeeded Reinhold in 1794, at a time when he was working on his *Theory of Knowledge*. Schelling became Professor of Philosophy in 1798, and Hegel first came to Jena in 1801, and between them the new philosophy of idealism was worked out. In those days students must have lived in a heady and exciting atmosphere of ideas of Enlightenment, cosmopolitanism and Idealism.

Thus the picture of Weimar culture in the 1790s is one of high civilisation, centring in the Duke and his mother. The talk is of literature, music, the theatre, music in the park on Sundays, Goethe reading aloud to the Court, amateur theatricals, meetings of the literary and philosophical society, papers read on science, scientific collections which developed into museums. In all Goethe remains the central figure and the main attraction. Not even the Napoleonic Wars entirely destroyed the charm and culture of Weimar, and years later, when Thackeray visited it, he wrote:

> I think I have never seen a society more simple, charitable, courteous, gentlemanlike than that of the dear little Saxon city, where the good Schiller and the great Goethe lived and lie buried.

It was an atmosphere in which men might well feel indifferent to the politics of the outside world.[1]

The Emperor Leopold I

If the Emperor Charles V (1519–55) gave new life to the old idea of the universality of the Holy Roman Empire, that idea finally perished during the Thirty Years' War and in the Peace of Westphalia. The Habsburgs were thrust back from North Germany and the European State-system took shape; the Turks were a constant danger to the east, Spanish power was uppermost in Italy, and France found a new strength under Richelieu and Mazarin. The Habsburg dominions had suffered dreadfully during the wars; great areas were devastated, agriculture and industries dislocated, and the population had de-

---

[1] On the whole subject see the brilliant study by Bruford: *Culture and Society in Classical Weimar*.

clined. Yet all was not loss, for the Habsburgs were to some extent thrown back upon their own dominions, and there began, very slowly at first, a policy of centralisation and consolidation which reached its climax in the second half of the eighteenth century.

The Emperor Leopold I (1658–1705) was a cold, phlegmatic man, sickly in health, blessed with the Habsburg lip, much attached to the formal dress and etiquette of the Spanish Court, a devout man, devoted to the Jesuits, with a preference for despotism which he was never strong enough to achieve. Like his predecessor, Ferdinand III, he employed all the forces of the Counter-Reformation to discipline his subjects and to glorify the Monarchy. He was a patron of the Marian cult (the exaltation of the Virgin Mary), and professors in the universities had to swear annually to belief in the Immaculate Conception of the Virgin. He brought in Italian and German artists to build and decorate Baroque churches and palaces, and he was devoted to Italian music and pictures. The suppression of the Bohemian revolt in 1620, and the forcible conversion of numbers of Bohemian protestants, gave the Habsburgs a taste of absolute power, which however was countered by the growing power and independence of the nobility in the Habsburg dominions. Extensive foreign wars could be fought only if the ruler had the support of his landed nobility. Moreover, economic dislocation increased the power of the landed gentry; war brought devastations to some provinces, and this was accompanied by a heavy decline in population. Bohemia, for instance, lost nearly half its population between 1618 and 1648. This meant a great increase in demesne farming, and a shortage of agricultural labour. Peasants therefore were increasingly tied to the soil, and labour services greatly increased, often during the seventeenth century from twelve days a year to three days a week. In other areas, where devastations had not taken place, there was a greatly increased demand for the produce of the land, wheat, timber, meat, wine and the like, and this favoured the growth of great estates and the subjection of the peasantry to serfdom. The power of the Habsburg Emperor rested squarely upon the support of his nobility, and in the provinces the nobility had virtually a political and economic predominance.

A specially difficult problem was presented by Hungary, and to understand this we should look back several centuries. In the tenth century A.D. wild Magyar horsemen conquered the area to the north of the Danube and reduced its Slav inhabitants to servitude. In the eleventh century the Magyars under its King, St. Stephen, were converted to Roman Catholicism, and thereafter Hungary became a potent State and an outpost of western culture. By the Golden Bull of 1222 the Magyar nobility limited the power of the King in their own interests, and they lorded it over the subject Slav and Roumanian peoples. They had a saying 'Extra Hungariam non est vita, et si est vita, non est ita' (Outside Hungary nothing exists, or if it does exist it does not signify). Still, for a time the Hungarian State served a European purpose of being a bulwark against the Turkish advance. John Hunyadi (1387–1456) and his son Matthias Corvinus (1458–90) were two of the hero-kings in the fight against the Turks. But in 1526 the Turks overwhelmed the Magyars at the great battle of Mohacs, and two-thirds of their land were occupied. In these desperate circumstances the Hungarians turned to the Habsburgs, and the Crown was offered to Ferdinand of Habsburg, brother of the Emperor Charles V. For a century the Turks maintained their hold on two-thirds of Hungary, and the country was divided into *sanjaks*. Only in the mountains of the north and west did the Hungarians remain free from the Turks, and they were reluctant to submit to Habsburg domination. The fact was that, though the Magyars needed the Habsburgs to protect them from the Turks, they were quite ready to play off Habsburg against Turk as a means to preserving their liberties. In 1658, when Leopold I came to the throne, his authority in Hungary was confined to the north and west of the country; Transylvania was a Turkish dependency, and the rest of Hungary was directly under Turkish rule.

Leopold's accession coincided with a notable revival of Turkish power under the Koprili.[1] In 1662 Akmed Koprili invaded Transylvania, conquered it, and invaded Hungary. Leopold appealed to Europe for aid, and the Imperial Diet, the Pope, Spain and Brandenburg all sent aid. In 1664 the able Austrian commander Montecuccoli routed Akmed at the battle of St. Gotthard. This might have been the moment for the Habsburgs to have driven the Turks completely out of Hungary while they were in confusion. But the Emperor preferred to make the Treaty of Vasvar (1664) leaving the Turks

[1] See Chapter 13.

in possession of all their conquests, including the fortress of Neuhäusel, and enabling them to turn away to attack Venice and to capture the island of Crete. It was a serious error on the Emperor's part,
for it convinced the Magyars that they had little to hope from the
Habsburgs, and that they had best make what terms they could with
the Turks. The result was conspiracies against the Habsburg power led
by Peter Zrinyi, which the French did their best to foment. Leopold
reacted sharply to the new threat, sent in an army of occupation, and
in 1673 established a provincial administration (*Gukernium*) sitting at
Pressburg to rule Hungary by means of an army of occupation.

Leopold's difficulties were the result of attempting to look two ways
at once. In making a speedy peace with the Turks he had been influenced by the prospect in 1664 of the early death of Philip IV of Spain
and his infant son. When Louis XIV began the War of Devolution in
1667,[1] Leopold did not join the Triple Alliance or seek to restrain the
French menace, but, accepting the policy of his Minister Lobkowitz,
entered into secret negotiations with France for the partition of the
Spanish Empire, by which he hoped to revive the ghost of the Empire
of Charles V. Not until 1672 did he take up arms against France, and
even then his modest war effort put a great strain upon his resources.
From 1678 to 1680 a great plague ravaged his lands, and in 1680 there
was a peasants' revolt in Bohemia, consequent upon the rapid extension of labour services. The revolt was savagely suppressed, and it
was followed by a Patent which significantly attempted to limit the
customary services of a peasant to three days a week.

Freed from the war in the west by the Peace of Nijmegen (1679),
Leopold turned to pacify Hungary. In 1681 he called the Hungarian
Estates, and made peace with them. He agreed to recognise the liberties of the Kingdom; the *Gubernium* was abolished, and the Estates
recovered their right to elect a Palatine (or governor). All offices of
State were to be filled by Hungarians, and the Estates were restored
to full participation in government. Finally, Protestant liberties were
guaranteed. The peace had been made not a moment too soon, for in
1682 the Turks under Kara Mustafa, in alliance with the Hungarian
rebel leader Thokoly, attacked again with an enormous army, reputed
to be 200,000 strong, and advanced to the very walls of Vienna.
Leopold, with one eye on Louis XIV's *Chambres de Réunions*, was

[1] See p. 96.

ill-prepared, and only at the last minute concluded an alliance with John Sobieski of Poland. When the latter arrived, he found the Imperial garrison of 11,000 in dire peril. Declaring to his troops: 'We have to save today not a single city but the whole of Christendom. . . . The war is a holy one', he attacked. The Turkish forces broke, and a terrible slaughter followed. This great defeat of the Turks, together with the Battle of St. Gotthard, broke for ever the legends of Turkish invincibility, and marked the last attempt of the Turks to carry their empire forward. The Austrian forces went on to capture Neuhäusel (1685), Buda (1686) and to rout the Turks again at Mohacs (1687) on the very field of the great Turkish victory 160 years before. A great war of liberation was fought throughout Hungary. Prince Louis of Baden conquered Transylvania. In 1697 Prince Eugène of Savoy became commander of the Imperial forces, and he destroyed the last great Turkish army at Zeuta. Turkish resistance was at an end, and the British ambassador at Constantinople negotiated the Treaty of Carlowitz (1699) by which the Turks renounced the whole of Hungary and Transylvania, except the Banat and Belgrade.

These victories were accompanied by a significant extension of the royal power. In 1687 Leopold forced the Diet of Pressburg to declare that the Crown was no longer elective, but hereditary to the Habsburgs, and the right of confederation and *insurrectio* (legal resistance to the monarch, specifically recognised by the Golden Bull of 1222) were abrogated. Thereafter the Diet ceased to meet for a time, and Hungary was virtually under a military occupation, with a provincial status like Bohemia. When Transylvania was conquered it was not incorporated with Hungary, but ruled directly from Vienna, though it retained its Estates and was granted religious liberty (a constitution which continued until 1848). The spread of Habsburg absolutism brought new revolts in Hungary in 1703, led by Francis Rakoczi, with the aid and encouragement of Louis XIV. If the French had won the Battle of Blenheim, one result would certainly have been the independence of Hungary. The allied victory was thus a blow to the rebels, but the revolt continued until 1712, when the new Emperor Charles VI ratified the Peace of Szatmar.

The defeat of the Turks and the liberation of Hungary and Transylvania from the Turkish yoke constitute the real glory of the reign of Leopold I, and account for the great prestige of the Habsburgs by the end of the seventeenth century. In the west the showing was less impressive. Vienna was saved in 1704 by Marlborough and the Allies, just as it had been saved in 1683 by John Sobieski. The campaigns of the Archduke Charles in Spain were a fiasco, and only in Italy did the genius of Prince Eugène of Savoy give the Habsburgs military success. Yet by the Treaties of Utrecht and Rastadt the Emperor gained the lion's share of the spoils of war: the Austrian Netherlands, Naples, Sardinia, the duchy of Milan and the Tuscan ports. Such extensive gains were in fact a recognition of three things, first of Habsburg prestige, second of the victories of Prince Eugène in Italy, and third of the importance of the Habsburgs to the balance of power in Europe.

The Emperor Charles VI

Leopold I was succeeded by his son Joseph I (1705–11), a gentle and refined monarch, devoted to the arts, who died (of smallpox) at the age of thirty-three, and was succeeded by his younger brother Charles VI (1711–40). Like so many of the Habsburgs, Charles VI was a cold, phlegmatic man, serious, it was said, even when he smiled. He had a deep sense of duty, and lived a life of the strictest morality. He had the most exalted sense of the Imperial dignity, and always deeply regretted the loss of the Spanish Crown. For years he ruled with the aid of a Spanish Council and continued to confer Spanish titles on his favourites. He was meticulous in the transaction of government business, and many despatches to his ambassadors were written in his own hand. Indeed his insistence that he should retain all business in his own hands meant that most business was behindhand. It was said that even the copy of the Quadruple Alliance of 1818 remained three months on his desk before he could be induced to sign it.

One of his first tasks was to ratify the Treaty of Szatmar with the Hungarians. It provided for the return of peace, a general amnesty for the rebels and a recognition of the liberties of Hungary. Charles went to Pressburg for his coronation as King of Hungary; the royal insignia were restored to Hungary, especially the Crown of St. Stephen. In future the Hungarian Chancellery was to be independent of the *Hofkammer* in Vienna. Finally, it was decreed that peasants were to be legally tied to their masters' land, a law made necessary by the steady flight from the land and the rapid decline in cultivation, both under the Turks and subsequently. The restoration of Magyar liberties was the price Charles VI was ready to pay for peace in Hungary. Moreover, a separate army was voted by the Hungarian Diet, which proved to be an important instrument of royal power; it was not directed by the *Hofkriegsrat*, but was directly under the royal authority. It was a small but professional army, much more efficient than feudal levies. The justification for this was the need to protect the southern frontier against the Turks, and for this reason the 'Military Frontiers' were withdrawn from the control of the Hungarian Diet and governed directly from Vienna. Thus liberties which were confirmed with one hand were subtly limited by the other. A period of internal peace ensued, and this was of the greatest importance to Charles VI in view of the central problem of the reign, that of the succession.

The Emperor Joseph I had had two daughters, and in 1703 it was agreed that if he died without male heirs, his brother Charles would succeed him, but that if Charles also died without male heirs, Joseph's daughters would succeed to the throne before his. In 1717 Maria Theresa was born, and in 1718 her sister Marianne, and thereafter it became clear that Charles VI would have no son. In Austria proper and in Bohemia the rights of succession could be decided by the ruler, so there was no difficulty in securing Maria Theresa's succession. But in the absence of a male heir the Hungarian Diet would regain its right to choose a king. Moreover, elsewhere in the Habsburg dominions it might be claimed that the Salic Law made a female succession invalid. In certain circumstances therefore the death of Charles VI might be the signal for the break-up of the Habsburg Empire. Charles VI's pre-occupation with this question has often been treated as though it were an absurdity, but the danger was real enough; the Habsburg hold on Hungary was too uncertain to be risked in a disputed succession. Charles VI's error was not that he concerned himself with the problem of the succession, but that he did not reinforce his policy with a full Treasury and a sound army.

Now it should be clear why he was so anxious to secure peace in Hungary. In 1720 he produced a document proclaiming that the Habsburg lands were indissoluble. All the Diets of the Empire, including the Hungarian (the only one which really mattered), accepted it, and thus the Hungarians virtually surrendered their right to decide upon the succession. In return for this, Charles VI again confirmed Hungarian liberties.

In 1720 Joseph I's elder daughter married the Elector of Saxony, and the younger married the Elector of Bavaria, both having recognised the Pragmatic Sanction. Spain recognised the precious document in 1725, Russia in 1726, Prussia in 1729, England in 1731, the Empire except for Bavaria and the Palatinate, in 1732 and Sardinia in 1739. For some of these agreements Charles VI had had to pay a heavy price, yet when the test came in 1740 each country pursued the policy which seemed to be in its own best interests.

To understand the problems of Habsburg government in the eighteenth century it is necessary to examine its form of government. The Habsburg dominions divided administratively into Austria, Bohemia, Hungary, Transylvania, the Netherlands and the Italian provinces. Even these divisions implied a good deal of administrative centralisation, for in fact the Emperor was duke of Upper and Lower Austria, margrave of Styria, duke of Carinthia and Carniola, lord of Swabia, count of Tyrol, king of Bohemia, margrave of Moravia, and king of Hungary, Transylvania, Croatia, Slavonia and Dalmatia, to say nothing of his Italian and Flemish titles. Each of these provinces had its local Estates. The main organs of the central government under the Monarch were:

1. The Privy Council (*Geheimer Rat*) in which matters of high policy were discussed.
2. The *Hofkammer*, which dealt with finance and trade.
3. The *Hofkriegsrat* or War Council.
4. The Imperial Chancellery, dealing with Imperial affairs.
5. The Court Chancellery, dealing with domestic affairs.
6. Similar Chancelleries for each of the administrative units, Bohemia, Hungary, Transylvania, the Netherlands and the Italian provinces.

As we have seen, Hungary occupied a special position, and had vastly greater liberties than other provinces of the Empire. Bohemia on the other hand had never really recovered from its conquest and suppression in 1620. Its Estates continued, but were docile, and its nobility found it advantageous to co-operate with the Monarchy, if only because the latter aided them in the extension of serfdom over the peasantry. The Moravian Estates were of little account, and Moravia was ruled by a nominated council sitting in Brno. In Hungary a *modus vivendi* had been reached by which the Crown respected Hungarian liberties in return for a standing army, while at the same time it maintained its direct authority along the Military Frontier, in Transylvania and in Croatia. Croatia was under a military government headed by a governor (*Ban*) directly responsible to the Emperor, although the Croatian Estates met in Zagreb. Although in certain important ways the royal power had advanced between the accession of Leopold I and the reign of Charles VI, yet, compared with the new monarchies of Louis XIV or Frederick William I in Prussia, Habsburg government remained essentially 'mediaeval'. That is to say, there was little administrative uniformity between one province and the next; each province retained its system of laws and customs; and in matters of finance and war the ruler was often dependent upon the support of the local Estates. In short, the Habsburg Empire was still federal and feudal in an age of centralisation and administrative absolutism. Nor had Charles VI and his Ministers any consistent policy to change the system. Prince Eugène of Savoy, the military genius of the age, had tried to carry extensive military reforms, but with little permanent effect.[1] The real head of the administrative system during the reign of Charles VI was Bartenstein, the secretary to the Privy Council, and the only non-noble among his Ministers, a time-server who made no attempt at reform.

The provinces were divided into lesser units, known as 'Circles', and these were chiefly concerned with the collection of taxes and with recruitment. Their officials were mainly appointed by the Estates from among the local nobility, and they formed a formidable obstacle to any increase of the royal authority. Thus, for instance, after 1729 Charles VI no longer summoned the Hungarian Estates, but as the Magyar nobility kept local administration in their hands, they prevented the Crown from carrying out its most needful reform. This was

---

[1] Prince Eugène was the son of Eugène Maurice, Count of Soissons and of Olympia Mancini, niece of Mazarin, and a direct descendant of Charles Emanuel I, Duke of Savoy. Born 1663, he had served under John Sobieski, Charles of Lorraine and the Elector of Bavaria, and was a close friend of the great Duke of Marlborough. He had defeated the French in Italy and was the hammer of the Turks, both in 1697–99 and in 1718–9. He was a man of wide culture and taste in the arts, and was devoted to the Habsburg cause, although he was never personally attached to Charles VI, who treated him coolly. All his life he struggled in vain against the incompetence of the Habsburg system.

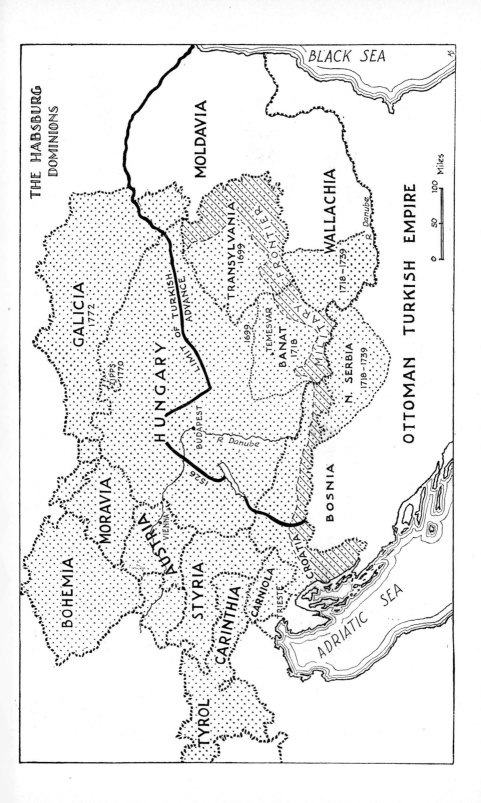

THE HABSBURG DOMINIONS

BLACK SEA

MOLDAVIA

GALICIA
1772

ZIPPS
1770

HUNGARY

LIMIT OF TURKISH ADVANCE

TRANSYLVANIA
1699

1699

TEMESVAR
BANAT
1718

WALLACHIA

1718-1739

R Danube

MILITARY FRONTIER

BUDAPEST

R. Danube

N. SERBIA
1718-1739

BOHEMIA

MORAVIA

AUSTRIA

VIENNA

1526

BOSNIA

OTTOMAN TURKISH EMPIRE

STYRIA

CARINTHIA

CARNIOLA

TRIESTE

CROATIA

TYROL

ADRIATIC SEA

0   50   100 Miles

the increase of the Hungarian contribution to the Emperor's exchequer. Hungary was much the wealthiest province of the Empire, yet it contributed far less than its fair share of taxation, and this was one of the fundamental weaknesses of the Habsburg monarchy in 1740.

To the prevailing power of the nobility must be added that of the Church, for the two were usually in close alliance. Jesuit influence exercised a stranglehold over the intellectual life of Austria and Bohemia, and while we in onay it was an important ally of monarchy, yet in its alliance with the nobility it could be a powerful check. Moreover, it was largely responsible for the constant waves of persecution of Protestants which went on in Bohemia, with their savage punishments of torture and the galleys. Joseph II's later hostility to the Jesuits sprang from a realisation that much was wrong with the old order under his grandfather.

The Habsburg dominions had an unspectacular share in the general economic expansion which marked most of western Europe during the period. Charles VI sensed the importance of trade, and spent months on elaborate plans for the formation of an Ostend Company (1722) which would establish trading stations in India, and participate in the rich trade of Spanish South America. But the promise of privileges from Spain did not materialise; the hostility of the English and Dutch East India Companies was too much for it, and the Company was wound up before the end of the decade. Charles VI also granted a charter to the East India Company of Trieste to open up routes to India, and Trieste and Fiume were made free ports. But again the opposition of the Maritime Powers proved too much for it, and communications between the ports and Austria were very difficult. Roads were built, one over the Semmering Pass, and the other the famous *Karlestrasse* in Croatia, but in the end Charles VI abandoned his project and sold his fleet to Venice. There was some industrial expansion; candle manufacture was started at Fiume, hosiery and cottons in Schwechat, linen at Linz, and porcelain at Vienna, but there was little capitalist organisation; industries were mainly domestic and governed by strong gild privileges. But if there was no startling economic achievement, yet it was a period of prosperity in many respects. Population grew steadily. There was extensive colonisation of the new lands of the Military Frontier. Agriculture was prosperous, although the burdens of serfdom were heavier and more general than ever before. Charles VI's reign may be regarded as the culmination of the period of the Baroque. It was the period of the magnificent palaces of Fischer von Erlach, built to the glorification of the nobility. Vienna was increasingly a city of fine streets, squares, fountains and statues. There had already begun a process which Maria Theresa was to encourage so successfully, by which nobles preferred to live in Vienna rather than on their estates. This had important political consequences, for they became increasingly attached to the Monarchy, increasingly dependent upon the Court for appointments, and less interested in the work of their local Estates. This was one of the reasons for the decline of the latter. In the arts Italian influence dominated. The best Court poet was the Italian Metastasio, who wrote many of the libretti for the opera for which Charles VI had a passion.

Maria Theresa

The greatest criticism of the reign of Charles VI must be that he left his Empire disastrously unfitted, both in internal organisation and preparedness, and in foreign relations, to meet the great challenge of Frederick of Prussia. We shall see the outcome of Maria Theresa's heroism during the War of the Austrian Succession. We must now examine the domestic aspects which made her reign one of the greatest in Habsburg history. When she came to the throne she found only 100,000 florins in the Treasury, and an army of only 30,000 men. Her Ministers were elderly. Count Sinzendorf, the Court Chancellor, was a courtier of the old style, frivolous and a dilettante. Count Starhemberg, President of the *Hofkammer*, was upright and honest, but with little head for policy, and practically in his dotage. Bartenstein was merely an efficient bureaucrat. Few reforms could be carried, or even contemplated, during the war, but once the war was over, the first period of reform began. It was heralded by a change of Ministers. Maria Theresa was greatly impressed by the work of Anton von Kaunitz in negotiating the Treaty of Aix-la-Chapelle; he became Chancellor in 1753, and henceforth for the rest of her reign he was the chief influence in determining Habsburg foreign policy. Count Ludwig Haugwitz, Chancellor of Bohemia and Austria, was a Silesian nobleman who won the confidence of the Empress by the plans he drew up for the reconstruction to repair the ravages of war. Finally Rudolf Chotek took charge of the finances.

The war had shown the danger of the Habsburg military dependence on the local Estates; the process was slow, uncertain and the resultant forces inadequate. The annual cost, met by the Estates, had been about 9 million florins. Haugwitz proposed a *Decennalrecesse*, by which the contribution should be voted, not annually, but for a period of ten years. The sum should be raised to 14 million florins, but in return the Estates would be freed from the burdens of foraging and quartering of troops. Maria Theresa declared that it was not her intention to limit constitutional liberties, but that the reform sprang from sheer necessity; the result would be a standing army of 108,000 men, the minimum for safety. To raise the extra money it would be necessary for the nobles and clergy to submit to taxation, new tax registers were to be compiled, and a new land tax worked out. There would also be an increase in customs duties. Maria Theresa proceeded warily; she refused to attempt to introduce these reforms in Hungary, for she had sworn to respect their liberties, and she was loath to create an internal conflict. In practice therefore the changes were confined to the Austro-Bohemian lands. They were submitted to the local Estates; there was much opposition, but one by one they were induced to agree, except the Estates of Carinthia, where the reforms had to be introduced by decree.

The changes had important administrative consequences. Previously, as we have seen, recruitment and taxation had been in the hands of the local nobility appointed by the local Estates. Now new bureaucratic institutions emerged. Each province was governed in future by *Repräsentationen und Kammer* (known variously in different provinces by such names as *Gubernium, Regierung, Landeshauptmannschaft*, etc.), and the Circles were placed under *Kreisämter*, both primarily responsible to Vienna, though the *Kreisämter* were nominally responsible to the Estates for certain things. At first they were responsible for military affairs, then for the collection of customs, and eventually for almost everything, such as road-building, trade, schools, agriculture and peasant affairs. But these changes were introduced gradually, almost imperceptibly. This was part of the genius of Maria Theresa's reforms. She could claim that she had not changed the constitution; the Estates remained, but they declined in importance as powers passed to the new bureaucratic machine.

Another important change was instituted in 1749. Hitherto there had been a Chancellery for Austria and one for Bohemia, and each had combined political and judicial functions. In that year a single administrative unit for Austria and Bohemia was created, under a *Directorium* with Haugwitz as President. Political and judicial matters were separated, and a Supreme Court (*Oberste Justizstelle*) was established for Austro-Bohemia. In this way a great piece of administrative centralisation was carried; in future the two lands were treated as a single unit and governed from Vienna.

Most of these reforms were instituted in the years of peace 1748–56. At the end of the Seven Years' War the Habsburg Monarchy emerged with greatly increased prestige. Moreover, the ideas of the Enlightenment were in the air. The new philosophy saw the ruler as appointed by God to protect the people against feudal domination and clerical obscurantism. The tide was flowing in favour of a secular and bureaucratic despotism, and Haugwitz advised Maria Theresa to take full advantage of it. There was much in the teaching of the Enlightenment she detested. She was devoted to the Catholic Church; she was deeply conservative in nature; she believed with unerring instinct that her dynasty rested upon the observance of pledges and upon the twin foundation of Church and Nobility. Yet she saw also that the continuance of a feudal State into the age of Frederick the Great was an anachronism, that it was a simple issue which faced her Empire: Change or Perish! So long as the reform was dictated by practical considerations, and not by some philosophical will-o'-the-wisp, she was ready to accept it. Political realism was one of her most striking qualities.

In 1760 Maria Theresa was persuaded to establish a new supreme Council of State, consisting of Kaunitz (Foreign Affairs), Haugwitz (domestic and finance), Daun (War), Blumegen (Police) and several others, capable of taking rapid political decisions. Finance was taken away from the Directorium, and a separate Chamber of Finance was set up. The Austro–Bohemian pattern of government in its final development became:

Whatever the particular name of the provincial government, its character was the same; its Governor was the representative of the central government, and responsible for all aspects of government. He presided over the Estates (from 1765), but the work of the latter was so circumscribed that many of the nobility no longer troubled to attend. Many of the great nobility gravitated to the Court, and the smaller nobility had not the power, nor perhaps the will, to resist encroachments of the central authority. At Court the nobility found an outlet; the chief Ministers, Haugwitz, Chotek, Hatzfeld, Kollowrat were all nobles. Many of the nobility were enormously rich and exercised enormous social influence: the Auersbergs, the Batthianys, the Czartoryskis, the Dietrichsteins, the Esterhazys, the Kaunitzs, all had

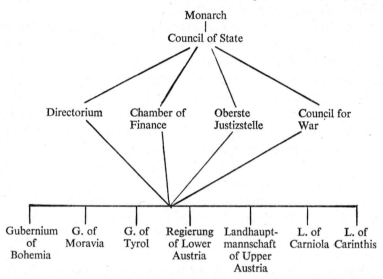

incomes of over 200,000 florins a year, and the Schwarzenbergs and Lobkowitzs paid two or three times that sum in taxes alone. It was a triumph for Maria Theresa that she was able to attach the nobility so successfully to the Monarchy. The Kreisämter were the links between the Government and the people. One of their most significant functions was to protect the peasants from the landlords. From 1769 the landlords gradually lost the right to try and punish their serfs; their justice had to be confirmed by the district officials, and gradually it fell into disuse.

Governmental interference in the relationship between landlord and serf had a practical necessity behind it, for if the peasant was to pay more in taxes to the State, he must needs pay less to the landlord, to whom he owed dues in money, labour services and kind. Thus in 1768 in Bohemia there was set up the *Urbarial-Hofcommission*, to draw up books called *Urbarien*, enumerating the duties of serfs to their lords, and these duties were not to be exceeded.[1] Other Commissions followed elsewhere, and gradually a pattern of services was worked out, and it was laid down that a peasant could make money payments in lieu of services (1773). It was an embarrassment to the Government that the rumour spread among the peasantry that the Government wished to abolish serfdom entirely but were prevented from doing so by the landowners; there were also religious discontents the result of continued persecution of Protestants. The result was the outbreak of a number of peasant risings which had to be severely suppressed. That the peasant rumours were not entirely without truth is suggested by the fact that the Venetian ambassador, Contarini, reported that but for the close relations which the Bohemian nobles had with Vienna, serfdom might have been totally abolished. On the royal estates serfs were in fact liberated.

The tendency during the reign of Maria Theresa was to create a unitary and absolute State in Austro-Bohemia. The great obstacle to its further extension was Hungary. The Italian historian Valsecchi comments:

> Austria had an administration without a constitution, Hungary had a constitution without an administration; one was a triumph of the State, the other of the individual... The Diet was the true Sovereign of Hungary.

We have seen that Charles VI's concern for the Pragmatic Sanction had enabled the Hungarians to obtain full recognition of their liberties. During the war Maria Theresa had been anxious not to offend the Hungarian Diet and thus endanger its military contributions. Yet the continuance of the right of the Diet to determine its financial contribution to the State was the greatest single weakness of the Habsburg Monarchy. Hungary represented about half the Habsburg

---

[1] The Report of Count Trautmansdorf, the President of the Commission, presents a grim picture of the conditions he found. He reported that the labour services were a grievous burden, that the peasants were brutalised, living in tumble-down shacks, sleeping on straw, their children running naked. 'Even their personal goods are not safe from the greed of the great lords. If they possess a good horse, a great landowner forces them to sell it. ... In each village market-place, or before the *Schloss* stand instruments of torture; recalcitrant peasants are put in irons . . . for the least little offence they receive 50 lashes; the serf who arrives late for service, even though it is only half an hour, is knocked almost senseless. Many flee to Prussia to escape this régime of terror. . . . The kingdom of Bohemia resembles a statue which crumbles because someone has removed the base. For all the charges of the kingdom are borne by the peasants who alone contribute.'

dominions, and almost half their population, yet their contribution to army expenditure was about 4 million florins, or less than one-quarter that paid by all the Habsburg lands. It would not be too much to say that the financial problem lay at the root of all the administrative changes of Maria Theresa's reign. The Habsburgs were usually beset with the problems of a financial deficit, and for this the inadequacy of the Hungarian contribution was a most important, but not the only, cause. Geography and traditional Habsburg ambitions had imposed an expensive expansionist foreign policy; since 1618 the Habsburgs had been more often at war than at peace. The Habsburg dominions lay off the main trade routes and lacked the capital resources which came with trade and industry. Expenses of government were high; Charles VI had spent 145 million florins in the course of his reign on the royal chapel, music and poetry. Maria Theresa spent much less on these (77 millions), but on the kitchens and entertainments a total of 649 millions. This was not mere extravagance, but sound policy, for it was her intention to attract to Court the greater nobility, and thus bind them more effectively to the dynasty. But the problem of the expenditure remained. In 1745 her total revenues were about 20 millions a year; ten years later they had doubled.[1] But the War of the Austrian Succession cost about 80 millions a year; the Seven Years' War about 50 millions a year. Even in peace time the army cost about 16 millions a year, and the costs of bureaucratic government steadily mounted. These figures are necessary to put the Hungarian problem into perspective. It was one, however, which Maria Theresa left to her successor. She never summoned the Hungarian Diet after 1765, but on the other hand she did not risk innovations in Hungary which would have been stoutly resisted. If politics is the art of the possible, the political acumen of Maria Theresa was of a high order.

In 1765 her amiable consort the Emperor Francis I died. Entirely excluded from the business of government, he had spent his life in amusements and in the harmless occupation of amassing a private fortune. Maria Theresa, who loved him very deeply, was unconsolable. Her eldest son Joseph had been born in March 1741 into a world torn by the strife of war, a month before the battle of Mollwitz. He

[1] The increased revenues came partly from a poll tax according to social position, ranging from 600 florins for a bishop to 24 for a peasant; and partly from a steady increase in indirect taxes on wines, foodstuffs, state monopolies of salt and tobacco. In all this the leading light was Rudolph Chotek.

had grown up a self-willed and passionate youth, a great problem to his mother, delighting in military matters, and longing for a share in political power. He married Isabella, daughter of Duke Philip of Parma, a delightful, romantic girl, who, however, died in 1763, when Joseph was only twenty-two. Joseph had learnt to love her deeply, and the loss was one from which he never recovered. All his life he had a deep strain of melancholy, from which he found relief only in work. He married again, but he cared nothing for his second wife, and remained for the rest of his life a solitary, lonely figure. In 1764, to his mother's joy, he was crowned King of the Romans, thus ensuring his succession as Emperor; German princes were not anxious to repeat the unfortunate experience of having a non-Habsburg Emperor. But even during the festivities he wrote to his mother (to whom, all his life he was devoted; his letters to her are an invaluable, and deeply human, source for the period):

> I am a man whom sadness penetrates through and through. I play a comedy, my lips smile and my spirit weeps.

With the death of his father he became Emperor, and also Co-Regent with his mother. Maria Theresa regarded him with a mixture of admiration and anxiety, admiration for his abilities and zeal, anxiety lest his impetuosity should land them into disaster.

Joseph II

Joseph's education was much neglected. By the age of twelve he had read little except a life of the saints. He never acquired a taste for the arts except music, and had no knowledge of the sciences. The governing fact of his early years was undoubtedly the wars with Prussia. His hero was always Frederick the Great. Joseph all his life admired military success; he was convinced of the backwardness of the Habsburg Empire. In a *Memoir* he wrote when he was twenty he painted a gloomy picture of the Habsburg lands threatened on all sides, by Prussia, by the Turks, by France, and even by Savoy. To survive, the Monarchy must be strong; it must expand; it must have a strong army, sound finances, industries and commerce; there must be administrative efficiency; luxury must be curbed, and so on. Joseph had all the instincts of a despot; he intended to govern as well as reign. He had unlimited confidence in himself; he was intolerant of opposition, or even of discussion. He saw clearly that the Habsburg Monarchy was a conglomeration of provinces, held together it is true by some community of interests, but above all by the dynasty. Charles VI and Maria Theresa had preserved the integrity of the Monarchy, except for Silesia. But more was needed. The whole must be welded into a single State, in the same way as the Hohenzollerns had done with their far more scattered dominions. It could be done only by the Monarchy. 'It needs great courage', he wrote, 'and still more great patriotism, to be an innovator in our century.' His instincts were more than reformist; he was by nature a revolutionary in the strict sense of the word. 'Great actions', he wrote, 'should be carried out with a single stroke.'

In the discussions on reform Kaunitz was inclined to take Joseph's side. He was devoted to the spirit of enlightened despotism. Like Joseph he was exasperated that so often there seemed to be no State policy, but only the policy of the Estates. He wrote in 1763: 'The other sovereigns of Europe more and more restrain the privileges of the nobility, for the true strength of the State rests on the majority of its servants, that is to say on the third estate: it is the latter who deserves the greatest attention.' Neither Joseph nor Kaunitz was led to this conclusion by a vague altruism, but because they were convinced that the strength of the State, a full treasury, a strong army, depended upon a growing and prosperous population, and greater centralisation. This was in Joseph's mind when he wrote in 1765: 'From the greatest possible number of subjects proceeds all the advantages which the State enjoys.'

But if Kaunitz agreed with some of Joseph's objectives, he often differed from him on method of procedure. Joseph wished to destroy the privileges and autonomy of the nobility. He saw no reason, for instance, why the sons of the middle class, or even of the peasantry, should not proceed by way of advanced studies to some of the highest offices of the State. All the instincts of Maria Theresa and Kaunitz were opposed to such a policy. Maria Theresa saw her monarchy resting on the firm supports of the nobility and the Catholic Church, and, though she was quite ready to curb the excessive independence of each, she feared the destruction of either. Kaunitz sided with Joseph on the issue of the Catholic Church, but with Maria Theresa on that of the nobility. The middle class and the peasantry, he wrote, should

1 John Locke (1632–1704) from a portrait painted in middle life.

2 Voltaire, the sage of Ferney. Bust by Antoine Coysevox (1640–1720).

3 Sir Isaac Newton (1642–1727), from a portrait by William Gandy 1706.

4 Bernini: Constantine the Great before the Vision of the Cross, at the head of the Scala Regia, Vatican, 1670.

5 Bernini: Saint Theresa in Ecstasy, in the Cornaro Chapel in S. Maria della Vittoria in Rome. The angel is about to plunge the fiery dart into the heart of St. Theresa, symbol of her mystical union with Christ.

6 Bernini: Piazza of St. Peter's, Rome: a magnificent piece of town planning, fully in the spirit of the Catholic Revival. The great colonnade symbolises the arms of the Church embracing the faithful.

7 The Trevi Fountain, the most splendid in Rome, the work of several artists between 1735 and 1762, based on a design by Bernini.

8 Piazza Novano, Rome. The central fountain was erected by Bernini and his pupils, and symbolised four great rivers. The fountain in the foreground, with masks and Tritons, was partly by Bernini.

9 Watteau: *Embarkation for Cythera*. The most delicate expression of the poetry and fantasy of the age.

10 Mme. de Pompadour by François Boucher (1703–70). Boucher, appointed *Peintre du Roi* in 1765, represents the supreme development of Louis XV painting.

11 High altar of the Cathedral of Freising, Bavaria; a representative example of Central European Rococo.

12 The Palace of Schönbrünn, Vienna, from the Gardens, by Bernardo Bellotto (1720–80), showing the formal garden in French style as it was in 1749. Leopold commissioned Fischer von Erlach to plan a new summer palace in 1692. It was begun in 1695 and partly completed in 1713. Between 1744–49 it was remodelled by Nicolaus Pacassi, as in this painting. Later it became the favourite residence of Empress Marie Theresa, and by 1780 decoration and gardens were greatly changed.

13 The Schloss of the rulers of Wurttemberg, near Stuttgart, one of the largest German palaces built in the eighteenth century. Style reflects the influence of Versailles.

14 View of Versailles, painted by Pierre-Denis Martin in 1722, as it was at the death of Louis XIV, and before the later additions of 1771. In the foreground are the carriages of Louis XV and the Conti family.

15 Louis XIV, marble bust by Antoine Coysevox, commissioned 1686, when Louis was at the height of his power, to stand in the Salle des Etats of the *Parlement* of Paris.

16 Charles XII of Sweden by J. D. Swartz, 1706. Sjöholm Castle, Sweden.

17 Louis XVI,
   from a portrait by Bosc.

18 Louis XV by Van Loo.
A good example of the
formal portrait which
Louis XIV had made the
fashion for French kings.

19 (*above*) The epitome of Absolutism and Enlightenment: Frederick the Great in his old age, by Anton Graff, at Sanssouci.

20 (*left*) Charles III of Spain in Hunting Dress by Goya (1746–1828). Goya painted with devastating frankness one of the most successful monarchs of his time.

21 (*below*) Frederick the Great reviewing his troops.

be taught trade and agriculture, but the study of the law, political economy and administration should be reserved for the sons of the nobility. Moreover, his political sense showed him the dangers of Joseph's autocratic desire to regulate and control everything as if government were a military operation. Joseph once proposed to forbid the nobility to wear ceremonial dress, in the interests of economy. Kaunitz wrote to Joseph: 'All prohibition is odious. . . . I think that it is very important not to interfere in all the insignificant details of the life of men. We should allow each at least the liberty of dressing as he will.' To Maria Theresa he wrote, preaching to the converted:

Too great a submission of subordinates to their superiors is the consequence of a constraint which stifles in us all idea of honour. I do not believe that Your Majesty would wish to introduce the mechanical discipline of the army into civil government; in the army obedience alone counts, whilst in civil administration it is necessary to think before acting; and these two principles are fatally opposed to each other.'

He knew that Joseph stood for the introduction of Prussianism into the Habsburg Monarchy, for the triumph of *raison d'état*. Joseph stood for one theory of monarchy, Maria Theresa and Kaunitz for another. Kaunitz wrote:

Despotic governments concern themselves with intimidation and punishment. But in monarchies, and above all when we have to do with civilised nations, we should equally be careful to reward merit and not to stifle a certain elevation of mind, love of prince and country, not to deprive ourselves of the advantages of works which create thought and feeling, nor to forget how much it is a joy worthy of a noble mind to govern free and thinking beings than to rule vile slaves.

Moreover, he knew the strength of the forces which would be ranged against Joseph. Kaunitz sought to reconcile monarchical power with the traditional interests; to carry the nobility along with the work of reform, as Maria Theresa had already done. Joseph thought that, relying solely on the power of the State, he could ride roughshod over all opposition. But, it is only fair to Joseph to say that he saw himself working against time. His State was in great danger; time appeared to be on the side of Prussia. His haste was not just a matter of temperament; it was dictated by a race for power which would decide whether the very power of the Habsburgs would survive.

Thus Joseph II placed himself at the head of the *Aufklärungspartei*

H

(party of Enlightenment),[1] those who had derived their ideas from the French Gallicans, Jansenists and *philosophes*, and thought of the Catholic Church as the purveyor of obscurantism and superstition. None of their ideas was new, but they were new to Austria. They supported the idea of the unified State and looked to the ruler as alone able to make progress possible. They believed in greater social equality; they glorified the great nobility as the vanguard of progress in the service of Monarchy; they detested the lesser nobility for their feudal oppressions and their tax exemptions. Above all they wanted to change the relations between Church and State. In 1763 Nicholas of Hontheim, bishop suffragan of Trier, better known as Febronius, published his famous pamphlet, which made two essential points: first, that the Catholic Church should be confined solely to the spiritual sphere, and second, that the Pope was subordinate to the Council of the Church. The same arguments were put forward in the writings of Stephen Rautenstrauch, who later was responsible for Joseph's reform of ecclesiastical studies (1775). Joseph was the patron of Martini and Sonnenfels, professors in the University of Vienna, who taught the new principles of Natural Law, and of Van Swieten, who reformed the medical faculty, and of Johannes Riegger, Professor in the University, and Reporter on ecclesiastical affairs in the Austro-Bohemian Chancellery, to whom the Church was merely an institution entirely within the jurisdiction of the State. All these men saw the ruler as the philosopher–king, the only hope of progress towards Enlightenment. In 1764 a Hungarian Adam Kollar published a book on the nature of political power, in which he claimed that the royal power was absolute to direct all affairs, secular and ecclesiastical, to administer justice and to interpret the laws. The Magyar Diet thought otherwise, had the book publicly burnt, and underlined their point of view by voting Maria Theresa less than one-third of the revenues she asked for in 1764. The incident isolates the factors in the situation: a reforming

---

[1] A French traveller at the time well summarised the opposing views: 'The first and strongest party in Austria . . . is always full of schemes for chastity-commissions, prohibition of books, exile of dangerous teachers and preachers, maintenance of papal absolutism and the persecution of the new philosophy. A large part of the nobility, whose rights are tied up with those of the clergy, supports this view. The second party is that of the Emperor, constantly at war with the other. It stands for the reform of justice, the promotion of agriculture, commerce and industry, the undermining of the power of bigotry, the diffusion of the new philosophy, the reduction of the unfounded rights of the nobility, and the protection of the weak against the strong.'

Monarchy, enthusiastic philosophers, and a recalcitrant Magyar nobility.

Joseph II and Kaunitz wished to make the Gallican Propositions of 1682[1] the basis of State policy towards the Church. In a Memorandum to the Empress dated February 10th 1769 Kaunitz outlined his policy: ecclesiastical possessions should be brought more under State control, ecclesiastical control of education should be limited, the wealth of the Church should be limited, the activities of the monastic Orders circumscribed, the excessive number of saints' days reduced, marriage should be a civil contract, and the activities of the Inquisition curbed; and all this should be done by the decree of the ruler. Maria Theresa would go some way in this direction. She agreed that papal Bulls should require the royal *placet*, and that excommunication required the approval of a special commission. She agreed to the establishment of an Extraordinary Commission for Ecclesiastical Affairs to limit the jurisdiction of the Church over laymen and the operation of *mortmain*. She sorrowfully acquiesced in the suppression of the Jesuits in 1773, which Joseph II regarded as one of his greatest triumphs. A report of 1773 showed that there were 5,600 Jesuits in the Habsburg dominions, possessing a capital of about 400 million florins, with an annual income of 4 million florins. This was seized and placed under an Aulic Commission for Studies, to be devoted to educational purposes. The controlling mind of the Commission was Van Swieten. In the University of Vienna new Chairs of natural law and political science were occupied by Martini and Sonnenfels. The Commission's reforms in the faculties of theology and philosophy were strongly supported by Trautsohn, archbishop of Vienna, who was anti-jesuit, and favoured Augustinianism. A new approach to history was revealed by Professor Gaspari, who argued that the Middle Ages were marked by ecclesiastical and feudal domination before the triumph of Roman law and the rise of the secular State. In the faculty of theology it was now necessary to study ecclesiastical history, canon law and biblical exegesis.

Some of these reforms certainly went beyond the wishes of Maria Theresa, and in two respects she was adamant. She refused to remove the strict censorship of books. On one occasion the Russian ambassador Galizin had the eighteen volumes of the complete works of

[1] See p. 91.

Voltaire confiscated at the frontier, and on another the Saxon ambassador was deprived of the *Lettres persanes* of Montesquieu. To strong protests Maria Theresa replied: 'I do not permit the introduction into this country of such horrible works, which serve neither science, pleasure nor religion.' She was equally adamant against the introduction of religious toleration. Protestantism and mysticism always flourished in Bohemia, in spite of persecution, and religious persecution had been one of the causes of the peasant risings in the 1770s. Joseph II was no friend to Protestantism, for Protestants were the natural allies of Frederick the Great, but he saw the futility of driving hundreds of peasant families either to revolt or to flight into Prussia. He appreciated Frederick's remarks that 'all religions are equally good if they teach men obedience', and that 'if Turks or pagans came to people my country, I would build them mosques or temples'. To Maria Theresa all heresy was sinful and hateful; to Joseph it was a matter of State expediency. So long as his mother lived he might argue, but he could not insist upon his views.

Maria Theresa died in 1780. The greatest achievements of her reign were to have preserved her dominions intact, except for the loss of Silesia, to have greatly enhanced Habsburg prestige, and to have effected a degree of centralisation by which alone the Habsburg Empire could survive in the new age of absolutism. She was in fact one of the most successful exponents of the administrative revolution. Whether she can accurately be described as an *enlightened* despot depends upon the exact interpretation of the word one favours. She was certainly no disciple of the *philosophes*; she feared and detested the new irreligion which she felt would undermine the social order. She was devoted to her Church and to her nobility, yet when they seemed to threaten the authority of the Monarch, she was ready to limit the independence of both. The final impression of the great Queen is of a woman of remarkable political sagacity, the greatest stateswoman of the eighteenth century, and the greatest of the Habsburgs.

Her prestige in Europe after 1763 was great; she was in a sense the grandmother of Europe. The Habsburgs had always been famous for judicious marriages,[1] and Maria Theresa pursued this policy to the full. Her daughter Marie Antoinette married the future Louis XVI of

---

[1] Cf. Matthias Corvinus's famous quip: 'Bella gerant alii! Tu, felix Austria, nube.' (Let other Powers make war! Thou, happy Austria, marry.)

France in an attempt to cement the Austro-French alliance; her daughter Caroline married Ferdinand of Naples, and virtually ruled Naples in the Habsburg interest; Maria Amelia married Ferdinand of Parma; and Maria Theresa's second son, Peter Leopold, was Grand Duke of Tuscany. In this way, since the Treaty of Aranjuez by which Spain abandoned interest in Italy, and the Austro-French alliance of 1756, the Habsburgs had a peaceful and unchallenged domination of Italy. Although the French alliance wore thin after 1763, it was not abrogated. Relations with Russia were still more uncertain, for Russia preferred a Prussian alliance, and an aggressive policy in Poland and against the Turks. And behind every intrigue in Europe she saw the enigmatic figure of Frederick of Prussia, whom she regarded as the very devil incarnate. Her last years therefore were full of care; she feared that she might again be dragged into war, or that Joseph might be hoodwinked by Prussia. Her tears at the partition of Poland were genuine enough, for she had witnessed the partition of her own lands, and she had a great respect for the established order. It was a comfort to her to know that her adventurous son would have Prince Kaunitz as guide in the difficult years following her death.

Anton von Kaunitz was the son of a governor of Moravia; his mother was the heiress of the last count of Rietberg. Born 1711, he studied at Leipzig, travelled widely and became a councillor of state to Charles VI. After appointments in Turin and Brussels, he made his name at the Congress of Aix-la-Chapelle. In 1751 he was sent as ambassador to Versailles, where he worked for a French alliance, and in 1753 he returned to take charge of foreign affairs. He at once reformed the organisation of the Chancellery. Sir Charles Hanbury Williams wrote to the Duke of Newcastle that Kaunitz had

> already put the office for foreign affairs upon a new footing, in imitation of those of England and France, and all his commis and clerks are persons of his own, very little known at Vienna.

He rapidly won the complete confidence of Maria Theresa, so that in after-years he was more like a dictator at Court than a Minister. He was tall, slender and a dandy; a contemporary described him as 'si frivole dans ses gouts, si profond dans les affaires'. He had adopted all the affectations of a French *petit-maître*, was inordinately vain, and spent hours a day at his toilet. He was so fanatical against fresh air that at the report of his coming the entire palace fled to secure windows and doors. But with all his absurdities, he was a man of great ability, wide knowledge of Europe and utter devotion to the Habsburgs, and he presided over Habsburg foreign policy from 1753 until Joseph's death in 1790. He was a complete product of the Enlightenment, detesting the powers and privileges of the Catholic Church, although his political sense prevented him from endorsing Joseph's most hasty steps towards a secular absolutism.

Joseph II in 1780 presented the picture of a ruler in a hurry; he appeared to be not so much inheriting a government as initiating a revolution. He had a formidable programme of social, political and economic reform, while abroad he looked to territorial expansion and the humiliation of Prussia. He at once instituted a régime of the strictest economy; he hated luxury and waste, and spent little on entertainment. He cut pensions, closed part of his palace, and was accustomed to wear a coat patched at the elbows. Under Joseph II there came to an end that traditional observance of Spanish etiquette which Charles VI had so delighted in, and Joseph left a tradition of austerity which was seen again in the Emperor Francis Joseph. Even to Mozart he spared a pension of only 800 florins; for music was a frivolity, and the ruler had more serious things to do with his money. He took up the business of government with the utmost seriousness. To him the sovereign ruled, not by divine right, but as the mandatory of his people, for their happiness. He was none the less an absolute ruler, for he alone knew best what his people needed. Joseph would recognise the rights of no intermediary body between himself and his subjects. He cared little for tradition and nothing for racial prejudices; his approach to government was that of the despot. But with all his limitations, no ruler has ever been more concerned than Joseph II to rule well and to serve the Habsburg State. In some ways he was the high priest of a new cult of the State; his motto might have been, as he once wrote: 'Do everything to the glory of the State!' All political decisions were his; he rarely summoned the Council of State, and preferred to consult his Ministers individually. Often he did not consult them at all, but simply sent them instructions. On the whole Kaunitz, Kollowrat and Cobenzl, his most important Ministers, were men of the Enlightenment and accepted his reforms, yet it cannot be said that Joseph aroused either enthusiasm or devotion. He knew this, and it increased his loneliness and sense of failure. Yet he never spared himself; he was a constant worker, rising early, working privately until 11 a.m., when he gave audiences until 3 p.m. At 3 p.m. he dined, then worked again until 6 p.m., when he received Ministers and issued detailed instructions. Whatever his failings, indolence was not one of them.

Judging from Joseph's correspondence, it might well be argued that the subject to which he gave prime concern was ecclesiastical affairs, for these occupy more space in his letters than any other. He was not hostile to religion; indeed, unlike Kaunitz, he was a good Catholic. But he could not permit the Church to continue to function as a State within a State; his concern was always with the power of the State, and in this the Catholic Church was a powerful obstacle. It exercised an intellectual domination over his Empire and hindered intellectual progress; it controlled education; it censored and banned books; it diverted revenues to Rome; it possessed great areas of land in mortmain; it hindered agricultural progress; it absorbed numbers of his subjects into the contemplative Orders; it hindered production by proclaiming too many Saints' days; it encouraged the persecution of the Emperor's Protestant subjects, and drove them to revolt or to flee to Prussia. These were the complaints which occurred so often in his letters. He was not an enemy to religion, but it must always be religion in the service of the State. The test he applied to any institution was how it served the State.

He wrote to the archbishop of Trier who protested against his reforms:

> Your Highness eats the bread of the Church and protests against all reform; I eat the bread of the State and therefore defend its interests, and I employ its prerogatives in every way possible.

His attitude is most clearly expressed in the letter he wrote to Cardinal Herzan, the Imperial Minister in Rome in October 1781:

> Since I have ascended the throne, and wear the first diadem in the world, I have made philosophy the legislator of my Empire. In consequence of its logic, Austria will assume another form, the authority of the hierarchy will be restricted, and *the rights of majesty* will be restored to their primitive extent. It is necessary I should remove certain things out of the domain of religion which never did belong to it. As I myself detest superstition and the Sadducean doctrines, I will free my people

of them; with this view, I will dismiss the monks, I will suppress their monasteries, and will subject them to the bishops of their diocese. In Rome they will declare this an infringement of the rights of God: I know they will cry aloud, 'The greatness of Israel is fallen'; they will complain, that I take away from the people their tribunes, and that I draw a line of separation between dogma and philosophy; but they will be still more enraged when I undertake all this without the approbation of the servant of the servants of God. To these things we owe the degradation of the human mind. A servant of the altar will never admit that *the State* is putting him into his proper place, when it leaves him no other occupation than the gospel, and when *by laws* it prevents the children of Levy from carrying on a monopoly with the human understanding. . . .

The rights of the bishops, *which I will re-establish*, must assist in reforming the ideas of the people; instead of the monk I will have the priest to preach, not the romances of the canonised, but the holy gospels and morality. I shall take care that the edifice, which I have erected for posterity, be durable. *The general seminaries are nurseries for my priests*; whence on going out into the world, they will take with them a purified mind, and communicate it to the people by wise instruction. Thus, after the lapse of centuries, we shall have Christians; thus, when I shall have executed my plan, the people of my Empire will better know the duties they owe to God, *to the country* and to their fellow creatures; thus shall we yet be blessed by our prosperity, for having delivered them from the overgrown power of Rome; for having brought back the priests within the limits of their duties, and for having subjected their future life to the Lord and their present life *to the country alone.*

A careful study of this letter will explain Joseph's fundamental attitude to the problems of statecraft. It makes clear what philosophy he intended to make 'the legislator of his Empire': it was the philosophy of the absolutism of the secular State. The words printed in italics make this clear. He did not seek to destroy religion, but to win over the priests trained in his seminaries to the idea of religion in the service of the State; they must learn to serve God *and their country*. It is an idea the twentieth century will readily understand.

Thus in 1781 he issued an edict of toleration for Protestants. To Van Swieten, his close collaborator in ecclesiastical affairs, he wrote:

Till now the Protestant religion has been opposed in my states; its adherents have been treated like foreigners; civil rights, possession of estates, titles and appointments, all were refused them. I determined from the very commencement of my reign to adorn my diadem with the love of my people ... consequently I granted toleration. ... Fanaticism shall in future by known in my states only by the contempt I have for it; nobody shall any longer be exposed to hardships on account of his creed. ... Tolerance is an effect of that beneficent increase of knowledge which now enlightens Europe, and which is owing to philosophy and the efforts of great men; it is a convincing proof of the improvement of the human mind, which has boldly reopened a road through the dominions of superstition ... and which has now become the highway of monarchs (December 1787).

He extended a similar toleration to the Jews. Good citizens should not be impeded from serving the State because of their religion. For the same reasons he took censorship in hand, and made Count Chotek and Blumauer ('the Austrian Voltaire') heads of a Censorship Commission. Joseph had been much impressed with Gustavus III's introduction of freedom of the press in Sweden in 1774, and he followed suit. There was not in fact complete freedom of the press; the works of Voltaire were still not permitted, but on the other hand attacks on the Pope and the religious Orders were freely permitted. Joseph himself led the attack on the monasteries, and he suppressed some 700 of the houses of the contemplative Orders, such as the Capucins and the Carthusians, and diverted their possessions to religious uses. With some of the money he established new parishes and increased the stipends of the lower clergy. He was extremely anxious to establish State schools wherein secular education could combat the excessive influence of the Church, and in this he achieved much, for within a few years over 200,000 children were in the new schools. Some of the wealth of the monasteries, estimated at 60 million florins, was devoted to extending the University of Vienna, and Van Swieten laid the foundations of Vienna's greatness as a medical centre. In 1782 Pope Pius VI made his famous and most unwelcome visit to Vienna to attempt to dissuade Joseph from his ecclesiastical policy. His visit was accompanied by the publication of a pamphlet *What is the Papacy?* by Eybel, professor of ecclesiastical law at Vienna, which argued that the Pope was merely the bishop of Rome; that the authority of the Vicar of Christ had devolved upon all bishops, and that the ruler derived his authority directly from God. Pope Pius found much religious enthusiasm in Vienna, but he failed to deflect Joseph from his purpose, and Kaunitz insulted the Pope by refusing even to call upon him. The Ecclesiastical Commission went ahead with its work, reorganising the seminaries which trained the priests, requiring them to study history and law; it ordered Mass to be said in German, it interfered with altars and shrines; it made marriage a civil contract. Many of its reforms were in exact accord with the Jansenist doctrines which flourished in France and Italy.

The second great domestic problem with which Joseph dealt was that of administrative centralisation. The two greatest problems which he inherited from his mother were that of serfdom and that of Hungary. The problem of serfdom had a twofold aspect; in the age of Enlightenment it seemed an offence against humanity, and in an age of centralisation it was an obstacle to economic progress and State power. In September 1781 Joseph issued his Patent against serfdom. It declared that 'the liberty to which every man has a right by nature and by law should be extended equally to the serfs'. Personal servitude was abolished; the peasant could leave his land, could marry, apprentice his son to a trade, without the consent of his lord. He still had to render labour services in lieu of rent, but these were limited by law. Against this decree there was a conspiracy of silence in Hungary; no attempt was made to implement it, and the Magyar nobility regarded it as inapplicable because contrary to Hungarian liberties. The time had come, Joseph felt, to grapple with the problem of Hungary.

Joseph began his reign with an omission; he was not crowned King of Hungary, in order to avoid having to take the oath to preserve Hungarian liberties, and he had the Crown of St. Stephen transferred to Vienna. He at once began 'scrambling' bureaucratic and military appointments, so that an increasing number of Germans were appointed in Hungary. Then in April 1784 he ordered government business in Hungary to be conducted in German instead of the traditional Latin. He would, he said, with engaging ingenuousness, have made the language Magyar, but so few of the German officials spoke Magyar! The Magyar nobility at once saw the innovation as a threat to their liberties. But there was worse to follow. We must not forget that the root of the problem was the need to increase Hungary's financial contribution, and for this Magyar liberties must be curbed. Traditionally the Hungarian Diet determined the size of Hungary's contribution, which was then distributed among the fifty-four 'congregations' and collected by the nobility. Joseph ignored this system and divided Hungary into ten administrative districts each under a commissioner of his own appointment. These districts were the equivalents of the *Gubernia* of Austro-Bohemia. The Hungarian Diet was ignored. Many changes were introduced, not by decree, but by administrative order. Hitherto Joseph's decree on serfdom had been ignored in Hungary, but in 1784 a peasant rising was stirred up by Hora, a Transylvanian serf from Zalatna, who claimed that he had laid the peasants' grievances before the Emperor, and had received his authority to lead the peasants to freedom. The revolt was severely suppressed, but the nobles blamed the Emperor for its outbreak, and certainly the Emperor was the hero of the peasants. In this way the foundations were laid for the alliance between Habsburgs and people which was so often a feature of nineteenth-century politics. But for the moment Hungary was restive.

The next step was for the Emperor to tackle the problem of taxation. Joseph was much impressed by the French Physiocrats and their doctrine that land was the source of all wealth, and therefore that the State should rely primarily on a land tax. This seemed to confirm him in his belief of the need to end the fiscal privileges of the nobility. He began compiling tax registers, in Hungary as elsewhere. The Hungarian nobility fiercely resisted. By 1789 they were on the verge of rebellion. Events elsewhere played into their hands.

The tendency of Joseph's reforms was to create a unified and centralised Empire, which took no account of local privileges and traditions. In some ways this was a condition for the survival of the Habsburg Empire; it was certainly the condition for economic development. But there were peculiar difficulties about attempting to centralise the administration of the Austrian Netherlands. Perhaps no area of Europe so small in size had so many customs, liberties and constitutions. In most provinces rights were traditional, but in Brabant there was a detailed charter of Philip the Good, called *La Joyeuse Entrée*, with an enumeration of customs, including the clause that if the Sovereign should cease to observe any article, his subjects might cease to obey him. Except in Flanders, each province had an assembly of three Orders, nobles, clergy and burghers, with the right of taxation. There were many different courts of justice and a multitude of different laws. Joseph neither understood nor respected such mediaeval survivals. Moreover, he wished to increase the economic strength of the Netherlands and their yield to the exchequer. On his visit to the

Netherlands in 1781, he was appalled by the backwardness of its administration and the power of the Catholic Church. The Belgian clergy bitterly resented the new ecclesiastical seminaries, and under Frankenberg, archbishop of Malines, they joined in resistance. Then in April 1787 the Emperor's representative Belgiojoso, a clumsy bureaucrat, called together the provincial Estates to have them vote an increase in the customs duties. The Estates of Brabant replied by quoting their charter, *La Joyeuse Entrée*, which empowered them to refuse any increase of taxation. Meanwhile a revolt spread in Brabant, led by Van der Noot. He was no democrat, but a reactionary and defender of aristocratic privilege. But the rebels wore tricolor cockades, and pelted Belgiojoso's carriage. In May 1789 insurrection spread to Brussels, and a great crowd demonstrated before the palace demanding the recall of Belgiojoso. The governor, Maria Christina, Joseph's sister, who had always detested Belgiojoso and feared the result of her brother's policy, agreed to all their demands. The crowd was jubilant; the bells were rung, flags were flown, and Van der Noot was drawn in triumph through the streets. By this time Joseph was deeply involved with his Turkish war and had few troops to spare; he might fume, but he could only submit. The Hungarian nobles did not need to revolt; they merely united to resist the Emperor's reforms. Kaunitz could only counsel concession. The offending decrees both in the Netherlands and in Hungary were cancelled.

Joseph sadly commented to the French ambassador that the French were in revolt because Louis XVI had failed to introduce reforms; his own subjects were in revolt because he had introduced reforms! He had given his people liberty of thought, reformed the law,[1] improved the economy, abolished serfdom, built schools and hospitals, yet his people did not love him. On his deathbed he declared: 'I do not regret leaving the throne. All that grieves me is that, despite such efforts, I have made so few men happy.' When Kaunitz heard the news of Joseph's death his only comment was: 'It was time.'

In economic affairs the reigns of Maria Theresa and Joseph II had seen a great extension of State activity. The years of war had gravely hampered the beginnings of industrial activity which Charles VI had

---

[1] His most important judicial reform was to abolish the death penalty, the main reason for which appears to have been economic. A criminal was of more value in the galleys than on the gallows.

done something to encourage, and the loss of Silesian industry was a heavy blow to the Habsburg State. Maria Theresa learnt that she must follow the example of Frederick the Great in encouraging industry; she must become a complete Mercantilist. Her first words on economics were a memorandum in 1743 in which she wrote:

> I see that in the provinces not enough attention is paid to commerce and manufacture, which are the only means of gaining wealth and earning foreign currency,

and she at once established an Aulic Commission for Commerce for Austria. Three years later it became the Directory of Commerce (*Kommerzdirectorium*) for the entire Empire, another step towards administrative centralisation. Commercial policy was directed by Rudolph Chotek, and after 1771 by Count Kollowrat. One of its activities was to open up river navigation, and it established internal free trade between Austria and Bohemia, but in general it achieved little. Joseph was very dissatisfied with economic progress, and attempted to stimulate production by high protective duties. He tried to develop the port of Trieste, but later wrote that his ships lay rotting in harbour. His Empire sorely lacked efficient communications. After 1770 there was a flood of physiocratic writing in Austria, and a demand for greater freedom of activity from government control, which Joseph fully endorsed, as when he wrote: 'In industry and commerce nothing is more necessary than liberty, nothing is more harmful than monopoly.' By 1780 the years of peace had brought increasing prosperity and ministerial reports dealt in particular with the industrial progress of Bohemia and Moravia. There are too few statistics available to be certain how far this was the result of government policy.

In foreign affairs it must be remembered that Joseph II had lived his whole life under the shadow of the great Frederick of Prussia. From him he had learnt the nature of power politics. He longed also either to regain Silesia or to find elsewhere an equivalent compensation for it. In these simple facts lie the mainspring of Joseph's foreign policy. After 1763 Habsburg foreign policy was complicated by the weakness of the French alliance, and by the rise of the Russian colossus under Catherine II. For a moment it had appeared likely that under the Russian threat Austria and Prussia would draw together, and this might well have been the soundest policy for both States. In

1769 Joseph met Frederick at Neiss, and again in 1770 at Neustadt, but nothing came of it, and in 1771 Frederick began the negotiations which led to the partition of Poland. Kaunitz' first reactions to the news was to mobilise and to sign an alliance with the Turks. But he was on weak ground, for the Habsburgs had themselves begun the partition by forcibly annexing the county of Zips in 1769–70 on the basis of a claim which dated from 1589. Moreover, Choiseul had just fallen in France; no help could be expected from that quarter, and the prospect of fighting Russia and Prussia was unthinkable. Maria Theresa was in a fever of anxiety lest war should break out, and in the end Joseph and Kaunitz preferred to join in the partition. Joseph's visit to France in 1777 failed to renew the French alliance, but already he was contemplating another adventure in foreign affairs.

The Habsburgs had a claim to Bavaria upon which no less than 288 books had been written; which dated from 1429 and was indeed of the most shadowy kind. It was madness for Joseph and Kaunitz to raise this claim without the most careful diplomatic preparation, in view of the hostility of Prussia. But in spite of this Kaunitz raised the question in 1777. Bavaria had been ruled between 1745 and 1777 by Max Joseph, one of the enlightened despots of the time. In his Will he designated Karl Theodore, the Elector Palatine, as his heir. Karl Theodore was a weak man, with many bastards to provide for, and was not averse from selling his inheritance. This was of the greatest importance to the Habsburgs, for twice during the century (in 1703–4 and 1741–42) Bavaria had threatened the very existence of the Habsburg power. For years the latter had tried to build up a pro-Austrian party in Bavaria, and Joseph had married a Bavarian princess as his second wife. In 1775 Joseph visited Munich incognito, dined daily with the Elector, and secretly made up his mind to annex it. The old Elector feared what was coming and made his Will accordingly. In January 1778 Karl Theodore agreed to sell about one-third of Bavaria, giving Austria a defensible frontier, and the rich salt mines and corn lands of the south. Joseph was jubilant, and thought that Frederick was too isolated to dare to move. But Prussia at once mobilised the opinion of the German princes against the Emperor. Austria and Prussia both put their armies on their frontiers, but neither side really wanted war. The deciding factor was Catherine II, who put 30,000 men into western Poland and then, with France, offered mediation. The ensuing Congress of Teschen was a triumph for Prussia. By the Peace signed in May 1779 Austria received the area of Burghausen, up to the Inn river, and Karl Theodor was confirmed as Elector of Bavaria. Joseph had allowed himself, for an insignificant gain, to appear as the aggressor in the Empire of which he was supposed to be the guardian, and Frederick was able to pose as the protector of the rights of the German princes. Moreover, the threat of Russian power had been felt in Germany as it continued to be felt during much of the nineteenth century.

The next diplomatic question Joseph raised was that of the Barrier Fortresses. Since the Barrier Treaty of 1715 the Dutch had garrisoned the Barrier Fortresses against France in return for an annual subsidy from the Habsburgs. Joseph inspected these fortresses in 1781, and found that most of them had been ruined by the French during the War of the Austrian Succession and had never been repaired; nor (for years) had the subsidy been paid. Joseph argued that such a treaty was an indignity to a sovereign Power, that it was quite ineffective, and that it was no longer necessary in view of the Austro-French alliance. He therefore asked the Dutch to withdraw their garrisons; they protested, but complied. But Joseph also had plans for the economic development of Belgium, and in 1784 he informed the Dutch that he no longer considered the river Scheldt closed except to Dutch and British merchants. The Dutch, however, seized Belgian ships which attempted to use the river, and Joseph broke off diplomatic relations and prepared for war. Eventually the French Foreign Minister Vergennes intervened and negotiated a settlement (1785) by which the Dutch paid the Emperor 8 million guilders to which the French added another 2 million, and the Emperor renounced all right to free transit of the Scheldt and to the fortress of Maestricht. Joseph's policy had been in line with his general policy of centralisation, but it is doubtful whether he had been wise to abrogate the Barrier Treaty which provided for the intervention of Britain and the Dutch to defend Belgium against a French attack.

There was, however, a very different reason why Joseph had wished to abrogate the Barrier Treaty, for he needed to possess the Netherlands in full sovereignty in order to implement another plan for expansion. He had not abandoned his plan to acquire Bavaria. Karl Theodor was childless, and his heir might be persuaded to exchange

Bavaria for the Netherlands, which might become the kingdom of Burgundy, and which in any case was a wealthier State than Bavaria. Joseph knew that Prussia, the princes of the Empire, the Dutch and the British would oppose the exchange, but thought he could rely on the support of France and Russia. But as soon as the proposal was bruited in 1785, Frederick of Prussia accused the Emperor of violating the constitution of the Empire, and raised such an opposition among the Princes, that the Elector of Bavaria withdrew his consent to the plan. Prussia used the opportunity to form a League of Princes (*Fürstenbund*) for the preservation of the liberties of the Empire. For a second time Joseph had enabled Prussia to pose as the leader and protector of the German princes.

Joseph was seriously hampered in all his foreign relations by the absence of a firm ally. France could not be relied upon to aid Austria in war, while an alliance with Russia could only mean Austrian assistance to further Russian expansion. The one alliance which would have accorded with Austrian interests would have been with Prussia, but this was impossible with Frederick the Great. Joseph felt his isolation severely in the years after the Russo-Prussian alliance of 1764. In 1781 he seized the opportunity to reverse the tables. The Prussian alliance no longer served Russian interests which were now directed towards war with the Turks; Catherine saw Joseph as a more satisfactory ally. An *entente* was made in 1781. Catherine sought the dismemberment of the Turkish Empire, and Joseph could now aid only in the dismemberment, and secure gains for himself. Yet in this he was a reluctant aggressor, for Kaunitz and he knew that the true interests of the Habsburgs lay, not in further Balkan acquisitions, but in preventing further Russian expansion. Both knew the risk they ran from French hostility to a war against the Turks, and also to the danger of a Prussian attack in the rear. But in 1787 Joseph accompanied Catherine the Great on her triumphal tour through the Crimea. The Turks knew what was coming and attacked first. At first everything went against Joseph's armies. During 1788–89 epidemics broke out and thousands of his troops died from fever; Joseph himself was desperately ill with it. Joseph failed to take Belgrade in 1788 and the Turks overran the Banat and devastated it. In 1789 the tide turned, and Marshal Loudon captured Belgrade and overran Serbia and Wallachia. Peace was made by the Treaty of Sistova in 1791, by which the Habsburgs gained the frontier region of Orsava in Hungary.

Joseph never recovered his health, and died in 1790. His last years were darkened by military defeats, the growing power of Russia, the revolt in the Netherlands and the beginning of the revolution in France. When he died he was only forty-nine. His later failures have tended to obscure his achievements, and some writers have written these off as non-existent. But this is not to see his work in perspective. His abolition of serfdom and his attempt to protect the peasant from exploitation in Austro-Bohemia was of permanent benefit. He created a link between the peasant and the dynasty which was never entirely lost so long as the Habsburg Empire survived. Much of his administrative centralisation remained, and the bureaucracy which Maria Theresa and Joseph created was one of the most important structures holding the Empire together during the nineteenth century. He increased the activities of the State, increased revenues from 54 to 92 million florins, and began the building of schools and hospitals. He limited the power of the Church. The work of Maria Theresa and Joseph equipped their dominions to withstand the whirlwinds of Napoleonic days. The areas of his Empire which most resented Joseph's reforms were the two most reactionary areas, the Netherlands and Hungary. Hungary presented the greater problem. If Joseph failed to solve the Hungarian question, so did all his successors, and the question remained a century later to drag Europe into war and the Habsburg Empire to its final destruction. In the Age of Absolutism and Enlightenment, Joseph II, more than any other monarch, combined in his person the ideals of each.

9: Russia from Peter the Great to Catherine the Great

The Problem of the Succession

One of the most urgent problems Peter the Great left to Russia was that of the succession. Peter married twice; by his first wife he had a son Alexis who was in every way his opposite, weak, scholarly and opposed to his father's innovations. In 1712 Peter married a second time and had a son named Peter. He demanded that Alexis should either endorse all his reforms, or renounce the throne. Alexis chose the latter, and in 1716 he suddenly fled to the Habsburg Court. News

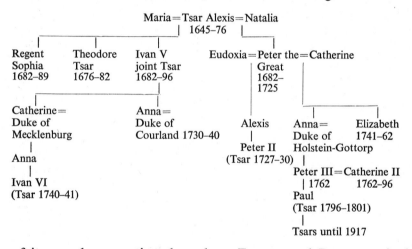

of it caused a sensation throughout Europe, and Peter promised Alexis pardon if he returned to Russia. He did so, but then enquiries showed the extent to which Alexis had been the centre of opposition to his father's reforms. The pardon was withdrawn, and a special court sentenced Alexis to death. However, before the sentence could be carried out, Alexis died from torture. In 1722 Peter the Great issued a new Law of Succession: the principle of hereditary succession was entirely ignored, and the ruler was given complete freedom to nominate his successor. But Peter made no such nomination. He died in 1725, at the age of only fifty-two, worn out by a life of constant toil. Alexis was dead; Peter's second son was dead. There remained his second wife, Catherine, who had been a Lithuanian peasant woman; Alexis's son Peter, Peter the Great's daughters, Anna and Elizabeth, and finally Ivan V's daughters, Catherine and Anna. As there was no principle of succession at all, the way was open for a period of Court intrigues and Palace revolutions. During the next thirty-seven years Russia was ruled by three women, two children and a half-wit, with all the attendant uncertainties and confusion in policy.

Peter the Great's friends, headed by Prince Menshikov, had his wife Catherine proclaimed Empress, not by the *Zemski Sobor*, as in the past, but by the Senate, acting under pressure from the Guards, who were demonstrating outside, Menshikov, who commanded the Guards, having suitably bribed them for the occasion. Catherine always remained the peasant woman she had once been, understanding little of affairs, and with a single interest in the pleasures of over-eating. On Menshikov's advice, she set up a privy council of six, composed of Menshikov, Galizin, Ostermann and three of their friends, as a suitable means by which Menshikov could continue to rule Russia. But in 1727 she died, having nominated Alexis's son Peter to succeed her, with the Privy Council as Regent. Peter II was aged twelve, and around him there surged the struggles between Menshikov and the Dolgoruky family for political power. Alexis and Ivan Dolgoruky represented the old boyar class, opposed to westernisation and reform, and they soon succeeded in ousting Menshikov from power and exiling him. If Peter II had lived for long, all the work of Peter the Great would have been undone. Local government rapidly slipped back into the hands of the nobility. But in 1730 Peter died of smallpox, without nominating a successor.

The Empress Anna

It might have been supposed that the choice would then fall upon Anna, Peter the Great's daughter, and widow of the Duke of Holstein. But the Privy Council preferred Anna, daughter of Ivan V, widow of the Duke of Courland, for it appeared likely that she would be of little account. The dominant figure in the privy council at this point was

Prince Galizin. In 1697, at the age of thirty-six, he had gone to western Europe to study, had built up a fine library of foreign books, including the writings of Pufendorf and Grotius. He had seen how Sweden had limited the power of its king after the death of Charles XII, and for a time he and his circle discussed the relative merits of the Swedish, English and Polish constitutions. The French Embassy Secretary wrote home: 'Here, in the streets and homes alike, there is nothing to be heard but talk of the English Constitution and the rights of the English Parliament.' Anna therefore, upon her nomination as Empress, was presented with a document, which she at first approved, requiring her to rule only with the advice of the privy council, and confirming that no nobleman could be punished without legal trial. This would have been to turn her into a constitutional monarch. It soon became clear, however, that the document did not carry the support of the great mass of the nobility. They had no quarrel with the autocracy, and no wish at all to be governed by Galizin and his privy council. What they wanted was relief from the burdens of State service which Peter the Great had imposed upon them. They wanted no share in the actual business of government, but a guarantee of the rights of property, freedom from arbitrary punishments, and freedom from compulsory service. In the face of their indifference or hostility, Anna was able to tear up the constitution, suppress the privy council, and arrest and execute some of its members. The nobility soon had to pay dearly for their support for autocracy.

Anna was a stout, masculine woman, cruel, delighting in coarse living, utterly incompetent in government. She distrusted Russians, and surrounded herself with German favourites. The Government was dominated by her lover, Count Bühren, who had followed her from Courland, and he and his German friends, according to Russian historians, plundered the Russian State. Foreign affairs were directed by Ostermann, a Westphalian, and the army by Münnich, a soldier of fortune, both Germans, and former servants of Peter the Great. Russia became a police state in which 20,000 Russians were sent to Siberia for so-called conspiracies against the Government. In government Anna used neither the old Senate, nor the privy council, but a new 'Cabinet' of two or three, who in fact governed for her.

She made a series of important concessions to the nobility. In 1730 the law of Primogeniture was abolished, and the division of estates was resumed. In 1731 it was decreed that nobles entered government service with the rank of officer, and a special Cadet Corps of Nobility was established for the sons of nobility. In 1736 it was decreed that the term of service was limited to twenty-five years, but the Turkish War meant that this had to be deferred. During the period the position of the peasant continued to deterioriate. One problem which caused the Government genuine concern was his constant flight from the soil. In less than a decade, it was estimated, some 200,000 peasants had fled to Poland, or the Ukraine or the steppes, with a consequent loss in tax-payers and army recruits, as well as tillers of the soil. It was partly to check this, and to curb the periodic peasant revolts, that the nobility in 1730 received increased police and judicial powers. They were now entirely responsible for the collection of the peasants' taxes, and for their good behaviour. But this they could not do if they were away on State service, and thus the decree which cut the term of service to twenty-five years also enabled fathers to keep a son at home to manage the estates. Moreover, estates were no longer held as service estates, but as hereditary possessions. Thus the nobility were effec-tively transformed into hereditary lords of the manor, with full powers over their serfs. In 1760 they obtained the right to send them to hard labour in Siberia (an area the State was anxious to populate). More-over, all peasants were treated as serfs, and the finer gradations of status were eliminated; for, if the lord was responsible for the taxes of peasants, they were regarded as his serfs. Thus in the decades follow-ing the death of Peter the Great the development of serfdom went on steadily.

In foreign affairs Ostermann and Münnich had considerable suc-cess. In the War of the Polish Succession they placed their candidate Augustus of Saxony on the Polish throne with little cost to Russia, and in 1739, by the Treaty of Belgrade, they gained Azov from the Turks, thus fulfilling one of the ambitions of Peter the Great. But these successes did nothing to reconcile the Russians to their German rulers. Anna died in 1740, having nominated her great-nephew, the two-months' old Ivan VI as her successor, with Bühren as Regent. But Bühren was soon overthrown by Münnich, and finally in 1741 the whole 'German party' were driven out in another palace revolution, organised by the Guards, and Peter the Great's daughter, Elizabeth was declared Empress. Her sister Anna Petrovna was already dead, but Elizabeth at once nominated Anna's son Peter as her successor, and, as a reassuring gesture to her subjects, she abolished the death penalty during her reign.[1]

The Empress Elizabeth

The Empress Elizabeth (1741–62) was a kindly, charming and beautiful woman, but without any real grasp of policy, so that the great events of her reign unfolded without much influence from her. She never forgot that she was Peter the Great's daughter; she loved the pageantry of ruling, and at her death left a wardrobe of 15,000 gowns. Yet her palaces were in squalor, with holes in the ceilings, and royal furniture was so scarce that she had to carry it from palace to palace as she moved. She spent 10,000,000 roubles on the building of the Winter Palace, but it was unfinished at her death. She was humane and enlightened, as her abolition of the death penalty showed, and was in many ways influenced by the western culture of the time. But the financial chaos, which dated from Peter the Great's time, continued to mount, and the position of the serf continued to worsen. She restored the Senate to power, but ruled mainly through her favourites. She early fell in love with a simple Cossack shepherd named Alexis Razumovsky, and kept him about her for the rest of her life, but he had little influence on affairs, though his brother became President of the Academy of Sciences. Government was conducted mainly by Ivan Shuvalov, a man of culture and ability, who founded the University of Moscow with the aid of his cousin Peter Shuvalov, who was in charge of finances, and Peter's brother Alexander Shuvalov, who was head of the secret police. Foreign policy was conducted by Count Michael Bestuzhev.

In general, Bestuzhev's foreign policy was to continue that inherited from Ostermann and Peter the Great. That is to say, Russia regarded her neighbours, Sweden, Poland and the Turks, as her enemies; and it followed therefore that France must be an enemy also. Thus Russia's natural ally was Austria. Russia fought numerous wars in the period, all in alliance with Austria, the Polish War (1733–35), the Turkish War (1736–39), a Swedish skirmish (1741–43), and the wars against Prussia (1746–48 and 1756–63). The general objectives were to advance to the Black Sea, to increase Russia's hold on Poland, and to

[1] She had to restore it ten years later at the insistence of the Church.

restrain the growing power of Prussia, in which Bestuzhev sensed the greatest threat to Russia's power in the Baltic. In all this from time to time French gold and skill in diplomacy acted as a disruptive influence, in an attempt to prevent the destruction of Polish independence. On the other hand, relations with England were always good. The British ambassador, Sir Charles Hanbury Williams, was on good terms with Bestuzhev, and did what he could to relieve pressure on Prussia during the Seven Years' War. He also gave £10,000 to the future Catherine the Great to encourage her to contemplate a *coup d'état* upon the death of the Empress. The death of Elizabeth in 1761 saved Frederick of Prussia from destruction at the climax of the Seven Years' War.

Peter III and Catherine

In 1762 Elizabeth's nominee, Peter III, succeeded quietly to the throne. The son of the Duke of Holstein, he had at first been thought likely to succeed to the Swedish throne, and though he came to live in Russia from the age of fourteen, he never understood or liked the Russians. Feeble-minded and cruel, he feared the people around him, and his love for Germans took the form of an irrational admiration for Prussia. He appointed Germans to command the Russian army. He admired Lutheran Protestantism, and openly jeered at Russian Orthodox ceremonies. His foreign policy appeared to lead to a subordination of Russia to Prussian interests. In one thing only did he please his nobility. In February 1762 he abolished the principle of compulsory service for the nobility; henceforth a nobleman could leave State service at any time. Thus was completed the process which had continued since the death of Peter the Great. The nobility of Russia were now a hereditary and privileged landowning class, the masters of their serfs, but no longer compulsorily servants of the State. But this concession did not save Peter in the eyes of his nobles.

In 1745 Peter III had married Catherine, the daughter of the Prince of Anhalt-Zerbst, one of the petty princelings of Germany who was in the service of the King of Prussia, for whom he was Governor of Stettin. The choice of bride had been made by the Empress Elizabeth, and had been furthered by Frederick, who sought to offset the influence of the anti-Prussian Bestuzhev in Moscow. Catherine soon found her husband 'childish. . . . I observed with astonishment his imprudence and lack of judgment on a number of matters.' Catherine dutifully became a member of the Greek Orthodox Church, learnt Russian, and observed intrigues which went on around the person of the Empress. She soon found her husband ridiculous ('small and infantile, talking of nothing but soldiers and toys', she wrote in her *Memoirs*), and, as she frankly admitted, 'the Crown of Russia attracted me more than his person'. Moreover, after an attack of smallpox in 1745, he became, she wrote, 'horrid to look at'. Peter utterly neglected her, and preferred to spend his time drilling his soldiers, and holding mock-courts-martial. Catherine soon learnt the art of duplicity, without which it would have been difficult for her to survive at the Russian Court, where she was suspected of being a Prussian spy. She even secretly took a lover, the first of at least twenty-one who during the next forty years sought to satisfy the appetites of this remarkable woman. In her *Memoirs* she hints that she took Serge Saltikov as a lover in order to provide an heir, and when her first child was born no one at Court seems to have been in much doubt who the child's father was. If her hints are true, there was no Romanov blood in any of the rulers of Russia during the nineteenth century, which, considering the mentality of Peter III, was perhaps just as well. Her son Paul was born in 1754. Meanwhile her feelings for her husband turned to loathing. On one occasion she came upon him flogging a small King Charles terrier; on another occasion he was holding a court-martial upon a rat. Her next lover was the handsome Stanislaus Poniatowski, soon to be, at her instigation, king of Poland. Meanwhile she devoured French literature, Montesquieu and the popular French novels of the time. There was a moment of crisis when her friend Bestuzhev was arrested for treason in failing to prosecute the war against Prussia during the Empress's illness. In this Catherine might well have been implicated, had she not hastily burnt all her papers. She describes in her *Memoirs* how she lay low for a time, amusing herself by reading the first volumes of *L'Encyclopédie*, and so the crisis passed.

A new crisis came with the death of the Empress in December 1761. Catherine was expecting a child by her new lover, Gregory Orlov. Orlov and his brothers gathered the nobility against the new Tsar. Peter, for his part, talked openly of putting away his wife. It was a simple struggle for survival between them, in which the superior ability of Catherine triumphed. The principal conspirators were the Orlovs, Count Nikita Panin, Princess Dashkov and the Guards. What brought matters to a head was the Tsar's decision to declare war on Denmark to regain Schleswig for Holstein. Orlov escorted Catherine to the Guards' H.Q. where they swore allegiance to her as Empress. On June 28th she issued a Proclamation that she would defend the Russian Orthodox Church and Russian foreign prestige. Peter failed to organise resistance, and fled to the country. Catherine entered St. Petersburg in state in one of the least bloody revolutions in Russian history. On July 6th 1762, the day on which she issued a Manifesto to her people, Peter was killed in a brawl with one of his jailors. The Manifesto declared:

> An Autocracy which good and philanthropic qualities in the Sovereign, ruling autocratically, do not check is an evil.

The *Nakaz* of 1767

Her years of loneliness, difficulty and intrigue had matured a most remarkable personality. A warm and sanguine nature was combined with a high intelligence, abundant energy and a cool determination to triumph. Beneath a passionate exterior there was the ruthlessness of a supreme egotist. The sentence quoted from her Manifesto is significant of her approach: the only restraint upon the will of an autocrat is his good sense. Her *Memoirs* make clear how purposefully she had aimed at the Crown, and no ruler could have a clearer grasp of the fundamental facts of power. And indeed, in 1762 she could not afford to ignore the facts, for she was a foreigner, until recently suspected of being a Prussian agent, dependent for her position upon a small group of nobles. The revolution which had been made so easily might be unmade equally easily. It followed that she must retain the loyalty of the Guards, and indeed of the whole noble class, by a government which was in their interests. It followed also that she must reverse the policies of her late husband. Frederick the Great told the French ambassador, Ségur, that Catherine was not so much the instigator of the revolution as its tool. Yet the remarkable fact was that she at once turned the revolution to her own advantage. It is true that she could rely on the devotion of the conspirators, and also upon the fact that Russia was accustomed to an autocracy. She did not even find it necessary to reverse Peter's foreign policy, for in 1764 she signed an alliance with Prussia.

Meanwhile she studied the predicament of her government: an inefficient administration, financial weakness, widespread corruption; no adequate government records; she did not possess even a map of the entire Russian Empire. She found that whereas 28 million roubles were collected in taxation, only 16 million actually reached the Treasury. The very laws of the country, she declared, bore little relation to the needs of a great country. She travelled widely, studying the facts. She immensely enjoyed the exercise of power, and she was saturated by the ideas of the Enlightenment, especially of Montesquieu and Beccaria. Gradually the notes and translations of her reading were put together during 1765–67 to form her famous *Nakaz* ('Instruction') of 1767. 'Nothing in the composition is mine', she wrote to Frederick the Great, 'beyond just the ordering of the material and an occasional word.' This was true, for 250 of the 526 articles were copied directly from Montesquieu, and over 100 on criminal procedure show the influence of the ideas of Beccaria. The following extracts will do more than any commentary to make clear the nature of this remarkable document.

The INSTRUCTIONS to the Commissioners for Composing a New Code of Laws

6 Russia is a European State.

9 The Sovereign is absolute; for there is no other Authority but that which centres in his single Person, that can act with a vigour proportionate to the extent of such a vast Dominion.

12 It is better to be subject to the Laws under one Master, than to be subservient to many.

13 What is the true end of Monarchy? Not to deprive people of their natural liberty, but to correct their actions in order to attain the Supreme Good.

15 The intention and end of Monarchy is the glory of the citizens, of the State, and of the Sovereign.

33 The Laws ought to be so framed as to secure the safety of every citizen as much as possible.

34 The equality of the citizens consists in this, that they should be subject to the same laws.

41 Nothing ought to be forbidden by the laws but what may be prejudicial either to every individual in particular, or to the community in general.

57 The Legislature ought to adapt its laws to the general sense of the nation. We do nothing so well as what we do freely and uncontrolled.

63 Every punishment which is not inflicted through necessity is tyrannical.

85 Experience teaches us that in those countries where punishments are mild, they operate with the same efficiency upon the minds of citizens as the most severe in other places.

94 It is unjust to punish a thief who robs on the highway in the same manner as another who not only robs, but also commits murder.

96 All punishments by which the human body might be maimed ought to be abolished.

123 The usage of torture is contrary to all dictates of Nature and Reason; even Mankind itself cries out against it, and demands its abolition.

210 Proofs from fact demonstrate to us that the frequent use of capital punishment never mended the morals of a people.

248 Finally, the most sure, but at the same time the most difficult expedient to mend the morals of the people is a perfect system of education.

261 A law may be productive of public benefit which gives some private property to a slave.

265 Russia is not only greatly deficient in the number of her inhabitants, but at the same time extends her dominion over immense tracts of land which are neither peopled nor improved. And therefore, in a country so circumstanced, too much encouragement can never be given to the propagation of the human species.

266 The peasants generally have twelve, fifteen and even twenty children by one marriage, but it rarely happens than one-fourth of these ever attains to the age of maturity. There must therefore be some fault, either in their up-bringing, their way of life or method of education which occasions this prodigious loss and disappoints the hopes of the Empire. How flourishing would be the state of this Empire if we could but ward off or prevent this fatal evil by proper regulations.

295 Agriculture can never flourish where no persons have any property of their own.

313 Agriculture is the first and principal labour which ought to be encouraged in the people; the next is the manufacturing of our own produce.

317 Commerce flies from places where it meets with oppression, and settles where it meets with protection.

350 It is impossible to give a general education to a very numerous people.

520 God forbid that, after this legislation is finished, any nation on
earth should be more just, and consequently should flourish more
than in Russia, otherwise the intention of our laws would be totally
frustrated, an unhappiness which I do not wish to survive.

It is clear that the document is infused with the spirit of Enlightenment. Catherine's prime purpose is a reform of the law, the definition
of rights, liberties and punishments. The Empress Elizabeth had
already suspended the death penalty; Catherine frowned on the use
of torture. A country lacking in inhabitants could not afford such
wastage of human life. Catherine repeats the arguments of the Mercantilists on the need to encourage the growth of population. She was
timid on the subject of serfdom, and at one point made clear that she
was not contemplating wholesale emancipation; yet she hinted that
there was something seriously wrong with the practices of serfdom
(Art. 266). There was no question of limiting Russian autocracy—
geography alone made autocracy the only government for Russia—
but in other respects the tone of the document was liberal.

The *Nakaz* was submitted to a Legislative Commission in June
1767. 565 deputies were summoned as representatives of the nobility,
towns, the Government, freemen, and even the peasants. An extraordinary fact was that whereas the nobility represented only 30 per
cent. of the whole, the towns, which played so small a part in Russian
life, were represented by 39 per cent. The implication is that Catherine
was seeking some national support other than that of the privileged
classes. During the following eighteen months the Commission met
203 times, at first in Moscow, later in St. Petersburg; there were long
discussions about the rights of the nobility, but no conclusions were
reached. When it broke up, it left a committee which lingered until
1774, and then disappeared. It is not difficult to see why the experiment failed. Russia was entirely unused to such an assembly and such
a commission; even the *Zemski Sobor* had long ago disappeared. The
classes represented had little in common with each other and could
not have been expected to come to any conclusions. Nor is it clear
what exactly they were expected to do; it was impossible that an
assembly of 565 people, untrained in the law, could draw up a new
law code, or that the nobility would voluntarily abdicate their rights.
Historians have been puzzled that Catherine, one of the political
geniuses of the period, should have acted apparently so naïvely, and

they have contrasted the idealism of 1767 with the realism of the rest of her reign. Russian historians have tended to be contemptuous of a document which seemed to them merely to repeat western clichés unrelated to the real needs of Russian society. The *Nakaz* did indeed register Catherine's reactions to the primitive conditions she found in Russia; it seemed to her that a civilised code of law was the necessary foundation for any western State. But she risked very little by her experiment of 1767; in some ways she gained, for on the one hand she fulfilled the desirable qualification of any usurper of being a reformer, without risking her autocracy, and on the other she learnt much about the essential character of the country she was to govern. Moreover, in the eyes of Europe, especially of the *philosophes*, she appeared in the exciting light of that new phenomenon, an Enlightened Despot. From the moment of her accession Voltaire had regarded her with the greatest expectation, and had entered into correspondence with her. Catherine was flattered by his letters, and sought, like Frederick the Great, to imitate his style. Voltaire for his part pronounced the *Nakaz* the finest monument of the century, and it is significant that whereas the publication of the document was forbidden in Russia (a strong argument against the idea that Catherine was seeking to build up some popular party in Russia against the nobility) it went through twenty-three separate editions in Europe within four years. It thus gave Catherine considerable moral status in Europe. The idea that she had some vague intention of following it by a constitution is entirely unsupported by the facts.

Her correspondence with Voltaire in the early years of her reign, with all its posing and gesturing, nevertheless gives one of the best insights into the workings of her mind at this period. She was at great pains to show herself an apt pupil of the *philosophes*. In August 1765 she gleefully described to Voltaire how she had tamed the Church in 1762 by imposing control upon its revenues, and how, when Arsenius, Archbishop of Rostov, opposed her plans, and lectured her about 'the principle of the two powers', she had had him reduced to the status of a monk. She proudly declared that toleration existed throughout her dominions, that she had sent to England for a certain Dr. Dimsdale to inoculate herself and her family against smallpox.[1] Much of the correspondence was taken up with her wars against the Turks, in which

[1] At that time a sign of advanced thinking indicating a belief in the new science.

Voltaire was always urging her on to ever greater efforts. Sometimes they discussed literature and philosophy, and in January 1774 she wrote delightedly that Diderot had reached St. Petersburg, and that she could talk with him 'all her life without wearying'. Sometimes the letters were mere flattery, as when Voltaire called her 'the northern star, towards which all eyes must turn', and Catherine replied that she was not the northern star, but merely the aurora borealis, reflecting Voltaire's light. But never for a moment in the correspondence was there any doubt that Catherine was the autocrat of Russia, and that her true motive was the pursuit of power. Years before, in 1757, she had written to Sir Charles Hanbury Williams: 'Neither my head nor my character will ever change'; and this was no more than the truth.

The Government of Catherine the Great

When the Commission broke up Russia was already at war with the Turks, and Catherine's energies were diverted to the stimulating task of foreign expansion. Before that war was ended in 1774 she had been led by Prussia into the partition of Poland (1772). In all she ruled as a complete autocrat, unlimited by Senate, Privy Council, or Cabinet, such as had from time to time emerged since the death of Peter the Great. Her Minister Nikita Panin did in fact suggest a permanent Council of State in 1762, and Catherine at first agreed, but when she saw that it would act as an effective check upon her power, the idea was dropped. Later, in 1769, when firmly in control, she did employ a Council of Ministers, but never allowed it to be a limitation upon her power.

In 1773, however, her régime received an unpleasant shock from the revolt of Pugachev. This was really only the most famous, and the most serious, of a long line of peasant revolts which disturbed Russia in the eighteenth century. We have seen already how Russian power had for a century been encroaching into the Ukraine, bringing with it the oppressions of State power, taxation, forced labour and serfdom. Emelian Pugachev was a Cossack, a soldier and a deserter, who declared himself to be Peter III, to whom he had a superficial resemblance. He set up an Imperial Court and announced the end of taxation, serfdom and military service. Social discontent gave the movement impetus, and it spread through the basins of the Volga and Ural rivers. The Government was taken entirely by surprise, and, in view of the Turkish War and the partition of Poland, had few troops to spare. The rebels took Kazan, and, if Pugachev had been more daring, he might have taken Moscow. But he had neither organisation nor plans, and could only wait for the Government to recover its strength. In 1774 the revolt was suppressed, and Pugachev was tried and executed.

The revolt had considerable influence upon Catherine; for her there had been moments of great danger. If there remained any ideas in her mind of lightening the burdens of serfdom, they were now banished. Her autocracy had been shown to rest squarely upon the support of the nobility, and it remained so for the rest of her reign. But the revolt did show the need for a more efficient organisation of local government, and in 1775 she introduced a major reform. Instead of the twenty provinces, or *gubernii*, which Peter the Great had established, she divided them into fifty smaller ones, each of from 300,000 or 400,000 inhabitants, subdivided again into cantons of 20,000 or 30,000 people. Each area was governed by a Governor (*gubernator*) and Council (*gubernia*), a police department, law courts and a treasury, with corresponding institutions for the cantons. There was some attempt to keep executive, legislative and judicial matters separate, but the plan made no provision for equality before the law, and in fact there were clearly defined courts for each social stratum. The plan was quite different from Peter the Great's, where the great object had been to bring the landowners under central control. In Catherine's plan every effort was made to enlist the co-operation of the gentry in the business of government. They in fact governed the provinces, in co-operation with the central government, as well as keeping law and order on their estates. It is true that the Governor and Council were appointed by the Empress, but they were drawn from the gentry class, and in all sub-committees the local gentry dominated in the business of local government. In short, the central government was recruited from the nobility; they appointed nobility to be Governors and Councillors, and the latter ruled the provinces in co-operation with the local nobility.

Ever since the death of Peter the Great, the Russian nobility had pursued the policy of transforming themselves from a service nobility into a hereditary landed gentry. Their attempts to impose checks upon the ruler, such as that of 1730, had been much less important or sustained than their attempts to free themselves from the inconveniences of arbitrary punishments and confiscations, and from long periods of State service. Peter III had released them from the latter obligation in 1762. The climax came when in 1785 Catherine granted her Charter of Nobility. This recognised the nobility as a privileged caste with defined rights. They were recognised as the absolute owners of their property, exempt from personal taxes, liable only to judgment by their peers, and free from the risk of all corporal and non-judicial punishments. In each district the nobility were an organised caste, represented by an elected Marshal of the Nobility, and in this corporate capacity they could directly petition the monarch. Thus Catherine crystallised a system of caste privilege which lasted down to 1917.

It was a corollary of this that serfdom was more firmly than ever fastened to the backs of the Russian peasant. As we have seen, serfdom in Russia was not a creation of the eighteenth century, but it extended steadily throughout the century in several ways. First, the poorer peasants were treated automatically as serfs; second, the burdens of serfdom, in taxation, labour dues and military service, increased as the powers of the State grew; and third, it extended to an ever wider area as Russia itself expanded. Indeed the granting away of serfs became the usual means by which a Tsar rewarded his favourites. Menshikov, the son of a palace groom, received gifts of 100,000 serfs from Peter the Great. Catherine, on her accession, rewarded her fellow-conspirators in the same way and granted away over a million serfs in the course of her reign. During the seventeenth and eighteenth centuries it had become increasingly necessary for landlords to be responsible for tax-collecting and good behaviour among their serfs, but Peter the Great had not regarded the peasants as the property of their masters. In 1762 a decree permitted owners to sell their serfs without the accompanying land. Peter had expressly forbidden this practice in 1721. Nor did the eighteenth century impose any limitations on peasant services. It is true that there never was a law expressly establishing serfdom as a condition of private possession, but this was the practical situation by Catherine's reign. In 1767, for instance, the Commission had been in doubt as to whether any punishment was due to a master who had beaten his serf to death. It is true that Count Peter Panin had urged Catherine in a memorandum in 1763 to limit the 'at present boundless power' of the landowner over his peasantry, and suggested that labour services be limited to four days a week, and dues to two roubles. Yet, as we have seen, her hints on this subject in the *Nakaz* were vague, and nothing was done. Instead, serfdom was extended throughout the Ukraine when in 1783 it was decreed that no peasant could leave his lord without his permission, and as late as 1792 the public sale of serfs was expressly permitted.

Historians have usually regarded these developments of Catherine's reign as retrograde steps. It has been argued that just at the time when the nobility had shaken themselves free from State service, they became a hard caste of privilege, while serfdom became a crippling burden to the State until 1861. It was not merely that privilege and serfdom were contrary to the principles of Enlightenment which Catherine had embraced; Enlightenment was in any case a word of many definitions. But Catherine knew that serfdom was contrary to the economic progress of the country. In 1765 a group of enlightened reformers whom she encouraged, called the 'Free Economic Society', reported to her that local agriculture was declining because of the excessive labour services, that serfdom was wasteful and uneconomic, there being great numbers of domestic serfs doing very little, and finally that the army suffered because landlords sent their least useful serfs for military service. Not only was serfdom a brutal system (Kliuchevsky quotes the punishment of 17,000 birch-strokes for absenteeism, after which the victim was permitted one week in hospital in order to recover), but it tended to keep labour tied to unproductive land while the richer areas were short of labour, and the moral effects of serfdom were disastrous. Thus a canker ate deeper into Russian society during Catherine's reign, and was only finally eliminated in 1917.

But to Catherine it appeared otherwise. Her decrees did not initiate the privileges of the gentry, nor the system of serfdom; she merely accepted as inevitable a process which had been going on since the death of Peter the Great, and one which she could not hope to reverse, without a social upheaval which might well have cost her her throne. And the compensations were great, for by recognising the privileges of the nobility her own autocracy was left unchallenged, and with the support of her nobility she made Russia the dominant State in eastern Europe. Catherine had always been more concerned with the facts of power than with chimeras of theory.

I

There is, moreover, another aspect of her policy which is too often overlooked, and one which shows her to be more consistent than is sometimes supposed. The *Nakaz* had shown her deep concern for a society based on legal status (e.g. Art. 33). With all his remarkable achievements, no one could say that this had been one of the objectives of Peter the Great, for in his day, though all men were held to serve the State, they were not free from the arbitrary will of the ruler. Catherine now gave legal status to a class, albeit a class of privilege. She went further, and by a Municipal Decree of 1785 set up a system of urban participation in the government of towns. Three legal categories were established of merchants, artisans and labourers. Municipal government in fact remained in the hands of magistrates appointed by the central government, but there was set up a general *Duma* of elected representatives, and a special *Duma* of six members sitting permanently as an executive, to deal with some aspects of local affairs. This was a seed of self-government, which however failed to sprout. The hand of the central authority always weighed heavily upon towns; taxation was heavy, yet towns contributed only 3 per cent. of the taxes raised in the country, and what trade there was remained in the hands of Jews and foreigners. Yet the reform was an indication of Catherine's intention to broaden the legal basis of Russian society. Even though she achieved it only for the privileged class, the way was open for its extension down the social scale during the nineteenth century. Moreover, the changes of her reign were not so far removed from those taking place elsewhere in Europe, as might be supposed. For in France, Spain, Prussia and the Habsburg dominions the monarchs had either been in conflict with their nobility, or had increasingly centralised their governments in co-operation with them. Catherine was merely attempting, with remarkable success, in the peculiar circumstances of Russia, what was being attempted elsewhere in Europe.

Social Development

We have said already that it is a mistake to judge the reign of Louis XIV from the exclusive standpoint of 1789, and it is equally a mistake to judge the reign of Catherine the Great from the standpoint of 1917. Serfdom ultimately proved to be a disease in the State, but in the eighteenth century its disadvantages appeared to be outweighed by its advantages, for it was the condition for a stable society. And in other respects the eighteenth century in Russia was a period of considerable progress. It appears likely that the Russian population actually declined under the burdens of Peter the Great, but between his death and that of Catherine the Russian population increased from 13 to 29 millions, or if we include Catherine's conquests, to 36 millions. The industries which Peter had established, especially in iron and copper, flourished. Indeed before 1770 Russia was the largest producer of both metals in Europe. The number of factories and workshops increased in the same period from 250 to 3,000, and the number of industrial workers may have exceeded 200,000. It is known, for instance, that one factory alone had 3,500 workers. Some factories were State-owned and worked by industrial serfs, but the textile industries around Moscow were mainly private concerns. On the whole, the Russian rulers of the eighteenth century pursued an enlightened economic policy, removing internal customs duties, and encouraging foreign trade. Moscow was an important commercial centre, and so were St. Petersburg, Riga, Kazan, Kaluga and Tobolsk. Russian foreign trade was mainly through the Baltic, and there was a rapidly increasing export of grain, timber, hemp, flax, tallow, and iron ore. At the end of her reign Catherine's conquest of Odessa opened up the possibility of Mediterranean trade. Imports tended to be in luxury goods, but they were always substantially less than exports. Half Russia's foreign trade was with Britain, which was a main reason for the good relations between the two countries during most of the century.

But in the eighteenth century 95 per cent. of Russia's population was still rural. Russia failed to develop a strong middle class. Serfdom and labour-services were to be found particularly in the 'black-earth' areas of the south, while in the sterner areas of the north, where occupations were mainly based on forestry and rye-growing, the landlord tended to receive his rents in kind. Serfdom still seemed the best system in a country of primitive agricultural method, where land was plentiful and unskilled labour could scrape a living. But the rents and services grew steadily during the century, and some peasants by the end of the reign were working five days a week for their lord.

During Catherine's reign the Russian Church suffered a heavy blow. One of the insistent teachings of the *philosophes* was that the

State should keep its clergy under control, and Catherine found it convenient to follow their advice. In 1764 she nationalised the church lands, in return for an annual subsidy of 450,000 roubles to the Church. This sum represented only about one-third the income from the lands, was quite insufficient to provide the clergy with an adequate living, and most of the Russian clergy lived in conditions little better than those of the peasants.

One problem never solved in the eighteenth century was that of finance. From Peter the Great's time onwards there was almost always a deficit, and at the end of Catherine's reign it amounted to about 10 million roubles a year on a budget of nearly 50 millions. The usual eighteenth-century methods of dealing with it were attempted. Catherine organised the national debt, and began State borrowing from abroad, especially from Holland. Taxes mounted steadily; paper money was issued, with a consequent depreciation and inflation. But these difficulties did not prevent Catherine from fighting constant wars, and from maintaining one of the most sumptuous Courts in Europe.

Catherine's reign was certainly a golden age for the Russian nobility. Numbering less than 1 per cent. of the population, they dominated the countryside, possessed most of the wealth of the country, held most of the important positions at Court, and increasingly acquired the veneer of western culture. There is much truth in the statement that Peter the Great introduced western technology, the Tsarina Elizabeth introduced western fashions and manners, and Catherine the Great introduced western ideas. There had been occasional men of western culture in Russian history before Catherine, Prince Galizin for example in the reign of Anna, or Count Ivan Shuvalov in the reign of Elizabeth, but, encouraged by the Enlightened Despotism of Catherine, they became a frequent occurrence by the end of the century. In every way they aped French customs, they spoke French, they wore the latest French fashions. Catherine adored French literature, corresponded regularly with Voltaire from 1765 until his death, and tried hard, but unsuccessfully, to bring d'Alembert to Russia to act as tutor to her heir. Hearing that Diderot was in financial difficulties, she paid 15,000 livres for his library, and appointed him as her librarian at 1,000 livres a year, an act which all Europe applauded. Her grandsons had as tutor a Swiss republican named La Harpe. One of the greatest of the nobility, Saltykov, had

Marat's brother as tutor for his children. Kliuchevsky tells us that Princess Dashkov, when a girl of sixteen, sat up at night secretly reading Bayle, Helvétius and Rousseau, and he sneers that whereas in Peter's time the nobility (at least) studied mathematics and navigation, now they studied Voltaire! But Kliuchevsky underestimates what was achieved. A number of Russians studied abroad, particularly at the University of Jena. In Peter's reign some 600 books were published in Russia; in Catherine's reign over 8,000. The first newspaper was founded in Peter's reign; in 1770 there were eight periodicals on western lines. Moscow University had been founded by the efforts of Count Ivan Shuvalov in 1755, but it had made slow progress, for Russia as yet had no elementary schools. But Catherine watched with considerable interest the educational schemes of Joseph II in Austria, borrowed his ideas, and even his textbooks, founded a teachers' training college, in 1783, and by the end of her reign had built 300 schools, educating 20,000 children.

During her reign the Russian language, spelling and grammar were regularised, rather as the French language was regularised in the age of Boileau, and English in the age of Addison and Defoe; and the first Russian dictionary appeared in six volumes at the end of the reign. Some of the literature of the reign was mere imitation of French models, and justly earned Kliuchevsky's contempt:

> In no other period of our history do we see our literature treat so extensively of subjects abstract and elevated. And in no other period do we see our literature so remarkable for absolute poverty of content.

Russia, he said, did not think for itself, but imported ideas ready-made. Many Russian nobles, for instance, celebrated the fall of the Bastille in the name of a liberty they ill-understood. But it was not all thoughtless imitation. Alexander Radischev (1749–1802) was a nobleman and a government official who had studied at the University of Leipzig, and had absorbed the ideas of the Enlightenment. In 1790 he published a work entitled *A Journey from St. Petersburg to Moscow*, the first attack upon serfdom by a Russian intellectual. He argued that serfdom was brutalising and degrading:

> Can a country in which two-thirds of the citizens are deprived of their civil rights, and are in part dead to the law, be called happy?

Moreover, the system was uneconomic, for no man will cultivate the field of another as well as he will his own, and society comes to rest on hatred and fear:

> Nothing is more hateful than to witness the relationship between master and slave, on the one side arrogance, on the other fear; between them there can only be the bond of force.

The result one day would be 'a great bursting of the dam', a bloody revolution:

> Death and fiery desolation will be the reward for our harshness and inhumanity.

Catherine studied the work carefully, even fearfully, for she thought it an invitation to another peasant rising, and Radischev was sent to Siberia, and narrowly escaped death.

In the other arts also Russia borrowed from the West. In architecture the Winter Palace, for instance, was designed by the Italian Rastrelli. Catherine was devoted to the theatre, which was developed on western lines. Levitsky painted portraits in the approved western manner. Kliuchevsky's patriotism bristled against such an importation of culture. But it must be remembered that *all* Europe borrowed from France in the eighteenth century, and not merely Russia. Russia has indeed borrowed from the West ever since, and made amazingly successful use of her borrowings. Catherine made Russia, politically and intellectually, more completely a part of Europe. In this she completed the work of Peter the Great and laid the basis for the State-system of the nineteenth century.

Foreign Policy

In the years after 1763 Russia towered like a colossus in eastern Europe. In many respects Catherine's foreign policy was a logical continuation of that of Peter the Great. Peter had defeated Sweden, but had failed to defeat the Turks; Catherine sought to dominate both the Turks and Poland. By the first Turkish War (1768–74) and the Treaty of Kutchuk-Kainardji Russia gained the port of Azov and the area around Kherson, thus bringing Russian territory to the Black Sea, and isolating the Crimean peninsula. Russia also obtained the right to interfere in the Balkans on behalf of the Balkan Christians, a power with considerable possibility for the future.

Meanwhile Catherine's attention was diverted by the Partition of Poland and by the Pugachev revolt. Her Foreign Minister, Panin, had failed to bring about his scheme for a 'Northern System', in the 1760s, an alliance between Russia, Poland, Prussia, Sweden, Holland and Britain. There was little clear purpose in the idea, and it came to nothing. Instead the Russo-Prussian alliance was made in 1764, and it was this which led directly to the Partition of Poland in 1772. Whether this event was really in Russia's interests we have discussed elsewhere,[1] but it certainly brought Russia into closer relationship with Prussia and Austria. Once the First Partition of Poland was completed it was necessary for Russia and Prussia to continue on close terms in order to concert their policy with what remained of Poland, and if Russia was to expand into Turkish territory Catherine required the good will of Austria.

The guiding spirit of her Turkish ventures was Gregory Potemkin, a man of enormous bulk and great energy, who became her lover in 1774. He was an able administrator who brought the Cossacks of the south into the Russian system. He fortified Kherson and began the building of a Black Sea fleet. Above all he carried an important series of army reforms which brought the Russian army into line with Prussian efficiency.[2] Since 1774 the Crimean khanates had ceased to be vassals of the Turks, and in 1782 Potemkin began the penetration of the Crimea. In 1783 he proclaimed their annexation. Kherson had not proved suitable for a naval base, and in 1784 Potemkin built Sevastopol and employed Sir Samuel Bentham, Sir Samuel Greig and John Elphinstone to construct a base and build a fleet. With Potemkin Catherine worked out the plan for her 'Greek Project'. She dreamed of expelling the Turks from Constantinople and Europe, and of establishing a Greek empire with her grandson, appropriately christened Constantine, as ruler. When she took over towns in the Crimea, she gave them classical Greek names, Taurida, Sevastopol, Eupatoria and Theodosia. Catherine first met Joseph II at Moghilev in 1780, and soon stimulated his appetite for new territory. The *entente* was confirmed by a most spectacular tour of inspection which Catherine made through the Crimea in 1787, the elaborate details of

---

[1] See Chapter 12.
[2] Although Prussian troop movements during 1778 showed how far the legendary Prussian army had deteriorated.

which were worked out by Potemkin. Fourteen great sledges and 124 smaller ones bore the Tsarina, the Emperor Joseph, the French ambassador, Ségur, the British ambassador, Fitzherbert and a brilliant concourse of Russian society to Sevastopol. On the return journey at Poltava Potemkin staged a re-enactment of the famous battle with 50,000 men.

The Turks did not wait to be attacked; in October 1787 they laid siege to Kinburn. It was then proved that Potemkin's preparations for war had been quite inadequate, and to some extent he had been taken by surprise. The main event of the war was the Russian capture of Ochakov in December 1788 after a siege of over a year. Thereafter the new Russian commander Suvarov covered himself with glory, and stormed Ismail in 1790. Austria withdrew from the war in 1791, and in 1792 Catherine was ready to accept the Treaty of Jassy, by which the Turks surrendered the Crimea, the port of Ochakov and the territory between the Bug and Dniester rivers. For the first time the whole of the northern shore of the Black Sea was Russian; the gains were in the strategic interests of Russia, but Catherine was a long way from achieving her 'Greek Project'. Her remaining years were concerned with the final partitions of Poland.

In the final estimate, the greatness of Catherine depends upon her success in establishing her despotism in Russia and in extending Russian influence in eastern Europe. Lord Malmesbury, the British ambassador, noted her 'incredible vanity', and how she was solely concerned with 'her own greatness and power', and this was true. She coarsened with the exercise of power; her early idealism was abandoned as she learnt to understand the complexities of the Russian situation, and thus her 'Enlightenment' was only skin-deep. Russia was too alien a country to be ruled by western philosophy.

10: Spain and Portugal in the Age of The Enlightenment

The Decline of Spain

In 1660 Spain was in full decline. Olivares' attempt between 1621 and 1643 to put the clock back, and endow Spain once more with a grandiose foreign policy, had failed lamentably. His attempt to continue the policy of Philip II and establish military ascendancy in western Europe imposed impossible burdens on the enfeebled State. In 1640 Portugal and Catalonia revolted against the Spanish Monarchy. In 1643 Spanish military power was broken by Condé at Rocroy, and in the following years Roussillon, Cerdagne, Flanders and Dunkirk fell into French hands. In 1648 Masaniello led a romantic revolt in Naples against Spanish rule. The Peace of the Pyrenees (1659) cost Spain Artois, Roussillon and part of Cerdagne, and might have been much harsher but for the internal difficulties of France.

The true core of the Spanish Monarchy lay in Castile; it was Castile which bore most of the taxation, and which in the sixteenth century provided most of the colonists and soldiers who had made Spain a great power. But in the seventeenth century its population was probably declining, and it was increasingly unable to bear the heavy burdens of taxation. Agriculture was in decay, and there was a steady drift of people from the countryside into the towns, so that whereas the rural areas declined, Seville doubled in size in half a century. The reasons for this rural decline have not been fully investigated, but most historians agree on the most probable causes. First, in the early decades of the seventeenth century a quarter of a million Moriscos were expelled from Spain, mostly from Aragon, and Valencia lost one quarter of its population. The consequences were disastrous; a mortal blow was struck at the economic life of the kingdom; formerly rich food-producing lands were often deserted. But this can hardly be the cause of the decline of Castile, for Castile had few Moriscos. In the

reign of Charles V there had been in Castile a prosperous cloth industry, and a profitable wine and oil trade. All these subsequently declined, and for this it appears that royal policy was primarily responsible. It was royal policy to encourage sheep-farming at the expense
of food production. As the *Mesta*, the powerful corporation of aristocratic sheep-farmers, grew in strength, the rural population
declined. This gave Castile a dangerously unbalanced economy, and
food supplies were increasingly imported from north and east Europe.
Not only was there a drift of population from the land, but those
who remained were so poor that they had little or no purchasing
power for the support of urban industries. Meanwhile the land fell
into the hands of fewer and fewer great landlords, most of whom
preferred to throng the Court rather than develop their estates, and
Castile suffered from all the disadvantages of absentee landlordism.
Then again, rural life steadily declined under the pressure of heavy
taxation, constant recruitment, and the burdens of the quartering of
troops. It was easier for many peasants to flee to the towns, or to join
the hordes of vagabonds and beggars who swarmed Castile, rather
than to keep up the unequal struggle upon the land. Areas which in
the sixteenth century had supported prosperous rural industries were
thus converted into the silent barren spaces which the modern traveller
associates with the interior of Castile.

There was little capitalist enterprise in Spain. The great ambition of
all was to become *hidalgos* and thus share in the prestige of nobility.
Young men of ambition became students, or entered the Church, or
became bureaucrats, and rarely looked to trade or industry for
careers. What little capital there was was loaned to the State, or to
private persons, and not invested in economic enterprise. The ideals
of society were closer to those of Don Quixote than to the modern
age of Capitalism. Thus even in industries in which Spain had once
been proficient, as in textiles and ship-building, foreigners tended to
dominate the Spanish markets by the seventeenth century. Nor is it
a fact that the Spanish American colonies ever provided the Monarchy
with as much revenue as is sometimes implied. The true source of
Spanish revenues was not the Indies, but Castile, which contributed
seven or eight times the revenues of the former, and was steadily bled
dry. The rest of Spain was quite unable to supply the deficiency.
Aragon's agriculture had been ruined by the expulsion of the

Moriscos; attempts to thrust more burdens on Portugal had led to its successful revolt; and in these circumstances the Franco-Spanish war had exhausted Spain. The lowest point was probably reached in the period 1650 to 1680, when the population, which is thought to have been about $7\frac{1}{2}$ millions in 1550, dropped to 6 millions in 1660 (Richard Herr's estimate of $4\frac{1}{2}$ millions is probably too low. Max Beloff hazards 5 millions.). There was certainly a drift of population from the interior to the coastal regions. It was a period of rapid inflation, punctuated by short periods of sudden, fierce deflation, with resultant economic chaos and hardship. As the American silver mines approached exhaustion, silver virtually disappeared from circulation. In Castile in particular there was a general atmosphere of impoverishment and decay.

In the last resort this must be a judgment upon the Government of the Spanish Habsburgs, but it was a judgment also upon Spanish society. Spain in the seventeenth century was increasingly separated from the main stream of intellectual development in western Europe, a tendency which may be dated from the policy of Philip II in isolating his dominions from the heretical influences of Protestantism. The ideals of Spanish society were religious orthodoxy, aristocratic exclusiveness and military achievement. Everyone wanted to be a *hidalgo*, living in pride and idleness, and patents of nobility were easily purchased from the Crown. The patentee then became exempt from some personal taxes, though he still had to render military service. Manual work was disdained; neither saving nor investment was thought to be compatible with nobility. There was a general belief that mercantile nations like the Dutch, English or French should manufacture the luxuries needed by Spain, while the *hidalgo* and grandee pursued a quixotic cult of honour. The reigns of Charles II and Philip V gave ample opportunity for the pursuit of military glory and the continuance of the fiction of Spanish military greatness. Merchants were few, though they were stronger in Catalonia than elsewhere, particularly in Barcelona. In Castile, the industries of Seville, Valencia, Toledo and Granada (silk, woollens and leather) were in full decline. Trade between Spain and the Indies fell catastrophically during the seventeenth century, and most of the manufactures exported to the colonies from Spain were of foreign origin. Probably two-thirds of the total of South America were smuggled.

In the social and economic life of Spain the Church played an enormous part. Much of the land (although the extent is not known) was held in mortmain, and ecclesiastical agriculture was no more progressive than that of the rest of Spain. In 1660 there were about 200,000 clergy. Not only did the Church, the bureaucracy and the army attract all the ambitions of the nobility, but great numbers of men and women found an easy refuge in the minor orders of the Church, and here sloth and ignorance predominated. The Church did its best to relieve poverty by alms-giving, but it is possible that indiscriminate charity did much to increase the number of beggars in a country in which poverty carried no social stigma. In intellectual affairs the Church had a stranglehold, and in the age of Descartes, Locke and Newton the thought of Spain was simply that of Molina and the Counter-Reformation. The predominant tone of literature was theological and philosophical, such as is found in the religious dramas of Calderón.

In architecture and sculpture the seventeenth century witnessed the triumph of the Baroque. But of all the arts it is in painting alone that Spain achieves a European importance, with the work of Ribera, Zurbaran, Murillo, but above all with Vélasquez, the great painter of Philip IV's Court, and the forerunner of realist painting, and Goya.[1]

Apart from the incessant wars there are few details worth recording of the period 1660–1701. Philip IV died in 1665, leaving a four-year-old son, the sickly and misshapen Charles II, as his successor. The regency of the Queen Mother lasted until 1675, but in both this period, and the subsequent reign of Charles II, politics and government largely consisted of Court intrigues around the pathetic figure of the hapless Monarch. For thirty years the early demise of the King was expected, and as all attempts to provide Charles with an heir failed, the Court became increasingly the scene of the rival intrigues of the French and Austrian ambassadors as they jockeyed for advantage in the expected succession crisis. In the general European tendency in the later seventeenth century towards growing State absolutism, Spain took no part. The greatest service which Charles II was able to perform for his country was his final attempt to maintain his dominions intact when in 1700 he made a Will adopting Philip of Anjou as his heir. Five weeks later he was dead. He left his country with a de-

[1] See p. 66.

crepit government, a feeble army, a fleet of twenty ships, a decaying economy, declining population and ruined finances. Spain had little reason to mourn the passing of the Spanish Habsburgs.

Philip V

The first reforms came with the French occupation. Philip V was neither a reformer nor an able ruler, and so long as his grandfather lived, Louis XIV was the real ruler of Spain. The latter was appalled at the backwardness of Spain, and French experts were introduced to bring order into chaos. It was the Frenchman Orry who began the reform of the finances, and the abolition of sinecures and pensions. There was a new emphasis upon centralisation and royal absolutism. Castile was already under royal absolutism under the Habsburgs, but Aragon, the Basque provinces and Navarre still retained considerable autonomy, had often thwarted the intentions of the ruler, and always bore a much lighter tax burden than Castile. Under Philip V the Basque provinces and Navarre preserved their autonomy, but Aragon gave some support to Charles of Habsburg, and Philip V replied by destroying its autonomy. He ceased to call the Cortes of Aragon, and merged their deputies with those of Castile, so that for the first time it might be said that there was a Cortes for Spain. In any case the Cortes was called during the eighteenth century only to swear allegiance to the heirs to the throne and to ratify important decrees. The Council of Aragon was abolished, and the Council of Castile became the supreme administrative body for Spain. Philip V also introduced five secretaries of state to act as Ministers, and governors or Intendants to head provincial administration, all on the model of France. These Intendants did invaluable work in introducing more efficient administration in such matters as tax-collection and the encouragement of industries, agriculture and ship-building. A new sense of honesty and efficiency permeated the administration. The War of the Spanish Succession provided a new national stimulus such as Spain had not known for sixty years.

Philip V's lack of energy was more than compensated for by his ambitious Queen, Elizabeth Farnese, and for twenty years her aspirations in Italy gave Spain the continued illusion of being a great power. Her Minister Alberoni was a man of great energy and inventiveness. He gave Spain a new fleet, encouraged trade, began the reform of the tariffs so as to exclude foreign manufactures, and build up home industries. He continued the Bourbon policy of centralisation, and would undoubtedly have made great impact on the Spanish economy had he not been hastened by Elizabeth Farnese into an ill-prepared foreign adventure, which brought his downfall in 1719. His most important successor during the reign was Don José Patiño, who had been employed by Alberoni as Intendant of Cadiz to reconstruct the Spanish fleet. By 1727 he had risen to be Minister of Finance and Marine, and in 1729 Chief Secretary of State. Without instituting any great reform, he showed great facility in raising revenues which between 1700 and the 1730s increased by one-third, and he built up a substantial fleet, which enabled Elizabeth Farnese to continue her active foreign policy.

One of the most important limitations upon royal absolutism in Spain was the liberties of the Roman Catholic Church, which had indeed grown during the seventeenth century, until two-thirds of Spanish ecclesiastical appointments were made in Rome, and the Pope drew large revenues from vacant sees and from the fees of ecclesiastical courts. In the colonies, however, and in Granada, the Monarchy had always had a much greater control over church patronage than elsewhere. The Spanish Bourbons sought to imitate Louis XIV's absolutism in ecclesiastical, as in other respects, and there was continual friction between Philip V's government and Pope Clement II. The elevation to the papacy of the conciliatory Benedict XIV in 1740 provided a new opportunity for negotiations, which, however, were prolonged until January 1753, when a new Concordat was signed. It amounted to a triumph for the Spanish Monarchy. The Pope retained the right to appoint to only 52 out of over 12,000 Spanish benefices; the remainder were made by the Crown. The revenues which had gone to Rome were abolished, and the Spanish Crown compensated the Pope with a small indemnity. The Concordat revolutionised the relationship between Crown and Church, and was an important step in the establishment of royal absolutism. It also greatly encouraged the Jansenist and anti-Jesuit campaign which at this time was sweeping Europe.

The Concordat of 1753 was the most important event of the reign of the melancholy and innocuous Ferdinand VI (1746–59). He showed little interest in either foreign or domestic affairs; his first act was to withdraw from the War of the Austrian Succession, and he maintained peace for the rest of his reign. His Minister Carvajal (1746–54) was interested in the development of the Spanish colonies, and for this he sought good relations with England, as the naval power best placed to threaten Spanish sea-power. The quarrel over the Asiento Treaty was settled by the Anglo-Spanish commercial treaty of 1750, and the pro-English foreign policy was continued by the Foreign Minister, Richard Wall. But all this was changed under Ferdinand's successor.

Charles III

Charles III (1759–88), formerly the Don Carlos of Elizabeth Farnese's ambitions,[1] had proved himself an able king of Naples. He was intelligent and industrious, and it was under him that the work of Absolutism and Enlightenment was resumed. His reign began with a disastrous intervention in the Seven Years' War (1761–63) and the loss of Havana and Manila to British sea-power. This, together with high taxation and resultant hardships, was blamed on his Italian Minister, Squillace. In 1766, following bad harvests and a severe winter, Squillace was stoned by a mob and driven from office. Only then was order restored by the new Minister Aranda, and the work of reform begun. In particular the work begun by the Concordat was continued. The example of the suppression of the Jesuits in Portugal in 1759, and in France in 1764[2] was not lost upon Spain. The Jesuits were made the scapegoats of the recent riots, and in 1767 Aranda quietly expelled them from Spain. In 1773 Charles III used his influence in Rome to secure the suppression of the Jesuit Order, and his agent in the affair was promoted to be the Conde di Floridablanca, who in 1776 succeeded Grimaldi as Foreign Minister. Most of the Spanish bishops approved of the suppression of the Jesuits; there was in Spain a tradition of veneration for the Monarchy which greatly eased Charles III's task.

Charles III was no enemy of the Church; he was a man of great personal piety, and this did much to endear him to his subjects. His object was the extension of royal power, but this was, as he conceived it, in the best interests of the Church, and many of the clergy supported him in his efforts. There were too many clergy and minor orders in Spain—some 2 per cent. of the population, which was two-and-a-half times the proportion in France—and many of them were

[1] See p. 274. [2] See p. 335.

ignorant and idle. Devotion to the Catholic religion was often carried to the most superstitious limits. The Church was undoubtedly the strongest force in Spanish society, and Charles III sought to raise standards, and not to undermine religion. He checked the control of the Jesuits in university teaching, and the writings of Febronius and Van Espen began to circulate. The Inquisition was left intact but only because it never conflicted with the royal power.[1] Charles's comment was 'The Spaniards want it, and it does not bother me'. By the end of his reign the Spanish bishops were outstanding in Europe for their austerity and zeal. The standard of education among the clergy had risen, and efforts, largely unavailing it must be admitted, were made to reduce the curse of beggary.

These developments were the result of the extension of the royal authority rather than the spread of the ideas of the Enlightenment, to which Spain remained largely impervious. An exception to this was Benito Freyjoo, professor of theology at Oviedo, who died in 1764 at the age of eighty-eight. He was a passionate reader of French literature, and in a series of essays under the general title of 'Teatro critico universal' he rejected the prevailing scholasticism, and called for the new experimental science of the West. He was contemptuous of the backward and superstitious society of Spain. None of his ideas was original, but they were widely read, and were entirely new to Spain. Yet he was an isolated figure. Spain remained almost entirely untouched by the new science, though by the 1780s, as we shall see, a small group of intellectuals did emerge. The French *Encyclopédie* was excluded by the Inquisition; so were Montesquieu, Voltaire and Rousseau. Beccaria was translated into Spanish in 1774; Rousseau's *Émile* circulated in spite of the ban; Condillac, Raynal and Mably were also translated. A few Spaniards studied abroad and picked up French ideas; the Duke of Alba, for instance, was a cultivated man, and a friend of the *philosophes*. But on the whole Spain remained outside the main current of European thought. This was not simply a matter of censorship and the suppression of ideas. Spanish thought was repelled by the irreligion of the *philosophes*. In Spain alone in western Europe did the Catholic faith keep the irreligion of Enlightenment at bay.

[1] For instance, it wisely resisted the temptation to prosecute Charles's reforming ministers.

The aspect of the new European thought which had greatest impact upon Spain was the thought of the physiocrats. The Spanish Empire had always provided the mercantilists with an object-lesson in the importance of gold and silver, but Spain had never produced a Colbert who would attempt a consistent plan for economic expansion. In the second half of the eighteenth century, for the first time, Spanish writers pleaded that the country with the most gold might still be the poorest country, that agriculture was the source of all wealth; that the expulsion of the Moriscos had been a misfortune; and that commerce and industry, together with a prosperous agriculture, were the only true sources of wealth. Some looked to Colbert's methods of State control; others preferred the greater freedom of Adam Smith, who was translated into Spanish in the 1780s. In either case they saw in economics 'the true philosopher's stone with which all nations can become happy' (as the professor of political economy wrote at Saragossa in 1784).

During the eighteenth century Spanish population, like that of most European countries, grew steadily, so that by 1787 it was nearly $10\frac{1}{2}$ millions, the great majority of whom lived on the land. The Crown was not an important landowner; often the Crown lands were the waste lands of the interior. How extensive Church lands were has never been fully investigated, but it appears likely that they were much less than those in the possession of municipalities. The chief burden of the Church on the land was in the form of tithes. Much of the land in private possession was entailed, and most progressive writers of the eighteenth century condemned entail as stultifying to progress. Quite apart from the private possession of estates, there were the general seigneurial rights, with the usual dues of hunting, fishing, milling and the like, which pressed so heavily on the peasants. These rights had been readily bought from the needy Habsburgs, together with the rights of nobility, and they were the chief source of wealth to the privileged classes. The highest rank of nobility was the grandee of Spain, of whom there were 119 in 1787; below them the *titulos de Castilla*, the *caballeros* (members of one of the four military orders) and finally the *hidalgos*, who in fact counted for little in the social structure of Spain. The status of the peasant differed greatly from one part of the country to another. In the Basque provinces, for instance, most land was possessed by the peasants, and 'here every peasant claimed he was an hidalgo' (Herr). In Catalonia on the other hand most of the land was under seigneurs who were treated as owners, though the peasants had security of tenure. The peasants of the north and east benefited from the export of wines, fruit, olive oil, silk and wool and thus shared in the general European prosperity. In the south, however, in La Mancia and Granada it was a different story, with two-thirds of the peasants landless hired labourers, dressed in rags, and often dwelling in caves.

Charles III's government took an active interest in agriculture. It sought to curb the predominance of sheep-farming and to encourage a prosperous peasantry by an increase of corn-growing. In 1767 a project was launched for the settlement of German and French immigrants on the deserted lands of the interior, and over 50 villages and towns were established in an area of over 1,000 square miles. In the 1780s Floridablanca established *montes pios* to lend money to farmers. The sheep-farmers of the interior had long been organised into the powerful corporation known as the *Mesta*, which had always under the Habsburgs been a privileged body. In the 1780s its power was broken, when Campomanes became its President and permitted enclosure and encouraged the change-over to corn-growing. Yet it would be easy to over-estimate the effects of government policy. The agriculture of the northern and eastern coastal regions was prosperous without much government help, and in the centre and south, where poverty was so marked, it is doubtful whether the impact of government policy went very deep.

More impressive was its industrial and commercial policy. In 1700 the trade of the Spanish colonies was largely in the hands of foreigners, either through Cadiz, or through smuggling. The Bourbons encouraged the formation of monopoly companies. In 1728 the Caracas Company was formed to develop the trade of Venezuela in cotton, indigo and tobacco. It flourished, and in 1785 it became the Philippines Company to develop a hitherto non-existent trade with the Pacific. Before 1765 all colonial trade had to go through Cadiz, but in that year the trade was thrown open to several ports, and in 1778 all Spanish ports were permitted to trade with all parts of Spanish America, except Mexico and Venezuela. Venezuela was thrown open in 1785, and Mexico in 1789.

Industrial policy was imitated from Colbert's work, whereby the

Government created factories and gave them monopolies. The first was a woollen factory at Guadalajara in 1718, and later there were tapestries in Madrid, mirrors and glass at San Ildefonso and silks at Talavera, all in Philip V's reign. Charles III established porcelain near Madrid and woollens at Sevogia. By the 1780s the cloth manufactory at Guadalajara employed 800 looms, 4,000 weavers and 40,000 spinners. Yet all these industries relied for survival on government privileges and financial aid, without which they could not have withstood foreign competition. In one respect Campomanes departed from Colbert's example. He broke down the restrictions of gilds, and established a considerable measure of freedom of commerce. Schools were established to teach poor children trades such as spinning and weaving. In 1773 permission was given to *hidalgos* to engage in trade, and in 1783 crafts were declared compatible with the rank of nobility. The import of an increasing number of manufactured goods, such as cotton and iron, was forbidden in the interests of home industries, although it never proved possible to prevent wholesale smuggling, especially from France. The three areas of particular industrial prosperity were Valencia, Catalonia and the Basque provinces (linen, silk, iron, woollens, cutlery and paper). Most of their industries reached a peak of prosperity in the 1780s, and in 1792 the Catalan cotton industry was reported to have employed 80,000 workers, and to be second in Europe only to that of England. Joseph Townsend and Arthur Young were both much impressed with the industrial conditions, and the latest machinery which they saw in Spain. Spain was more prosperous at the end of Charles III's reign than it had been for over a century. To some extent, no doubt, this was merely that the country was participating in the general economic expansion of Europe, but government policy in establishing free trade with the colonies, encouraging industry, breaking gild restrictions, and establishing banking and credit facilities, had much to do with it.

In the kingdom of Castile the story was less happy. Taxation was higher there than in the rest of Spain. With the destruction of the autonomy of Aragon higher taxes were imposed there, but they were never so heavy as in Castile; and Navarre and the Basque provinces always preserved some rights of autonomy, and therefore low taxes. The odds therefore were weighted heavily against Castile, with its high taxation, severe climate, long droughts, soil erosion and absence of communications. Charles III did begin building good roads, mainly from Madrid to the Basque lands, and along the Mediterranean coast from Valencia to the French border, but most of Castile remained untouched, and without transport the kingdom remained backward and poverty-stricken.

At the centre of all the activities of the reign was the grave and devout Charles III. No European king of his time was more successful in winning the devotion of his subjects. His reign had indeed started badly, but after the dismissal of Squillace and the appointment of Aranda a change began. The most successful ministers of the reign were Aranda, Campomanes and Floridablanca, the last of whom was in the last years of the reign a close confidant of the King. Charles III was hard-working, deeply religious, hating waste and extravagance. His private life was above reproach; his one luxury was hunting, his one passion, apart from his Church, was the welfare of his subjects. It was largely due to him that Enlightenment, in so far as it had an impact upon Spain, did not destroy the essential unity of the nation as it did elsewhere. An ambassador wrote to Floridablanca in 1789 that in Spain 'One finds religion, love for the king, devotion to the law, moderation in the administration, scrupulous respect for the privileges of each province and the individual . . . and a thousand other things that the French lack.' Richard Herr has endorsed this view, and has concluded:

> Charles III did more for Spain than any monarch since Isabel. Among the enlightened despots of his own day none was a more successful ruler.

On the whole Spanish society remained impervious to the main intellectual trends of European Enlightenment, except in economic affairs. In 1764 the Conde de Peñaflorida, who was deeply imbued with the atmosphere of the French salons, founded the 'Basque Society of the Friends of the Country', the members of which, all noblemen, set out to study agriculture, industry and the sciences. In 1775 the Royal Economic Society of Madrid was founded for the same ends, and by 1789 there were fifty-six similar societies in other towns It is not likely that their impact was very great, but they did something to disseminate a new attitude to change. The leading members of the Government, Campomanes, Cabarrus and Jovellanos, were all members of the Madrid Society. Something of the new learning slowly reached the universities. In 1771 the Reales Estudios de San Isidro was established in Madrid, with courses in experimental physics, law and logic. After the expulsion of the Jesuits, the universities were reformed. Pablo Olavide reorganised the University of Seville in 1769, and introduced Cartesianism where scholasticism had previously reigned unchallenged. The University of Salamanca, Spain's leading university, resisted attempts to enforce the study of science and mathematics; but the University of Valencia was more progressive, and the writings of Locke, Hume, Montesquieu and Leibniz were known to a select few. Gradually the study of the law of nature and of nations began to infiltrate, and Charles III required all lawyers to study it if they wished to practise in Madrid. Joachim Marin, professor at the Reales Estudios, wrote in 1776 the official textbook of natural law, which, although it did no more than repeat the ideas of Grotius and Pufendorf which had been current in Europe for a century, was new to Spain. It stated the theory of the social contract; that society exists for the welfare of the governed; that kings should rule according to the fundamental law; that the good of the people was the supreme law, and so forth. In general, however, the teaching of philosophy remained in the hands of the Church. The influence of the new experimental philosophy is seen on the new textbook of philosophy written by the Capuchin friar Villalpando in 1778. The Augustinians were well versed in the new ideas, but the Dominicans remained the champions of orthodoxy, and some French Dominicans coming to Spain at the end of the century said that it was like passing from the eighteenth to the fourteenth century.

A new spirit of social criticism was reflected in the periodicals of the time, like *El pensador*, started in 1761 by Joseph Clavijo, and *El censor*, started by a Madrid lawyer. These papers often attacked the false values of Spanish society, and the obscurantism of the Church, while among the things to be praised were English institutions, the rule of law, social responsibilities and the thought of Descartes and Newton. But it was not easy for such criticism to escape the vigilance of the Inquisition. An enormous number of books were placed on the Spanish Index (including Dante, Montesquieu, *Robinson Crusoe*, Kepler, Grotius, Pufendorf and Montesquieu). The most famous trial of the century was that of Olavide, a great exponent of French ideas.

In 1778 he was condemned to imprisonment and the loss of all his property, a sentence which had the full approval of the orthodox king. In 1780 Olavide fled to France, where he was given an ovation by the *philosophes*. Other writers were similarly dealt with, and if they were few it was because orthodoxy was stronger in Spain than anywhere else in Europe.

In 1787 the centralising policy of Charles III was completed with the establishment of a Council of Ministers (Junta de Estado) under Floridablanca. When the King died in December 1788 his Monarchy seemed secure; the Cortes which met under his successor Charles IV was utterly submissive. Floridablanca saw to it that the first news of the French Revolution was excluded from Spain. He wrote in July 1789:

> It is said that this enlightened century has taught man his rights. But it has also taken away, besides his true happiness, the peace and security of his person and family. We want here neither so much light nor its effects.

In April 1793 Spain declared war on the revolution in France.

Pombal in Portugal

In Portugal in 1750, when Joseph I ascended the throne, there was a long tradition of conflict with the Papacy over the royal rights of patronage. Benedict XIV had been conciliatory, had been accommodating over finding benefices for John V's bastards, and had even conferred upon him the title of *rex fidelissimus*. Joseph I's Minister of the Interior was Sebastiano José de Carvalho, better known to history by the title he acquired in 1770, as the Marquis of Pombal, and for the rest of the reign, until 1777, Pombal was the absolute Minister of Portugal. Trained as a diplomat, Pombal had had experience in Vienna and England. In Vienna he had married the daughter of Marshal Daun; in England he had learnt to appreciate the importance of trade and good government, and he found Portugal with a government which had almost ceased to function, and an economy which was stagnant. The King was so indolent that, although he loved music, the theatre and hunting, he could hardly be induced to sign a document. Pombal was a product of the Enlightenment, industrious and determined, bent on centralising the administration, and on encouraging industry and trade along the lines of the Physiocrats. His methods were ruthless, and he made Portugal something of a police State. The *Cortes* had not met in Portugal since 1697, and the Monarchy was as much an absolutism as any other in Europe at the period. Pombal saw the Catholic Church as the great obstacle to progress, and he treated the bishops and clergy with great ruthlessness, imprisoning and banishing those who stood in his way. Above all, he was hostile to the Jesuits. So long as the Queen Mother lived he had to tread warily, but she died in 1754, and Pombal was free to act. He made full use of the constant stream of accusations against Jesuit activities in Paraguay and Maranhao. More unbiased research will have to be carried out before it is possible to judge how much truth there was in the charges; certainly some of them were exaggerated by the enemies of the Jesuits. But Pombal accused them of opposing the royal will, misgoverning and stirring up rebellion. In 1757 the Jesuits were excluded from Court. In 1758 he demanded of the Pope that he either reform the Order or abolish it. Pope Benedict appointed Cardinal Saldanha to report on the activities of the Order; a significant choice, for the Cardinal was a relative of Pombal's.

At this point Pope Benedict XIV died. He had been a gentle and conciliatory Pope, fighting a rearguard action against the disruptive forces within and without the Church. His successor, Clement XIII, was a noted patron of the arts, but was not equipped to withstand the onslaught which the governments of Europe were preparing for him. Meanwhile Cardinal Saldanha suspended the Portuguese Jesuits from participating in all trade, and from preaching and hearing confessions. In September 1758 an attempt was made on the life of Joseph I, and in January 1759 twelve of the nobility were executed for the crime. The evidence connecting the Jesuits with the attempted assassination was vague, but Pombal seized the opportunity to accuse them of complicity, and in January 1759 a decree confiscated the property of the Order. Saldanha proved himself a mere tool of Pombal. While negotiations were still continuing with Rome, Pombal suddenly expelled the Jesuits from Portugal, and in October 1759 he had 133 of them landed at Civita Vecchia; in fact they were already at sea when the royal decree of expulsion was issued in September. In all about a thousand were sent to Italy. In June 1760 the Papal Nuncio was expelled from Portugal. In all this it was clear that Pombal had simply used the Jesuits as the spearhead of a general attack upon the Church, and with this was coupled an attack upon the nobility also. In this way he sought to weaken the two enemies of absolutism and reform.

Bishops and clergy were frequently imprisoned; ecclesiastical appointments could not be made without the express approval of the Government; the ecclesiastical Orders were discouraged from taking new novices. The Pope made repeated efforts at reconciliation. Finally in December 1767 the nuncio reported that reconciliation depended upon the complete suppression of the Jesuit Order. Pombal regarded the suppression of the Jesuit Order in 1773 as the consummation of his anti-clerical policy.

11: The Balance of Power, 1713-63

The New Europe

In 1713 England was the most recent of the great Powers to have emerged. William III and Marlborough had cemented the Anglo-Dutch alliance, given England a fine army and made her the keystone of the Grand Alliance. England was rapidly becoming a naval, commercial and colonial Power, with extensive strategic interests in the Baltic, the Mediterranean, the Low Countries, the Atlantic sea routes, the West Indies and India. These interests were too closely connected with European affairs ever to permit her again to turn her back upon Europe. Moreover, the new king was also Elector of Hanover. George I had been a dashing and able soldier, deeply concerned with the fate of the disintegrating Swedish Empire, anxious to annex the territories of Bremen and Verden which would give Hanover an outlet to the sea, and deeply conscious of the insecurity of his English throne. The enemies of England abroad might give aid to the Jacobites, and thus it was particularly necessary to secure peace in Europe, and the general observance of the Peace of Utrecht, which had specially recognised the Hanoverian succession in England. Above all, this meant good relations with France.

The military setbacks of France during the War of the Spanish Succession had done little to diminish her prestige in Europe. France had the largest population in western Europe; it was by far the wealthiest country; its military strength far exceeded that of any other country. The Monarchy of Louis XIV was the grandest spectacle of the age. French civilisation, literature, architecture, government, were the admiration of Europe. Colbert had given France a strong mercantile and naval power, and at home a commercial and industrial basis for overseas trade and colonies. After 1715 France had some great pioneers in her colonies, Imperialists of vision and enterprise. But the French government never gave them more than half-hearted support. Europe always seemed more important. Until 1756 France could rarely resist the opportunity to make alliances with German princes against the

Emperor, and some princes, like the Archbishop of Cologne and the Elector of Bavaria, were traditionally pro-French and anti-Austrian. Yet French aims in Europe were confused and uncertain. With over two centuries of rivalry with the Austrian Habsburgs, the policy had become a tradition. Yet in the eighteenth century there was little substance in it. So long as the Habsburg–Bourbon rivalry was a fact, the French policy in eastern Europe of alliance with Sweden, Poland and the Turks made good sense, for they were useful allies who could be induced to attack France's German allies in the rear. But in the first half of the eighteenth century France lost her predominating influence in Poland, and in the second half of the century her alliance with the Habsburgs largely neutralised French policy in eastern Europe. Yet with all these uncertainties of policy, throughout the century the culture of the *ancien régime* continued to exercise a civilising influence on Europe, and France was still thought of as the leading Power.

In 1713 Habsburg power in Europe stood a great deal higher than could possibly have been foretold a decade earlier. Thirty years before, the Turks had been hammering at the very gates of Vienna. In 1704, but for Marlborough, Vienna would have fallen to Louis XIV. Yet by the Peace of Utrecht Charles VI of Habsburg had acquired the Netherlands, the Milanese, Naples and Sardinia, and thus the political domination of Italy. Only a man as unimaginative and blindly devoted to Spain as Charles VI was, could have failed to see the extent of his good fortune. But his position was also fraught with danger. The possession of the Netherlands might embroil him with France, and the existence of the Barrier Treaty was an indication that the Habsburgs were not expected to be able to defend their distant possessions. In Italy it was unlikely that Spain would accept the loss of so much territory without an attempt to regain it. Savoy was a potential enemy, for the House of Savoy longed to possess the Milanese. In the south-east the Turks were about to begin another war of aggression. Above all, before he had been on the throne many years, Charles VI, with two daughters, was concerned with problems of the succession, which he sought to remove by issuing the fundamental law of the Pragmatic Sanction.

Even after the Treaties of Utrecht and Rastadt there continued a virtual state of war between Charles VI and Philip V, for the former had not renounced his claims to Spain. He still regarded himself King of Spain; he retained his Spanish Council, and in October 1716 by an Imperial decree, written in Spanish, he conferred the title of Grandee of Spain upon his city of Milan, which, among other things, conferred upon its patricians the right to wear their hats in the presence of the king of Spain. He had not been named after Charles V for nothing; the idea of the universality of the Empire died hard.

By 1700 Spain had become the Sick Man of Europe. However unjust the partition of the Spanish Empire at the Peace of Utrecht might appear, it was no more than a recognition of the hard fact that Spain was no longer capable of ruling so vast an area. The French under Philip V made some attempt at administrative reorganisation. Louis XIV found his grandson as pliable to his instructions as he could have wished, and he largely ruled Spain through the agency of Philip's Queen, Maria Louisa of Savoy, and the powerful Princess des Ursins. But in 1714 Maria Louisa died. The doctors feared for the sanity of Philip V, and it was felt necessary to hurry through a speedy second marriage. The Minister in Madrid of the Italian State of Parma, Giulio Alberoni, a man of low birth and high ambition, saw his chance. He proposed to Mme. des Ursins that Elizabeth Farnese, daughter of the Duke of Parma, was a docile and simple girl, and would make an admirable instrument for Madame's purpose. In 1714 the marriage was concluded. On Alberoni's advice, one of Elizabeth Farnese's first acts was to bundle Mme. des Ursins back to France, and henceforth the two of them virtually ruled Spain. Their policy and significance will not be understood if they are thought of simply as the Queen of Spain and her Minister; this would be to miss the point. The explanation is to be found in the fact that both were Parmesans; both therefore had been brought up to detest Imperial power, and both were concerned with the impending fate of the tiny duchy. The following table will make the danger apparent:

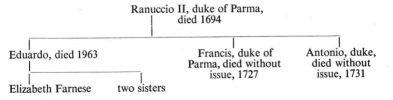

If the rights of female succession were ignored, as was usual in Italy, then it appeared likely that the House of Farnese was doomed to a speedy extinction, and in that event Parma reverted to the Imperial power. This Elizabeth Farnese and Alberoni were determined to prevent. At the very time when Charles VI was seeking to secure European recognition to the claims of his daughter Maria Theresa, it seemed to Elizabeth Farnese a reasonable solution to the question of Parma that her own son, Don Carlos (b. 1716) should inherit the duchy. And not merely Parma, for she had some claims to Tuscany, where the House of Medici was also facing extinction. As her ambitions grew, Elizabeth Farnese envisaged a large north Italian principality, which might include the Milanese, Mantua, Parma and Tuscany. The great dream was the liberation of Italy from the Imperial yoke. This in a sense might also be a Spanish aim, which would seek to reverse the decision of Utrecht and Rastadt, but it was not Spanish interests which Elizabeth Farnese and Alberoni sought first to serve.

The Anglo-French Entente

The Whigs in England had opposed the terms of the Treaty of Utrecht which Bolingbroke negotiated with such skill, because they thought it dangerous to British interests that a Bourbon should be allowed to retain the throne of Spain. That there was some danger in this is shown by the later Family Compacts between the French and Spanish Bourbons in 1733 and in 1761. But once the Treaty was made, and George I securely on the throne, they became the firmest supporters of the Treaty, as the best guarantee of peace, security and the balance of power in Europe. They assumed that France would seek to overthrow it, and hence they supported the Barrier Treaty of 1715 with the Dutch, and in May 1716 signed the Treaty of Westminster with the Emperor. These were skilful steps in a policy designed to tie England, the Dutch and the Emperor together in a perpetual defence of the peace settlement. They had a further success. In France the Regent Orleans soon felt the hostility of Philip of Spain. The latter believed that no treaty or agreement could deprive him of his right to the succession to the throne of France, should the young Louis XV die. According to the Treaty of Utrecht the claims of Philip V were ruled out, so long as he was king of Spain, and thus the Duke of Orleans was heir to the throne of France. There were special circumstances therefore why France should cease to desire the overthrow of the Treaty, and thus in October 1716 Stanhope and Dubois signed an

Anglo-French alliance. The Whigs also found themselves sought after by Alberoni, who concluded with England two commercial treaties in December 1715 and April 1716. But Alberoni intended that the price of these treaties should be British support for, or at least acquiescence in, Elizabeth Farnese's ambitions in Italy. The other outstanding issue between Britain and Spain was the possession of Gibraltar. Its seizure had been an indication of the importance Britain attached to the Mediterranean trade routes, but Stanhope was not averse from surrendering it for the sake of peace with Spain.

Altogether British influence in Europe at this time was very great. Britain had alliances with the Dutch, the Emperor and the Regent of France, and commercial treaties with Spain, paid a subsidy to aid Charles VI in his Turkish war, and in 1718 successfully negotiated a Peace between him and the Turks. In the Baltic a British squadron protected her interests in the Russo-Swedish War. Earl Stanhope proved himself one of the most brilliant foreign ministers in our history. Alberoni was soon to test the strength of his system.

Alberoni

The Spanish Minister gave a lively, though short-lived, impetus to Spanish administration and economy, and rapidly built a strong fleet. His diplomatic preparations were shoddy, but spectacular. He stirred up intrigues against the Regent in France. The continuance of the Turkish war would weaken the Emperor. England might be managed by a combination of trade concessions and threats of support for the Jacobites. Savoy might be won over by the prospect of gaining the Milanese. Hearing that Charles VI was negotiating with Savoy, by which the latter would cede the island of Sicily in return for Sardinia, Alberoni declared that this was a breach of the Peace settlement. Declaring that 'God wishes that they shall be punished for all the cruelties they have committed in our poor land', in August 1717 Alberoni sent the Spanish fleet to attack Sardinia, and in the following year Sicily also. But then he found himself faced with the united opposition of the Great Powers. Charles VI hastened to sign an alliance with Britain, France and the Dutch, so that the Triple Alliance became the Quadruple Alliance (August 1718). (This also permitted him to exchange Sardinia for Sicily.) At the same time a British fleet under Admiral Byng destroyed a Spanish fleet off Cape Passaro, in Sicily, and a French force crossed the Spanish frontier. For some months Alberoni threatened war, and a small Jacobite force actually sailed against Scotland. But the forces ranged against Spain were overwhelming. Cellamare, the Spanish ambassador, was arrested in France for conspiracy, and finally in 1719 Philip V dismissed Alberoni as the first condition for peace. Alberoni cannot be rated more highly than as an adventurer with some sentiments of Italian patriotism and a hatred of German rule; who directed Spanish affairs with vigour, but without a head for reality in a Europe he failed entirely to understand. Italian historians have often seen Alberoni as something of an Italian patriot; he was certainly anti-Habsburg, and it was this which persuaded the Pope to give him the cardinal's hat in 1717. His main service to Spain was to help create the illusion that Spain was still a Great Power. His fall did not for long deflect Elizabeth Farnese from her intentions.

Negotiations were carried on between Spain and the Quadruple Alliance during 1720–21, and finally Spain reaffirmed the Treaties of Peace, and recognised the Emperor's acquisition of Sicily. In return, the Allies agreed to submit all outstanding disputes between Spain and the Emperor to a Congress to meet at Cambrai. This ill-suited Charles VI, who placed every conceivable obstacle in the way of the Congress; it was not able even to meet until 1724, and thereafter, in interminable sessions, it failed completely to achieve any agreement.

On the events of the period 1716 to 1720 two conclusions would seem to be justified. The first was the brilliant way in which Stanhope directed European diplomacy in the interests of British policy. His success rested on the Anglo-French alliance. British influence in Europe has often been most effective when Britain has acted in alliance with France. The second was the effective way in which the Quadruple Alliance had served as complete protection for the Habsburg Monarchy. Charles VI would have done well to have made the continuance of that alliance the cornerstone of his policy. But after 1720 the Quadruple Alliance went into rapid dissolution, and with it came the decline of British influence.

The Treaties of Vienna 1725 and 1731

The first reason for the break-up of the Alliance was the reaction in France against the Regent's foreign policy. This had taken the form of close relations with Britain, support for the Emperor, and even the coercion of Philip V. But the pro-Spanish party pointed out that this made nonsense of the War of the Spanish Succession; that the natural ally of France was now Spain, and that the Regent had become a mere tool of British foreign policy. In 1721 there was a change of emphasis, and Orleans and Dubois arranged a double marriage with Madrid, by which Louis XV was to marry the daughter of Philip V and Elizabeth Farnese (as yet a child of five), and the heir to the Spanish throne was to marry a daughter of the Regent Orleans. Britain could only watch this *entente* with apprehension. Moreover, in 1723 the Regent died, and the special circumstances which gave rise to the Anglo-French *entente* passed away. The second reason was a cooling of Anglo-Austrian relations consequent upon the chartering of Charles VI's Ostend Company in 1722. This was a monopoly commercial company which was intended to give the Austrian Netherlands some taste of the commercial prosperity which similar companies had brought to the Dutch, the English and the French. It at once aroused the opposition of the merchants of the three rival countries. Moreover, at the Congress of Cambrai, Charles VI was disappointed with his failure to secure the acceptance by his allies of the Pragmatic Sanction. For some time his mind had played with the idea of a possible direct agreement with Spain, and at Cambrai in 1725 the Spanish envoy Ripperda was filled with the same thought.

Ripperda was a Dutchman, a native of Groningen, who had once been a colonel in the Dutch army and a friend of Prince Eugène's. He had then in 1715 become Dutch envoy to Spain, was favoured by Alberoni, and was fired by the idea that, with Dutch ideas on commerce and administration, Spain might become a rich commercial Empire. He dazzled Philip V and Elizabeth Farnese with plans for development; the most daring of all was that Spain and the Emperor should restore the old alliance of the days of Charles V. If Spanish ambitions in Italy could not be obtained by hostility to the Habsburgs, they might be fulfilled by direct agreement. The Emperor might be won over by offers of commercial concessions for his Ostend Company within the Spanish Empire, and the agreement might be cemented by a marriage treaty between Don Carlos and Charles's daughter Maria Theresa. Nothing might have come of this but for the clumsy action of the Duke of Bourbon, chief Minister of France, who, in 1725, decided that the succession in France was too perilous to defer any longer the marriage of the young Louis XV, and that as the Spanish Infanta could hardly marry for another five years, another bride should be sought. Thus the Infanta was unceremoniously returned to Spain, and Louis XV married Marie Leszczynska, the daughter of the ex-King of Poland. The indignation of the Spanish Court knew no bounds, and Elizabeth Farnese hastened Ripperda into negotiating an alliance with the Emperor (Treaty of Vienna, April 1725). The terms were secret, and Europe feared the worst. This unexpected development could mean only a conspiracy against the Utrecht settlement. In September 1725 Lord Townshend negotiated a renewal of the Anglo-French alliance (Treaty of Hanover), a good illustration of the almost mechanical precision with which the principle of the balance of power worked in the eighteenth century. This had the reverse of the effect intended, for it drove Spain and the Emperor into a second agreement (November 1725) committing them to the very terms Townshend had feared to be a part of the first. The two sons of Elizabeth Farnese were at some future date to marry the two daughters of Charles VI, and the Emperor, in return for commercial concessions in the Spanish Empire, agreed to support Spain in the recovery of Gibraltar and Minorca.

The Emperor's position appeared to be a strong one, for to the alliance with Spain he added treaties with Russia and Prussia (1726). In this respect his position might be said to foreshadow that of his daughter in the period 1753–56. In fact, however, it was far less sound. From the Spanish alliance he hoped to gain commerce and wealth, recognition of the Pragmatic Sanction and peace in Italy; yet he must have known that the reality of that alliance depended solely on his willingness to gratify the ambitions of Elizabeth Farnese in Italy and elsewhere. Further thought convinced him that he could not agree to the Spanish marriages; he was reluctant even to contemplate the succession of Don Carlos to Parma. To Elizabeth Farnese, however, the Habsburg alliance was worth fighting for, and for some years she still clung to the hope that it would lead to the marriage treaty. In fact, however, Spanish policy rapidly got out of hand. Ripperda, on his return to Madrid, was openly boastful of the prospects of a European conflagration in which the Emperor and Spain would give the law to Europe. When the Imperial ambassador asked for his dismissal, he fled to the British ambassador and revealed, not only the secret terms of the Treaties of Vienna, but also the enormous bribes he had received from the Emperor. He was dismissed in May 1726, but not before serious damage had been done. A desultory war followed between England and Spain, in which the Spanish attempted a feeble and unsuccessful blockade of Gibraltar, and a British fleet under Admiral Hosier blockaded the treasure fleet in Porto Bello (1726–27).

The key to the situation lay in the new chief Minister in France, Cardinal Fleury, the skilful successor to the blundering Duke of Bourbon. Fleury's policy was simple, even if his methods were often involved. To him the natural enemy of France was the Emperor, and the natural ally of France was Spain. At the same time he abhorred the intrigues and ambitions of Elizabeth Farnese, and looked to close relations with Sir Robert Walpole in England to maintain peace and the superiority of French interests in Europe. By patient diplomacy, with English help, he detached the Emperor from the Spanish alliance by a treaty of May 1727, by which it was agreed to submit outstanding questions to a new Congress, this time at Soissons, not far from Paris. In March 1728 Spain signed the Convention of the Pardo, bringing the hostilities with England to an end. The Congress of Soissons, which met in 1728, was no more successful in playing the part of a United Nations than the Congress of Cambrai had been. By that time Elizabeth Farnese was convinced of the failure of the Habsburg alliance, but her nuisance value was such that she could win the support of France and England to the claims of Don Carlos. Thus in November 1729 she signed the Treaty of Seville with Britain and France. Spain cancelled her concessions to the Ostend Company, and Britain and France recognised the succession of Don Carlos to Parma. For a time it looked like war between Spain and an angry and outmanoeuvred Emperor. The war of 1733 might very well have broken out three years earlier, for Fleury's Foreign Minister Chauvelin was hot for war. The question became critical early in 1731 when the last Duke of Parma died, and Don Carlos became entitled to succeed him; but the Emperor at once occupied Parma with his troops. At this point Sir Robert Walpole's diplomacy took charge of events. He was ready to pay a price for peace in Europe. The result was the Second Treaty of Vienna (in fact there were two treaties). England paid the price Charles VI had sought for years, and recognised the Pragmatic

K

Sanction. The Emperor agreed to suspend the Ostend Company, to recognise Hanover's annexation of Bremen and Verden, and the succession of Don Carlos in Parma. The settlement was a triumph for Elizabeth Farnese. Her son was now Duke of Parma; in 1732 Europe was treated to the spectacle of the British fleet escorting Don Carlos to Italy to take possession of his new duchy.

The settlement of 1731 marked the end of the Anglo-French alliance. Fleury had been secretly angry at the way in which Walpole had secured for the time being the diplomatic lead in Europe. The birth of an heir to Louis XV had removed any threat to France from Philip of Spain. The Anglo-French alliance had been the product of the special needs of the time, and those, so far as France was concerned, were now removed; there was a powerful party in France demanding closer relations with Spain. But the Anglo-French alliance had played an important part in preserving the Peace of Utrecht for twenty years, and had been an invaluable basis for British power and influence in Europe at a time critical for the Hanoverian dynasty. In the following years a different pattern of Europe emerged.

The War of the Polish Succession

The death of Augustus II of Saxony and Poland in February 1733 was the signal for a general war in Europe, and for this the Emperor Charles VI was much to blame. Augustus' son and successor in Saxony signified his readiness to accept the Pragmatic Sanction, and at that Charles VI immediately supported his candidature to the Crown of Poland. To Europe he declared his intention to support the constitution and the principle of free election in Poland (an ominous declaration!) and that he was supported in this by the Tsarina Anna and the King of Prussia. This was a direct challenge to the French government, whose candidate for the Polish throne was Stanislas Leszczynski, father-in-law to Louis XV. It was an act of stupidity on the part of Charles VI to risk a conflict with the West, so soon after the settlement of 1731, and on an issue which had so little real value for the Habsburgs. For the brunt of a war would fall on Austria, but the benefits of a French defeat in Poland would go to Russia. When in 1772 Maria Theresa wept over the partition of Poland, it is not recorded whether she reflected that it was her father who had done much to bring it about.

France, as should have been expected, took up the challenge so ostentatiously thrown down to her. The war party in France was headed by Marshal Villars, Marshal Berwick, the Comte de Bellisle and the duc de Noailles, encouraged by Chauvelin; the latter was retained in power by Fleury as the man of action who might be used, or blamed, as events unfolded. The French nobility had little to occupy their time, and, with few openings of a political nature available to them, their only hope of winning fame and glory was in war. It was foolish of Charles VI to provide them with so good an opportunity. In September 1733 French gold secured the election of Stanislas by the Polish Diet, but the minority withdrew, placed themselves under Russian protection, and declared the election of Augustus III. In a war in Poland France was at a hopeless geographical disadvantage, and Stanislas was forced to take refuge in Danzig. Thus Augustus III was king indeed, and Charles VI could congratulate himself that it had not been necessary to send a single soldier into Poland. But in the West he was forced to fight alone; to his great disappointment Frederick William of Prussia preferred neutrality, and so did Walpole in England. Although the war gave rise to the danger of Franco-Spanish preponderance in the West, which was certainly the concern of England, yet there was some excuse for Walpole thinking that it was an unnecessary war, and largely of the Emperor's making. Equally important for Charles VI was his failure to win the alliance of Piedmont.

Victor Amadeus II of Savoy had brilliantly directed policy during the War of the Spanish Succession. He crowned this by useful domestic reforms between 1713 and 1730, and when he abdicated, he left to his son, Charles Emanuel III, a well-governed State, a full treasury capable of standing two years of war without resort to loans, and an army capable of expansion to 60,000 men. Piedmont was a neighbour the Habsburgs would have done well to respect. In one respect certainly Piedmontese and Habsburg interests coincided: neither could look with favour upon the return of the Spaniards to Italy. This might have been made the basis for an agreement. Negotiations did take place in 1732, and if Charles VI had offered Piedmont some reward for her alliance, perhaps the territory of Piacenza, an alliance would most likely have been concluded. But Charles refused to make any substantial concession, and Charles Emanuel turned to listen to more alluring offers from France. Some interesting fencing took place in the correspondence between Charles Emanuel and Cardinal Fleury. Charles Emanuel wrote at the end of 1732 that:

> the vivacity and suddenness of the queen of Spain, and her willingness to change sides should make one consider how little would be gained by her alliance, especially if another Power should offer her more advantageous terms for her sons. This being so, I should prefer to remain neutral rather than be constrained to take up arms against my allies.

Fleury replied with alluring offers: the balance of power must be restored; Piedmont must be strengthened:

> The vast designs of the Emperor are today no longer hidden; he aims at making himself master of Europe, if he is not opposed in time by a powerful league. It is necessary to make Your Majesty powerful enough to balance the authority of the Emperor in the peninsula, and with the aid of Spain there will be no insuperable obstacle.

These were the words Charles Emanuel wished to hear; the alliance was signed in September 1733. The negotiations had extended over nine months, during which time no substantial counter-offer had come from Vienna. Piedmont was to have the Milanese; Don Carlos was to have the Two Sicilies; Piedmont would then be willing to cede Savoy to France. Nothing less than the prospect of gaining the whole of the Milanese would have persuaded Piedmont to aid in winning such advantages for the sons of Elizabeth Farnese. The treaty had two main defects. First, Spain was not a party to it, and there was no guarantee that Elizabeth Farnese would observe it; and second, no mention was made of Mantua, in some ways the key to the whole north Italian plain. Charles Emanuel certainly hoped to annex it to Piedmont; Elizabeth Farnese planned Mantua as part of a territory for her second son, Don Philip. On these weaknesses the alliance was ultimately to break.

In November 1733 the Family Compact was signed between France and Spain. The two Powers guaranteed each other's possessions, and agreed to make common cause against the Emperor, and also against the commercial and naval power of England. The inclusion of the latter clauses makes it more difficult to justify Walpole's neutrality. The War of 1733 was really the attempt of France and Spain to recommence the War of the Spanish Succession, and to reverse the Settlement of Utrecht. This was not an issue to which England could afford to be indifferent. But the French skilfully avoided giving offence to England, and the Austrian Netherlands were not attacked. Walpole could therefore claim that English interests were not directly threatened. But English neutrality gave great offence to the Emperor, and was regarded by Prince Eugène with consternation. He wrote to his agent in London:

I need not tell you, what is well known, that I was always inclined to the union with the Maritime Powers. But I cannot refrain from avowing my astonishment at their present conduct. Will it be a matter of surprise, should the Emperor, abandoned by those on whom he ought most to rely, be reduced to the extreme necessity of consenting to a measure, on which he cannot reflect without horror [i.e. the marriage of Don Carlos and Maria Theresa]? What then will become of the liberty of Europe; and who can justly reproach him for having taken the only step which can take him from destruction? Should he not take that step, should the House of Bourbon continue in possession of her present conquests, and those she is likely to make, will the liberty of Europe be more firmly established? Can the Maritime Powers imagine that the Emperor is too formidable, and the House of Bourbon too weak? Or can anyone, attached to the interest of the King, believe that His Britannic Majesty will not feel the fatal effects of the weakness to which the Emperor may be reduced; and that the House of Bourbon, to attain universal monarchy, will not raise herself on the ruins of that of Austria, destroy the commerce of the Maritime Powers, and establish the Pretender on the throne of England!

The war north of the Alps was of little account. Danzig surrendered to the Russians after an eight months' siege, and in June 1734 Stanislas fled into Prussian territory. There is no evidence that Fleury cared much about the Polish question, and he made only a meagre attempt to aid his candidate. On the Rhine his troops occupied the Imperial fortress of Philipsburg. But the main theatre of operations was in Italy. There the outbreak of war took the Austrians by surprise, and Marshal Daun, governor of the Milanese, had only 12,000 men, while Charles Emanuel commanded a combined force more than four times greater. In November 1733 the French and Savoyard allies crossed the frontier, and in December Charles Emanuel entered Milan and proclaimed himself Duke. Spanish troops were disembarked at

Genoa and Leghorn, and in March 1734 Don Carlos left Parma, joined them, and marched on Naples. The Austrian garrisons in the kingdom of Naples collapsed, and in May Don Carlos proclaimed himself King of the Two Sicilies, upon the authority of Philip V of Spain. The Habsburgs had always found it impossible to defend southern Italy, and their rule ended there without regret on the part of the inhabitants. Charles Emanuel was less popular in Milan, but militarily the campaign had been a complete success. The Austrian power was confined to Mantua. Concerted action between Piedmont, Spain and France could hardly fail to conquer Mantua. But Charles Emanuel refused to advance until he had assurances as to his claims to Mantua. Fleury could only reply that Elizabeth Farnese was intending the duchy of Mantua for Don Philip. It was clear to Charles Emanuel that he was riding as dangerously near the wind as his father had done during the years 1700-3. Elizabeth Farnese was bent on restoring a Spanish domination of Italy. With Don Philip in Mantua, Don Carlos in the Duchies and the Two Sicilies, the Emperor hostile, and England alienated, Piedmont would be reduced to a state of dependency on France. In these circumstances Charles Emanuel refused to lift a finger for the capture of Mantua, and thus 1734 passed with no decisive action. In 1735 Fleury opened secret negotiations with Vienna, and in October peace preliminaries were signed. Charles Emanuel learnt of them twenty-four days later, when Louis XV wrote to inform him that he had had to make a speedy peace to forestall a peace between Madrid and Vienna! The terms were that Charles VI should give up the Two Sicilies to Don Carlos, but retain Milan and Mantua, and, in compensation for the loss of the Two Sicilies, should annex Parma and Piacenza. Charles Emanuel would receive Novara and Tortona from the Milanese. Stanislas Leszczynski would receive the duchy of Lorraine, which on his death should revert to France. The present duke of Lorraine, Francis Stephen, who was to be the consort of Charles VI's daughter, Maria Theresa, was to become the grand duke of Tuscany upon the death of the last Medici, Gian Gastone. Finally, France recognised the Pragmatic Sanction. Charles Emanuel protested at the terms, and Elizabeth Farnese loudly proclaimed the French betrayal, but both had no choice but to accept, and Elizabeth Farnese certainly had little enough to complain of. The details took many months to work out, and the Treaty of Vienna was finally signed in November 1738. Charles Emanuel did not accede to it until February 1739. Its terms make the Treaty one of the most remarkable of the century. During the war the Habsburgs had come near to losing their Italian possessions, yet by the Peace, although they lost the Two Sicilies (too distant for them to defend against a strong enemy), they were more strongly entrenched in North Italy than before. The acquisition of Parma and Piacenza, and the accession of Francis Stephen, the future husband of Maria Theresa, to Tuscany, were of the greatest strategic advantage to Austria. Such favourable terms could not have been obtained had the Franco–Spanish alliance been closer, and had not Fleury made a separate peace. This *rapprochement* between France and the Emperor in some ways foreshadows the Diplomatic Revolution of 1756. The reversion of Lorraine to France was a substantial gain which completed the work of Louis XIV on the French frontier. Apart from this, Charles VI came out of the war more successfully than perhaps he had had any right to expect.

The War of the Austrian Succession

Before the Treaty of Vienna was signed, Charles VI was engaged in a disastrous war with the Turks, and in 1739 he was completely defeated.[1] Apart from his tenuous alliance with Russia he was isolated in Europe. Worry over his position in Europe hastened his end. He died in October 1740, aged fifty-six, the last of the male line of the House of Habsburg, which had continued unbroken for 400 years. He left his daughter Maria Theresa a sad inheritance. Her complaint that she 'inherited a Crown without an army, without money, without credit, and without experience or knowledge', was no exaggeration, but a simple statement of fact. He left her the Pragmatic Sanction, which ensured her succession to all her dominions, but gave her no protection against foreign enemies. It was a great misfortune for the Habsburgs that Frederick William of Prussia should have died a few months earlier, leaving to his son Frederick II a fine army, a full treasury, and an itch to cut a fine figure in Europe. But for the action of Frederick II it is possible that her accession would have been peaceful.

Frederick II, as he said, was anxious to keep an appointment with

[1] See p. 317.

glory.[1] In December 1740 he suddenly invaded Silesia, while at the same time sending an audacious message to Maria Theresa offering her his alliance in return for the cession of Silesia, an offer which was rejected with contempt. In April 1741 he fought his first battle against the Austrians at Mollwitz. Frederick had to learn the art of war by hard experience; his cavalry was shattered; he was convinced the battle was lost and he fled the field. But in his absence the Prussian Commander, Schwerin, won the battle, and a shamefaced king returned next day to acclaim the victory. The battle of Mollwitz decided the fate of Silesia, and, but for the character of Maria Theresa, might have decided the fate of the Habsburg Monarchy.

The ease with which Prussia seemed to succeed brought a host of flies buzzing around what was commonly supposed to be the carcase of the Habsburg Monarchy. Louis XV, Elizabeth Farnese, Augustus of Saxony, Charles Emanuel of Piedmont and Charles, Elector of Bavaria, all had designs upon Habsburg territory.[2] In France there was a war party, headed by Marshal Belleisle, of idle nobility who longed for a military promenade at the expense of the old Habsburg enemy. Mentally they still lived in the days of Richelieu. Fleury, by his peace with Austria (1735–38), had been feeling his way towards a general *entente* with Austria. Now the hotheads among the French nobility wished for their own glorification to fight battles which had no purpose which accorded with the interests of France. Fleury as usual bowed to the storm. France had been the last Power to accept the Pragmatic Sanction; now he declared that the acceptance was conditional upon the non-appearance of a better claimant than Maria Theresa. Marshal Belleisle was sent to Germany, and by May 1741 he had negotiated alliances with Spain, Saxony, Bavaria and Prussia, for the dismemberment of the Habsburg Empire. In September a Franco-Bavarian army reached Linz, on the Danube, within striking distance of Vienna.

In her hour of peril, Maria Theresa showed magnificent courage. She was now aged twenty-four, a woman of great beauty, commanding presence and regal quality. She was deeply religious, and always had a simple, child-like faith in God's Will, and in the mission of the

---

[1] See p. 177.
[2] Both Augustus of Saxony and Charles Albert of Bavaria, of the House of Wittelsbach, had shadowy claims to the Habsburg inheritance through marriage.

Habsburgs. She was well aware of the antiquated nature of her government, and necessity made her a reformer. Her attitude to government was matriarchal, and she knew how, by an ineffable quality of personality, to win the love of her people. Never for a moment did she contemplate failure or defeat. Perhaps her most famous act was that of 1741, when she threw herself upon the loyalty of the Hungarian Diet, to beg for their aid:

> The very existence of the kingdom of Hungary, of our own person, of our children, and our crown, are now at stake.

and the Magyar nobility, touched by her heroism, cried:

> We will die for our king, Maria Theresa!

The heroics of the event have obscured its true significance. Maria Theresa was so hampered by an outworn and feudal constitution in Hungary that she was entirely dependent upon the goodwill of the Diet. It is true that in moments of crisis the Hungarian nobility prided themselves upon their loyalty, but even so they voted their Queen only 25,000 men, and Maria Theresa had had to buy their loyalty by a confirmation of their privileges. This was not the way to defeat the trim Prussian despotism.

Luckily for Austria, the French and Bavarians turned from Linz to invade Bohemia; Vienna was saved, but in November the French captured Prague. In January 1742 the Elector of Bavaria was elected Holy Roman Emperor as Charles VII. Maria Theresa, as a woman, was ineligible, and her attempts to secure the election of her husband failed. The election was unanimous, but it was to prove an empty dignity, for Charles VI was soon to learn that it brought him neither revenues nor armies, but a host of troubles.

Thereafter Maria Theresa's fortunes rapidly improved. The fall of Walpole in England brought Lord Carteret into power, and his policy was one of vigorous support for Austria. Frederick of Prussia was concerned at the growing power of the French in Germany, and in October duped his allies by signing the treaty of Klein-Schnellendorf with the Austrians, by which he was left in possession of Silesia, and the Austrians were able to turn away and overrun Bavaria. Charles VII was therefore soon an Emperor without a capital, for Munich was occupied in February 1742. In Italy Spanish troops had begun to disembark in 1741. The success of the Gallospans (as continental historians call the French and Spanish allies) depended largely on a renewal of their alliance with Piedmont. But Charles Emanuel was not to be caught a second time without a clear understanding on Spanish intentions. In 1742 he issued his claims to the Duchy of Milan, by right of his descent through the female line of Philip II of Spain. But Spain refused to countenance it, and in February 1742 Charles Emanuel signed a military convention with the Austrians. This was of enormous importance to Maria Theresa. So long as the 'Austro-Sards' stood together in North Italy, France and Spain were not strong enough to destroy them. Moreover, in August 1742, Commodore Martin and the British fleet threatened Naples with bombardment, and forced Charles III (formerly Don Carlos) to announce his neutrality.

By 1742 therefore there was a spectacular reversal of Maria Theresa's fortunes. Prussia made peace in June (Treaty of Breslau), retaining Silesia. Saxony followed suit. The Austrians were in occupation of Munich. Carteret had put a 'Pragmatic Army' into Hanover, and in June 1743 it defeated the French at Dettingen on the Rhine. In September 1743, by the Treaty of Worms, Carteret completed the negotiations for the alliance between Austria and Piedmont. It was his crowning achievement. Charles Emanuel renounced his claims to the Milanese, and received Piacenza, Vigevano, Anghiara and part of Pavia. Carutti, the historian of the House of Savoy, declares that Charles Emanuel always regarded the treaty as his crowning achievement. France replied to the Treaty of Worms with a renewal of the Family Compact with Spain (October 1743). France was thus committed to continue the war in the interests of Elizabeth Farnese, and with no clear objective of her own.

In 1744 the character of the war again changed dramatically. France at last found a soldier of genius, Maurice de Saxe, illegitimate son of Augustus II of Poland. War was declared against England, and Marshal de Saxe began an invasion of the Netherlands. In the following year, he defeated the Allies under the Duke of Cumberland at Fontenoy (May 1745), and thereafter overran the Netherlands. In 1744 Frederick II decided that Maria Theresa had recovered her position to a dangerous extent, and that if she became too strong she would seek to regain Silesia. He therefore re-entered the war, but his position was now isolated. In 1745 the Emperor Charles VII died, and

Maria Theresa seized the opportunity to make peace with his son, the new Elector of Bavaria, the eighteen-year-old Maximilian Joseph. He was restored to his Electorate in return for his vote for Francis Stephen of Lorraine as the new Emperor. To Maria Theresa's delight, her husband was elected Emperor in September 1745, with only Prussia and the Palatinate voting against him. Frederick, without an ally (he declared that the Battle of Fontenoy was of no more use to him than the capture of Peking), was in a difficult position, and after defeating the Austrians in a series of minor engagements, he was glad to make peace again (Treaty of Dresden, December 1745).

In Italy Maria Theresa's forces in 1744 found themselves in difficulties which were largely of her own making. Her alliance with Piedmont, which had cost her so dearly in territory, she justified only by the prospect of the recovery of the kingdom of Naples. She bitterly resented the loss of that territory to Don Carlos in the previous war. In 1744 therefore the Austrian army in Italy, under Prince Lobkowitz, was ordered to march to the attack on Naples. In his absence Charles Emanuel was defeated by the Gallispans. Lobkowitz failed to take Naples, and his attack brought Charles III into the war. Charles Emanuel was in a desperate military position, and was bitter at the Austrian desertion. He was ready therefore to listen to French terms.

Since 1737 the French Foreign Minister had been the Marquis d'Argenson. Like his predecessor, Chauvelin, he was convinced that the old Habsburg–Bourbon struggle was in its final stages, and that the Habsburg Monarchy was about to break up. In November 1745 therefore, following the military disasters, he presented Charles Emanuel with an Italian plan. It was, he said, nothing less than 'de former une République ou association éternelle des puissances italiques, comme il y en a une germanique, une batavique et une helvétique'. Both Spain and the Habsburgs were to be expelled from Italy; Piedmont was to have the Milanese; Italian princes were to form a federation, with a Diet, and a federal army commanded by the King of Piedmont. There was, in short, to be a loose federation on the lines of the Holy Roman Empire in Italy. D'Argenson believed that once the Habsburgs were excluded from Italy, the long Habsburg–Bourbon struggle might be considered to be at an end. The proposals were, therefore, a sincere effort to solve a European problem, and as such were received with enthusiasm by the *philosophes*. Voltaire, for instance, proclaimed it the most useful political idea which had been launched in Europe in the previous five centuries.

But the plan found no favour in Italy at the time; nor has it ever aroused enthusiasm among Italian historians since. To begin with, the idea was a century ahead of its time. An assembly in which the rulers of Italy sat together was unthinkable in 1745. Worst of all, to the King of Piedmont, was the proposal to abolish all Imperial titles in Italy. It must be remembered that, until the time of Napoleon, Imperial law remained the basis of the legal systems of the greater part of Europe. Most of the territories of the King of Piedmont were held under this law.

The Imperial connection had ceased to be a hardship, and it did provide a fundamental law to which a ruler could appeal in case of danger. Charles Emanuel saw the French proposal as a trick to sever all Imperial connections between Italy and the Emperor, after which Piedmont would be entirely at the mercy of France. It is worth grasping the reasoning of Charles Emanuel here, for it throws much light on the eighteenth-century attitude to the Empire, and to the place of the Habsburgs in the European system.

Piedmont rejected d'Argenson's plan, and in 1746 the military situation was reversed. With the Peace of Dresden in Germany, Austria sent ample reinforcements to Italy. Don Philip was driven from his occupation of Milan, and from Parma as well. At that point Philip V died. His successor Ferdinand VI had no affection for Elizabeth Farnese and her sons, and no intention of squandering Spanish resources on their account. Spanish troops were ordered home, notwithstanding the protests of the French and Don Philip. 1747 saw the failure of an Austrosard attempt to invade Provence, and equally of the French to take Genoa. In the Netherlands the French defeated Cumberland at Lauffeldt, though they failed to capture Maestricht. In the colonies the English had captured Louisburg, the main French naval base in North America, and in India the French had captured Madras. At sea the British by 1747 were masters, and the French fleet was virtually confined to port. Prussia and Spain had already retired from the war; France, England and the Dutch found it difficult to see any objective in continuing the war. Only Maria Theresa seemed content that it should continue, but she was deserted by her allies. At the Congress of Aix-la-Chapelle she found Britain more anxious to placate Spain than to gratify Austria. The Preliminaries of Aix-la-Chapelle were signed in April 1748. Prussia's acquisition of Silesia and Glatz, and Charles Emanuel's gains in the Milanese, were confirmed. France evacuated the Netherlands. There was a mutual restoration of Madras and Louisburg. Spanish pride was satisfied by the recognition of Don Philip as Duke of Parma.

The War of the Austrian Succession did not finally resolve the Austro-Prussian conflict (that was not achieved until 1866), nor the Anglo-French colonial rivalry (that was not achieved until 1904). But Prussia had undoubtedly emerged as a Great Power, confirmed in the possession of Silesia. In all other respects, the war was a triumph for Maria Theresa. In 1740 the Habsburg Monarchy had appeared about to collapse; in 1748 its prestige was high, and internal reform was strengthening and mobilising its resources. The war marked the end of Spanish ambitions in Italy, and of the ambitions and influence of Elizabeth Farnese. Her objectives had been almost entirely dynastic, and only incidentally related to the interests of Spain. Yet she belongs to a fortunate few in history who can say that they had achieved what they set out to achieve. Both her sons ruled in Italy, although Habsburg power was more securely entrenched there than ever. The most remarkable terms of the Peace were those concerning France. France had been in occupation of most of the Netherlands, yet she gained nothing by the Peace. She fought with no clear objectives; she made no gains. The futility of French policy after the death of Fleury in 1743 is almost incredible. Frederick the Great was amazed at the absurdity of his ally. Piedmont had reached the maximum extent it was to achieve before the Treaty of Vienna in 1815, and for the rest of the century had to learn to live with his Habsburg neighbours. Russia had been Maria Theresa's ally during most of the war. The Tsarina Elizabeth had not provided much material aid, but she had learnt to detest Frederick of Prussia; her outlook was increasingly European, and the war marks another stage in the advance of Russia as a European Power.

The Diplomatic Revolution

The period of peace was of short duration, in America and India because it was hardly observed at all; and in Europe because Maria Theresa was determined to make another attempt to recover Silesia. In preparation for this, she instituted both a great programme of internal reform,[1] and abroad one of the most brilliant programmes of diplomatic achievement in the history of Europe. The Treaty of Aix-la-Chapelle forced upon the Habsburg government the necessity of hard thinking about its European position and future policy. Maria Theresa was profoundly dissatisfied. The loss of Silesia had deprived her of one of her richest provinces, and had left her with a frontier difficult to defend. In Italy Charles Emanuel had bitten deeply into the Milanese. The areas ceded were integral parts of the economy of the Milanese, and strategically the Habsburgs were left with an indefensible frontier. The loss of Parma, and the restoration of the Duke of Modena, had made communications with Tuscany more difficult. In the Netherlands the Barrier Fortresses had been ruined by the French, and the Habsburgs could not afford to rebuild them. Moreover, Maria Theresa was profoundly dissatisfied with her English alliance. Carteret's policy had been to persuade Austria to patch up a peace with Prussia by giving up Silesia, in order to concentrate her forces upon the French invader. Similarly, he sought to persuade her to win the Piedmontese alliance by giving up part of the Milanese, in order that the two Powers could stand firmly against France and Spain in Italy. Maria Theresa complained that the assistance she received from her allies consisted chiefly in advice as to how best to surrender her territory. This was not entirely fair; her position had appeared desperate; Britain had paid her subsidies, and Carteret had put the Pragmatic Army in Germany. But the lecturing tone adopted by British diplomats did much to justify her resentment. She wrote in answer to one of the lectures from England:

> If the House of Austria has derived useful succours from her alliance with the Maritime Powers, she has frequently purchased those advantages with the blood and ruin of her subjects; while her allies have opened to themselves new sources of aggrandisement and riches. . . . Could any consideration diminish our gratitude towards the Maritime Powers, it would doubtless be their endeavours to represent those succours as purely gratuitous, which have been the consequence of measures dictated by their own interests.

It did not take much therefore to persuade her to look elsewhere for allies. She sought now to achieve by diplomacy what she had been unable to achieve by war.

[1] See p. 209.

In this her principal adviser was Anton, Count (later Prince) Kaunitz-Rietberg.[1] His diplomatic skill early caught the attention of the Empress, and still more the revolutionary ideas he submitted to her on foreign policy. He argued that the British alliance could never be of much use to Austria in the recovery of Silesia. Britain was a sea power; her interests were overseas. Moreover, Hanover was too close to Prussia for George II to risk more than defensive operations against Frederick. The Habsburg–Bourbon conflict had burnt itself out; it lacked substance. Austrian policy should therefore be to win a French alliance against Prussia. In 1750 Maria Theresa, half-convinced by his argument, sent him as ambassador to Versailles. He moved easily in the cultured society of the French Court, and became a favourite with Mme. de Pompadour. All his life Kaunitz remained a devotee of the philosophy of the Enlightenment. But he found it impossible to make much progress with his idea of Habsburg–Bourbon *rapprochement*. In 1753 Maria Theresa recalled him to take charge of affairs, with the title of Chancellor.

One of the chief aims of a French alliance was the neutralisation of Italy in the coming war. Ferdinand VI of Spain had no further ambitions in Italy. But if Charles III of Naples, or Don Philip of Párma, were attacked, prestige might require the intervention of Spain. It was thus in the interests of both Madrid and Vienna to provide against such a contingency. Accordingly, in May 1752 the Treaty of Aranjuez was signed by Spain, Piedmont and Austria. The three Crowns guaranteed the Treaty of Aix-la-Chapelle, and each guaranteed the territories of the other. The Treaty was a great triumph for Maria Theresa's diplomacy (perhaps the first real success of Habsburg diplomacy since 1721). It virtually established the *status quo* in Italy; Spain recognised the Habsburg hegemony of Italy. Once the Habsburg alliance with the French was complete, Piedmont was deprived of an independent foreign policy. A peace settled over Italy which remained unbroken until the French Revolutionary Wars.

Maria Theresa's most important ally after 1748 was the Tsarina Elizabeth of Russia. The Russian alliance dated from 1726, when Russia had recognised the Pragmatic Sanction. It was renewed in 1746, and continued so long as the Tsarina lived.

Frederick of Prussia watched the success of Maria Theresa's

[1] See p. 219.

diplomacy with growing concern. He had no doubt that the outcome would be a general war. He was contemptuous of the French government, with its frivolity, its shallow politicians and its entire lack of policy. During 1755 the idea grew in his mind that he might be able to make use of George II's pre-occupations with the safety of Hanover in the event of war to detach Britain from the Austrian alliance. He saw the wealth of Britain as the invaluable ally of his own impoverished kingdom. That war between Britain and France was coming few could doubt. The colonists had failed to capture the French Fort Duquesne, on the Ohio, and in 1755 General Braddock was killed and his force wiped out. Admiral Boscawen, though he had failed to take a French convoy, had captured two of their ships and thus made war inevitable. In preparation for the coming struggle, in September 1755 George II signed a subsidy treaty with Russia for the hire of 55,000 Russian troops for the defence of Hanover. In the same year Maria Theresa decided that in the event of war she would not defend the Austrian Netherlands. This was a serious blow to England; it destroyed the *raison d'être* of the Austrian alliance which had continued since 1716. It was an indication that Maria Theresa no longer was interested in the English alliance. Frederick II leapt at the opportunity. He at once offered George II that he himself would defend Hanover in the event of a French attack. George II readily accepted, and the Treaty of Westminster was signed in January 1756. Its advantages to Prussia were obvious. He had removed the danger of Russian troops occupying Hanover; he sorely needed British subsidies; he had detached an important Austrian ally; he did not think for a moment that this would cost him his French alliance. Instead, he hoped that he might be able to patch up the colonial conflict, and unite the Maritime Powers against Austria. In his *Memoirs* he freely admits that he did not contemplate the possibility that France and Austria could come together. He thought he had dissolved the anti-Prussian alliance, not hastened its completion. News of the Treaty of Westminster had immediate effect in both Russia and France. The Tsarina was furious at the cavalier way in which George II had discarded his Russian alliance. The French government, alarmed at the desertion of their ally, signed with Austria a defensive alliance, the Treaty of Versailles (May 1756). This was the most spectacular part of the Diplomatic Revolution. The Habsburg–Bourbon rivalry, which had been an accepted fact in Europe for two-and-a-half centuries, was at an end. Twice it had been foreshadowed in the previous half-century, once at the time of the Quadruple Alliance, and once in the time of Fleury. Now it was effected by the brilliant diplomacy of Maria Theresa (with the assistance of Frederick the Great). Kaunitz's great plan had come to pass, and with it an alliance of the most formidable dimensions against Prussia. Maria Theresa had neutralised Italy, secured the neutrality of Spain and Piedmont, renewed the alliance with Russia, and brought France into her system. Prussia faced a coalition of Europe, with England his only ally.

It cannot be said that the French had worked for an Austrian alliance; rather they had felt themselves deserted by Prussia, and had then readily accepted Kaunitz's offer. Louis XV and Mme. de Pompadour were strongly in favour of it. There was certainly an advantage in being free from military commitments in southern Europe, if the main intention of the war was the conquest of the colonies. Yet France was ill-prepared for her struggle, whether in North America, in India or on the sea. She had brilliant servants in the colonies, the Marquis Duqesne, Montcalm, Bussy, the Comte de Lally; but they were ill-supported from France. In Europe France aimed at little but the invasion of Hanover. Her alliance with Maria Theresa deprived France of opportunities in the Netherlands, and also in eastern Europe: Poland, for instance, had virtually to be abandoned to Russian influence. In vain did Louis XV attempt a 'double' policy by means of the 'King's Secret'.[1] During the Seven Years' War French prestige was to fall to its lowest point in the century.

The Seven Years' War

There is no doubt that Austria intended to attack Prussia when preparations were complete. Frederick decided not to wait for the coming attack; in August 1756 he suddenly invaded Saxony, and by October its conquest was complete. He was condemned by the Imperial Diet (January 1757), but this made little material difference to Prussia. Austria rapidly renewed its alliance with Russia, agreeing to pay Russia an annual subsidy. In May 1757, by a second Treaty of Versailles, Maria Theresa promised France territory in the Netherlands if Silesia was reconquered; France, for her part, agreed to pay Austria

[1] See p. 338.

a large annual subsidy and to put 100,000 men into the field in Europe. This was an absurd development of French policy. The first Treaty of Versailles was reasonable as an act of disengagement, giving France peace in Europe, while she concentrated upon her colonial war. The second Treaty committed her to a major European war, fought presumably for the sake of gain in the Netherlands.

The war began well for France. The Duke of Newcastle, the English Secretary of State, expected an attempted invasion of England, and neglected to defend the Mediterranean. Marshal Belleisle therefore switched his attack to Minorca. Admiral Byng failed to relieve the garrison in May, and the French were left to complete the conquest of the main British naval base in the Mediterranean. In October 1756 news arrived in England of the capture of Fort Oswego by Montcalm, and at the same time of the Black Hole of Calcutta. In 1757 the French launched a full-scale attack upon Hanover, and in July the Duke of Cumberland was completely defeated at Hastenbeck. His attempt to hold the line of the Weser failed; the French occupied the towns of Brunswick and Hanover. Cumberland's nerve gave way, and he signed the Convention of Klosterseven, by which he agreed to disband his army and return to England.

In the campaign of 1757 Frederick II, still pursuing his policy of attack as the best form of defence, invaded Bohemia. A series of costly engagements followed, and in June Frederick was completely defeated at Kolin, with the loss of 14,000 men. With the French in occupation of Hanover, it was a moment of crisis for Prussia. The Austrian forces overran Silesia, and at one time reached even Berlin. The Russians were in East Prussia, and the Swedes were threatening from Pomerania. In November 1757 Frederick was encamped with a diminutive force near the castle of Rossbach, facing a greatly superior army of Austrians and French. Seeing the Prussians strike camp, the Allies assumed they were in retreat, and swarmed forward carelessly to attack. They came under murderous fire, and in less than half an hour were routed, with 4,000 killed and wounded and 7,000 prisoners. Prussian losses were said to be 300. The battle was of the greatest importance. The French fell back across the Rhine; Prussian morale was restored. Pitt was now convinced that Prussia could win, and was ready to make an advantageous subsidy treaty. But Silesia was still in the hands of the Austrians. In November, by forced marches,

Frederick approached Breslau, and in December, just a month after Rossbach, routed the Austrians, under Prince Charles of Lorraine, on the field of Leuthen. With an army of 30,000 he inflicted losses (killed, wounded and prisoners) of some 27,000 on an Austrian army more than twice as large. It was a shattering blow to Austrian morale, and thus ended the most brilliant of Frederick the Great's campaigns.

In July 1757 William Pitt came into power in England. His policy was a vigorous prosecution of the war against France in the colonies and at sea. But he had long since repented of his early attacks upon the 'Hanoverian' policy of Lord Carteret. He now took the Hanoverian army into British pay, and made Prussia an annual subsidy of £670,000. He saw, as he said, that Canada might be won on the banks of the Elbe, by tying down French troops in Europe; and thus France was committed to a continental war which was increasingly irrelevant to her needs. The new Hanoverian army under the brilliant Prince Ferdinand of Brunswick[1] succeeded during 1758 in driving the French out of Hanover and across the Rhine, with the loss of 10,000 men. Thus England's services to Prussia were considerable, not only in money and supplies, but in covering Frederick's right flank from the French. In addition, during 1758 Pitt despatched commando attacks against the French coast, at St. Servan, St. Malo and Cherbourg. In themselves they were not of great importance, but they did destroy shipping and harbour installations, and they did tie down some 30,000 French troops in France, which might have been sent to the colonies or Germany.

Thanks to Pitt's aid, Frederick II had only to deal with the Russians and Austrians in 1758. Elizabeth of Russia had been concerned at Frederick's victories at Rossbach and Leuthen, and in January 1758 invaded East Prussia. Frederick determined on a speedy attack on the Austrians before the full Russian attack developed, and in April invested Olmütz. If the town fell, Vienna would be endangered. But Daun, the Austrian Commander-in-chief, and an extremely able newcomer, General Loudon,[2] put up a skilful defence, and Frederick had

---

[1] Brother of the Duke of Brunswick, and brother-in-law of Frederick the Great.

[2] Loudon was a Livonian of Scottish descent, a soldier of fortune who had once served the Russians, had offered to serve Prussia, but Frederick II had refused to employ him. He was to prove to be the ablest Austrian soldier of the century after Prince Eugène.

to withdraw. Meanwhile the Russians had ravaged East Prussia, and had advanced across Poland into Brandenburg. In August Frederick, after a march of 270 miles in 20 days, was before the town of Custrin, which the Russians were besieging and reducing to ashes. On August 25th Frederick attacked, and there followed the Battle of Zorndorf. Frederick lost almost one-third of his army of 36,000 men, to the Russian loss of 20,000. But the latter retreated into Poland, and for the moment Prussia was safe. Meanwhile Daun had turned his attention to the invasion of Saxony, and Frederick had to dash away from the scene of Zorndorf to save Dresden from the Austrians.

He received a check at the hands of Daun at Hochkirch, in October, but Dresden was saved. Marshal Daun had shown himself to be slow and over-cautious. There was no co-ordination between the military efforts of the three allies. Yet it should have been clear to them that only a careful co-ordination of their attacks upon Prussia would ensure Frederick's defeat.

The most significant facts for the campaigns of 1759 were, first the careful plans of Pitt for the conquest of Canada, and second the rise to power of the Duc de Choiseul in France. The French naval base of Louisburg had been taken in 1758, and in 1759 the British capture of the forts on Lake Champlain, and Wolfe's brilliant capture of Quebec, provided the most spectacular events in Pitt's famous Year of Victories. The Duc de Choiseul, a Lorrainer who had become enormously rich by a wealthy marriage, was a vigorous and sanguine man who saw Britain as France's chief enemy, and who wished therefore to concentrate French military efforts in the colonies and at sea, rather than against Prussia. But it was too late in the colonial war for Choiseul to effect the ultimate outcome, and considerations of prestige prevented the French from withdrawing from the German war. Choiseul could do little more than watch the British conquer Canada, secure command of the sea, dominate the West Indies, and drive the French from India. In Germany, however, the French launched an offensive with the object of overrunning Hanover, and thus gaining counters with which they might bargain for a reasonable peace with England. In August they captured Minden and threatened Hanover. But Prince Ferdinand counter-attacked and completely defeated the French in the Battle of Minden. French prestige was already so low that this was a shattering blow. Finally, in November, the French fleet was destroyed by Admiral Boscawen in Quiberon Bay; French hopes for an invasion of England were at an end.

While England went from strength to strength, Prussia in 1759 appeared to be reaching the end of its resources and of human endurance. Kolin, Leuthen, Zorndorf, Hochkirch and numerous minor engagements, had inflicted great losses upon the Prussian army, and put a superhuman strain upon the King, though he remained optimistic, and daily found time for reading his favourite books, Racine, Cicero and Lucretius, and talking with his Boswell, Henri de Catt. But the quality of his armies necessarily declined, while that of the Austrians improved with experience. For one thing, they had learnt the wisdom of closer co-operation with the Russians. Thus in August 1759 the Austrians and Russians were together at Frankfort-on-Oder, on Prussian territory, only forty-eight miles from Berlin. At Kunersdorf in August Frederick, with 50,000 men, attacked a combined Austro-Russian army of 70,000 men, and was completely defeated, with the loss of half his army. In the following month Daun occupied Saxony, and at Maxen captured a force of 15,000 Prussians. Yet neither of the Allies made much use of their victories; the Russians retired into Poland, and Frederick was saved for another year.

For Frederick the prospect for 1760 was grim, but there were two rays of hope. First, Russia's victories, and their occupation of East Prussia, were turning Poland into a Russian puppet. Neither France nor Austria could be indifferent to the rise of Russian power, and this might be expected to weaken the alliance against Prussia. Second, the Tsarina's health was bad; she might be expected to die at any time. Her heir, Peter, a poor, half-witted youth, was known to be a fanatical admirer of Frederick II. His accession might be the salvation of Prussia.

In 1760 the centre of operations was in Silesia. The Austrians had a great preponderance of manpower, but were handicapped by the slow and plodding caution of Daun. Relying on the element of surprise, Frederick suddenly attacked and defeated the Austrians at Leignitz in August. Still, with his limited forces, Frederick could not defend more than one theatre of operations at any time. Thus in October a force of 20,000 Russians and 15,000 Austrians raided up to the gates of Berlin, and for a short time occupied the capital. Frederick had to dash from Silesia to relieve his capital, and, when the invaders retired, he had to hurry to Saxony to hold Leipzig against the Austrians. Here in the closing weeks of 1760 the last battles of the German war were fought.

By 1761 both Prussia and Austria were exhausted. The French had been completely defeated in the colonial war, and had entirely lost command of the sea. Choiseul had one final card to play. The Don Carlos who had been King of Naples, in 1759 succeeded to the throne of Spain, leaving his son Ferdinand King of Naples. He had good reason to fear the growth of British sea-power, and also for the fate of the Spanish Empire if Britain was triumphant in America. It was a brilliant stroke of diplomatic success for Choiseul that in 1761 he persuaded Charles III to renew the Family Compact with France, and to enter the war against Britain in 1762. Pitt knew of Choiseul's intrigue, and in 1761 had wished to forestall Spanish intentions by an attack on Spain, but his Cabinet had not supported him, and he had resigned. But the outcome was much the same. Spain lost to Britain the richest jewel in its Imperial crown, the great city of Havana, and also Manila in the Philippines. British sea-power had triumphed equally over France and Spain.

In Europe 1761 was a year of manoeuvring, with both Prussia and the Austro-Russians avoiding battle. But the outlook for 1762 appeared desperate for Prussia, for Prussia would have found it difficult to raise more than 100,000 troops, and this meant that he would be outnumbered by more than three to one. But in January 1762 the Tsarina Elizabeth died. The half-witted Peter III who succeeded her immediately offered peace to Prussia, his sole demand being the award of the Order of the Black Eagle. The delighted Frederick readily complied, and much enjoyed the absurdity of the situation. He was now able to concentrate all his forces against Austria. A stalemate ensued, in which it was obvious that the chance of Maria Theresa's recovering Silesia had gone.

All Powers were now anxious for peace. It remained only for Choiseul to try by diplomatic skill to mitigate the harshness of the peace terms, and fortunately for him he had to deal, not with Pitt, who would have sought permanently to cripple French naval power, but with the earl of Bute and the duke of Bedford, who were in favour of a more moderate peace in the interests of the principle of the balance of power. By the Treaty of Paris (February 1763)

Britain gained Canada, St. Vincent, Tobago, Dominica and Grenada in America, and Senegal in Africa, and regained Minorca in Europe. The French lost their political power in India, but were allowed to retain five trading factories. They also regained Guadeloupe, Martinique and St. Lucia, Goree and Belleisle, and also their fishing rights off Newfoundland. Spain surrendered Florida, and received Louisiana, west of the Mississippi, as compensation from France. She also regained Havana and Manila. In Germany there could be only one settlement. By the Treaty of Hubertusburg there was a simple recognition of the existing situation, with Prussia left in possession of Silesia and Glatz.

The Significance of Frederick the Great's Policy

The wars of 1740 to 1763, and the concluding peace treaties, had brought about a new situation in Europe and the world. Britain had won a complete victory over France in the colonies and on the seas, but it was always recognised by some observers that the removal of the French threat from Canada to the American colonies would greatly weaken the relationship between the American colonies and the mother-country. The failure of the French was the result of a lack of clear objectives, the futile pursuit of outworn shibboleths in foreign policy, the feebleness of her Ministers until 1758 and the extraordinary absence of able military commanders. Napoleon saw these French military defeats as essential preliminaries to the coming French Revolution. The prestige of the Monarchy was shaken, and the financial position, though not yet irreparable, was greatly worsened. Austria, on the other hand, though she had lost Silesia, came out of the war with great prestige. The Habsburg Power was greater in 1763 than it had been at any time since 1721.

Prussia came out of the wars utterly exhausted, but undoubtedly with the rank of a Great Power. On the rape of Silesia and the subsequent struggle there have tended to be two schools of thought among German historians. Prussian historians of the nineteenth century tended to glorify the Prussian victory as the victory of the new German State over the old, outworn Habsburg Imperialism. They saw Frederick's work as the necessary preliminary to the work of Bismarck and the unification of Germany under Prussian leadership in 1871. A smaller, but nonetheless discerning, school of thought has blamed Frederick for deliberately dividing and weakening Germany by instituting a great Austro-Prussian struggle at a time when France was still a powerful enemy, and above all when a united German attitude would have prevented Russia from dominating Poland and becoming (as she certainly emerged in 1763) the dominant Power in eastern Europe. The argument continues that Frederick opened a new age of international immorality; he proclaimed to the world the doctrine that Might is Right; the Partitions of Poland were therefore the logical outcome of the seizure of Silesia; and Frederick the Great was the supreme exponent of the political philosophy of *Realpolitik*. Thus both on moral issues, and on the practical considerations of dividing Germany and aiding the rise of Russia, Frederick has been severely criticised. It is unrealistic to seek to blame Frederick II for any European predicament a century, or even two centuries, after his own time, and happily we are not called upon here to have to choose between these two schools of thought. They are themselves historical phenomena, and may well be modified by time. What is important is that we should understand why Frederick acted in the way he did. The whole tendency of the eighteenth century was towards expansion. Small countries might in many respects be happy countries, but they were poor countries. The Prussian kings were forced by geographical position to retain abnormally large armies; the burden to the State was enormous. The temptation to Frederick to add 16,000 square miles of valuable territory and a million subjects was too great to be resisted. A similar line of reasoning influenced the Habsburgs. Once Silesia was lost, Joseph II could not rest until he had found compensation elsewhere. In a sense all Joseph's foreign policy, in Poland, in Bavaria and against the Turks, can be explained in the light of that nagging urge to consolidate and expand. Neither Frederick the Great nor Joseph II was thinking in terms of German national unity, but in terms of his own State power.

12: The Partitions of Poland

When in 1386 Jagellon I established a personal union between the kingdom of Poland and the Grand Duchy of Lithuania, and was received into the Roman Church, he established by far the greatest Power in eastern Europe. At a time when the Grand Duchy of Moscow was struggling into existence as the power of the Golden Horde receded, the Polish-Lithuanian Monarchy included the vast area of Poland, Lithuania, Little Russia and the Ukraine, and it appeared as a great bastion of Romanism against both Greek Orthodoxy and paganism. Yet there were grave weaknesses in the Polish State which led ultimately to its disappearance from the map of Europe. The first was geographical; it was a country without natural frontiers. The very factor which enabled the Polish-Lithuanian power to expand over the great east European plain, enabled the power of Russia and the Turks to roll the conqueror back again, once they were strong enough to do so. For a time Poland asserted a suzerainty over East Prussia, but never came near to absorbing the Teutonic Knights and their successors into the Polish State. Against the Habsburgs the Carpathians provided a good frontier, but against the rising power of Brandenburg-Prussia there was again no natural frontier. Moreover, the State lacked racial cohesion, for it consisted of Poles, Lithuanians, White Russians, Ukrainians, Germans and Jews, and racial differences were expressed especially in religious dissensions. For whereas the Poles and Lithuanians were Roman Catholics, White Russians and Ukrainians were partly Uniate[1] and partly Greek Orthodox, while the Germans were Lutherans.

The second weakness was constitutional. When the Jagellon dynasty came to an end in 1572, there was established the principle of elective monarchy. The occasion of the election of a monarch was also the occasion for bargaining with him about his powers, and thus the powers of the Monarchy were frittered away with successive elections. As the powers of the Monarchy declined, the liberties of the Diet

[1] i.e. retaining Greek Orthodox rites, but acknowledging the supremacy of the Pope.

(*Sejm*) increased. It consisted of a House of Senators and a House of Deputies. The Senate consisted of bishops and high government officials, both drawn exclusively from the nobility. The deputies represented only the nobility; towns were unrepresented. The deputies represented strictly local interests and carried out the detailed wishes of their electors. The prime concern of the Diet was to preserve the local liberties and independence of the nobility, and thus had evolved the extraordinary principle of the *liberum veto* (first adopted in 1652), by which all votes of the Diet had to be unanimous, and a single vote cast against a measure not only defeated the measure, but vetoed all other decisions taken during the session, and brought the session to an end. As the Diet met every other year, and as in the period 1652–1763 48 sessions out of 55 had been brought to an end in this way, it is clear that Polish government often appeared to be little better than a form of legalised anarchy. Another characteristic institution was the right of Confederation. This was the legal right of any group of nobility to combine to resist, by force if necessary, any act of the executive of which they disapproved. The principle had been widespread in mediaeval Europe, but by the eighteenth century survived in its pristine form only in Poland (although the Hungarian nobility sometimes claimed it also, and so did Brabant, in the Netherlands).

Such a constitution was merely the visible expression of the social organisation of Poland. Poland was a land of peasants and nobility; the proportion of the nobility was very high, in some areas as high as 10 per cent. of the population, and the constitution was specially devised to preserve and extend their liberties. Many of them lived in great magnificence, in a style imitated from France, with ornate palaces built by Baroque architects from Italy, with exotic gardens and parks. Town life decayed; there was no strong burgher class, and what trade there was was in the hands of Jews and Germans. There was equally a decay of learning; the intellectual life of Poland was moribund as the Jesuit stranglehold was strengthened. The once great University of Cracow was by the eighteenth century a backwater. As the nobles objected to paying taxes, the revenues were small, and the Polish army ridiculously inadequate.

The decline of Poland may therefore be dated from the establishment of the elective monarchy in 1572. Sigismund III (1587–1632) was the first Saxon king of Poland. A fierce and intolerant Romanist, he was known as 'the King of the Jesuits', and his persecutions brought him into conflict with Lutheran Sweden and Brandenburg, and Orthodox Russia. But the great testing-time of the Polish State was during the reign of John Casimir (1648–68), the last of the Polish Vasa, when the Muscovites invaded Poland from the east and the Swedes from the north. Warsaw was occupied by the Swedes in 1655, and by the Peace of Oliva (1660) Poland lost Livonia to Sweden, and gave up the suzerainty of East Prussia. By 1667 Poland had lost her eastern provinces, east of the Dnieper river, including Smolensk, Kiev and part of the Ukraine, to Russia. In 1672 Poland lost Podolia and a further part of the Ukraine to the Turks. The balance of power in eastern Europe had permanently shifted against Poland. For a time the decline appeared to have been arrested when John Sobieski (1674–96), a Polish magnate, was elected king. He was a good soldier, and proved to be the last strong king of Poland. In 1683 he helped to save Vienna from the Turks. But at his death there was a return to the Saxon line in the person of Augustus II (1696–1733), and the decline went on apace. For years Poland was overrun by the armies of Charles XII of Sweden. All attempts to reform the constitution were defeated; the Diet failed to vote enough money to maintain a respectable army. Religious conflicts gave the foreigner ample opportunity for interference. It is an interesting fact that as the weakness of the Polish State became more manifest, the Polish reaction was not a determination to reform the State, but a determination to exterminate the non-Romanist religious minorities. There was a renewed persecution of the 200,000 Lutherans (most of them Germans in the towns), the demolition of their churches and the closure of their schools. There was thus ample excuse for Prussian intervention. Still more ominous was the power of Russia, which, after the defeat of the Swedes, never really left Poland alone. The Russian ambassador was always a power in the land, and in 1720 Russia and Prussia signed a secret agreement to maintain the political anarchy in Poland in the guise of protecting the religious minorities in Poland. A Russo-Prussian agreement would in any case spell the doom of Poland, but it was madness for the Poles to provide the excuse for intervention by the continuance of religious persecutions.

The reign of Augustus II was thus a period in which, in spite of a superficial revival of economic prosperity after the devastations of three-quarters of a century of war, the fate of Poland was sealed. He was unpopular with the Poles, and, quite powerless, he preferred to abandon his turbulent kingdom and spend most of his time in Saxony. Some Polish nobles already thought that the only solution was to come to terms with the Russian colossus; others were simply in Russian pay. Others looked to France for aid, and French gold produced ephemeral support for Stanislas Leszczynski as the king to succeed Augustus II. This party had the support of the Potockis, the most powerful family in Poland, who had already secured for themselves some of the greatest offices in Church and State, and looked to the time when they might become a real Venetian oligarchy. Opposed to them, and more patriotic, were the Czartoryski family, who looked to a real reform of the State as an escape from Polish weakness. When Augustus II died in 1733 most of the Polish nobility, including the Potockis and Czartoryskis, supported the candidature of Stanislas Leszczynski. The inane foreign policy of Fredrick William I of Prussia made him a negligible factor, and Austria and Russia agreed to support the Saxon candidature: an absurd policy for the Emperor Charles VI to pursue, since the outcome would be primarily to the advantage of Russia. When 30,000 Russians marched into Poland, many Polish nobles changed sides, and Augustus III was proclaimed king. The Emperor Charles VI found himself burdened with a war in the west, while Russia fastened her tentacles more securely around the Polish State. Augustus III disliked Poland, could not speak Polish, and spent most of his time in Saxony hunting and collecting art treasures. In Poland he was powerless, and Polish history became a dreary story of the family quarrels of the Potockis and the Czartoryskis. The former looked to France, the latter looked to Russia to sponsor a programme of internal reform. But neither party would agree to the taxation necessary to raise an army, and out of the fifteen Diets of the reign fourteen were 'exploded' by the use of the *liberum veto*. Prussia or Russia saw to it that every proposal for reform was defeated. During the Seven Years' War Russia used Polish territory as a base for operations against Prussia, and Frederick the Great looted Polish territory and extracted a profit of 20 million thalers from it.

In June 1763 Augustus III died suddenly. The Saxon line had presided over the decline of Poland into the position of a Russian puppet.

There had been an utter failure to carry any constitutional reform, and the Saxon kings had done little more than use Poland to further their own interests. Polish society was corrupted by the bribes which France, Russia and Prussia scattered among the nobility, and by the ever-present menace of Russian troops. It was not that the Poles were indifferent to politics; indeed they talked politics more constantly than any other people in Europe, but Russia and Prussia saw to it that talk of reform came to nothing. With political anarchy there went also economic stagnation. When James Harris entered Poland from Prussia in 1767 his first reaction was:

> I confess that I found the air of a Republic refreshing, after having passed so long a time in a despotic country.

But when he came to take a closer look, he came to a different conclusion:

> bad houses, in ruins, great appearance of poverty, and crowds of Jews and beggars . . . the few towns I passed through on the road are of the most pitiful sort. . . . Villages, such as they are, frequent; but the greatest poverty reigns. No houses, but huts: all the family in one miserable room. . . . I must remark that, in every place worthy to be called a town, there were Russian troops.

A previous British envoy had come to much the same conclusion when George Woodward commented:

> If this is liberty which one seees here, the Lord preserve us from such liberty.

In 1763 Europe was exhausted after the Seven Years' War. England retired into a period of isolation, and was on such bad terms with Prussia that there was no question of renewing the war-time alliance. In France Choiseul was anxious to repair the damage to French prestige by a war of revenge against Britain, and also by diplomatic success in Poland. After 1763 Maria Theresa became the most pacific of monarchs, and hoped only for the maintenance of the *status quo* everywhere in Europe. Prussia was utterly exhausted by war, and it followed that the maintenance of peace became a major object of policy. After 1763 Frederick the Great no longer feared a Habsburg attack; the nightmare now was the rising power of Russia under Catherine II. The problem was therefore how to remain on good terms with Russia and yet prevent a Russian domination in eastern Europe. The two possible directions of Russian advance were into Poland and into the Ottoman Empire. The chief European function of the Polish State had been to hold back the Muscovite advance, and its eastern provinces were Russian in population. It was inevitable therefore that once the tide turned, once Russia had a strong government, it would seek to regain those provinces. In 1763 it appeared only too likely that Russia would absorb the entire Polish State. It was imperative to Frederick to prevent this, and also to secure for Prussia the area of Poland known as West Prussia, together with the port of Danzig, and thus link up East Prussia with Brandenburg.

This was the situation when Augustus III died in 1763. Catherine at once determined to make her own candidate king of Poland. This was Count Stanislas-Augustus Poniatowski, one of the most elegant and cultured men in Poland, and a son on his mother's side of the Czartoryskis. He had travelled widely in the West, had been received at Versailles and visited England, and in 1755 had been introduced by the British ambassador to the young Catherine, who was fascinated by his grace and culture, and took him as a lover. They had had a daughter in 1757, but then political circumstances had intervened and Stanislas-Augustus was sent back to Poland. He was still devoted to Catherine, and on the other hand had much to commend him to the Poles, for he was the son of a famous soldier, had a fine presence, was a remarkable speaker, was deeply imbued with the enlightened ideas of the time and devoted to the arts and letters, and moreover was a patriot who might seek to reform the State. His peaceful election, however, must depend upon the support of Prussia, and Frederick was ready to agree only at the price of a Russo-Prussian alliance which would relieve him of all fears of further Russian aggression. In April 1764 this alliance was signed, and on August 28th Stanislas-Augustus was elected king.

Henceforth Catherine was the real ruler of Poland. The task of Stanislas-Augustus was an impossible one. He wished to restore vigour to his kingdom, and yet remain loyal to Russia, but every act of independence was frowned upon by Catherine, and every act of subservience was condemned by the Poles. Behind Stanislas-Augustus there was always the Russian ambassador. Catherine indeed wished only for peace in Poland, but there were two sources of conflict. The first was the growing Polish resentment at Russian domination, and the formation in 1764 of a Confederation for constitutional reform, in spite of a Russo-Prussian warning that there must be no tampering with the *liberum veto*. In 1767, when the Bishop of Cracow openly attacked Russian influence in the Diet, he was seized and transported to Russia. The second cause of conflict was the continued persecution of the religious minorities ('the Dissidents') which provided continual opportunities for foreign intervention. This was particularly in the interests of Prussia, who had no desire to witness a peaceful Russian absorption of Poland, and preferred to keep the pot of discontent boiling. In 1768 Russia and Prussia forced the Polish Diet to concede freedom of worship. In reply the exasperated opposition formed the Confederation of Bar to resist further Russian encroachments. It amounted to a nationalist revolt; France sent money and arms, and the Turks demanded that the Russians should evacuate Poland, and on their refusal declared war (1768). If Russia had been defeated in the Turkish war, the Polish revolt might have succeeded.

The Turkish war brought Catherine great difficulties. Russian troops occupied Moldavia (1769) and their fleet was victorious at Tchesmé (1771), but Russian victories were slow and Austria was restive at the Russian advance. In these circumstances it was imperative to seek peace in Poland and to retain Prussian goodwill, if only as a precaution against an Austrian attack. In 1771 Frederick proposed the partition of Poland. From his point of view this would have the advantage of gaining western Prussia from Poland, deflecting Russian interest from the Turks, renewing the Russo-Prussian alliance, and preventing an Austro-Russian war. Austria was faced with the alternative of resisting the partition single-handed, or participating in the scramble for a share. Joseph II and Kaunitz prevailed over Maria Theresa, and the Habsburgs joined in the conspiracy. Catherine seized the offer as the easiest way out of her difficulties, and in 1772 an astounded Europe was informed of the peaceful partition of Poland. Russia took provinces up to the Dvina and Dnieper; the Habsburgs took Galicia, with its rich salt mines, and Prussia took West Prussia (though not Danzig) and thus united East Prussia with Brandenburg. Austria's share was the richest, Russia's the most easily assimilated, and Prussia's the most valuable.

Stanislas-Augustus still hoped to rebuild an independent Poland,

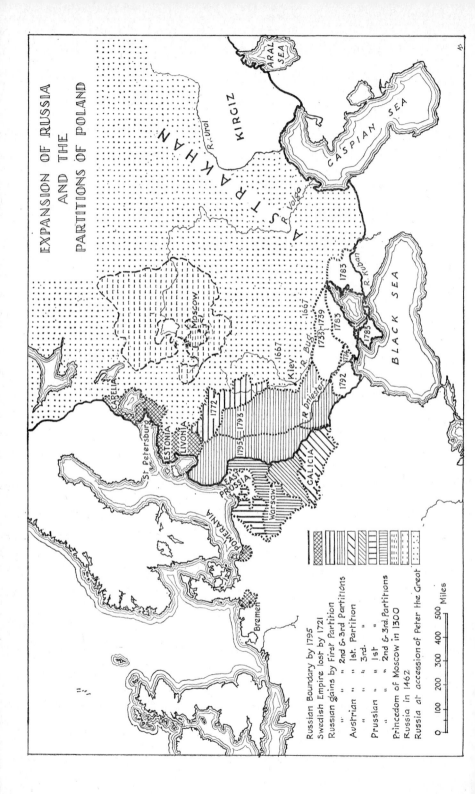

EXPANSION OF RUSSIA
AND THE
PARTITIONS OF POLAND

Russian Boundary by 1795
Swedish Empire lost by 1721
Russian gains by First Partition
Austrian   "   "   1st. Partition
    "   "   "   3rd.
Prussian   "   "   1st   "
    "   "   "   2nd & 3rd. Partitions
Princedom of Moscow in 1300
Russia in 1462
Russia at accession of Peter the Great

0   100   200   300   400   500   Miles

for he still had 150,000 square miles and 7 million people, and his subjects had had a salutary shock which would pre-dispose them to reform. The period 1773–92 was indeed a period of national awakening. The King was the chief patron of Polish literature; French influence was strong, and Enlightenment and Romanticism vied with each other in a cultural outburst. It was the period of the poet Krasicki, and the great national historian Naruszewic, author of a six-volumed *History of the Polish Nation*, and of the political philosophy of Staszic. But always there remained the Russian ambassador and the threat of further intervention. The national movement culminated in a plan for constitutional reform presented to the Diet in May 1791, by which the Monarchy would become hereditary, the *liberum veto* be abolished, and Ministers be responsible to the Diet. The best hope for the Poles had been that Russia and Prussia would disagree, and this had appeared likely when in 1788 Russia, again at war with the Turks, had withdrawn troops from Poland. But in 1792 Catherine made peace with the Turks and turned on Poland. The feeble Prussian government which succeeded that of Frederick the Great had contemplated a Polish alliance against Russia, but now preferred to join in the prospect of further partition. Thus in 1793 Catherine dictated the terms of a Second Partition. Austria was deeply engaged in the French war and could safely be omitted. Russia took the large area sometimes known as Black Russia, and Prussia took the area to the south of West Prussia. In 1794 the exasperated Poles of the truncated State which remained broke into a heroic but hopeless revolt under the patriot Kosciuszco. His first battle was a surprise victory over the Russians near Cracow, and the revolt spread throughout the land. But in June he was heavily defeated, and in October he was wounded and captured, and the revolt was crushed. Austria, Russia and Prussia then agreed to a final Partition, and Poland disappeared from the map.

Eighteenth-century Poland has always remained the classic instance of a State which disappeared from the map because it mistook anarchy for liberty, and thereby deprived itself of the means of defending itself against its neighbours. The Partitions of Poland have always seemed the outcome of the most cynical Power politics, but it is also possible to argue that no State can afford to be so weak that it is a standing temptation to its neighbours. In a wider historical perspective it appears that the great Polish-Lithuanian State, without

L

geographical or racial unity, must needs fall once the Russian State had risen to strength. More debatable is the question whether the Partitions were in Russian interests. In the first and even the second Partitions Russia could claim that it was annexing essentially Russian provinces, but the complete elimination of the Polish State brought Russia up to the boundaries of Austria and a greatly strengthened Prussia, and this had incalculable consequences for Europe during the next 110 years. Some Russian historians, for instance Kliuchevsky, have therefore severely criticised Catherine for being the dupe of Frederick the Great in 1772. They argue that the whole of Poland was already a Russian puppet, and that Russia gained less by partition than by continuing the life of the puppet régime. But against this there is the consideration that the situation in 1772 was extremely restive, and Catherine had good reason to seek a more permanent solution to her difficulties there. The question has recurred for Russia in the twentieth century.

13: The Decline of the Ottoman Turkish Empire

By the eighteenth century the Ottoman Sultanate had lasted some 400 years. It derived from the great leader Othman (d. 1326), the founder of a political power which conquered Bithynia at the beginning of the fourteenth century. In 1356 Ottoman power first crossed into Europe, and by 1389 it had conquered much of the Balkans, from which it extorted plunder and slaves. The Turks were essentially a nomadic and military people. They owed their success partly to military organisation, partly to religious fervour, partly to a succession of great leaders, and partly to the chronic disunity of Europe. It was usually true that when Europe threw up a great leader and there emerged some sort of European alliance, the Turkish advance could be held. Turkish power tended in any case to surge forward in waves, which were, however, followed by periods of regression, and Europe rarely took advantage of those periods of regression to push back the Turkish power before the eighteenth century. In the fifteenth century the Hungarians were the heroic defenders of Europe, and John Hunyadi (d. 1444) and Matthias Corvinus (1459–90) inflicted great defeats on the Turks. But Constantinople fell in 1453, and when Mohammed the Conqueror died in 1481, Ottoman power ran from the Danube and Albania to the Euphrates. His grandson Selim I conquered Syria, Egypt and Palestine, and moreover brought to an end the Caliphate of Bagdad, so that in future there was a single leader of the Islamic world, and he was the Sultan.

The great period of conquest comprised the first ten Sultanates, and ended with Suleiman the Magnificent (d. 1566). His greatest achievements were the capture of Belgrade and the great battle of Mohacs (1526), leading to the collapse of Hungary. Henceforth the Habsburgs were the great defenders of Europe. For another two centuries the Turks could from time to time threaten Europe, but in fact internal decay had set in, and decline had begun.

One cause of this was the constant struggle of sons and brothers of the Sultan to gain the throne. Hence the decree of Mohammed the

Conqueror enjoining his descendants to mark their accession by putting to death all their brothers. The Sultans were autocrats, limited in theory only by the Sacred Law of the Prophet. Many, however, were merely ciphers. In the 150 years following the death of Suleiman the Magnificent six Sultans were deposed, and two of them were murdered. Often they were merely the scapegoats for others' failures.

The Ottoman Turks showed little talent for political organisation; they were primarily nomads and warriors. What they had learnt of political organisation was derived from the Byzantine Empire; they borrowed little or nothing from the West before the eighteenth century. The original Turkish army was largely cavalry, the *Spahis* who received land in return for military service, and lived off plunder and the dues of their peasants. But this did not produce a large enough army, and the practice had early grown up of taking male children of their Christian subjects as tribute, reducing them to slaves and training them for service to the State. Entirely divorced from their homes and background, they grew up entirely dependent upon the Sultan. 'Slave' is in fact an unfortunate word, for it carried with it no social stigma, and half the highest offices of State were held by slaves. The Sultan was often the son of a slave woman, and he often preferred to rely upon a faithful non-Moslem slave than upon the doubtful loyalty of the Moslems. Many of the Christian boys received a rigorous military training and then went to make up the famous *Janissaries*. Others became officials in the Sultan's Household.

Before the nineteenth century the Ottoman Turks had singularly little difficulty in ruling their Christian subjects. Conquered territories fell into one of two categories, those directly controlled by the central administration, and those which merely paid tribute. Thus in Europe Dubrovnik (Ragusa), Moldavia and Wallachia were tribute-paying; the rest of the Balkans was of the first category. Moldavia and Wallachia were governed by *Voievodas* (or *Hospodars*) chosen by the Sultan, but most of its officials were non-Moslems. It is quite wrong to suppose that Turkish rule was some hideous tyranny; in fact it was tolerant, interfering little with the life of the Christian peasantry, so long as tribute was paid, and often was less irksome than the rule of their former masters. There was a good deal of provincial autonomy, and the tribesmen of Albania and Montenegro, for example, were virtually independent. By the eighteenth century, however, administrative standards had seriously declined, and there was widespread corruption among the ruling class, which went far to destroy the prosperity of some of the provinces.

Signs of the coming Turkish decline were present as early as the sixteenth century. The early Sultans were half-warrior, half-religious leader, but the startling success of their conquests was often measured in booty, and with this the Sultans surrounded themselves with luxury and pomp. It was an Empire which rolled forward under its own momentum so long as opposition was weak, but once the conquests ceased, plunder ceased also, and by that time the Sultans and their Vezirs were accustomed to a luxury they could no longer afford. They were, moreover, conquerors, not statesmen. Their Empire was over-large and unwieldy; its very extent and shape made a defensive policy difficult, if not impossible. The power of the Sultan, in theory absolute, in fact was often usurped by his Grand Vezirs, and government too often became a matter of intrigue. In the seventeenth and eighteenth centuries, when conquests ceased, and with them the flow of booty, the Sultan's government found it impossible to maintain both luxury and an efficient army. To raise money every office was bought and sold. By the seventeenth century the Janissaries had become too numerous, ill-trained, often unpaid and therefore rebellious. They were now allowed to marry, live out of barracks and engage in private trade. By the eighteenth century the Janissaries were in complete disorganisation, and it is surprising that the Turkish power did not suffer worse than it did.

This was partly because the Turkish power could still throw up some remarkable leaders. It had always been the case that when the Turks were led by a great leader, they made remarkable achievements, and this was so with the Koprili Vezirs. Mohammed Koprili, the first of the line, was of Albanian descent, started life as a kitchen-boy in the palace of the Sultan, and at the age of seventy had worked his way up to the office of Grand Vezir. His chief work was to check corruption in the administration, and it was said that in five years (1656–61) he had no less than 35,000 people executed. At the time of his death in 1661 he was vigorously pressing the war against Venice and the siege of Candia. He was succeeded by his son Akmed Koprili, the most eminent of the line. He was a great administrator and a tolerant man. Most of his period of office (1661–76) was spent at war. In 1664

L2

he suffered the great defeat of St. Gotthard at the hands of the Austrians under Montecuculi, which shattered the Turkish legend for invincibility which had been established by the battle of Mohacs in 1526. The Habsburgs might well have turned their victory to good account, but instead they preferred to make peace at Vascar leaving Akmed in possession of his conquests, including Neuhäusel, and he was able to turn aside to complete the conquest of Crete. In 1672 he overran the Polish province of Podolia, and defended it against repeated Polish attacks, and in 1676 the Poles made peace leaving Podolia in Turkish hands. Akmed died a few days later. He had apparently halted Turkish decline, and had once again set in motion a Turkish advance into Europe.

How much depended upon personality was shown in 1683, when the Turks under the new Grand Vezir, Kara Mustafa, were before the very gates of Vienna, with a huge army which may have been 200,000 strong. The Turks were in the very act of battering down the walls of the city when news arrived of the advance of John Sobieski and 50,000 Poles to the relief of the city. Kara Mustafa was a luxurious decadent who carried with him a great treasure and 1,500 concubines; at the approach of the Poles he massacred 30,000 Christian prisoners, mainly women and children, but he delayed the final assault on the city. At Sobieski's attack the Turks broke, and a terrible slaughter followed. The Austrians went on to capture Neuhäusel (1685), Buda (1687) and Belgrade (1688). The Turkish army was seething with mutiny, and the Janissaries were rioting in the streets of Constantinople. At this point Zadé Koprili, brother of Akmed who had died thirteen years before, became Grand Vezir. He at once took strong measures to restore discipline in the army, and in 1690 recaptured Belgrade. But in 1691 he was killed in battle, and thereafter Turkish resistance collapsed. Prince Eugène of Savoy crushed a Turkish army at Zeuta on the Danube (1697), at which 26,000 Turks were slain and another 10,000 drowned, and he went on to overrun Bosnia. The British ambassador, Lord Paget, then negotiated the general Peace of Carlowitz (1699), by which Austria retained conquests in Hungary and Transylvania, Venice kept the Morea and Albania, Poland regained Podolia, and the Russians took Azov. The Peace of Carlowitz is the treaty from which the 'Eastern Question' may be said to have begun, for the Ottoman Empire never recovered from its internal weaknesses, and henceforth was the concern of the East European Powers, no longer on account of its aggression, but because of its weakness. The fourth and last of the Koprili, Hussein Koprili, a cousin of Akmed, was Grand Vezir 1699–1702, and he attempted to reform the administration, but he died before achieving much.

In 1711 the Turks attacked the Russians, caught Peter the Great unprepared, surrounded the Tsar and his army, and forced it to capitulate. The Turks might have annihilated the Russians, but preferred to give them terms, by which they recovered the port of Azov. In 1715 they were at war with Venice for the recovery of the Morea, and there took place the siege of Corinth, the subject of Byron's poem. The Morea was taken, but in 1716 Austria declared war. Prince Eugène was at the height of his powers; he inflicted a loss of 20,000 men on the Turks before Belgrade, captured the city and overran Serbia. George I of England and Hanover then negotiated the Treaty of Passarowitz (1718), at which the remainder of Hungary, and part of Serbia and Wallachia and the great fortress of Belgrade, were ceded to the Habsburgs. The Treaty was the high-water mark of Habsburg power in the Balkans in the eighteenth century, and the situation was never so favourable again.

In 1730 a mutiny of the Janissaries forced the Sultan Akmed to abdicate. The new Sultan Mahmoud was quite unfit to rule, and for the twenty-four years of his reign all power was wielded by his chief eunuch, Bashir, an Abyssinian slave who made and unmade sixteen Grand Vezirs in twenty-four years. In 1735 the Russians attacked the frontier posts near Azov, and goaded the Turks into war. This was part of the Austro-Russian plan to dismember the Turkish Empire, to which Charles VI so readily agreed. The Russians captured Azov and Ochakov (1737), but the Austrians were routed and Belgrade besieged (1739). The Emperor was glad to take advantage of the mediation of Villeneuve, French ambassador to Constantinople, and to make peace, without reference to the Russians. The Russians, who had run into military difficulties, could only follow suit, and by the Treaty of Belgrade (1739) Austria gave up Belgrade, and the areas of Serbia and Wallachia that had been acquired in 1718. Russia kept Azov, but without the power to fortify it. The main reason for the Austrian failure was their own inefficiency, but the Turks had been skilful in concentrating their attacks upon them. There opened in

1739 a long period of peace for the Turks, but one in which the disintegration of their Empire went on apace.

In the period of almost continuous war from 1656 to 1739 an active military tradition had been kept alive, but it died in the succeeding thirty years of peace. The Habsburgs indeed were fortunate that no Koprili governed in Constantinople in 1740–41 to take advantage of Maria Theresa's difficulties; if there had been, she might have found them overwhelming. In fact, however, the period saw the complete disintegration of the military system of the Janissaries. The final straw came with the practice of selling the rank of Janissary to anyone who would pay for it, without any form of training. They became therefore an expensive and turbulent corps, utterly useless in war. The Turkish artillery had often in history been superior to that of their European enemies, and in the years before 1735 it was well organised and trained by the Frenchman the Comte de Bonneval, who became a Moslem with the name of Akmed Pasha. But after his death in 1735 it fell into decay. Also the military fiefs of the Spahis became private estates without military obligation, and the famous Turkish cavalry seriously declined in numbers. In the time of Suleiman the Magnificent they had numbered 200,000; by the eighteenth century they were not more than 25,000. The Sultans in war had to rely largely upon what troops the provincial governors chose to lend him, and these governors often set up as semi-independent princes.

With the accession of Catherine the Great in Russia, the Turks watched with apprehension the growth of Russian power in Poland, for they knew that their turn would come next. In 1768, when the Poles appeared to be on the verge of revolt, and the Confederation of Bar had been formed, the Turks demanded the Russian evacuation of Poland and declared war. Catherine had been caught unprepared, but Turkish military weakness was now revealed. The Russians overran Moldavia and Wallachia, and the Russian Baltic fleet, sent into the Mediterranean under the command of Admiral Elphinstone, defeated the Turkish fleet of Tchesmé. In the Caucasus the Turks were driven from Georgia. Prussia's proposals for the Partition of Poland had as one of their objects to relieve the pressure on the Turks, and this object was achieved, for Catherine offered the Turks very moderate terms at the Treaty of Kutchuk-Kainardji (1774). Russia annexed Cherson, Azov and the land to the south of Azov, but gave up Moldavia and Wallachia. The Sultan had to surrender suzerainty over the Crimea and to recognise Russia's right to protect the Christians of the Balkans. The Treaty thus marks the beginning of the dismemberment of the Turkish Empire. Russia proceeded to annex the Crimea in 1784, and the Turks knew that this was a preliminary to Catherine's 'Greek Project'. Russia and Austria declared war in 1788, and although Joseph II ran into serious difficulties, Austria captured Belgrade in 1789. The death of Joseph in 1790 disrupted the alliance for aggression, and his successor made peace with only a slight adjustment of frontiers. The Russians had again occupied Moldavia, Wallachia and the Kuban, but by the Treaty of Jassy (1792) Catherine annexed only Ochakov and the territory between the Dniester and Bug rivers. By this time all Europe was aware of the significance of the Eastern Question, and of the Russian threat to Constantinople. The Turkish Empire showed itself incapable of internal reform or regeneration, and the rising forces of nineteenth-century nationalism completed the disruption which administrative and military weakness had for so long foreshadowed.

14: The Monarchy of Louis XV

The Regency

In 1715 Louis XV was a child of five; there was therefore a Regent who by custom was the next in succession to the throne, excluding Philip V of Spain. This was the Duke of Orleans, nephew of Louis XIV, a genial and accomplished man, a good soldier, but notorious for his evil living, a sceptic in religion and a dabbler in the new science and philosophy. Louis XIV's Will sought to reduce his power to a shadow by making him dependent for all political decisions upon a Council of Regency consisting of the royal bastards, headed by the Duke of Maine. But Louis' Will was an abnegation of his own principle of Divine Right Monarchy, for once a king was dead his successor was absolute. The first act of the regency was to set aside the Will. In this he had the support of all the nobility, who were restive at the continued absolutism of the old king, and also of the *Parlement*, proud at being the repository of the Will, and anxious to show that they were still the guardians of the French constitution. Saint Simon has described the solemn ceremony at which the Will was set aside, and the Regent assumed the powers of absolutism.

The atmosphere of the Regency was one of renewed gaiety. In the language of Chapter 3 we may say that it was the period in which the grandeur of Baroque finally gave place to the delicate *insouciance* of Rococo. Of course it would be wrong to draw too sharp a line across history in 1715, but it is true that the atmosphere of the Regency was relaxed and pleasure-loving. Politically it marks the beginning of the Aristocratic Reaction which historians have come to see as a general characteristic of eighteenth-century France. For the *noblesse d'épée* were never reconciled to their loss of political power under Louis XIV. They yearned for a return to the days when they were the real rulers of France. The eighteenth century showed a new interest in the reading of history, and one reason for this was undoubtedly the nostalgia for those past days of power. This explains also the continuing prestige of the *parlements* as the last guardians of the mediaeval French constitution.

The change was symbolised by the flight from Versailles. For years an increasing number of the nobility had preferred their comfortable *hôtels* in Paris to the discomforts of Versailles, and there they had held their salons, of which we have spoken already, signs of a vigorous intellectual life quite independent of the Monarchy. The Regent always hated Versailles, and took up residence in the Palais Royal, while the young Louis XV occupied the Tuileries. Here the Regent attempted a new system of government. Instead of continuing Louis XIV's system whereby all government was conducted by the King through his Controller-General or his Secretaries of State, he set up a *Polysynodie*, composed of six councils, each of ten members, half of whom were nobles. Whether he intended really to rule through these councils, or merely to win the approval of the nobility, is uncertain, but in either case the experiment, serious or not, failed completely, and was abolished in 1718. The reason was that the nobility were quite inexperienced in government, and business virtually came to a standstill. Louis XIV's absolutism could not be ended so easily.

Saint-Simon has left a vivid picture of the idleness and debauchery of the Regent, and of his suppers where he entertained those he called his *roués* (i.e. deserving to be broken on the wheel), where the conversation was licentious and the drinking gargantuan. He preferred Paris to all places, because its theatres and its underworld gave him full scope for his pleasures. At Mass he would relieve the tedium by reading Rabelais. On his evening exploits he met all kinds of people. One of them was a clever young Scotsman named John Law, who had had to flee from his homeland because he had killed a man in a duel. He was a financial genius who had a clearer idea than most people of his day of the true nature of the commercial revolution which was taking place in western Europe. He understood that wealth was not the same thing as money, that the prosperity of the Dutch and the English depended upon the development of credit. He saw the commercial system of France hampered by lack of credit and currency. He believed that paper money would enormously increase circulation. He found in the Regent a ready listener, for Orleans was susceptible to new ideas.

Moreover, the financial state of France appeared desperate. The financial system had been one of the greatest weaknesses of Louis XIV's government, and the Regent found almost the entire revenue anticipated for the coming year. A Chamber of Justice had been set up to punish financial irregularities, but this did nothing to repair the rotten system. In 1716 Law was permitted to found a bank and issue notes. In view of the debased coinage of the time the bank's notes soon stood at a premium, and there was a welcome stimulus to trade. In 1717 Law obtained a controlling interest in the Mississippi Company, a derelict company founded in 1712, and renamed it the Company of the West, with an authorised capital of a hundred million livres, three-quarters of which was to be in State bonds. In 1718 by decree Law's Bank was transformed into the national bank (*Banque Royale*) with an authorised issue of 110 million livres of notes. In 1719 the Company of the West took over the monopoly of the tobacco trade, and indeed the entire trading monopoly of the East India Company together with the trade with Senegal. He also took over the coinage of money and the farm of the revenues. Finally he took over the National Debt of 1,500 million livres, for which he asked only 3 per cent. The shares in his Company rocketed during 1719–20 to ten times their value, and his bank proceeded to issue 800 million livres in notes in return for coin. As the notes were at par value and the coins were debased, this was a popular move. In 1720 Law was appointed Controller-General of Finances, and he was soon busy planning a number of reforms which would have been of great value to France, such as a reform of tax-collection, and the imposition of a direct tax from which there would be no exemptions. But he had made many powerful enemies among the tax-farmers and other financiers. His propaganda machine had grossly exaggerated the profits to be expected from Mississippi trade, and by 1720 France was in the grip of a whirlwind of inflation and over-speculation. Some of the greatest ladies in the land consented to faint on Law's doorstep in order to gain admittance to the great man in the hope of purchasing shares. But in May 1720 he had to cut the value of all notes in circulation by one-quarter. A panic ensued; the *Parlement* refused to register the decree, and it had to be withdrawn. But confidence was shattered; the bubble had burst. Law's paper money collapsed, and in December Law fled to London. Some had made fortunes from the speculation, others were ruined. As with the South Sea Bubble in England, the ruin of Law's scheme did something to impede the development of investment and commercial expansion in France, and meanwhile the financial problems of the Government remained unsolved.

In only one aspect of government did the Regency achieve a positive success, namely in foreign policy. In foreign affairs the Regent relied for guidance on his old tutor, the Abbé Dubois, a man of low birth and habits, but a most skilful diplomat. Faced with the hostility of Philip V of Spain (who regretted his exclusion from the succession now that the survival of Louis XV seemed so doubtful a matter) the Regent in 1716 sent Dubois in disguise to the Hague to meet Earl Stanhope, the English Secretary of State, and later the conversations were continued in Hanover. The result was an Anglo-French treaty, which with the adherence of the Dutch in 1717 became the Triple Alliance. Guaranteeing the Utrecht Settlement, it secured the Regent against the machinations of Philip V, such as the plots of the Spanish ambassador Cellamare in 1718, and it led to the defeat of Alberoni and Elizabeth Farnese in the following years. In 1721 Philip V recognised Orleans's right of succession in France, and a new era of good relations was inaugurated by the betrothal of an infant Spanish *Infanta* to Louis XV. For his services to peace Dubois received a cardinal's hat. While the Triple Alliance lasted it was a powerful instrument of diplomacy. Both Dubois and the Regent died in 1723.

The Period of Cardinal Fleury

As the next in line among the Princes of the Blood, the Duke of Bourbon succeeded the Regent Orleans. He was a singularly stupid man, largely under the influence of his mistress, Mme. de Prie, and his short period of office is memorable for one thing only. Louis XV was now aged fifteen, and if he married the Spanish princess, who was a child, France must wait some years before there could be an heir to the throne. Bourbon therefore bundled the *Infanta* back to Spain and married Louis to Marie Leszczynska, daughter of the ex-king of Poland. As she was aged twenty, and her father was a mere pensionary of France, it seemed to Bourbon that she would make a suitable Queen, satisfactorily grateful to Bourbon and Mme. de Prie for their favour. The marriage took place in 1725. Elizabeth Farnese bitterly resented the insult to Spain, and the *entente* which Dubois had so carefully constructed was broken.

Bourbon soon over-reached himself in another direction. Louis XV was extremely attached to his old tutor André-Hercule Fleury, Bishop of Fréjus. Bourbon tried to remove Fleury as a dangerous rival, but he underestimated Fleury's skill. In 1726 Louis XV dismissed Bourbon, and Fleury succeeded to his place. Cardinal Fleury (as he was later to be) was indeed a remarkable man. Quiet, modest, affable, he was now aged seventy-three, and had never played any notable part in politics. He now revealed qualities hitherto unsuspected. Under his reserved and cautious exterior there was an iron will, and a clear grasp of the nature of power. He was devoted to the service of his master and to the maintenance of the power of France, and for the next seventeen years he gave France the best government she was to experience during the reign of Louis XV. To understand this it is necessary to recall the nature of the French system of government. As established by Louis XIV, the French system was a despotism in which all political power rested with the King himself. As we have seen, Louis XIV never appointed a Prime Minister, and himself took all the important political decisions. His system of councils exercised just as much, or as little, authority as the King chose to give it at any one time. His Secretaries of State and his Controller-General carried on the business of government, but merely in the capacity of chief executives, carrying out the will of the King. Everything depended in the last resort on the remarkable qualities of the King himself. But between 1715 and 1789 France never again had a King capable of continuing the system of Louis XIV. Louis XV had some of the external attributes of monarchy; he was handsome, regal in appearance, and with a great sense of kingly dignity. But he was quite incapable of the sustained application, the hours of daily grind, which Louis XIV had had to devote to the business of government. Moreover, in 1726, he was aged only sixteen. So long as he lived, Fleury exercised the powers of monarchy, and gave government its unity and sense of direction. The title of *premier ministre* had been revived successively for Dubois, Orleans and Bourbon between 1722 and 1726; Fleury never actually used the title, but that was his true function. After Fleury's death Louis XV attempted to take over the direction of government himself, there was no further *premier ministre*, and French government lost its sense of direction at a crucial time in its history.

Fleury is often compared with Sir Robert Walpole in England. He was no innovator or reformer; by nature he was a conservative and a man of peace. He was convinced that after the constant wars of the previous half-century France needed peace, in which trade and industry could recover, and an attempt could be made to repair French finances. In Europe, French interests required the maintenance of peaceful relations with England, in order to restrain the ambitions of Elizabeth Farnese of Spain, but at the same time the cultivation of peaceful relations with Spain in order to satisfy the pro-Spanish party at Court. His handling of the War of the Polish Succession was characteristic of his equivocal approach to foreign affairs. When the Emperor Charles VI blazoned forth the Austro-Russian support for Augustus III of Saxony, the war party in France, headed by Chauvelin, the Keeper of the Seals, were hot for the support for Stanislas, father-in-law of Louis XV. Fleury allowed the war to ensue, and saw to it that France ultimately gained Lorraine as a price for her intervention, yet he strove to keep the war within limits, and opened negotiations for peace at the earliest possible moment.[1] Chauvelin had been allowed to make the war; by 1737 he had outlived his usefulness. Fleury knew all about his intrigues against him, and he was dismissed. Fleury could claim that the war increased French prestige, and brought a solid gain in the shape of the reversion of Lorraine. Moreover, in 1739, French diplomacy was brilliantly successful in negotiating a Peace between the Emperor and the Turks. Fleury could also congratulate himself upon his success in keeping good relations with Walpole during the war.

At home there were no spectacular reforms, but France was well governed. D'Aguesseau, the Chancellor, continued the legal reforms begun by Colbert. D'Angervilliers, Secretary of State for War, maintained an efficient army, and Maurepas increased the strength of the navy. Orry, the Controller-General, by careful administration, concealed the defects of the financial system until war put too great a strain upon it. For France these were years of growing prosperity. Business-men and financiers grew increasingly wealthy and powerful. When Fleury wanted advice upon the issues of peace and war, he called in Pâris-Duverney, the most powerful financier in France, to advise him. The Controller-General of France was too dependent upon the goodwill of such men to treat them other than with respect, and the financiers for their part found it more profitable to lend money to the Government than to invest it elsewhere. The forty

[1] See p. 284.

Farmers-General, who every six years made a new contract with the Government, were powers in the land. They were often of humble birth, but they lived in fine houses and moved freely in aristocratic society. Trade rapidly recovered in the new stability Fleury established, particularly with the colonies, the West Indies, Canada, the Mississippi, Senegal and India. In this period in fact there was a flowering of the seeds which Colbert had planted. Cities like Bordeaux, Nantes, Le Havre and Marseilles grew rich on the trade in fish, sugar, slaves, and on the export of wines and luxuries. All over France there was growing evidence of the spread of wealth and gracious living, the building of fine town houses, the laying out of new streets and squares, the growing demand for pictures, fine furniture, tableware, and serious books in their magnificent eighteenth-century bindings. Industry expanded more slowly than trade, because all the old restrictions continued, though there was a gradual movement to greater freedom of trade. Even as late as 1789 there were still sixteen hundred customs barriers on the rivers of France, but the restrictive practices of gilds were slightly mitigated. In 1754 the hosiery industry, which previously was limited to seventeen towns, could be carried on anywhere. An ordinance of 1755 threw open all towns, except Paris, Lyon, Rouen and Lille, to any craftsman who had completed his apprenticeship. But there was no relaxation of government controls; Colbert's system continued, and between 1715 and 1789 there were well over 300 *règlements* controlling industry. French industry always suffered from a shortage of capital, for men preferred to invest in government stock, or use their capital to buy expensive offices, rather than invest in industry. To some extent in this respect France still felt the cold hand of Colbert, for he had fostered the great tradition of State enterprise, such as at the Gobelin works, rather than that of private enterprise. Industry was still in any case largely organised on a small-scale domestic basis, with workshops consisting of a master and two or three apprentices and journeymen, though there were some large-scale capitalist works, especially in the iron industry.

The historian, when he is studying the eighteenth-century French Monarchy, may well feel that he is observing the slow running-down of a complicated political mechanism. The central authority was declining in effectiveness and sense of direction, but certain parts of the governmental machine retained their efficiency. This was particularly true of the Intendants. It may well be true that they were the greatest administrative achievement of the French Monarchy; they were certainly the part of the French administration which most clearly fulfilled their purpose. The offices were never sold; the Intendants were simply efficient servants of the Controller-General, masters of their administrative areas, responsible for everything, the organisation of industry, famine relief, public health, recruitment, road-building. The latter was in fact one of their most distinctive achievements. During the eighteenth century France received the finest network of highways in Europe, built by trained engineers under the direction of the Intendants, with the use of *corvée*, or forced labour from the local inhabitants, financed by the Controller-General, who recouped himself by increased road charges. Arthur Young, later, in his travels in France, was amazed at the high quality of the French highways. The *corvée*, however, pressed heavily upon the already overtried peasants, some of whom were prosperous enough, but many of whom practised primitive agriculture in conditions of great poverty. To this subject we shall return later.

So long as Fleury lived there was strength and direction in the French Government. But his last years were darkened by intrigues of those who hoped to succeed the aged Minister. There was, moreover, a conflict over the direction of French foreign policy. Chauvelin, who had been dismissed in 1737, not only hoped to succeed Fleury, but stood for a vigorous anti-Habsburg foreign policy in close alliance with Spain. When in 1740 Maria Theresa was attacked by Prussia, Fleury could no longer restrain the popular demand among the young nobles at Court headed by the Comte de Bellisle, for a vigorous war. In 1743 Fleury died at the age of ninety and with him French foreign policy lost its sense of direction.

The Age of Mme. de Pompadour:
Jansenists, the *Parlements* and the Suppression of the Jesuits

Louis XV disappointed those who had hoped to succeed Fleury, and decided to act upon the injunction of Louis XIV that he should be his own Minister. But Louis XV had not the makings of a great, or even of an effective king. With all his kingly presence and his early popularity (he was styled *le bien-aimé*)[1] he was a weak man. Government bored him, the Court bored him, sustained effort was wearisome to him, and he was constitutionally incapable of taking political decisions. He sought refuge from his boredom either in hunting or in a long succession of mistresses, most of whom wearied him after a few weeks, and of whom only Mme. de Pompadour and Mme. du Barry deserve to be remembered. Yet with all his boredom, he could not forget that he was king; his conscience frequently bothered him, though never for long. After Fleury he trusted no one; he kept the prerogative of monarchy strictly in his own hands, but as he had no policy to pursue, the result was stagnation. The Marquis d'Argenson, one of the ablest Ministers of the time, describes the exasperation of sitting in Council when nothing was properly discussed, and with a king quite incapable of ever taking a clear decision. His only real political interest was in foreign affairs, and with this he was able to combine a fondness for intrigue to produce the famous *secret du roi*.

This was the result of conflicting ideas in French foreign policy after 1748. The close alliance between Austria and Russia made it difficult for France to continue to exercise much influence in eastern Europe, especially in Poland. When, in 1756, France entered into alliance with the Habsburgs, Louis' Ministers concluded that they should abandon the tradition of a Polish alliance. Louis XV, however, preferred to attempt to keep it alive, and thus there was the ridiculous situation in which French envoys to Poland received virtually two contradictory sets of instructions, one from the Foreign Minister, and the other from the King's Cabinet. In all this the Prince de Conti was a willing ally of the King, in the hope that he might be the French candidate for the Polish throne, but the only result for France was increased confusion and ineffectualness in foreign relations.

In 1745 a new interest relieved the tedium of Louis XV's existence; he gained a new mistress and created her the Marquise de Pompadour. She was the daughter of a servant in the great banking-house of the Pâris brothers, and was married to the nephew of one of the Farmers-

---

[1] The name given to him in 1744, when he fell very ill and was expected to die. Public opinion was roused at the fears of political confusion which would follow the King's death at such a time. Louis underwent a moral reformation which lasted only as long as the fear of an early death.

General. We have already seen that the financ ers were not on y men of wealth, but were already a power in the land. They were, moreover, men of culture and refinement, patrons of the Enlightenment, in whose houses the polite world of literature and philosophy were accustomed to gather. Mme. de Pompadour was a great beauty, as the exquisite portraits of Boucher show, but also a woman of wit, culture and good taste. She surrounded herself with the finest artistic products of the age, books, jewellery, porcelain, china and tapestries. She loved the music of Rameau and Couperin. She imposed her exquisite taste upon the Court, redecorating and refurnishing the royal apartments, or the Petit Trianon, or her miniature château at Bellevue, all with the same touch of natural and delicate gaiety. Her orders alone kept an army of craftsmen busy. It used to be said that this was shameless extravagance which helped to ruin France, but recently historians have taken a more balanced view. The ruinous state of French finances was the result of more fundamental defects in the French State, and expenditure on craftsmanship could never be entirely without social benefits. In any case, succeeding ages have good reason to be grateful for the artistic influence of Mme. de Pompadour. For five years she continued the King's mistress, and until her death continued to be his close friend and confidante, with a perceptible influence on the course of events.

After the death of Fleury, Ministers were apt to change frequently, and some of them are hardly worth remembering. The man who hoped to succeed Fleury was the Comte de Bellisle, but he was passed over, and the Marquis d'Argenson became Foreign Minister. He was a man of ideas, but never succeeded in giving a clear direction to the Austrian War. In fact the only Frenchman to give lustre to that war was Marshal de Saxe. Orry, Fleury's capable and careful Controller-General, was dismissed in 1745, and was succeeded by the former Intendant of Valenciennes, Jean-Baptiste de Machault. The war had put great strain upon the finances, and in 1749 he attempted a most important reform, the introduction of a new *vingtième*, a tax of one-twentieth on all incomes, from which there would be no exemptions. That French finances were by no means beyond reform is shown by the fact that this reform, with attendant good management, would have wiped out the annual deficit and established stability. But at once Machault encountered the united opposition of the nobility, the clergy and the *parlements*. The clergy in particular, who were exempt from taxation except for a small *don gratuit* they made to the Crown, raised such a storm that the King gave way, and Machault dropped the reform. It is interesting to note that Mme. de Pompadour strongly supported the reform, but her influence was outweighed by the privileged Orders. The attitude of the clergy appears especially incongruous at this time. The French Church was enormously wealthy, with annual revenues of between 100 and 200 million livres, yet its *don gratuit* amounted to only 2 or 3 millions. It had never been more worldly, with its bishoprics and wealthy benefices the preserve of the nobility. Internally it was split by continuing Jansenist–Jesuit conflicts, and externally it was challenged by Deism and the philosophy of Enlightenment. Yet this was the time the Church chose to attack the Monarchy in its most vulnerable spot, namely the finances, and to make it impossible for Ministers to achieve financial stability. In fact the Church was only one branch, so to speak, of the privileged orders who were becoming increasingly accustomed to combine to limit the power of the Monarchy. It included also the *noblesse d'épée* and the big financiers, the powerful magistracy known as the *noblesse de robe*. And the most effective mouthpiece of them all was the *Parlement*.

In France there were about eleven hundred *parlementaires*, men of wealth and power, headed by such great families as that of Lamoignon and Molé. In the eighteenth century it was a closed corporation, increasingly confined to men of noble birth. They were lawyers by profession, but the office went from father to son with little regard to fitness, and carried with it great powers and social prestige. The importance of the *Parlement*[1] in the eighteenth century arose from its claim to have the exclusive right of registration of royal decrees. If it disapproved of a decree it could draw up a *remonstrance*, and if it refused to register it, it could be overawed only by a *lit de justice*, by which the King himself attended and ordered registration, or even by exile under a *lettre de cachet* to some distant town. In fact the *parlements* gave Louis XIV little trouble, he was too strong for them; but from the Regency onwards they again raised their heads and voices. They readily set aside the Will of Louis XIV, and they became the

---

[1] There were thirteen *parlements*, but that of Paris was much the most important, and it is to that that we shall pay most attention. The chief interest of the provincial *parlements* seemed to be in thwarting the Intendants in their attempts to carry useful reform.

mouthpiece of Gallicanism and Jansenism against the Jesuits and *dévots* of the Court. They opposed every attempt at reform, such as Machault's introduction of the *vingtième* in 1749. They never lost an opportunity to defend the feudal rights of privilege of the nobility. They even condemned the new practice of inoculation against smallpox.

Recent historians, in searching for the origins of the French Revolution, have come to recognise the great importance of the claims made by the *parlements* in their *Remonstrances*.[1] They claimed that they were all that remained of the ancient *curia regis*, supposed to have begun with the Franks. They refused to admit that the King of France was absolute; he was a constitutional monarch, bound by fundamental laws, of which the *Parlement* was the guardian, and there existed a Contract between the ruler and his people. They made frequent use of the word liberty, but the liberty they had in mind was not that of 1789, but the feudal liberty of past ages. In fact they made current the language of revolution decades before 1789. They hindered reform and weakened the Monarchy by spreading abroad a spirit of disobedience. They are a measure of the difference in character between the Monarchy of Louis XIV and that of Louis XV.

The part played by the *Parlement* in the intellectual and religious affairs of the time can best be illustrated by some characteristic incidents. In 1751 a certain Abbé de Prades submitted to the Sorbonne a doctorate in theology which, after a public examination, was approved with acclamation. But a fortnight later the *parlement* of Paris denounced the thesis as heretical. De Prades was in fact a friend of Diderot and d'Alembert, and as the first volume of the Encyclopaedia had appeared in the same year, the *Parlement* was on the alert. The Sorbonne at once reversed its previous decision and condemned the thesis, and the abbé fled to Holland to escape imprisonment. From there he went to Potsdam, under the protection of Voltaire, and eventually obtained a benefice in Silesia.

The publication of the Encyclopaedia, which began in 1751, brought into the open the conflict between the *philosophes* and the established order. The storm burst in 1758 when Helvétius, a former farmer-general, a *philosophe*, though not a contributor to the

---

[1] The best short treatment of this subject is by Professor Cobban in *History*, vol. XXXV.

Encyclopaedia, published his materialist '*De l'Ésprit*'. It was condemned by Jesuits and Jansenists alike, by the Sorbonne and also by the *Parlement*. But at Court the Encyclopaedia found powerful friends in Mme. de Pompadour, Choiseul, Malesherbes (the Court librarian), and even Louis XV, who said that 'there were some good things in the *L'Encyclopédie*'; and Diderot stoutly defended his work. Eventually the *Parlement* decided that in some respects the Encyclopaedia was useful, and it was allowed to appear under the eye of the censor, and thus the thirty-six volumes continued one by one to appear.

The *Parlement* not only acted as censor, but it took an active part in the religious conflicts of the time. In 1746 there was enthroned a new Archbishop of Paris, Christophe de Beamont, a pious young man (he was not yet forty), but a singularly stubborn one, and a firm supporter of the Bull *Unigenitus. Unigenitus* had made a new Gallican and Jansenist party in France, and Christophe despaired of the weakness of the Government in failing to suppress it. In 1749 he took extreme measures; he threatened excommunication against those who refused to accept the Bull, and he refused the last rites and ecclesiastical burial to those who had failed to obtain a *billet de confession* of their acceptance.[1] In that year Charles Coffin, Rector of the University, and author of some noted hymns, died without receiving the last rites because he refused to produce a *billet de confession.* The priest did not dare to refuse him burial, and the funeral took place in the presence of a great concourse of dignitaries of the University intended as a demonstration against the Archbishop. When his nephew fell ill and was also refused the last rites (even though he offered to confess), the *Parlement* stepped in and imprisoned the priest. The nephew was then allowed to confess, and received the last rites. Similar subsequent refusals of the sacraments occurred during the next few years, and the *Parlement* repeatedly condemned the attitude of the Archbishop. Finally, in 1753, when the sacraments were refused to a seventy-eight-years-old nun named Sister Perpétue, the *Parlement* threatened to bring the Archbishop to trial before his peers.[2] But at this the King

---

[1] In this he was not an innovator, and was only carrying out the instructions of Pope Benedict XIV. What was new was that it should be attempted in Paris.

[2] This proposal raised most important constitutional issues. Had the *Parlement* the right to summon the Peers to judgment? Once they had done so, could the King's Council take the matter out of their hands? It would not be a great step from this to a declaration that the King was a constitutional monarch.

intervened and ordered silence, and when the President of the *Parlement* Maupeou went to protest, Louis told him that his judgments were not to be questioned. The reply of the *Parlement* was to draw up the *Grandes Remonstrances* of April 9th 1753. These amounted to nothing less than a treatise on the rights of the Crown in ecclesiastical affairs, and the *Parlement* appeared as the great protector of the rights of Catholics against the intolerance of Jesuits and *dévots*. They were able to argue that it was no heresy to reject the Bull *Unigenitus*, and in this they certainly had public opinion behind them, as is shown by the fact that 20,000 copies of the *Remonstrances* were sold in a few weeks.

Everything at this point really depended upon the strength of the Crown, and in an absolute monarchy it was not possible for even a Louis XV to disregard so vital an issue. He had always preserved a genuine religious feeling, the result of Fleury's teaching. To him the Bull *Unigenitus* was the law, in both Church and State, and therefore the Jansenists were disturbers of the peace; and in this view he was supported by the pious Queen Marie Leszczynska and her *dévot* friends. But against this was the influence of Mme. de Pompadour, and such Ministers as Machault, the Controller-General, Jansenists like Marshal de Noailles, and friends of the *philosophes*. Moreover, the constant interference of the *Parlement* seemed to him to be a defiance of the royal prerogative. In the end his policy pleased no one, and was damaging to his own position. He delayed action for too long and thus allowed the forces of disruption to grow. On one occasion the bishop of Amiens wrote:

> It is easy to see what the *Parlement* wants, but for the life of me I cannot see what the king is aiming at.

To the Papal Nuncio it had seemed throughout a simple matter: if the King once and for all deprived the *Parlement* of the right to interfere in ecclesiastical affairs, Jansenism would be deprived overnight of its most powerful ally in France. Meanwhile the *Remonstrances* of the *Parlement* had been blazoned abroad; many people had hung copies of them at the head of their beds along with the images of the saints. Printed jokes were circulated inviting people to the funeral of 'the most noble lady, Madame la Constitution Unigenitus, daughter of Clement XI, who died suddenly in the Great Hall of the *Parlement* in

Paris'. The idea was now current in Paris that the nation was above the king, and that the *Parlement* was its special representative. The King himself had referred to the *Parlement* as an assembly of republicans, though he had added characteristically that he supposed the system would last his time. On one occasion when the Dauphin and his wife were driving to Notre Dame, they were surrounded by a crowd of women demanding bread. The Papal Nuncio wrote prophetically to Rome in May 1752 that the King was preparing his own downfall by his weakness towards the *Parlement*, and that religious upheaval would mean political upheaval as well. Posters with the words 'Long live the *Parlement*! Death to the King and the bishops', had already appeared in Paris. When therefore musketeers handed notices of exile to the members of the *Parlement* in May 1753 the damage had already been done. In the ensuing months legal business virtually came to a standstill in Paris, for no one would use the temporary royal Court, and when the King recalled the *Parlement* in September 1754 they were welcomed back with bonfires and celebrations. As they had not modified their claims in any degree respecting their powers in ecclesiatical affairs, the victory remained with them. In 1755 the *Parlement* fined the canons of Orleans 500 livres, and banished four of them, for refusing the Sacraments to a Jansenist. A similar fine of 3,000 livres was imposed on the Bishop of Troyes. The Archbishop of Paris was banished to his country residence of Conflans by the King for the same offence. After this, twenty-six bishops declared that *billets de confession* were unnecessary, and the practice was gradually discontinued (1755). In 1755 the *Parlement* decreed that the Bull *Unigenitus* was invalid, but the Royal Council in turn invalidated the decree. Finally in 1756 an Encyclical from the Pope modified the attitude of the Church, and *Unigenitus* was no longer declared 'a rule of Faith'. The reply of the *Parlement* was to ban the Encyclical in France.

A further battle might have ensued, but in January 1757 an attempt was made on the life of the King by Damiens, when Louis was slightly wounded by a penknife. The motive was interpreted according to one's political views, for Damiens had been once educated in a Jesuit College; on the other hand he had imbibed his hatred of the King by listening to the debates of the *Parlement*. Both sides, however, were disposed by the incident to moderation, and the influence of the Foreign Minister, the Abbé (and later in the year Cardinal) Bernis, was salutary in this respect.

During the period the Jesuits were increasingly under fire. A good illustration of the issues involved is to be seen in the case of Isaac Berruyer. Berruyer was a French Jesuit who had written a book on the Old Testament in which he had attempted to re-tell the old stories in the light of the new naturalistic attitude of the age of the Enlightenment. The book had been popular, and he followed it with a book which sought to do the same for the New Testament, called *History of the People of God from the Birth of the Messiah to the End of the Synagogue* (1753). Berruyer was at once accused of heresy; the book was placed on the Index, and the Archbishop tried in vain to suppress its circulation. It was answered at once by the theologian Jean-Baptiste Gaultier in his *Lettres théologiques*, and Gaultier put his finger on what he felt was the theological weakness of the Jesuit heresy:

> Père Berruyer's book discloses a mystery which the [Jesuit] Society has for a long time kept hidden. It is not simply to the dogmas of predestination and grace, and to the truths which depend upon them, that the Society confines its attention. It has views which are much more extensive. It has overthrown morality and discipline in order to accommodate the passions of men. It now wishes to abolish mysteries in order to accommodate what the world calls the intellectuals (les beaux esprits). Deism is the fashionable religion; it is necessary therefore to relieve Religion of what these *philosophes*, whom the world adores, reject. The mystery of the Trinity shocks them. That of the Incarnation scandalises them. Nothing which passes the boundaries of their feeble reason with them merits any belief, however evident should be the reasons for belief. The Reverend Fathers ask what to do with men so difficult, and reply that if the *philosophes* do not wish to place their minds under the yoke of religion, let us place religion under the yoke of the *philosophes*. We have lifted the barriers which impede the passions; let us lift those which restrict the mind.

Needless to say, the book was also condemned by the *Parlement*, and publicly burnt, but for a different reason; not for its faulty theology, but because it served to spread 'the ultramontane doctrine of the infallibility of the Pope'. If to this we add the attacks of the *philosophes* upon the Jesuits for their obscurantism, their adherence to Scholasticism, and their Ultramontanism, the unhappy position of the Jesuits will be appreciated.

The expulsion of the Jesuits from Portugal in 1758 greatly increased the attacks on them in France, and a flood of pamphlets appeared against them. The final disaster was occasioned by the case of Antoine Lavalette. Lavalette was a Jesuit who since 1725 had worked in the missions of Guadeloupe and Martinique, and, in order to supplement the finances of his mission, had acquired an estate worked by several hundred slaves, and had engaged in private trade in sugar, contrary to the strict rule of his Order. But the onset of war with England in 1755–56 ruined him, and he was faced with an enormous debt of 4½ million livres. Instead of settling the debts as quietly as possible, the French Jesuit Order foolishly allowed the case to come before the *Parlement* of Paris, their natural enemy. In May 1761 the *Parlement* gave judgment against the Order, whereby the latter had to make good all Lavalette's debts, a very popular decision in Paris. But the *Parlement* did not stop there. With the excuse that they wished to see what were the regulations of the Order on the subject of private trade, the *Parlement* insisted that the Jesuits lay before them the latest copy of their Institute, and then proceeded to pronounce upon the character and organisation of the Jesuits. The Jesuits were attacked as being subjects of a foreign power (i.e. the General of the Order); their Institute was declared opposed to the laws and liberties of France; it had never been registered by the *Parlement*, therefore the Jesuits had no legal existence in France. In August 1761 twenty-four Jesuit books were burnt by the executioner at the command of the *Parlement* as attacking the powers of the secular ruler. Again the King allowed the attack of the *Parlement* to gather momentum without a check; on this occasion France was at war, and the goodwill of the *Parlement* was needed if financial provisions were to be registered without difficulty. So the attack of the *Parlement* continued. In March 1762 it published a large work setting forth its attack on the teachings of the Jesuits. It was a gross distortion of the truth, in which the Jesuits counted no less than 758 deliberate falsifications. In April all Jesuit schools were closed in Paris, and all their estates were confiscated. In August it was declared that the Society of Jesus was incompatible with any well-ordered system of government; that its teachings were contrary to natural law; that it was an enemy of the secular power, that its rules offended the principles of the Gallican Church, and that its morals were corrupt. All who did not abjure the rules of the Order were required to leave France within a week. Similar declarations were carried by the other *parlements* of France (though they did not extend to Flanders, Alsace and Franche-Comté). Finally in December 1764 at a plenary session of the *Parlement*, attended by the peers of France, the decree was read in which Louis XV declared that by virtue of his supreme authority, the Society of Jesus ceased to exist in France. The reasons he gave for the act were, significantly, the threat to internal order and the force of public opinion. Some 3,000 Jesuits thus abandoned their vows or left France. The Pope condemned the act in the Bull *Apostolicum pascendi*, which, needless to say, was banned in France by the *parlements*.

The loss of the Jesuits left a perceptible gap in French education, for they had been some of the best teachers in France. The popular idea that the Society was rich was a myth, and the confiscations did not amount to much. The suppression of the Jesuits had a quite different and twofold significance. First, it marked the triumph of the *philosophes*, the philosophy of the Enlightenment over Catholic traditionalism. Second, and still more significant for the future, it marked the triumph of the *Parlement* over the Monarchy. In this the *Parlement*, in a curiously distorted way, had come to represent the nation, the constitution, natural law, against the will of the Sovereign. The royal decree abolishing the Jesuits had come, almost as an afterthought, two and a half years after the *Parlement* had declared them suppressed and had confiscated their property. It was an occasion on which all men could see the degree to which the Monarchy had lost the initiative in France. It is for this reason that the suppression of the Jesuits in France was one of the most significant events in the reign of Louis XV. The point may be made in another way. As we have seen, the French clergy defeated and weakened the Monarchy in 1749 by defeating Machault's financial reforms. In 1762–64 the *Parlement* and Monarchy together weakened the Church by the suppression of the Jesuits. Both events in a way could be represented as a triumph for privilege, both certainly weakened the Monarchy, and both induced an attitude of mind which led ultimately to the destruction of the *ancien régime*.

Failures in Foreign Policy

Nor could Louis XV claim that he had offset domestic difficulties by a successful foreign policy. The War of the Austrian Succession failed to achieve any solid advantage for France. Marshal Bellisle's attempt at destroying Habsburg power in Germany and Italy and setting up a Bavarian Emperor in place of a Habsburg, failed completely. The Prussian alliance proved to be a doubtful factor. The Italian adventure was more in Spanish than in French interests, and more to the advantage of Elizabeth Farnese's sons than to either. French aid to the Jacobites raised hopes which were never fulfilled. In the colonial field the issues at stake in the Anglo-French struggle were hardly appreciated by French Ministers and French sea-power was shown to be inferior to the British. Only Maurice de Saxe's victories in the Netherlands continued the legend of French military strength, but brought no permanent benefit to France.

After the war France appeared to have, not one foreign policy, but three, for while the Foreign Ministers of the period (mostly nonentities) tried to retain the Prussian alliance, the King was pursuing his *secret* through the Comte de Broglie, French ambassador to Poland; and Mme. de Pompadour leaned towards an Austrian understanding. Kaunitz, as we have seen, worked steadily towards the same goal, and in the negotiations of 1756, when France was alarmed at the news of the Anglo-Prussian treaty of alliance, Mme. de Pompadour used the Abbé de Bernis as a special agent to carry on the Austrian negotiations. The result was the Diplomatic Revolution of 1756, with all its great consequences for France and for Europe.

The Diplomatic Revolution (or the Reversal of Alliances, as the French historians term it) could be justified, if at all, on two scores. First, the Anglo-Prussian alliance having already been signed, France had to have an ally, or else remain neutral in the coming war. Second, the Austrian alliance relieved France from fear of an attack anywhere in southern Europe, and thus would enable her to concentrate upon the colonial and maritime war against Britain. Yet this was not the strategy upon which France based the Seven Years' War. Instead of concentrating upon the overseas theatres of war, France lost the command of the sea, and engaged in a full-scale war in Germany, which could not be justified by any claim that it was aimed primarily against Hanover. The result was the great defeats of Rossbach (1757) and Minden (1759). Overseas there was complete defeat, and the loss of Canada, the West Indies and India. The Abbé de Bernis continued as

Foreign Minister until 1758, when he was quietly replaced by another of Mme. de Pompadour's favourites, the Duc de Choiseul. Choiseul was a trained diplomat and courtier, a man of energy, determined to put a new vigour into the war, and if possible, to save the situation for France. His great achievement was the *pacte de famille* with Spain in 1761, by which he brought Spain into the war. But it was too late to save France from the disastrous Peace of 1763. The feebleness which France showed in foreign affairs during the period merely reflected the general malaise which was affecting the whole French government, and which was as apparent in internal as in foreign affairs.

The Duc de Choiseul

But here a clear distinction should be made between France and the French government. For France itself was still enormously prosperous, and above all it was the intellectual and cultural centre of Europe. Its language was the language of diplomacy and of culture throughout Europe. It was the high-water mark of the influence of Voltaire, Montesquieu and *L'Encyclopédie*. Rousseau's influence was different, but none the less profound. The prevailing note in France was not one of defeat, but of energy and reform. It was the period of Quesnay, Turgot and the Physiocrats. The spirit of change was abroad, and was reflected in the literature, the periodicals and the correspondence of the time.

In some ways Choiseul typified this aspect of the period. A member of the *noblesse d'épée*, he was a man of culture; he was also a man of energy and vigour; not a great statesman, but one who for a time gave the French government a sense of direction. He was loyal to the Austrian and Spanish alliances, and wished to make them the basis for the restoration of French influence in Europe. He gathered the key offices of Foreign Affairs, Marine and War under his control (his cousin, Choiseul-Praslin, was Minister of Marine). As he wished to pursue an active foreign policy he wanted peace at home, and this is one reason why the *Parlement* was allowed to hunt down the Jesuits without much hindrance from the Court. Moreover, Choiseul, though a Catholic, was hostile to the Jesuits, and favoured the *philosophes*. He began a reform of the army, introducing greater centralisation, and striking a blow at the practice of captains of deliberately under-manning their companies, which Louvois had attacked, but not entirely eliminated. He insisted upon annual manoeuvres. The artillery was re-organised and the new inventions of Gribeauval introduced. Even so, he aroused much opposition among the old officers of the Seven Years' War, and soon found it necessary to tread warily in the face of growing opposition, but he certainly produced a more efficient army. During the years following the Seven Years' War he doubled the effective fighting strength of the French navy. Choiseul was influenced also by the thought of the Physiocrats, and was much interested in the development of agricultural method and greater freedom of trade in grain. To give greater governmental direction to agriculture he appointed a fifth secretary of state, Bertin, and he and the Controller-General, Laverdy, saw to it that the Intendants encouraged agricultural and commercial development in the *généralités*. The Intendants, in fact, were the most efficient and progressive men in the French administration, and but for them a breakdown in the *ancien régime* would have come much sooner than it did. One significant omission in Choiseul's period was any financial reform, and without this the French Monarchy was ultimately doomed.

In foreign affairs Choiseul did much to restore French prestige in the years following the Peace of Paris (1763). In 1766 France had a windfall when Stanislas Leszczynski, the duke of Lorraine died, and his duchy reverted to France, a legacy really of Fleury's foresight. Thus the work of Louis XIV was completed, and France had a strong eastern frontier. Choiseul was anxious to take advantage of the Spanish alliance to make the western Mediterranean a French preserve, and in 1766 he purchased the island of Corsica from the Genoese republic for 2 million livres. In 1770 he renewed the French alliance with the Habsburgs, when he arranged the marriage of the dauphin with Maria Theresa's daughter, Marie-Antoinette. But his provocative maritime policy pointed to a conflict with England, and in 1770 the prospect of war arose. A dispute between Spain and England over the possession of the Falkland Islands seemed to Choiseul an opportunity to cement the Franco-Spanish alliance and at the same time to inflict a defeat upon England. He was ready for war. But at this his enemies at Court saw their chance. It was pointed out to the King that France could not afford a war in the serious state of French finances. A fierce argument ensued in the royal council in the presence of Louis XV. But to Louis it seemed absurd that there should be a war over some remote islands which were no concern of the French. Choiseul and his cousin were dismissed. Their enemies at Court had triumphed, but they left office amidst popular acclamation, and to the genuine regret of the *philosophes*.

Meanwhile in internal affairs the French Monarchy reaped the whirlwind which was the result of its feeble policy towards the *parlements* during the previous decade. The events culminating in the suppression of the Jesuits in 1762–64 had been a triumph for the *parlements*. Their pretensions knew no bounds, and moreover they had awakened everywhere a spirit of reform which they were ludicrously inadequate to satisfy. For the *parlements* stood, not for reform, but for privilege. They were strong enough to destroy the prestige of the Government, and to thwart useful reform, but able to achieve little else. Yet in the eyes of popular discontent, they were heroes, the conquerors of the Jesuits, the champions of 'liberty' (whatever that might mean) and natural law, the enemies of despotism. Moreover, the struggle was no longer merely with the Paris *Parlement*; the provincial *parlements* were equally active in resisting the encroachments of royal power.

During the Seven Years' War a determined effort was made by the Governor of Brittany to build an effective system of roads connecting the province with the capital. This could only be done by the employment of the system of royal *corvée*. But Brittany had always been one of the most independent parts of France; it still retained its provincial Estates, and had first received a royal Intendant as late as 1689. The Estates at once resisted the *corvée*, and were supported in their resistance by the *Parlement* of Rennes. The attacks of La Chalotais, the *procureur général*, upon the royal authority were such that the Governor had him arrested. At this the *Parlement* of Paris took up the cause of their colleagues in Rennes, and thus for the first time there was a declaration of solidarity against the Monarchy on the part of all *parlements*. It was a further step in the growth of the idea that there was a constitution limiting the royal power. The conflict was most embarrassing to Choiseul. As we have seen, he wanted only domestic peace, and had always been favourable to the *Parlement*. But here was a direct threat to the royal power, and at Court he had many enemies, including the Dauphin and the *dévots*. The challenge of the *parlements* could not be ignored. With a determination he had never before shown, Louis suspended the *Parlement* of Rennes, and, in a *lit de justice* in the Paris *Parlement*, declared:

> What has occurred in my *Parlement* of Rennes does not concern my other *parlements*. I have dealt with this Court in this affair as my authority requires, and I am answerable to no one. In my person alone resides the sovereign power; from me alone my Courts take their existence and their authority; to me alone belongs the legislative power, without dependence and without division; public order emanates entirely from me, and the rights and interests of the nation, which some have dared to separate from those of the monarch, are necessarily united in my hands and rest only in my hands.

But Choiseul was not the man finally to settle accounts with the *Parlement*. He was by birth one of the *noblesse d'épée*; his secret sympathies were with the *Parlement* who had so recently destroyed the Jesuits. The situation was complicated by the duc d'Aiguillon who, dismissed from his governorship, demanded to be heard by his peers in the *Parlement* of Paris. In 1770 the King forbade the trial, but it took place all the same. Defiance of the Crown had now become open and sustained.

Choiseul's position at Court rapidly weakened. His friend Mme. de Pompadour had died in 1764, at the age of forty. Louis XV was deeply moved at the loss of one who had become to him a counsellor and friend. In 1768 there was established at Court a new mistress, Mme. du Barry, whose scintillating beauty was the wonder of all who saw her. For some reason which has never been satisfactorily explained, Choiseul soon made an enemy of her, and this weakened his position with the King. In 1768 Maupeou became Chancellor, and in 1769 the Abbé Terray became Controller-General. As Maupeou had been president of the *Parlement*, and Terray had been a councillor in the *Parlement* for ecclesiastical affairs, they were especially fitted to deal with that institution. They were both clever enough to sit at the feet of Mme. du Barry, and soon were openly opposing Choiseul's handling of affairs. In particular, his foreign policy appeared likely to lead to a war with England, and Terray was able to show that French finances would not bear the strain. As we have seen, in December 1770 Louis XV supported Maupeou and Terray, and Choiseul was dismissed.

The Triumvirate

Maupeou, Terray, and the new Secretary of State for Foreign Affairs, d'Aiguillon, were known as the Triumvirate. They could count on the support of Mme. du Barry and also the *dévot* party. To the *philosophes* this was a reactionary government, yet it was the Government which most successfully took up the challenge of the *parlements*. In January 1771, when the *Parlement* again defied the Crown, Maupeou exiled 130 of their members and their families to Auvergne, and forced them to travel through all the discomforts of the winter snows. In February an edict re-organised the administration of justice, abolished the purchase of offices, by which the *parlementaires* had become virtually hereditary, set up a new *Parlement* appointed entirely by the Crown, and divided the jurisdiction of the old Paris *Parlement* into six areas, each with a Court of its own. It was more than a judicial reform; it was a political and social revolution of the greatest importance. The privileged classes combined in opposition, and were supported by public opinion, while the *dévots* and some of the more discerning of the *philosophes*, such as Voltaire, supported Maupeou. Maupeou planned a complete judicial reform for France with a new plenary Court for the registration of royal decrees. Although he was unable to complete this, he had shown that, with a display of determination, the Crown still had considerable power.

Meanwhile Terray was able to turn with a new freedom to the next most pressing problem, that of the state of the finances. He had to resort to drastic measures, for there was a national debt of 110 million livres and an annual deficit of 63 millions. He began by suspending payment on a number of government debts, which amounted to a recognition of partial bankruptcy, and he introduced a number of new indirect taxes. He re-allotted the assessment of the *vingtième* on a more equitable basis, though this was a small reform compared with the mountain of inequality there was in taxes. He made a new bargain with the tax-farmers which gave the State an extra $3\frac{1}{2}$ million livres. There was now no *Parlement* to block his path, though he must have been the most unpopular Controller-General of the reign. In 1773 there were riots against his prohibition of the export of grain, following a series of bad harvests, and the rioters declared that the King, du Barry and Terray were making a fortune out of speculation in grain.

But Terray and Maupeou were not easily defeated, and a few more years of the Government might have given the Monarchy an opportunity to find a new stability. Louis XV had at last come to understand the seriousness of internal affairs, though in foreign policy he had a set-back in 1772 with the Partition of Poland. Meanwhile his life was the usual round of gaiety, with its fêtes, entertainments and the fascinating du Barry. But in April 1774 he was stricken with smallpox, and died in the following month. Not a single Mass had been said in Paris for his recovery, and at his funeral his body was carried to Saint-Denis to the cries of 'Voilà le plaisir des dames!' It was a fair comment. His reign had been mainly one of drift, and great forces had arisen during its course which the Monarchy failed either to harness or to stem. Yet the cause of Monarchy was not yet lost; the Triumvirate had shown that there were reserves of strength. Much depended upon the character of the new King.

15: The Coming of the French Revolution 1774-89

Louis XVI and Turgot

Louis XVI, the grandson of the late king (for the Dauphin had died in 1765), was aged only twenty. He was well-intentioned and pious, and had been carefully educated, but he had all the indecisiveness of his grandfather and none of his *mystique*. He neither looked nor acted like a king. Extremely unsure of himself, he was all too ready to rely upon others. He rarely saw the larger issues at stake, and was happiest when keeping his personal accounts (which he did meticulously, down to the last sou), or in making locks, which he did expertly. He would have made a good shopkeeper, and would have been happier at that than at being a king. The Queen, Marie-Antoinette, the beautiful and vivacious daughter of Maria Theresa, had an unhappy time at Versailles, bullied as she was by the King's aunts, especially Mme. Adelaide, who hoped to rule the Court, and stifled by the etiquette of Court, which bored her so. She was closely watched by the Austrian ambassador, the comte de Mercy, who reported her every move to the Empress, and she was constantly lectured by her mother for her indiscretions. She was increasingly the victim of vicious rumours in which there was no truth. For years, through the incapacity of Louis, she was unable to bear a child, and had to keep silent at the calumnies against her. The Court was no longer the centre of the nation as it had been sixty years before. But it would be quite wrong to suppose that the reign opened in an atmosphere of gloom. In fact there were great hopes of the new king; the philosophy of Enlightenment appeared to be triumphing, and reform was on everyone's lips; not least on those of the *parlementaires* who now witnessed the fall of Maupeou.

To emphasise the new era of conciliation, the Triumvirate were dismissed, and on the advice of Mme. Adelaide, Louis XVI appointed the comte de Maurepas as his Minister. Maurepas was aged seventy-three, had served Louis XV for thirty years, but was a courtier rather than a Minister. He disliked taking responsibility, and could be relied upon to choose the easiest way out of any difficult situation. The extraordinary thing was that Louis had not recalled Choiseul, generally recognised as the leader of the 'patriot party'. But Louis disliked Choiseul for his hostility to his father, and the intention was to avoid both the Choiseulists and the *dévot* party. In the end Maurepas constructed a government which had much to commend it. Vergennes, favourite of Mme. Adelaide, and formerly ambassador to Sweden, became Foreign Minister, to the delight of the *dévots*; and Turgot, formerly Intendant of the Limousin, became Controller-General, to the delight of the *philosophes*. In the serious state of the finances, Turgot held the key position in the Government.

Turgot, born in 1727, came of a family of lawyers. He was destined for the Church, but at the Collège de Bourgogne he imbibed the philosophy of Newton, Locke, Montesquieu and Voltaire. He chose the law, and in 1753 he became a councillor in the *Parlement* of Paris. There he watched the *Parlement*'s defiance of the King in the 1750s, and he developed a bitter hatred of their principles. He came to believe in toleration, and above all in the absolute monarchy of France as the only institution capable of carrying through the programme of Enlightenment. In Paris he moved through the salons of the time, and was the friend of Mlle. de Lespinasse, d'Alembert, Condorcet, Grimm and d'Holbach. He contributed five articles to the Encyclopaedia, although he declared: 'I am not an encyclopaedist, since I believe in God.' He was particularly interested in the teachings of the Physiocrats, who in 1757 began to meet regularly in Quesnay's rooms to hear the theory that land was the source of all wealth, that taxation should be low and that capital should be allowed to flow freely. In 1761 he was appointed Intendant of Limoges, a backward and remote *généralité*, where he showed himself to be a model administrator. His predecessors had begun a great programme of road construction, by means of the hated *corvée*. Turgot considered the system unjust, and introduced payment for work done, providing the money from increased impositions, which consequently increased more than 800 per cent. between 1762 and 1789. This was a heavy burden on trade, but it gave the Limousin a fine road system which Arthur Young described as

> much more like the well-kept alleys of a garden than a common highway . . . without dust, sand, stones or inequality, firm and level, of pounded granite.

Turgot greatly encouraged new agricultural experiments, tackled practical problems such as plant and cattle disease, grain storage and new agricultural methods, and made great efforts to persuade the peasant to grow the potato, against which there was an unreasoning prejudice. Meanwhile among the *philosophes* he was regarded as one of the most important men in Europe.

In 1774 there was a general demand from the privileged orders for the restoration of the old *Parlement*. Turgot alone among the Ministers was opposed to it, but the decision was taken almost before he had entered office. In November Louis XVI recalled the *Parlement* of Paris; it was a most popular measure, but a disastrous one. The *Parlement* returned in all its magnificence, and with a greater determination than ever for ultimate victory. But reform was in the air, and meanwhile Turgot had submitted to the King a programme which he wished to implement, based on the new physiocratic principles. He was faced with an annual deficit of 48 million livres. He sought to repair this, without increase of taxation, by stimulating the economy. According to physiocratic theory, man was essentially a good and intelligent being, who needed an atmosphere of freedom in which to flourish. Turgot was an idealist, but he was also a practical administrator. In September 1774 he began by instituting internal free trade in grain. Export of grain was always forbidden, except in times of plenty, when it was permitted by a special *arrêt du conseil*. But internal regulations governing the trade were even more onerous than external. Corn and flour could be moved from province to province only by special permit. In so far as these regulations had a purpose, it was to prevent local famine, but in fact they produced far more distress than they prevented. In 1763 the Controller Bertin had decreed internal free trade in grain, but prejudice was hard against it. Grain riots followed, and the Triumvirate returned to the internal restrictions. Turgot now again attempted internal free trade (except for the Paris area, which other Ministers refused to accept). But the current harvest was poor, and in March and April 1775 there were further grain riots. In April a crowd of demonstrators reached Versailles, and when the chief of police took fright and sold them grain at two sols a livre, they went off to Paris and looted bakers' shops. Such was 'la guerre des farines'. Order was soon restored, but opposition to Turgot began to grow.

Meanwhile Turgot pressed on with his reforming plans. He wished to introduce a new and equitable tax assessment on land, which he had been able to effect in Limousin, and which he wished to extend throughout France. He wished also to put the general farm of taxes under State supervision, to ensure that the maximum sum reached the treasury. He appointed twenty new managers of the farm, and made with them a contract highly advantageous to the State, including an immediate advance of 6 million livres. He reassessed the *octroi* duties on goods entering and leaving Paris, so that they pressed less heavily on the poor, and more on the privileged classes. He introduced State economies, cutting his own salary from 142,000 livres to 82,000, and surrendering valuable perquisites. He reduced subsidies paid to foreign princes. He even managed to effect some economies at Court. The result was a remarkable achievement, for at the end of 1775 he had eliminated the annual deficit, and replaced it by a surplus of 5 millions.

Thus gradually the object which Turgot had set himself began to emerge. It was, first, to restore the financial strength of the Monarchy, and then to put the Monarchy again in touch with the progressive and reforming elements of the nation, as it had not been since the death of Colbert. His reforms could succeed only if he could win the support of public opinion, because only thus could he hope to defeat the great alliance of privilege which, he knew, must be opposed to him. But Turgot, like many other enthusiastic reformers, wished to proceed too quickly. In 1776 he produced his famous Six Edicts. They proposed (1) to suppress dues on grain for Paris, as had already been achieved elsewhere in France, (2) to suppress the royal *corvée* in road-building, and replace it by a tax on all land-owners without exemption, (3) to abolish all gilds and *jurandes*. The other three concerned the freeing of trade in Paris, such as the suppression of the *caisse de Poissy*, an oppressive means of controlling the meat trade. When the Six Edicts were submitted to the *Parlement* for registration, they immediately drew up a remonstrance against them. For tactical reasons the *Parlement* concentrated upon the abolition of *corvée*, because in this they could count upon the support of the nobility and clergy. At the head of the opposition was the Prince of Conti, who stood to lose 50,000 livres a year if gilds were abolished. Among the Ministers Turgot could count on the support only of Malesherbes, of the *Maison du Roi.* The argument against the abolition of *corvée* was that it put a new burden on the land which had not existed before, but Turgot's answer was

> The expenses of government, having for their object the interest of all, should be borne by everyone, and the more a man enjoys the advantages of society, the more he ought to hold himself honoured in contributing to those expenses.

It was a revolutionary idea, incomprehensible to those accustomed to the traditional ways of eighteenth-century thinking. Similarly, to the argument of the *avocat général* Seguier in the *Parlement* that the abolition of the gilds would mean the loss of great sums to the magistrates, Turgot replied with the revolutionary idea that the right to work was founded upon natural law. It was a principle received with enthusiasm by the great mass of the workers of Paris; it was a triumph of physiocratic thought. Moreover, in spite of the doubts of his other Ministers, Louis XVI stood firm, and on March 12th held a *lit de justice* to enforce registration.

But Turgot soon found ranged against him all the forces of wealth and privilege, the tax farmers, financiers, bankers, nobility and magistrates. Maurepas was ready to desert him, and against them all Turgot could rely only on the King. He tried to strengthen the feeble will of that Monarch:

> Never forget, sire, that it was weakness which placed the head of Charles I on the executioner's block.

For a time Louis remained silent. He never understood the great issues at stake, nor the far-reaching plans of his Minister. Turgot had hoped, for instance, for complete religious toleration in France and had submitted to the King a memorandum on the subject. He had toyed with the idea of a national system of education from which all citizens should benefit. He wished to see the final suppression of feudalism, and the union of the nation behind a reforming monarchy. He was entirely opposed to French intervention in the American war, which, he saw, would wreck all efforts at financial reform. If Turgot had had his way he would have converted France into an Enlightened Despotism, have put the Monarchy at the head of the nation in the work of reform and progress. There was ample public opinion on his side, but it was quite unorganised, and Turgot was quite unable to organise it. Instead he was borne down by the powerful forces of privilege. For some weeks he waited for a word from the King; when it came on May 12 1776, it was an order for his dismissal. The *philosophes* were in despair. Voltaire denounced the 'rogues' (*frippons*) and 'reptiles' who had opposed Turgot, and declared that his dismissal was a thunderbolt which had struck him to the heart. On the whole, history has agreed with him.

France and the American Revolution

In the months following Turgot's dismissal the topic which seized the French imagination was the American Revolution. It was natural that many Frenchmen, still bitter with the humiliations of 1763, should enjoy seeing the British in difficulties on the very scene of their former triumphs. But French enthusiasm went deeper. The comte de Ségur put his finger on a deeper cause when he wrote:

> This unexpected apparition produced upon us a greater effect in consequence of its novelty, and of its occurring precisely at the period when literature and philosophy had circulated amongst us an unusual desire for reform, a disposition to encourage innovations and the seeds of an ardent attachment to liberty.

The American Revolution occurred just at the point when the thought of the *philosphes* had reached a wide audience. Ideas of liberty, natural law, reform, however ill-defined, were on the lips of the nobility, magistrates, financiers and middle classes, all those in short who thought themselves progressives. Ségur wrote:

> Liberty, royalty, aristocracy, democracy, prejudices, reason, novelties, *philosophes*, all together joined to make our days happy. . . . It was a great point of honour to be in opposition: to be so seemed a duty to the more enlightened, a virtue to the generous, a weapon useful to the *philosophes*, a way of making a stir, a fashion which the youth of the kingdom seized on.

In a sense the French were already 'Republicans'. This does not at all mean that they were already hostile to Louis XVI, or that anyone contemplated a French republic; the meaning is more complex. The educated Frenchman of the day was deeply imbued with the classical spirit; he had relived in imagination the great days of the Roman republic, and knew well what the Romans meant by *virtus*. He had read also the *philosophes*, had imbibed the ideas of the rule of law, natural reason, toleration and the rejection of traditionalism, while Rousseau had re-enforced his belief in the natural goodness of man. From such sources there had sprung a sense of social solidarity, transcending institutions, which may for convenience be termed 'Republican'. There was much idealism; it was a springtime of human hopes and endeavours, and the American cause seized upon the imaginations of the French. For the Americans were fighting for liberty; they were a simple people, living close to nature, with a moral strength which far transcended that of older, more sophisticated European peoples. Thus when Benjamin Franklin arrived in France in December 1776 he was lionised by society, and was at once provided with a fine house by a wealthy admirer. In Paris it became the fashion to have his portrait over the mantelpiece, and even Turgot became lyrical with his latin tag that Franklin had 'snatched lightning from the heavens and the sceptre from the hands of tyrants' (*Eripuit caelo fulmen sceptrumque tyrannis*).

To Vergennes, the Foreign Minister, motives for intervention in the American War were more mundane, though perhaps no more substantial. The Austro-French alliance of 1756, renewed after the Seven Years' War, had curiously limited the extent of French influence in Europe. In particular it had deprived France of its traditional 'Eastern' policy of alliance with Sweden, Poland and the Turks. Choiseul reacted to the changed situation by fostering the *pacte de famille* with Spain, and by showing renewed interest in France's maritime position. Still, the Partition of Poland of 1772 was a serious diplomatic set-back to France, and did much to render unpopular the renewal of the Austrian alliance, which the marriage of Louis with Marie-Antoinette was intended to seal. Vergennes' policy therefore was to recede still further from Europe, and concentrate upon maritime, colonial and commercial expansion, even to the extent of war. It was a policy of the utmost stupidity. By intervention in the American War France could hope to embarrass and weaken Britain, but could not hope to reverse the decision of 1763 so far as France was concerned. France could win independence for the Americans, but could not hope to gain much of permanent benefit for herself. At the time when France should have concentrated upon the colonial war,

N

between 1740 and 1763, she was engaged in major conflicts in Europe. Now, when European affairs, particularly the fate of Poland and Turkey, required the intervention of France, in the interests of the balance of power, France concentrated exclusively upon a colonial struggle which no longer much concerned her. For this France paid a heavy price of national bankruptcy, the extension of revolutionary ideas in France, and the diminution of French influence in Europe.

In 1776, two years before war was declared, expenditure on the French fleet shot up from 32 to 62 million livres. Vergennes helped Beaumarchais (the author of *Le mariage de Figaro*) to establish a dummy firm of Roderique, Hortalez and Co. under cover of which he could ship supplies to the Americans. Sartine, the Minister of Marine, was building up, at considerable expense, a first-class fleet, commanded by excellent admirals of the calibre of d'Estaing, de Grasse and Suffren, the best fleet France had had at any time during the eighteenth century. At the same time the comte de Saint-Germain, the War Minister, an old soldier of wide experience carried important reforms in the army. He rapidly expanded the army, though by no means as much in reality as it was made to appear on paper. A great admirer of Prussian military discipline, he tried to introduce it into the French army, but the changes were unpopular among French officers and were usually defeated. He established 12 military schools (*Écoles militaires*), with 600 scholarships for the sons of poor nobility (in which Bonaparte was later to study). Much of his work was thwarted by the opposition from the nobility, who eventually succeeded in driving him from office. In 1781 they had a great success when they secured a decree requiring an officer above the rank of captain to show four generations of nobility. But in spite of this, Sartine and Saint-Germain deserve to be numbered among the reforming Ministers of the period, and they did give France military success in the American War. But in some ways the victory was illusory, for in 1783 France was much weaker militarily than she appeared to be.

But the new expenditure upset the financial balance Turgot had achieved, and to repair the damage Maurepas agreed to call in Jacques Necker. Necker was a Genevan, who had lived in Paris since 1747. In 1763 he had the good fortune to gain advance knowledge of the signing of the Treaty of Paris, had speculated heavily in East

India stock, and had made a fortune of 8 million livres. He then opened his own banking house in the rue de Cléry, and soon acquired the reputation of being a financial genius. He moved in high society, delighted in displaying a superficial culture, and in being a friend of the *philosophes*. His wife's Friday salon became a famous meeting-place for the *beaux esprits* of the time. But he was a shallow man, with few ideas, and none of the reforming genius of a Turgot. He was quite uninfluenced by the thought of the Physiocrats, and in fact was regarded as a leader of the opposition against the new ideas.

His task was in any case a difficult one. State expenditure before the war was somewhat over 300 million livres a year; during the war it was over 500 millions, but the strength of privilege was such that he was quite unable to increase taxation, and moreover the extravagance of the Court greatly increased as the influence of Marie-Antoinette grew. Her friends, the Polignacs, and the princess de Lamballe, made inexhaustible demands upon the generosity of the frivolous queen, until people whispered that it was the days of Pompadour and du Barry over again. In these circumstances Necker could only borrow money, and at this he was very successful, though at cruel rates of interest between 8 and 10 per cent. Financiers trusted him, and thus he was indispensable to Maurepas and his time-serving colleagues. He did attempt, during 1778–79 by holding assemblies in three *génér-alités*, in Berry, the Haute-Guyenne and Moulins, to bring the no-bility, clergy and middle class into a greater share of government by discussing administration with them. But the discussions became attacks on government, especially the work of the Intendants, and the experiment was not repeated. He next tried a revolutionary means of strengthening his position, both with the financiers, and with public opinion. In 1781 he published the *Compte rendu au roi*, a financial statement of the state of the nation. No such statement had ever been made before, for the finances had always been treated as the private concern of the Monarch. This appeal to the nation was a most signi-ficant development; it was a clear recognition of the fact that there was a public opinion to which to appeal. 100,000 copies of the *Compte rendu* were sold and eagerly discussed. By careful omissions, and numerous inaccuracies, Necker was able to give a false picture of the state of French finances, to suggest that the budget was balanced, and that therefore there was no need for alarm. Necker appeared to be the most popular man in France; he now sought to dominate the Government. He demanded that the Ministers of War and Marine be placed directly under the Controller-General,[1] and he demanded to be admitted to the *Conseil d'en haut* with the title of Controller-General. Maurepas had watched Necker's rise with growing jealousy. Necker's demands were refused, and he was dismissed. By 1781 war and reckless borrowing had ruined French finances. At the same time, the *Compte rendu*, by suggesting that all was well, had made it difficult for any successor to institute drastic financial reform.

When the war ended in 1783 French finances were in utter confusion. The war had cost some 2,000 million livres, and the national debt had become mountainous. This had meant an enormous increase in the importance of *rentiers* and other financiers, and an increase in taxation upon those who were least able to pay. In these circumstances it is doubtful whether any Controller-General could have saved the situation without a political and social revolution. In any case the new Minister, Charles de Calonne, was no revolutionary. He was an old and experienced administrator, formerly Intendant, first of Metz and then of Lille, a man of culture, but no reformer. He stood on good terms with the financiers, and had able assistants in his work, in particular Dupont de Nemours, the noted Physiocrat, whom he made director of commerce. But in general he could think of no better course than to continue Necker's policy of borrowing, and this at a fantastic level and at high rates of interest. Some were direct loans, perhaps 80 or 100 million livres at a time. Still more were indirect loans, such as from the city of Paris. There was also a greatly increased sale of offices, many of them created for the sole purpose of sale. In all Calonne must have borrowed some 800 million livres. As the total annual budget was only 550 millions, Calonne made the bankruptcy of France all but certain. Moreover, so much activity brought about inflation and a wild burst of speculation, in which many financiers made great profits. Few financiers sought to invest in commerce and industry, when they could earn high profits by lending to the Government. There was thus a great deal of spurious economic activity, much foreign investment in Paris, lavish government expenditure, and a consequent rise in prices without any comparable benefit to the great mass of the French people. Finance and politics

[1] In itself a sensible proposal if there was to be a curb to excessive expenditure.

had become a great game, and many a shady financier disported himself with a new-found ostentation. In the prevailing chaos the Government of Louis XVI had almost ceased to function.

Calonne and the *Révolte nobiliaire*

Yet there was a programme of reform already in existence, which might save the situation. It was that which Turgot had had in mind ten years before. In 1786 Calonne submitted it to the King: he proposed the removal of fiscal immunities, the adoption of a uniform method of assessment and collection, a new land tax to replace the old *vingtièmes*, the abolition of the royal *corvées* and a uniform customs tariff. These reforms, he calculated, would give an increase of revenue of 70 millions and a decrease of expenditure by 40 millions, and thus reduce the annual deficit, which was now 112 millions. If such a plan could be carried out the Crown would again have placed itself at the head of the nation; it would amount to a political and social revolution, and the disappearance of privilege from France. But it could no longer be carried by decree; this would merely have been to renew the old conflict with the *Parlement*. Calonne proposed the summoning of the Assembly of Notables. But this was to suppose that the nobility would voluntarily surrender their privileges, a wild hope. In fact, the summoning of the Assembly of Notables merely gave the opportunity for the *révolte nobiliaire*. To the privileged orders it appeared to be the ultimate victory in the long struggle with the Monarchy which had continued since the days of Louis XIV. Louis XVI hesitated long before he gave his consent, but eventually the Assembly was summoned for January 1787.

The Assembly of Notables consisted of 144 nobles and prelates. The fourteen prelates immediately exercised a dominating influence, especially Loménie de Brienne, archbishop of Toulouse, and the archbishop of Narbonne. Calonne at once presented them with the facts. He showed that with a deficit of 112 millions, the problem was urgent, and asked for their co-operation. His proposals were coldly received. They were in fact discussed only for the purpose of demolishing them, and the meeting turned into a general attack upon his administration. Louis was told that the only way of appeasing the nobility was to dismiss Calonne, and to this Marie-Antoinette added her influence. On April 8th Calonne was dismissed.

The King was still nominally in favour of the reform plan, and now the leader of the aristocratic opposition, de Brienne, was appointed to the royal council of finance. He at once resorted to a new loan, but when he came to examine the facts could only suggest a new land tax on the lines Calonne had proposed. But the nobles were no more inclined to submit to Brienne than to Calonne, and in May they were dissolved. Their opposition must be clearly understood. It was not that they doubted the seriousness of the financial situation, but they saw that the predicament of the Government had placed the Crown in their hands. They wanted to use their opportunity to extort important concessions from the Government. They wanted, in fact, to convert the Monarchy of France into an aristocratic republic. It was a measure of the degree to which the Monarchy had lost touch with the nation that the nation appeared to be behind the revolt of the privileged orders. How little truth there was in this the events of the next two years would reveal.

In the course of the reign of Louis XVI the fruits of the struggles of the previous reign with the *parlements* finally matured. During that period they had come to regard themselves as *corps intermediares*, as a constitutional body intermediary between the King and the people. Thus had grown in the popular mind the idea that France was a constitutional monarchy, and thus, as financial troubles grew, there grew also the demand for the summoning of the States General. Once this became the general cry the *parlements* began to sink into second place. To the general policy of borrowing, the *parlements* had given little opposition, but with the dismissal of the Assembly of Notables they again became obstreperous. The situation was desperate, for people had begun to fail to pay taxes, and government was near to collapse. Lamoignon, the Keeper of the Seals, returned to the policy of Maupeou. In May 1788 the *parlements* were suspended, some of their members were arrested, and forty-seven new courts were set up to take their place. But this merely cemented still further the alliance of the privileged orders against the Government. The Assembly of the Clergy, called in 1788 to vote a *don gratuit*, merely protested at the suspension of the *parlements*, and renewed their claims to exemption from taxation. The whole of privileged France appeared to stand united against the Crown. The King capitulated. The Ministers were dismissed; the States-General was summoned for the following May, and in August, amidst popular acclamation, Necker was recalled to office. One of his first acts was to recall the *Parlement*, which made a triumphal entry into Paris in September 1788. To them, more than to any other institution in France, the triumph of the privileged orders had been due. Yet privilege was one of the first casualties to the National Assembly in 1789, and six months after the meeting of the States General the *parlements* were quietly abolished.

Freemasonry and the Court

A characteristic development of the Age of the Enlightenment was the Freemasonry movement. Beginning in England at the end of the seventeenth century, where it was at first Jacobite, it spread to France in the 1720s, and reached Paris in 1725. Its objects seem to have been a vague humanitarianism, tolerance and peace, ideals particularly associated with the Age of Reason. It often took on an anti-Catholic bias, and in 1738 the Pope forbade Catholics to take part in the movement. Many notable figures of the period were Freemasons, Frederick the Great, Voltaire, Diderot, d'Alembert, Hélvetius and Baron d'Holbach. In Bavaria in the 1770s a similar secret society, known as the *Illuminati*, paid much attention to social and political reform, such as the abolition of feudalism, toleration, freedom of trade and the press and the pursuit of liberty and equality. In 1787 they were suppressed by the Bavarian government, but continued as an underground movement. In France by 1789 there were several hundred Freemasons' lodges, and some writers think that they had some influence upon the coming of the French Revolution, for most of the great names among the revolutionaries were Freemasons.

It is perhaps significant that the age which had so often rejected traditional religion in the name of Reason should have found new religious ceremonies in Freemasonry, and should have believed the impostures of Cagliostro and Mesmer. Cagliostro was a Sicilian who practised spiritualism, and for a time imposed upon the credulity of some of the greatest names of French society before he eventually fell a victim to the Inquisition. Mesmer was a doctor of medicine of the University of Vienna, and claimed to cure all diseases by the use of magnetism, successfully practised hypnotism, and was also for a time a great success in Parisian society. Some writers have interpreted all this as indicative of the character of French society, but too much should not be made of this, for all ages have their freaks and their frauds. It did, however, involve the Court, in the famous affair of the Queen's Necklace.

Marie-Antoinette often found life at Versailles tedious, and while Louis XVI hunted or amused himself with manual labour, she was drawn into the frivolities of the Court and Paris. Her friends were unfortunate, and in 1777 Mercy reported to Vienna that she was incurring gambling debts of nearly half a million livres without any means of paying them. Horse-racing had recently been introduced to France from England, and Marie-Antoinette often attended. There was also the craze for the masked ball, at which she was too often accompanied by the comte d'Artois, the King's dandy brother. She also dabbled in politics, although without much consistency, so that her brother Joseph II wrote to her:

> How do you come, my dear sister, to be concerning yourself with dismissing Ministers, with sending this one away to his estates, with giving a department to that one? Have you ever asked yourself by what right you are interfering in the affairs of government and the French monarchy? What studies have you made? . . . You, an amiable young person who thinks only of frivolity, of your toilet and your amusements. . . .

In 1785 a scandal burst upon the Court. The Cardinal de Rohan, the immensely wealthy archbishop of Strassburg and Grand Almoner of France, had fallen in love with the Queen. Partly under the hypnotic influence of Cagliostro, he entered into an absurd plan by which he should enjoy a silent midnight meeting with someone posing as the Queen, and then that he should buy her an expensive diamond necklace. Needless to say, the necklace was stolen by those who organised the plot. When eventually the story came out, Rohan, Mme. de la Motte and others concerned were arrested, and de la Motte was sentenced to life imprisonment. But although the Queen was innocent of any part in the affair, the incident did her much harm as it was thought typical of the frivolous life she led. To her enemies she was known as *Madame Déficit*, or simply as *l'Autrichienne*. Napoleon, with great exaggeration, said that the Affair of the Necklace marked the beginning of the Revolution, but there was this truth in it that it did much to destroy what remained of the *mystique* of monarchy. In this respect the spirit of the age was reflected best in Beaumarchais in his *Barbier de Séville* and *Mariage de Figaro* (1783). Re-capturing something of the wit and sparkle of Molière, he portrayed in his plays the sensuous world of a decadent aristocracy, the world of Fragonard now faded with autumnal tints, in which while the aristocracy make love and deceive each other, their servants show themselves superior to their masters and mistresses. It would be wrong to overestimate the social content of these sparkling plays, but they are as characteristic of the period as the Dresden shepherdesses or a La Tour portrait.

Social and Economic Background of the Coming of the French Revolution

It is difficult in a short space to do justice to the intellectual atmosphere of the decade before the French Revolution. The period still reflected the optimism of the earlier period. Ideas of change, reform and progress were everywhere, and if sometimes the changes instituted seemed retrograde, as with the decree of 1781 requiring four quarterings of nobility for a command in the army, many were undoubtedly progressive and humanitarian. In the 1780s torture was abolished. In 1784 the special tax on Jews was abolished. In 1784 also the general complaint against the use of *lettres de cachet* led to a general inspection of prisoners held under their order, and it was actually decided to demolish the Bastille, which no longer served much purpose in Paris. The prevailing interest was in science. Diderot's *Encyclopédie raisonnée des sciences et des arts* was a popular work spreading abroad the teachings of experimental science. The age could not boast of a Galileo, a Newton or a Huygens, but the *Académie des Sciences* in Paris encouraged the work of lesser lights such as Laplace and Lagrange. Lavoisier, one of the farmers-general, discovered the composition of the air and the nature of oxygen, and made useful contributions to plant biology. Buffon, the naturalist, followed his fifteen-volume *Histoire Naturelle* (1749–67) with *Epoques de la nature* (1778) in which he sought to distinguish the main ages in the earth's history. Lamarck (1744–1829) worked out a new method of plant classification in 1773, and began a great work in zoology which was to lay a basis for Darwinian theories of evolution. In most of the main provincial towns agricultural societies were formed for the discussion of new methods and the application of the new science.

Voltaire and Rousseau had both died in 1778. By then Voltaire's influence had done its work. He had successfully dissolved away, with his mordant scepticism, the intellectual foundations of the *ancien régime*. Rousseau's influence continued to be a powerful factor up to 1789, and even more so after the Revolution had begun. In painting, Boucher had died in 1770, and Chardin in 1779, but La Tour, a fine portrait painter, lived till 1788, and Fragonard and Greuze lived on into the years of revolution. In music, after Rameau (d. 1764) and the Couperin family, France had nothing to compare with the great German achievement of Glück and Mozart. Perhaps the most characteristic mind of the last years of the *ancien régime*, and the one which will give us clearest insight into the thought of the period was that of Condorcet (1743–94).

The marquis de Condorcet, like Voltaire, Diderot and Turgot, had been educated by the Jesuits. He early showed great aptitude for mathematics, and became Permanent Secretary of the Academy of Sciences in 1773. He was received by Voltaire at Ferney, and became an assistant to Turgot when he became Controller-General in 1774. Thereafter he gave less time to mathematics and more to politics and philosophy. He was a friend of d'Alembert and lesser *philosophes*, and his salon was noted in Paris in the years before the Revolution. When the Revolution began he became a Girondin, but in 1793 he had to go into hiding. He was tried and condemned in his absence by the Revolutionary Tribunal in October 1793. He lay concealed until April 1794, when he was denounced and arrested, and during the night he took poison. The supreme irony of his career is that, while he lay in hiding he wrote his chief work, the *Progress of the Human Mind*. It is written entirely without bitterness. It exudes a naïve belief in progress and the inestimable blessings which experimental science could confer on mankind. For man was a rational being, capable of profiting by experience. This experience was preserved, recorded and sifted by experimental science, and the progress of the work was the process we know as history. From what has been achieved so far we can estimate what may still be achieved in the future, and this gives man great grounds for hope.

> Such is the object of the work I have undertaken; the result of which will be to show, from reading and from facts, that no bounds have been fixed to the improvement of the human faculties; that the perfectibility of man is absolutely indefinite; that the progress of this

perfectibility, henceforth above the control of every power that would impede it, has no other limit than the duration of the globe upon which nature has placed us. The course of this progress may doubtless be more or less rapid, but it can never be retrograde; at least while the earth retains its situation in the system of the universe, and the laws of this system shall neither effect upon the globe a general overthrow, nor introduce such changes as would no longer permit the human race to preserve and exercise therein the same faculties, and find the same resources. . . .

The process was not a difficult or dangerous one. It became easy once writing was discovered, for progress could then be recorded. From that moment

> Philosophy has no longer anything to guess, has no more supposititious combinations to form; all it has to do is to collect and arrange facts, and exhibit the useful truths which arise from them as a whole. . . .

For progress proceeds as a whole, and not piecemeal, because 'nature has indissolubly united the advancement of knowledge with the progress of liberty, virtue and respect for the natural rights of man'. When this is generally understood, all men will have become *enlightened.*

> After ages of error, after wandering in all the mazes of vague and defective theories, writers upon politics and the law of nations at length arrived at the knowledge of the true rights of man, which they deduced from this simple principle: that *he is a being endowed with sensation, capable of reasoning upon and understanding his interests, and of acquiring moral ideas.*

From this it followed that man entered society only as a means of securing his rights. It followed also that every decision of a community should be a majority decision, and that all men should participate in government. All this followed from the certainties of the scientific method, for

> The only foundation of faith in the natural sciences is the principle that the general laws, known or unknown, which regulate the phenomena of the universe, are regular and constant; and why should this principle, applicable to the other operations of nature, be less true when applied to the development of the intellectual and moral faculties of man?

At present Enlightenment is confined to the French, the English and the Americans, but one day it will spread throughout the world. This is one of the main reasons for hope for the future, for it means the progress towards equality for all mankind:

> Will not every nation one day arrive at the state of civilisation attained by those people who are most enlightened, most free, most exempt from prejudices, as the French, for instance, and the Anglo-Americans? Will not the slavery of countries subjected to kings, the barbarity of African tribes, and the ignorance of savages gradually vanish? Is there upon the face of the globe a single spot the inhabitants of which are condemned by nature never to enjoy liberty, never to exercise their reason?

The basis of hope for man is that he is a reasonable being; the means of progress is experimental science; the goal is the freedom and harmony of all mankind.

Thus Condorcet argued under the shadow of the guillotine. His *Progress of the Human Mind* forms a fitting conclusion to the thought of the Age of Enlightenment which we set out to trace in the first chapter. For though he was not a profound thinker, he had imbibed the ideas which had grown in western Europe since the age of Newton and Locke, and, unlike most of the *philosophes*, he lived long enough to believe that the French Revolution was the beginning of the millennium.

.   .   .   .   .

In comparison with the great upheavals which followed it, the eighteenth century is often regarded as a period of peace and tranquillity. But in human affairs peace and tranquillity are merely comparative terms, and in any absolute sense could mean only death. The eighteenth century in France was in fact a period of great social tension. There was first a great resurgence of the aristocracy.

Louis XIV had left the nobility their social privileges, but excluded them from political power and subjected them to the governance of Ministers and Intendants, drawn from the middle class. But even Louis XIV's Ministers became ennobled and founded noble families. Colbert may have been the son of a draper, but his son was a marquis and his grandson a duke. Eighteenth-century Ministers were drawn frequently from the nobility, and in the reign of Louis XVI almost every Minister came of aristocratic families (though Turgot and Necker did not).

The term *noblesse* was an indication of privilege, for instance exemption from the *taille* and *corvées*, but in the eighteenth century it told one little else about the status or wealth of the individual. The old *noblesse d'épée* were men of ancient lineage and great wealth, often playing a notable part at Court. But many of the provincial nobility were impoverished, mere *hobereaux*, working their own lands and walking behind their own ploughs. Again, many of the nobility were of recent creation, *noblesse de robe*, their titles created for their service to the Crown, and many of them had purchased their titles from an impoverished monarch. There were in France some 400,000 *noblesse*, but only about 4,000 of them were great nobles of ancient lineage, accepted at Court and playing a significant part in affairs. Their chief occupation was a command in the army, where they hoped to win fame and glory; they were indeed a significant factor making for war, especially in 1733, 1740, 1756 and 1778. Others became ambassadors, where great wealth was necessary to create the right impression abroad, and others took high preferment in the Church. The lesser nobility resided on their estates. Feudalism was all but dead in France, but there remained seigneurial privileges, such as the *banalités* which required the peasant to use the lord's mill and wine-press, hunting-rights whereby the peasant could not protect his crops from the lord's deer or pigeons, and numerous payments in cash or kind. It is impossible to generalise about how burdensome all this was to the peasant, for conditions differed in different places, and some lords were more exacting than others. But in general it seems probable that these rights and customs were governed by ancient usage, and it was difficult for the lord to increase them without causing a disturbance. But with the fall in the value of money the money payments from the peasants were worth less and less. Landlords did therefore attempt to raise rents in the decades before the French Revolution, to the increasing discontent of their peasant. Historians have termed this process the *seigneurial reaction* and regarded it as a a contributory cause of the Revolution.

Many of the impoverished nobility found it wise to marry wealthy heiresses of the *bourgeoisie* or *noblesse de robe*. Lafayette's father had had to make such a marriage. This restored the family fortunes, and it also created a bond of solidarity between the nobility and the magistracy, bankers and lawyers. This bond should not be over-emphasised, for there was much class distinction, but the dividing line did not run neatly between nobles and non-nobles. For while the nobility at Paris or Versailles would mingle in the salons with tax-farmers and middle-class *philosophes*, they might regard with distant amusement the provincial *hobereau*.[1] Arthur Young commented that there were many families of *noblesse* who subsisted on 50, and even 25 louis a year (equal to £50 or £25 in English currency).

The middle class grew in wealth and social influence. The two most important professions were those of lawyers and financiers. The most sought-after of all legal positions were in the *parlements* of Paris or the provinces. These offices were either inherited or purchased for great sums. The salaries were not, by comparison, very great, but the perquisites of office were many, and the social prestige was very great indeed. Altogether they made twelve hundred of the most important men in France. Some of them, like Montesquieu, were men of culture, and most of them were bound together with a strong corporate sense. They were also closely connected with the bankers and financiers, for financial decrees and loans had to be registered in the *parlements* like other decrees. It is significant that the *Parlement* never attempted to hinder the loans of Necker or Calonne. Bankers and financiers grew in importance during the eighteenth century, partly with the growth of trade, but much more because of the increasing dependence of the Government upon loans. By the reign of Louis XVI it had become of first importance to the Government that the *rentiers* should be kept happy. Their new importance can be assessed by the fact that Necker thought it worth while publishing the *Compte rendu* specially in order to deceive them. Commercial activity and industrial development lagged behind, partly because of gild restrictions, partly because of continued government controls and partly because capital was directed into government loans rather than into industry. There was expansion in some industries, especially in large-scale industry in iron in the north-east, and Calonne did much to encourage the activities of the East India Company. But some industries, like the silk industry of Lyon, suffered decline and depression in the second half of the

[1] Professor Sagnac (*La Fin de L'Ancien Régime*) writes: 'What a gap between the great *noble d'épée*, living near the court, provided with a regiment, or a general command, and the *petit noble*, withdrawn to his estates, handling the plough, laboriously raising a large family, claiming for his sons places at the *École militaire*, without always obtaining them, and for his daughters education at the maison de Saint-Cyr!'

century. After 1770 there was serious industrial decline, especially in the cloth industry, which by 1789 had come almost to a standstill.[1] The most prosperous part of the French economy after 1770 was in foreign trade, especially with America, the West Indies, Africa and India. Ports like Bordeaux, Nantes and Marseilles were among the most prosperous cities in the world. French exports increased in the twelve years before 1789 from 259 to 354 million livres, and imports from 207 to 301 million livres. But France still lagged behind England or the Dutch in banking, credit facilities and the machinery for a commercial economy.

Taxation was a grievous burden upon the unprivileged classes, all the more because of its inequalities and injustices. Direct taxes, the *taille* (originally a military tax on personal and real estate, most arbitrarily assessed; privileged classes exempt), *vingtièmes* (in theory one-twentieth of income; privileged classes exempt), *capitation* (a poll-tax), ecclesiastical tithes, customs dues on all trade, *lods et ventes* (feudal dues to landlords), *gabelles* (indirect taxes on such articles as salt), *corvées* (labour services on roads and bridges), these were some of the burdens which pressed inequitably on tradesmen, shop-keepers, workers and peasants. The Bourbon monarchy had never been strong enough to reform the tax system, and to the end continued to defend feudal dues. As late as 1776 the *Parlement* condemned as seditious a pamphlet entitled *Les inconvénients des droits féodaux*. Taine, the great French historian of the Revolution, showed that in 1875 the French peasant was 93 per cent. better off than under the *ancien régime*, and Arthur Young showed that he was 76 per cent. less well off than the English peasant in 1787. Taine showed that after paying taxes the great mass of the peasants had no more than 25 or 30 livres left a year which he might spend on himself.[2] Such figures do not, however, tell us as much as they seem to tell, for most peasants were in the main self-sufficient, and bought very little.

Recent research has considerably modified the traditional view of the French peasant in the eighteenth century. He was not, for instance, everywhere oppressed by a feudal seigneur. In fact the nobility possessed far less land than is usually assumed. In Artois it was only

---

[1] This was partly the result of the Commercial Treaty with England in 1786, for French industry found it impossible to stand up to English competition.
[2] Say 30s. of English currency.

29 per cent. of the land; in Limousin only 15 per cent. The Church possessed a good deal less. Moreover, much of the land of nobles and clergy consisted of woods, useful for hunting, but of little other value. In the northern parts of France some 16 per cent. of the land was owned by members of the bourgeoisie who had turned land-owners. France was, in fact, as Arthur Young shows, already in the eighteenth century a land of peasant proprietors. Nor is it true that the most wretched peasants were to be found on the estates of the nobility and the Church. The exact opposite was often true. Some of the most prosperous peasants were tenants of the *noblesse*, but it is also true that the *métayers*, who were numerous in the midi and the west, were to be found on large estates, and they were the most wretched of French peasants. The system of *métayage* was one in which the peasant received everything, land, tools, seed, from the lord, and shared with him the resultant crops, perhaps on a fifty-fifty basis. Arthur Young called it 'a miserable system, that perpetuates poverty and excludes instruction'.

What is certain is that agricultural method in France was still often primitive. There was no widespread enclosure in France as in England. Intensive cultivation was unknown; the system of fallow was in general use. The result was a miserably low crop yield, of something like 1 in 4 in Limousin, though it was as high as 1 in 11 in Flanders. But agricultural improvement was in progress. Many Intendants, as did Turgot, encouraged the formation of agricultural societies for the discussion of new methods. The Physiocrats showed great interest in agricultural progress, and some of the nobility were both men of the Enlightenment and reforming agriculturists, such as the Duc de la Rochefoucauld, with whom Arthur Young had such interesting discussions. There was much interest in botany, and Lavoisier and du Tillet made useful scientific discoveries. The Crown made its contribution, and royal decrees of 1764–66 exempted drained and reclaimed land from taxation, and some advantage had been taken of this by 1789, although not much. The biggest cause of wretchedness among the peasantry was that the land-holdings were often too small. Five hectares of land could support a family comfortably, but in some *généralités* 60 per cent. of the peasants owned less than a hectare, and consequently had to eke out an existence by day-labouring.

In Guienne, for instance, Arthur Young met many beggars:

All the country girls and women are without shoes or stockings; and the ploughmen at their work have neither sabots nor stockings to their feet. This is a poverty that strikes at the root of national prosperity. . . . It reminded me of the misery of Ireland.

And this was an area in which peasant proprietorships were usual. On the other hand, in Béarn (also an area of peasant proprietorships) Arthur Young was full of praise for what he saw:

A succession of many well-built, tight, and comfortable farming cottages, built of stone and covered with tiles; each having its little garden, enclosed by clipped thorn hedges, with plenty of peach and other fruit trees. . . . To every house belongs a farm, perfectly well-enclosed, with grass borders mown and neatly kept around the corn fields. . . . It is all in the hands of little proprietors. . . . An air of neatness, warmth and comfort breathes over the whole.

The same contrast can be found with the nobility, for when in Poitiers he commented:

Whenever you stumble on a Grand Seigneur, even one that was worth millions, you are sure to find his property desert.

and he complained of 'the melancholy spectacle of ruined châteaux in so many parts of France'. The Marquis de Mirabeau, in his *Traité de la population* (1756), said that this was the consequence of nobility preferring to live at Versailles or in Paris to tending their estates. But at Liancourt Arthur Young gave a very different picture:

At a village near Liancourt, the Duke has established a manufacture of linen and stuffs mixed with thread and cotton, which promises to be of considerable utility. . . . It gives employment to great numbers of hands who were idle, for they have no sort of manufacture in the country though it is populous. . . . The daughters of the poor people are received into an institution to be educated to useful industry; they are instructed in their religion, taught to read and write, and to spin cotton. There is another establishment of which I am not so good a judge; it is for training the orphans of soldiers to be soldiers themselves. The Duke of Liancourt has raised some considerable buildings for their accommodation. . . .

But the Duke of Liancourt was one of the great reforming seigneurs of the time, and cannot be taken as typical of more than a few.

It is certain that on the whole the position of the peasant was better in the eighteenth century than it had been in the reign of Louis XIV.

It is true that agriculture was on the whole prosperous in that reign, but there were periodically dreadful famines, in which thousands died. In 1675 the Governor of Dauphiné declared that most of the peasants were living on acorns and roots. In Maine in 1685 it was said that peasants lived off buckwheat and roots, slept in straw and possessed no furniture or change of clothes. After 1715 conditions improved, and the picture can no longer be painted in such black colours. In the reign of Louis XIV there were frequent agrarian insurrections, which were harshly suppressed, but there were no such risings in the eighteenth century. There was a steady growth of population, and this implies improved conditions, though population was always pressing on the margin of subsistence. There were well-to-do peasants and there were those who still lived near the subsistence-line. There were many who had shaken off feudal dues, and there were some who were still subject to their annoyances. Labrousse shows that rents paid by peasants to landowners increased by 98 per cent. in the years before 1789. Moreover, whereas dues were accepted with silent resignation in, say, 1680, they were deeply resented by 1780. It was not merely that the burdens had become heavier, but that resentment to them had become general. There were frequent conflicts between peasants and landlords, and it was by no means always the landlord who won. When, for instance, the Marquis de Mirabeau wished to enclose some common land to prevent its deforestation by his peasants, he peasants resisted, and eventually Mirabeau's orders were cancelled by the *parlement* of Aix (1771).

The period of 1778–90 was one of special economic problems. The French historian C. E. Labrousse has shown that the general economic development of the period 1733–89 may be roughly illustrated thus:

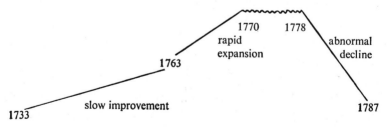

In the first period prices rose steadily, and this gave a stimulus to the economy, though it brought no special benefit to the peasant who was self-sufficient. But rents rose less steeply than prices and thus the leasing farmer benefited. Wine prices rose and benefited the wine growers. There was also a rapid increase in industrial production and an increased demand for colonial products, especially sugar and coffee. All this continued until 1770, which Labrousse called 'the height of the economic prosperity under the *Ancien Régime*'. Thereafter the tendencies were reversed. In a period of economic contraction wine prices were halved and grain prices fell heavily. In the towns the pressure of population brought about a steady deterioration in the position of the workers. Between 1740 and 1789 prices increased by 65 per cent., but wages by only 22 per cent. Industry languished and the volume of trade declined. In 1788, following devastating hailstorms, the grain harvest was bad, and this helped to spark off the final political crisis. But there had been many years when the grain crop had been no better, and they had not been followed by revolution. In the towns at the same time the cloth industry virtually collapsed, and there was an unemployment rate as high as 50 per cent. In 1789 cloth production amounted to only one-half that for 1787.

If we seek to relate the French Revolution to economic causes it is clear therefore that there are two generalisations which are at first sight contradictory, but if properly understood are both true. The eighteenth century was on the whole a period of economic improvement. The bourgeois classes were more numerous, more powerful and more important in 1789 than they were in 1715. Before 1715 peasants, during a period of famine, died in great numbers; there were no such catastrophes after 1715. When the French Revolution began it was the middle classes (a term admittedly very difficult to define) who asserted control, and it may well be argued that they were the ultimate recipients of the benefits of the Revolution. All this will suggest that the Revolution was the result of improved economic conditions. The nation was like some sturdy plant which breaks through a crusted surface which is impeding its growth. But it is also true that the Revolution was, as Michelet and Taine saw it, a revolt against poverty, hunger, unemployment and oppressive feudal burdens.

Both these aspects of the Revolution gave it impetus and direction. They help to explain why the Revolution took the course it did. They

do not quite explain why it began. Perhaps it is wrong to speak of
A French Revolution, as if it were a single, coherent movement. There
was not one French Revolution; there were at least three, an aristocratic revolution, a bourgeois revolution and a peasant revolution,
and there may have been others. If we ask what set the process of
revolution in motion, the answer is: the decline of monarchical despotism and the consequent break-down of administration, leading to
a loss of control of events, an inability to carry reform, and eventually
financial bankruptcy. Bankruptcy led directly to the *révolte nobiliaire*,
and thus to 1789. Any attempt which seeks to explain the French
Revolution simply in economic terms is bound to give a false picture
of the situation. It is equally true that any attempt to understand the
course of the Revolution without understanding the economic forces
which lay behind them would also be false. No historian today would
seek to explain the coming of the French Revolution simply in terms
of the teachings of the *philosophes*, for most of the *philosophes* were
admirers of Enlightened Despotism, and were no revolutionaries. But
it is true that the new humanism of the eighteenth century, which we
call Enlightenment, created an attitude of mind which dissolved away
the old loyalties in Church and State. It was not that men had become
increasingly resentful of State authority. In fact the French Revolution and Napoleon established a State far more powerful than had
ever existed before. It was that the Bourbons had ceased to exercise
State authority to the benefit of the nation. Repeatedly the men who
might have saved the situation, Machault, Turgot, perhaps even
Calonne, were thrust aside. Thus the Bourbons became an irrelevance,
and as such they were eventually superseded.

Suggestions for Further Reading

Chapter 1

The best reading would be of the works of the *philosophes* themselves, mentioned in the text. Also

A. R. Hall: *The Scientific Revolution, 1500–1800.* 1954
H. Butterfield: *Origins of Modern Science.* 1957
Palmer: *Catholics and Unbelievers in 18th-century France.* 1939
D. Mornet: *Les Sciences de la nature en France.* 1911
C. L. Becker: *The Heavenly City of the 18th-century Philosophers.* Yale, 1932
P. Hazard: *La Pensée européenne au XVIIIe siècle.* 1946
B. Willey: *The Eighteenth Century Background.* 1946
A. Cobban: *Rousseau and the Modern State.* 1950
R. Grimsley: *Jean d'Alembert.* 1963

Chapter 2

Sir George Clark: *The Seventeenth Century.* 1947
Eli Heckscher: *Mercantilism*, trans. Shapiro. 1956
Schmoller: *The Mercantile System.* 1885
Cole: *Colbert and a Century of French Mercantilism.* 1939
H. Sée: *Histoire économique de la France*, i. 1948
E. Coornaert: *Les Corporations en France avant 1789.* 1953
Vlekke: *The Evolution of the Dutch Nation.* 1951
Wilson: *Anglo-Dutch Commerce and Finance in the 18th Century.* 1774
Kulischer: *Allgemeine Wirtschaftsgeschichte*, ii. 1929
P. Geyl: *The Netherlands in the 17th Century.* Pt. II. 1964

Chapter 3

Victor-L. Tapié: *The Age of Grandeur.* 1960
Schonberger & Soehner: *The Art of Rococo.* 1960
Wittkower: *Bernini.* 1951
Summerson: *The Palladian Movement.* 1946
Blomfield: *History of French Architecture, 1661–1774.* 1911
E. de Ganay: *Les Jardins de France.* 1949
Dunlop: *Versailles.* 1956
Huyghe & Adhemar: *Watteau.* 1950
Verlet: *Le Style Louis XV.* 1943
S. Sitwell: *Spanish Baroque Art.* 1931

Desdevises du Dézert: *Les Arts en Espagne au XVIIIe siècle.* 1903
Dehio & Pauli: *Geschichte der deutschen Kunst,* iii–iv.   1931–41
Bukofzer: *Music in the Baroque Era.*   1945
Carse: *The Orchestra in the 18th century.*   1940

Chapter 4

P. Sagnac: *Louis XIV (Peuples et Civilisations* X).   1952
Lewis: *The Splendid Century.*   1953
Boulanger: *Le Grand Siècle.*   1930
Ashley: *Louis XIV and the Greatness of France.*   1948
Ogg: *Louis XIV.*   1923
Wallace Haddrill: *France; Government and Society.*   1957
Lord Acton: *Lectures in Modern History.*   1906
E. Lavisse: *Histoire de France illustrée,* VIII.   1920–22
H. Fréville: *L'Intendance de Bretagne, 1689–1790.*   1948
A. Rebillon: *Les Etats de Bretagne, 1667–1789.*   1950
Gazier: *Histoire Générale du Mouvement Jansenists.*   1922

Chapter 5

Klouchevsky: *History of Russia.*   1911–31
Riasonovsky: *A History of Russia.*   1963
Sumner: *Peter the Great and the Ottoman Empire.*   1947
Mirsky: *Russia, a Social History.*   1953
Sumner: *Survey of Russian History.*   1947
Hanisch: *Geschichte Russlands.*   1940
Waliszewski: *Peter the Great.*   1897
Milioukov, Seignobos & Eisenmann: *Histoire de Russie.*   1932

Chapter 6

Bengtsson: *Charles XII, King of Sweden, 1697-1718.*   1960
Ingvar Andersson: *A History of Sweden.*   1956
R. N. Bain: *Gustavus III and His Contemporaries, 1746-92.*   1895
B. Boethius: *New Light on 18th-century Sweden,* in *Scand. Econ. Hist. Review.* 1953

Chapter 7

Ludwig Reiners: *Frederick the Great.*   1960
Edith Simon: *The Making of Frederick the Great.*   1963
W. L. Dorn: *The Prussian Bureaucracy in the 18th century. Pol. Science Quarterly.* 1931–32
Carsten: *The Origins of Prussia.*   1954
Carsten: *The Great Elector and the Foundation of Hohenzollern Despotism. Eng. Historical Review.* April 1950

Hans Rosenberg: *Bureaucracy, Aristocracy and Autocracy.* Harvard: Oxford University Press. 1958
Frederick the Great: *Memoirs of Henri de Catt, 1758–60.*
Mémoires de Frédéric II, ed. Boutaric et Campardon.
V. Valentin: *Some Interpretations of Frederick the Great.* '*History*', XIX.
M. Braubach: *Der Aufstieg Brandenburg–Preussens, 1640 bis 1815.*   1933
H. Brunschwig: *La Crise de l'état prussien à la fin du XVIII*ᵉ *siècle.*   1947

Chapter 8

W. Coxe: *History of the House of Austria.*   1860
Marczali: *Hungary in the 18th Century* (trans. H. Temperley).   1910
F. Valsecchi: *L'Assolutismo illuminato in Austria e Lombardia* (an indispensable work).   1931
J. Redlich: *Das osterreichische Staats—und Reichsproblem.*   1920
Von Arneth: *Marie Antoinette, Joseph II und Leopold I; Ihr Briefwechsel.*   1880
W. Andreas: *Das Theresianische Osterreich und das 18 Jahrhundert.* 1930
G. P. Gooch: *Maria Theresa and Other Studies.*   1950
E. Winter: *Der Josefinismus und seine Geschichte, 1740–1788.*   1930
There is no good biography of either Maria Theresa or Joseph II in English, although S. K. Padover: *The Revolutionary Emperor; Joseph II* is good in parts. Fejto: *Joseph II; Un Habsbourg Revolutionnaire,* is a very readable book.

Chapter 9

In addition to those mentioned at the end of Chapter 5:

G. P. Gooch: *Catherine the Great and Other Studies.*   1954
W. F. Reddaway: *Documents of Catherine the Great.*   1931
Lady Craven: *A Journey through the Crimea, 1789.*
D. Maroger: *Memoirs of Catherine the Great.*   1955
Übersberger: *Russlands Orientpolitik in den letzten zwei Jahrhunderten.* 1945
Mediger: *Russlands Weg nach Europa.*   1950
Soloveytchik: *Potemkin.*   1948

Chapter 10

Richard Herr: *The 18th-century Revolution in Spain* (indispensable). Princeton: Oxford University Press.   1958
W. Coxe: *Memoirs of the Kings of Spain of the House of Bourbon.* 1815
E. Armstrong: *Elizabeth Farnese, the Termagent of Spain.*   1892
J. Sarrailh: *L'Espagne éclairée de la seconde moitié du XVIII*ᵉ *siècle.* 1936

E. J. Hamilton: *War and Prices in Spain, 1651–1800*. Harvard: Oxford University Press.   1947
E. J. Hamilton: *The Decline of Spain. Econ. Hist. Review*.   1938
answered to some extent by:
J. H. Elliott: *The Decline of Spain*. Past & Present. November, 1961
J. H. Elliott: *Imperial Spain, 1469–1716.*   1961
F. Rousseau: *Règne de Charles III d'Espagne, 1759–88.*   1907
P. Castagnoli: *Il Cardinale Giulio Alberoni* (excellent).   1932
Baudrillart: *Philippe V et la Cour de France.*   1937
M. Cheke: *Dictator of Portugal; the Marquis of Pombal.*   1938

Chapter 11

A. Sorel: *L'Europe et la Révolution française*, i.   1895-1904
R. Lodge: *Great Britain and Prussia in the 18th Century.*   1923
D. Carutti: *Storia della diplomazia della Corte di Savoia*, iii, iv.   1880
E. Rota: *Le Origini del Risorgimento*, i and ii.   1938
B. Williams: *Stanhope.*   1932
R. Lodge: *Studies in 18th-century Diplomacy, 1740–48.*   1930
A. von Arneth: *Geschichte Maria Theresias.*   1863-97
Z. E. Rashed: *The Peace of Paris, 1763*. Liverpool University Press.   1951
G. Zeller: *Le principe d'equilibre dans la politique internationale avant 1789*. Revue Historique, 1956.
P. Vaucher: *Robert Walpole et la politique de Fleury, 1731–42.*   1924
A. M. Wilson: *French Foreign Policy during the Administration of Cardinal Fleury*. Harvard: Oxford University Press.   1936
Duc de Broglie: *Le secret du roi, 1752–74.*   1880

Chapter 12

The Cambridge History of Poland. 3 vols.   1941
R. H. Lord: *The Second Partition of Poland*. Harvard: Oxford University Press.   1915
A. Sorel: *La Question d'Orient au XVIIIe siècle.*   1878
J. Fabre: *Stanislas-Auguste Poniatowski et l'Europe des lumières.*
H. de Montfort: *Le Drame de la Pologne: Kosciusko, 1746–1817.*
O. Halecki: *Modern Poland until the Partitions, 1506–1795*, in *Handbook of Slavic Studies.*

Chapter 13

Gibbs & Bowen: *Islamic Society and the West* (indispensable).   1950
A. Sorel: *La Question d'Orient au XVIIIe siècle.*   1878
J. Ancel: *Manuel historique de la question d'Orient.*   1931
M. S. Anderson: *Gt. Britain and the Russo-Turkish War of 1768–74.* E.H.R. 1954.

C. R. von Sax: *Gëschichte des Machtverfalls der Türkei*. 1908
Hasluck: *Christianity and Islam under the Sultans*. 1929

Chapter 14

A Cobban: *A History of France* 1957 (excellent).
Muret: *La preponderance anglaise* (1715–63).
P. Sagnac: *Le Fin de l'Ancien Régime* (vols. XI and XII of the *Peuples et Civilisations: Histoire Generale*). 1952
E. Lavisse: *Histoire de France illustrée*, vols. VIII and IX. 1911
F. L. Ford: *Robe and Sword*. Harvard, 1953
G. Pages: *Études sur l'histoire administrative et sociale de l'ancien régime*. 1938
A. Cobban: *The Parlements of France in the 18th Century. History*, 1950.
H. See: *Histoire économique de la France*. 1948
H. M. Hyde: *Life of John Law*. 1948
A. Gazier: *Histoire générale du mouvement Janséniste*. 1922
J. Parguez: *La Bulle Unigenitus et le Jansénisme politique*. 1936
H. I. Priestley: *France Overseas through the Old Régime*. 1939
Goodwin: *The European Nobility in the 18th Century*. 1953
P. Sagnac: *La Formation de la société française moderne*. 1950

Chapter 15

Funck-Brentano: *The Old Régime in France* (trans. Wilson). 1929
Maxwell: *The English Traveller in France, 1698–1815*.
D. Dakin: *Turgot and Ancien Régime in France*. 1939
J. M. S. Alison: *La moig non de Malesherbes*. Yale: Oxford University Press. 1938
P. Jolly: *Calonne*. 1949
A. de Tocqueville: *L'Ancien Régime*. 1856
G. Lefebvre: *The Coming of the French Revolution. Vintage*, 1957
G. Weulersse: *La physiocratie sous les ministères de Turgot et de Necker*. 1950
C. E. Labrousse: *Esquisse du mouvement des prix et des revenues au XVIIIᵉ siècle*. 1933
C. E. Labrousse: *La crise de l'économie française à la fin de l'Ancien Régime et au début de la Revolution, 1771–1791*. 1944
Lavaquerie: *Necker, fourrier de la Révolution*.
Gaston Martin: *Cahiers de la Révolution française*. 1927
D. Mornet: *Les origines intellectuelles de la Révolution française*. 1954
A. Goodwin: *Calonne and the Assembly of French Notables, 1787*. E.H.R. 1946
P. Sagnac: *La formation de la société française*. 1950
A. Davies: *The Origins of the French Peasant Revolution of 1789*. (*History*, February, 1964)

INDEX